Kant on Intuition

T0399591

Kant on Intuition: Western and Asian Perspectives on Transcendental Idealism consists of 20 chapters, many of which feature engagements between Kant and various Asian philosophers. Key themes include the nature of human intuition (not only as theoretical—pure, sensible, and possibly intellectual—but also as relevant to Kant's practical philosophy, aesthetics, the sublime, and even mysticism), the status of Kant's idealism/realism, and Kant's notion of an object. Roughly half of the chapters take a stance on the recent conceptualism/non-conceptualism debate. The chapters are organized into four parts, each with five chapters. Part I explores themes relating primarily to the early sections of Kant's first *Critique*: three chapters focus mainly on Kant's theory of the "forms of intuition" and/or "formal intuition", especially as illustrated by geometry, while two examine the broader role of intuition in transcendental idealism. Part II continues to examine themes from the Aesthetic but shifts the main focus to the Transcendental Analytic, where the key question challenging interpreters is to determine whether intuition (via sensibility) is ever capable of operating *independently* from conception (via understanding); each contributor offers a defense of either a conceptualist or a non-conceptualist reading of Kant's text. Part III includes three chapters that explore the relevance of intuition to Kant's theory of the sublime, followed by two that examine challenges that Asian philosophers have raised against Kant's theory of intuition, particularly as it relates to our experience of the supersensible. Finally, Part IV concludes the book with five chapters that explore a range of resonances between Kant and various Asian philosophers and philosophical ideas, with a special emphasis on the nature of philosophy itself.

Stephen R. Palmquist, Professor of Religion and Philosophy at Hong Kong Baptist University since 1987, has over 190 publications, including 100 refereed articles and book chapters. His 12 books include *Kant's System of Perspectives* (1993), *Kant's Critical Religion* (2000), *Cultivating Personhood: Kant and Asian Philosophy* (2010), and *Comprehensive Commentary on Kant's Religion Within the Bounds of Bare Reason* (2016).

Routledge Studies in Eighteenth-Century Philosophy

For more information about this series, please visit: www.routledge. com/Routledge-Studies-in-Eighteenth-Century-Philosophy/book-series/ SE0391

Kant on Intuition

Western and Asian Perspectives
on Transcendental Idealism

Edited by Stephen R. Palmquist

Routledge
Taylor & Francis Group

LONDON AND NEW YORK

First published 2019 by Routledge

2 Park Square, Milton Park, Abingdon, Oxon, OX14 4RN

605 Third Avenue, New York, NY 10017

Routledge is an imprint of the Taylor & Francis Group, an informa business

First issued in paperback 2020

Library of Congress Cataloging-in-Publication Data
Names: Palmquist, Stephen, editor.
Title: Kant on intuition : western and Asian perspectives on
    transcendental idealism / edited by Stephen R. Palmquist.
Description: 1 [edition]. | New York : Taylor & Francis, 2018. |
    Series: Routledge studies in eighteenth-century philosophy ;
    18 | Includes bibliographical references and index.
Identifiers: LCCN 2018039560 | ISBN 9781138589247
    (hardback)
Subjects: LCSH: Kant, Immanuel, 1724–1804. | Intuition. |
    Idealism, German—History—18th century. |
    Transcendentalism.
Classification: LCC B2798 .K223644 2018 | DDC 121/.3—dc23
LC record available at https://lccn.loc.gov/2018039560

ISBN: 978-1-138-58924-7 (hbk)
ISBN: 978-0-367-73252-3 (pbk)

Typeset in Sabon
by Apex CoVantage, LLC

To Anthony Luke
Truly an East–West synthesis of intuition and thought

Contents

Figures

Editor's Introduction

Stephen R. Palmquist

1. The Enigma of Kantian Intuition: Grist for the Mill of an Academic Conference

While few topics in Kant studies are wholly devoid of controversy, none is *more* contentious, while at the same time being *so crucial* to a proper understanding of Kant's Critical philosophy, than his theory of intuition, which plays a key role in his ground-breaking theory of transcendental idealism. What does Kant mean by "*pure* intuition", and how does it give rise to mathematics? If all Kantian intuition is an activity of the mind, then in what sense are *objects* of "outer intuition" genuinely *outside* us? If Kant's theory of transcendental idealism requires all intuitions to be synthesized with concepts in order to play a constitutive role in cognition, then would it be possible for intuitions to exist without having any conceptual content? If such intuitions do exist, then how could it make sense to talk about such *objects*, given that we cannot *cognize* objects without conceptualizing them? Moreover, is Kant justified in denying that human beings have *intellectual* intuition, such that all our empirical intuition must be *sensible*? Does not his own practical philosophy require something akin to intellectual intuition, in order to explain our immediate awareness of the moral law? These questions are only a sampling of the plethora of highly debatable issues surrounding Kant's rich yet enigmatic theory of intuition.

In early 2016, when the newly formed Programme Committee for the second Kant in Asia international conference first considered how best to design a sequel to the first conference,[1] we selected "Intuition, East and West" as the theme for four main reasons. First, we were confident that its highly debatable nature would make for a series of lively scholarly discussions—a prediction that was entirely fulfilled during the conference itself. A second reason was that, considering how immense its importance is for understanding Kant's philosophy, intuition had received relatively little attention in the literature until quite recently; moreover, we were aware of no previous conference that had been devoted to this specific theme. A third consideration made this topic *ideal* for our purposes, given the East–West focus that is implied by the "Kant in Asia" label: intuition has been a primary emphasis for much of the Asian scholarship on Kant. As Western Kant scholars are increasingly coming to recognize, the Chinese philosopher, Mou Zongsan (1909–1995), not only translated all three *Critiques* into Chinese, but also made Kant the focal point of his efforts in comparative (Chinese–Western) philosophy. Among his various adaptations and criticisms of Kant's position, none is more influential than his claim that Kant's denial that human beings can have intellectual intuition is proven false, at least for the Chinese people, by the fact that the whole history of Confucianism depends on and provides examples of Chinese philosophers who *have* had intellectual intuition. A fourth reason may have been the deciding factor: since January of 2016, three committee members had been working on a project whose aim was to do a detailed analysis of the various ways Kant uses the German terms, "*Objekt*" and "*Gegenstand*" (both normally translated as "object"). As soon as one member suggested intuition as a potential topic, we all recognized immediately that a conference on this theme would provide us with many relevant talking points relating to our budding theory. As evidence of its relevance, we have presented initial results of our (ongoing) study in Chapter 1 of this volume.

The conference took place from December 17th–20th, 2016.[2] One of the main secondary themes that emerged as the four-day event proceeded was the debate between "conceptualism" and "non-conceptualism". Indeed, this debate is a main topic of eight chapters in this anthology (including all five chapters in Part II; see §2, below): Chapters 3 (Nan), 5 (Chun), 6 (Allais), 7 (Chen), 8 (Hu), 9 (Orlander), 10 (Zhang), and 20 (Moss); it is also mentioned briefly or by implication in too many of the other chapters to list here. Hence, a brief preliminary introduction to the debate is in order. Kant famously argues that empirical cognition (i.e., our ability to affirm facts about sensible objects that we experience) can occur only if two essential components are combined in and by the human mind: *intuition* and *conception*. The precise nature of this necessary combination, however, is open to debate. *Conceptualists* emphasize that Kant says intuitions are "blind" if they are not connected to concepts (A51/B75) and argue that there is no way even to talk about the "nonconceptual content" of our experience, except on the assumption that our experience *has* conceptual content from the very start; only when philosophizing can we abstract from that content and pretend to talk about intuition on its own. *Non-conceptualists*, by contrast, insist that Kant's account of intuition provides ample evidence that he *did* assign a distinct role to intuition, which takes place prior to and without any involvement from the understanding; the categories may shape the conceptual side of human cognition, but conceptual thoughts are "empty" without intuitive content. In the broad spectrum of positions held by Kant–scholars nowadays, those who lean toward the extreme of positivism are more likely to support conceptualism, while those who lean more toward the mystical are more likely to support non-conceptualism.

Among the numerous other themes that emerged during the conference and also play a significant role in this anthology, four are worthy of special mention. First, the nature and significance of intellectual intuition, mentioned above, was raised by roughly half of the chapters: Chapter 18 (Wong) gives it the most thorough treatment, but Chapters 6 (Allais), 15 (Pathak), and 19 (Lo) all include a substantial discussion of the issue, and several others (including Chapters 1, 10, 14, and 20) mention it in passing.[3] Second, an equally obvious secondary theme that emerged during the conference was the nature and/or validity of transcendental idealism, a major topic of Chapters 1 (Palmquist, Lown, and Love) and 5 (Chun), discussed in some detail in Chapters 6 (Allais), 11 (Zammito), and 14 (Moskopp), and mentioned in Chapters 2, 9, 10, and 17. Third, the possibility that Kant's philosophy might have implications for mysticism is raised in Chapters 5 (Chun), 10 (Zhang), 11 (Zammito), 14 (Moskopp), and 15 (Pathak), as well as being mentioned in Chapters 12 and 19.[4] Finally, a less obvious secondary theme is the possible relevance of the aforementioned *Objekt/Gegenstand* distinction for a proper interpretation not only of Kant's theory of intuition but also of his broader theory of transcendental idealism. The opening chapter deals with this issue head on, and several other chapters make a point of mentioning one or both of the key terms (including Chapters 3, 9, and 17), while Chapter 19 (Lo) explicitly affirms the distinction's importance. The conference motto, quoted from the third *Critique*, was selected because of how effectively it shows the relevance of this fourth theme to intuition: "the concept of nature indeed makes its objects [*Gegenstände*] representable in intuition, but not as things in themselves, rather as mere appearances, while the concept of freedom makes a thing itself representable in its Object [*Objekte*], but not in intuition" (5:175).

A word about this anthology's subtitle is in order. The reference to "Western and Asian Perspectives" is not meant to imply that there is only *one* approach from the West and one from the East. Rather, the intended connotation of the plural word, "perspectives", is that different perspectives on interpreting Kant (especially his transcendental idealism, with its accompanying theory of intuition) exist in *both* Asia and the West. Indeed, to a large extent the range of possible positions can be reflected by philosophers on both sides. Two examples will suffice to illustrate this point. First, Western interpreters of Kant are often classified into "two worlds" and "two aspects" approaches; in Chapter 17, Chun-yip Lowe demonstrates that two of the main Chinese interpreters of Kant in the twentieth century exhibited essentially the same two approaches, though the details of their applications of these two approaches differ somewhat from those exhibited by Western interpreters. Second, while Western interpreters nowadays may be accustomed to thinking of intellectual intuition as a theory that *no Western philosopher* would take seriously, this bias neglects the fact that, prior to Kant, notions similar to intellectual intuition were quite commonly defended by Western philosophers. As such, Asian philosophers are far from being completely alienated from the West in their insistence that such intuition is possible.

The present volume consists of 20 chapters,[5] organized into four parts with five chapters each. Part I ("The Role of Intuition in Geometry and Transcendental Idealism") explores themes relating primarily to the Prefaces, Introduction, and Transcendental Aesthetic sections of Kant's *Critique of Pure Reason* (1781/1787): three chapters focus mainly on Kant's theory of the "forms of intuition" and/or "formal intuition", especially as illustrated by geometry, while the other two (the first and the last chapters in Part I) examine the broader role of intuition in transcendental idealism. Part II ("The Function and Status of Intuition in Human Cognition") continues to examine themes from the Aesthetic but shifts the main focus to the Transcendental Analytic, where the key question challenging interpreters is to determine whether intuition (via the faculty of sensibility) is ever capable of operating *independently* from conception (via the faculty of understanding); each contributor offers a defense of either a conceptualist or a non-conceptualist reading of Kant's text. Part III ("The Sublime and the Challenge of the East on Intuiting the Supersensible") includes three chapters that explore the relevance of intuition to Kant's theory of the sublime, followed by two that examine challenges that Asian philosophers have raised against Kant's theory of intuition, particularly as it relates to our experience of the supersensible. Finally, Part IV ("East–West Perspectives on the Role of Intuition in Philosophy") concludes the book with five chapters that explore a range of resonances between Kant and various Asian philosophers and philosophical ideas. The following section offers a synopsis of each of these twenty chapters in the context of the book's four parts.

2. Overview of the Chapters

Part I of *Kant on Intuition* begins with a chapter co-authored by three members of the conference Programme Committee: Brandon Love, Guy Lown, and I had been working together for about a year (prior to the conference) on a research project that started with Guy's hunch that the terms *Objekt* and *Gegenstand* have distinct meanings for Kant that had not yet been sufficiently unpacked in the literature. Kant scholars typically treat them as synonyms; but if they are distinct, then properly *understanding* the distinction could be crucial for understanding transcendental idealism in general and his theory of intuition in particular. After assessing several past attempts to distinguish these terms, we argue that a *Gegenstand* is a representation generated from either what is given in intuition (and destined to become a *phenomenon*) or what is merely thought (and thereby is properly regarded as a *noumenon*), while an empirical *Objekt* is a fully determined thing that is conceptualized as existing *independently* of (but *for*) the human subject. Kant's famous attempt, in his Refutation of Idealism, to resolve the "scandal of philosophy" (Bxxxixn) in response to Jacobi illustrates the significance of this distinction. We explain why he refers only to *Gegenstände* in arguing that transcendental idealism grounds a robust empirical realism: Jacobi only challenged Kant's view of *Gegenstände*; moreover, Kant had already sufficiently demonstrated the reality of *Objekte* in the Deduction. We conclude the chapter by examining the distinction's role in the transition from theoretical to practical philosophy. In morality, "*Gegenstände*" expresses the relationship between the will and actions, thus determining the value of *Objekte* (good or evil) and leading to the ultimate *Objekt*, the highest good.

In Chapter 2, also co-authored, Hoke Robinson and Dan Larkin seek to justify Kant's defense of Euclidian geometry in the first *Critique*'s Transcendental Aesthetic. In dialogue with a recent article by Michael Friedman, which critiques a group of studies proposing a new "diagrammatic" interpretation of Euclid that allegedly also fits Kant's spatial theory, Robinson and Larkin present a thought experiment whereby the role of Euclidean geometry is compared to the role of rules in playing a game. Without substantially disagreeing with Friedman, they argue that their alternative way of justifying Kant's use of Euclidian geometry has various advantages over Friedman's, from (at least) a pedagogical point of view. Following Friedman, they distinguish between a "form of intuition" (i.e., in this case, space) and a "formal intuition" (i.e., a rule that guides our understanding of phenomenal/Euclidean space). As regards the functioning of geometry in relation to Kant's wider theory of space, they argue that Kant's view of Euclidian geometry exhibits some interesting similarities to Einstein's view of non-Euclidean geometry, particularly with regard to the function of making choices that are essentially arbitrary.

Staying with the focus on geometry, Xing Nan explains in Chapter 3 what Kant means when he calls geometrical concepts "formal intuitions". Examining the enigmatic footnote at B160n, which has become a central focus of the recent debate between conceptualist and non-conceptualist interpretations of Kant's theory of intuition, Nan defends a non-standard version of the conceptualist reading. He recommends replacing the terms "conceptualism" and "non-conceptualism" with "intellectualism" and "sensibilism", so that interpreters are less likely to conflate Kant's notion of "conceptual content" with the way contemporary philosophers of mind use the latter term. "Formal intuition", Nan argues, refers to the givenness in intuition of a geometrical figure; as such, a formal intuition necessarily involves geometrical concepts, though it need not involve pure concepts of the understanding (i.e., categories). Nan thus refers to this new version of conceptualism as "conceptualist sensibilism".

Gregg Osborne, in Chapter 4, scrutinizes Kant's elusive distinction between "pure intuitions" and "pure *forms* of intuition". In the Aesthetic, Kant purports to show (1) that *our representations of* space and time are pure intuitions, and (2) that space and time *themselves* are pure *forms of* intuition. His attempts to explain what these claims mean, however, are problematic. Osborne identifies and offers plausible solutions to several of the most perplexing problems. With the help of passages from outside the first *Critique*, he shows that (1) must mean that our representations of space and time are intuitions and that with respect to their *nature* (as opposed to their *existence*), they do not depend on sensations. Likewise, he shows that (2) should mean that space and time themselves are aspects of sensible things which arise as the various things that affect the senses are coordinated by a certain natural law of the mind, and that (again with respect to their *nature* as opposed to their *existence*) they do not depend on sensations. Osborne admits that these solutions entail a substantive revision of Kant's own account as he presents certain details in the Aesthetic; but this revision is the only way to avoid a troublesome regress.

Effectively complementing Osborne's emphasis on the *nature* of space and time, Chapter 5 concludes Part One with Jack Chun's impressive account of the centrality of the *existence* of the external world in Kant's theory of intuition. Chun portrays intuition, being *concept-blind*, as the only mechanism whereby the subject can ever *touch* the raw reality and the particulars in existence. In reconstructing Kant's arguments for this special function of intuition, he starts with Kant's abstraction of space and time as the necessary forms of intuition. He then interprets Kant's argument from empirical consciousness in time to the presupposed existence of spatial objects. Chun reads Kant as attempting to close the ontological and the epistemic gaps between inner and outer objects through the transcendental unity of apperception. Not only in the Refutation of Idealism, Chun demonstrates, but throughout his discussion of intuition, Kant argues that the experience of unity we have, when we look inwardly (i.e., when we experience what Kant calls "inner intuition"), could not take place if something permanent and *real* outside of us did not exist (i.e., if what Kant calls "outer intuition" did not present to us genuinely existing *objects*).[6] Although Kant's superstructure is spectacular, Chun questions whether it can be anchored to reality in the way Kant seems to think it is. In order to consider reality as more than the subject's fabrication, Kant must introduce the transcendental object, whose existential independence is supposed to explain the objective reality of the subject's intuition. The status of the transcendental object, as part of what Chun calls the "transcendental package", paradoxically illustrates how intuition helps construct and yet also disrupts Kant's transcendental idealism.

Part Two begins with a chapter by Lucy Allais, the first of the conference's three keynote speakers. Human cognition (*Erkenntnis*) being a central notion in Kant's Critical philosophy in general and a main topic of the first *Critique* in particular, she begins with a synopsis of her view on the role of intuition in Kant's answer to the question of how cognition of synthetic *a priori* propositions is possible. Kant famously argues that we cannot have cognition of things as they are in themselves, and also that we cannot have cognition of what he calls the supersensible, which includes God, our souls, and our freedom. Allais moves on from a consideration of these theoretical issues to examine Kant's claims, in the second *Critique* and elsewhere, that we *can* have cognition of freedom through practical reason, and that this also provides rational grounds for belief in God and the immortality of our souls. While intuition is a crucial ingredient in all theoretical cognition, Kant portrays practical cognition as occurring without intuition. Both theoretical and practical cognition have concepts, the other central ingredient in theoretical cognition, so something in practical reason must take the place of intuition. Allais concludes by reflecting on whether there is some equivalent to intuition in practical cognition, given the absence of *sensible* intuition there, and assesses the plausibility of Mou Zongsan's famous claim that something like *intellectual* intuition must be at work, at least in the practical realm, though not in the theoretical, as Mou had claimed.

In Chapter 7, Xi Chen defends a conceptualist interpretation of Kant's theory of intuition, in opposition to scholars such as Allais. In order for non-conceptualism to hold true, Chen argues, intuitions would need to be capable of referring to objects without using any concepts; however, this would make it difficult (if not impossible) to explain how concepts can *ever* be applied to such non-conceptual sensory intuitions. She devotes much of her attention to the task of demonstrating that the B Deduction does not entail any essential change from the A Deduction, even though the subject–object relation exhibits a "symmetric" structure in A and an "asymmetric structure" in B. The A Deduction's symmetric structure assumes a subject–in–itself as the substratum underlying all representations of "I", whereas the B Deduction avoids making this assumption. Instead, Chen argues, Kant portrays the subject as *pure activity* in the B Deduction, and since concepts play a necessary role in all cognitive activity, all sensory representations of the objects combined by such activity have to be conceptual; moreover, non-conceptual sensory intuitions, as well as sensibility itself, must also be deeply affected by the subject's rule-governed activities. She takes the B Deduction to entail a refutation of the non-conceptualist reading of Kant's theory of cognition. As such, intuitions could not be experienced or even be taken as "real" in any meaningful sense, if they were not first synthesized through the process of conceptualization.

Jieyao Hu demonstrates in Chapter 8 that both non-conceptualist and conceptualist interpretations have a legitimate grounding in Kant's texts, though she eventually sides with the non-conceptualists, for the following reasons. While it is, indeed, the case that (as conceptualism claims) Kant argues that intuitions must be conceptualized *if they are to produce knowledge*, Kant never claims that this fact prevents us from experiencing intuitions that are *not* (or that cannot be) so conceptualized; rather, it only means that the latter sort of intuitions have not attained (and possibly could never attain) the status of full-fledged empirical cognition. Moreover, the debate can best be resolved by clarifying the difference between intuition and perception in Kant's theory of cognition. Accordingly, Hu distinguishes between "content non-conceptualism" (which does not require non-conceptual *perceptions*) and "relational non-conceptualism" (which does interpret non-conceptualism as a theory about perceptions) and regards the former as more defensible, and more faithful to Kant, than the latter.

Chapter 9 shifts the topic of Part Two from an explicit emphasis on the conceptualism/non-conceptualism debate as such to a more focused assessment of Kant's claim that *empirical knowledge* can occur only when intuitions and concepts work together: Sebastian Orlander offers a reading of the notoriously difficult Schematism chapter, paying special attention to Kant's several references to the image of drawing a line. He argues that the Schematism is more relevant to the long-standing debate over conceptualism and non-conceptualism than is often recognized. Surprisingly, many commentators have neglected to comment on what seems to be Kant's favorite image for characterizing the activity of the imagination in applying the categories to the forms of sensibility, an activity generally understood to be integral to the process of schematizing. Using some hints from a phenomenological understanding of time-consciousness, Orlander offers a way of understanding what Kant could have meant by defining schematism in terms of time-determination and by focusing on Kant's treatment of number. Given that the problem of how the categories are applied to sensibility is central to the whole Schematism chapter, Orlander interprets Kant's image of drawing a line in intuition as offering more weight to non-conceptualist readings of Kant's position. Nevertheless, he concedes that his considerations also pose some problems for understanding what it would mean for Kant to be a non-conceptualist: the fact that the Schematism places such great importance on understanding magnitude in numerical terms seems like a step toward a *conceptualist* understanding of cognition.

Part II concludes with Ellen Y. Zhang signaling the importance of taking into account Asian perspectives on the issues discussed in Part Two: she argues in Chapter 10 that the classical Indian philosopher, Nāgārjuna (150–250 C.E.), had an account of "negative certainties" that directly challenges what she takes to be the traditional Kantian (*conceptualist*) notion of the "togetherness" of intuitions and concepts. Viewing this "togetherness principle" from the perspective of Madhyāmika Buddhism, via Nāgārjuna's arguments on the relationship between intuitions and concepts, as well as on the twofold nature of truth (i.e., "conventional truth" [*samvrtisatya*] and "ultimate truth" [*paramārthasatya*]), Zhang explicates Nāgārjuna's skeptical view of the semantic dependence of intuition on concepts in light of his notion of "conceptual proliferation" (*prapañca*). She then argues that the "togetherness principle" fails to distinguish conceptual and non-conceptual intuitions, as Kant himself seems to do when he defends "pure intuition", identifying consciousness with objectively representational content that is essentially independent of concepts. She concludes by appropriating Kant's notion of non-conceptual intuitions in conjunction with his Critical position on mystical experience, thus bringing Kant into conversation with Nāgārjuna and post-Nāgārjuna Ch'an (Zen) Buddhism. Zhang contends that we need to draw a line between "intuitive experiences" and discursive, "post-experiential interpretations"; the latter, as maintained by Nāgārjuna, belong to conventional truth—i.e., they are always conceptually dependent.

Part Three begins with the conference's third keynote speaker, John H. Zammito, who presents in Chapter 11 an analysis of how the third *Critique* portrays human beings as having various types of "intuitions of the ultimate". Zammito begins by pointing out that alleged intuitions of the ultimate, so characteristic of Asian thought, have typically met with a sharp measure of skepticism from Western thinkers, as famously instantiated in Sigmund Freud's suspicion of any "oceanic feeling". Freud viewed this feeling as indicating a person's failure to advance from an infantile state. But Kant was hardly guilty of infantile thinking, for as Zammito skillfully demonstrates, his third *Critique* explores such experiences richly and in considerable depth, under the notions of the "sublime", the "supersensible substrate", and "spirit". While Kant retained his first *Critique* scruples about our ability to obtain empirical cognition of such metaphysical ideas, his exposition of these three themes in the third *Critique* makes it clear that he thought of such deeply felt experiences as being crucial for humankind and even a *requirement* of reason itself. In a series of endnotes, Zammito responds to feedback given by Robert R. Clewis, who had served as the invited respondent to his keynote lecture during the conference. In order to allow readers to appreciate the specific points Clewis had raised, his response is included as an Appendix to Chapter 11. Chief among Clewis' key concerns with Zammito's approach is that Kant's own text emphasizes the *practical* far more than the spiritual (or even mystical) overtones that Zammito underscores. Zammito grants Clewis' point, admitting that he is emphasizing what might be only a secondary theme in the text of the third *Critique*; but he insists that it *is there* nonetheless.

In Chapter 12 Bart Vandenabeele adopts a more cautious interpretation as he explores the complex roles of intuition and exhibition (*Darstellung*) in Kant's account of the sublime. He observes that in §26 of the third *Critique,* Kant argues that "nature is sublime in those of its appearances whose intuition carries with it the idea of their infinity" (5:255). Kant argues that judging the mathematically sublime involves not a mathematical method of measuring, but a (vain) attempt to perceive an overwhelmingly large object (*Gegenstand*) in a single intuition through aesthetic comprehension. Through the human imagination's effort to comprehend aesthetically the size or power of, for instance, a huge canyon or volcano, we are made aware of our limited capacity to intuit overwhelmingly large objects, and we thus become aware of "the feeling of a supersensible power in us" (§25, 250)—namely, reason. Furthermore, Kant insists that the sublime is a matter of aesthetic exhibition (also sometimes translated as "presentation"), but he is adamant that sublime pleasure (*rührendes Wohlgefallen*) is ultimately grounded in our susceptibility to *moral* ideas (§26, 252). In his account of Kant's overall theory of the sublime, Vandenabeele points out several significant flaws in Kant's argumentation, noting in particular that Kant unwarrantedly downgrades the aesthetic nature of the sublime and hence makes it impure in a way that he does not appear to acknowledge.

In Chapter 13, Zhengmi Zhouhuang[7] offers a third, highly systematic perspective on Kant's theory of the sublime, portraying it as no less important a part of aesthetic judgment than his theory of beauty, in spite of the complexity of the argument Kant constructs to explain what Zhouhuang interprets as essentially a turn from the faculty of sensibility to the faculty of reason. She clarifies the logical construction of the argument and the functional position of the sublime in Kant's philosophy by contrasting his description of the sublime with his accounts of beauty and moral feeling. The sublime can be systematically distinguished from the latter two types of feeling by regarding it as a mixture of intuition and exhibition, as based on a turn from sensibility to reason, and as resulting from a combination of contemplation and movement. Moreover, in discussing the implications of the four moments in the judgment of the sublime, comparing them with Kant's account of judgments of taste, Zhouhuang clarifies how judgments of the sublime do belong to pure aesthetic judgment—Vandenabeele's protests notwithstanding. She goes on to explain the distinctions between the mathematical sublime and the dynamical sublime and their penetration into each other. Finally, she further elucidates the connection and differences between the sublime and moral feelings, thus effectively clarifying why Kant regards these as two types of feeling.

While not dealing with the sublime as such, the last two chapters in Part Two interpret aspects of Kant's theory of cognition in the first *Critique* as being so profound as to raise them almost to the level of sublimity. Werner Moskopp argues in Chapter 14 that by recognizing the ubiquity of transcendental apperception in Kant's theory of cognition, we can better appreciate why he regards his transcendental idealism as also constituting empirical realism. Transcendental idealism guarantees the relation of things as appearances to the ego, which in turn is given as an appearance to inner sense. The feature that Kant calls "synthesis" completely permeates the intentional capabilities of the human mind. Hence, Kant's ultimate justification of transcendental idealism depends neither on the intuition of the outer senses nor on any intellectual intuition. Rather, it rests on the synthesized awareness conveyed by transcendental apperception—i.e., by actual first-person experience (*"Erleben"*). As such inward "experiences" can be articulated only after a person has them, Moskopp asks why Western philosophy classifies the mystical evidence of *Dasein* as "ineffable", whereas nothingness/emptiness in Asian philosophy tends to be seen as giving people access to phenomenal consciousness. Associating Kant's *Critique* with Eastern philosophy in this way has several consequences: the universality of the forms of intuition and conception can now be read as ubiquity instead of merely as generality; the spatiotemporal world appears to be in a steady, mind-dependent transformation (here and now); it no longer has to be regarded merely as a sequence of variations of a substance (soul, world, or God), but instead constitutes full-fledged empirical cognition.

This emphasis on the affirmation of mystical experience, so prevalent in Asian philosophy, is further explored by Krishna Mani Pathak in Chapter 15. While he takes Kant's position on the role of intuition in cognition to be that of a conceptualist, Pathak critically examines the plausibility of such a position by comparing Kant's definition of intuition, as (re)presentation of objects to the human mind, with that of the Indian philosopher and religious teacher, Jiddu Krishnamurti (1895–1986). Krishnamurti takes intuition to be an independent form of intelligence, which is neither identical with past experience nor even dependent on it. After giving an introductory account of Kant's epistemology (assuming a conceptualist understanding of the necessary connection between concepts and intuitions), Pathak compares and contrasts Kant's theory of mental representation in general, and of intuition in particular, with that of Krishnamurti. Based on his reinterpretation of the role intuition plays in Kant's theory of cognition, whereby he portrays Kant as defending what could be regarded as a version of intellectual intuition, Pathak concludes by demonstrating that the philosophies of Kant and Krishnamurti exhibit a surprising degree of symmetry: both regard intuition as integrally bound up with the human intellect, in one way or another.

Chapter 16 begins Part IV, while completing this book's gradual transition from Western to Asian perspectives, with the conference's second keynote speaker, Tze-wan Kwan, who examines Kant's view of the nature of philosophy itself: philosophy should always bear the mark of "situatedness"; rather than being just an intellectual game, it should be directed at the world that confronts humanity. After discussing Kant's distinctions between mathematics (which *constructs* its objects) and philosophy (which deals with objects that are *given*) and between philosophy in a scholastic sense (which emphasizes sheer, scholarly mastery of philosophical doctrines) and philosophy in a cosmic sense (which entails the free and active use of reason in solving the "worldly" issues that haunt humanity), Kwan presents etymological evidence that this Kantian legacy is quite unexpectedly prefigured in Chinese antiquity: the archaic Chinese character "*zhe*" (meaning "wisdom") dates back at least to the pre-Chin[8] Chinese classics and was used by Japanese academia in the late nineteenth century, and subsequently by the Chinese themselves, to translate the Western term "philosophy". Kwan draws on his prior research into various archaic Chinese script tokens to show that the notion of "wisdom", central to "*zhe*", arises by the compounding of several visual–semantic script components, which refer in turn to "discerning" (or "discriminating"), to observation, to deliberation, and to the living ethos or "situation" where the need for discernment arises. These components are universal traits that pertain to Kant's "philosophy in a cosmic sense". Kwan concludes with observations on several Kantian claims that are entailed both in Kant's general notion of philosophy and in moral practices as described in the Chinese classics: the "primacy of practical reason", the concept of "choice" (*Willkür*), and the "motto of enlightenment".

The book's four remaining chapters draw out several more specific examples of how themes relating to Kant's transcendental idealism have also been defended by Asian philosophers. First, Chun-yip Lowe devotes Chapter 17 to the task of showing how Mou Zongsan and Lao Szekwang (1927–2012), two influential interpreters of Kant's philosophy in the Chinese-speaking world, echo the two main sides of a key debate that Western Kant scholars have also struggled with. Mou argues that, at least from the practical point of view, Confucianism demonstrates that human beings have intellectual intuition, and that this reveals a serious weakness in Kant's philosophy. However, Lao thinks that, with the help of Carnap's theory of linguistic frameworks, Kant's philosophy can be regarded as an explanatory language to justify the conditions of experience, but not as a metaphysical language to describe any metaphysical entities. The difference between these two ways of reading Kant aptly illustrates the debate among Western interpreters, between the two-world interpretation and the two-aspect interpretation, respectively. Lowe argues that the contemporary tendency toward postmetaphysical thinking causes Mou's metaphysical interpretation of Kant's philosophy to seem outdated: such an interpretation tends to give rise to a closed system that refuses to communicate with other philosophical systems. He therefore supports Lao's two-aspect interpretation as the superior alternative.

Chapter 18 follows, with Simon Sai-ming Wong *defending* Mou Zongsan against those such as Lowe, who prematurely reject Mou's reading of Kant. Wong argues that Mou's well-known criticism of Kant's denial of intellectual intuition (*intellektuelle Anschauung*) actually results from

Mou's misinterpretation of several of Kant's key theories, and that this, in turn, is caused by certain inaccurate and misleading translations of Kant's technical terms. Mou's criticism is motivated by a desire to defend a Confucian concept that is best translated into English as *"intelligible intuition"*, a term whose meaning (contrary to Mou's assumption) is fundamentally different from that of Kant's concept of *intellectual* intuition. Wong vindicates Mou's apparently rather audacious claim by showing that Kant's philosophy actually allows room for the Confucian account of *intelligible* intuition, properly understood, without compromising Kant's insistence that *intellectual* intuition is impossible. Wong accomplishes this feat by offering a Kantian interpretation of several interrelated concepts in the teachings of Liu Zongzhou (1587–1645). Liu's philosophy effectively illustrates the context within which the Confucian account of intelligible intuition should be understood and thus helps contemporary readers of Mou's work to put his criticism of Kant's theory of intellectual intuition into its proper perspective.

In Chapter 19 Suet-kwan Lo highlights the profoundly revolutionary nature of Kant's doctrine of *Anschauung*, whose nuanced meaning in the German, as marking out the limits of our sensible cognition, is not adequately conveyed with the English term, "intuition". Armed with this innovative theory, Kant shows not only that supersensible things are possible, but also tells us how we must think of them. Lo points out that for Kant, we seek the cognition of supersensible things not from supersensible objects (*Gegenstände*) themselves, but through reflection on the nature of the morally practical subject, the bearer of free will. That is, Kant shows that the proper way to understand supersensible things is through the domain of (practical) freedom (as argued in the third *Critique*; see e.g., 5:176). Lo recalls Kant's two key claims, that (1) we must no longer view cognition as conforming to the object, but rather the object conforms to our cognition, and that (2) we must divert our self-cognition from fruitless and extravagant speculation to a fruitful practical employment (see e.g., B421). Throughout her chapter, Lo argues that these aspects of Kant's moral philosophy are prefigured by the classical Chinese philosopher, Mencius (372–289 B.C.E.), especially in his theory of the "original mind", which exhibits many of the same features that Kant later defends in his Critical philosophy—though in Mencius the mystical overtones are overt, whereas many readers would find them absent in Kant (but see note 4, below).

Finally, Gregory S. Moss concludes Part Four and the book by defending the claim, in Chapter 20, that the criticism of Kant's theory of representation put forward by the Japanese philosopher, Keiji Nishitani (1900–1990), highlights a paradox that Kant never fully faced and yet is at the very center of the focus of much Asian philosophy. As was already reiterated at several points throughout previous chapters of the present book, Kant's first *Critique* demonstrates the impossibility of gaining knowledge of the thing in itself by means of either concepts or intuitions. Without disputing this key Kantian claim, Nishitani points out that the first *Critique* does not demonstrate that it is impossible to know (in the sense of *kennen*, gaining an *awareness* of) the thing in itself through purely *non-subjective*, *non-representational*, and *non-conceptual* means. With this possibility in mind, Moss reconstructs Nishitani's formulation of *the paradox of representation* and shows how his method of resolving the paradox illuminates the non-conceptual means by which the thing in itself may be known. For Nishitani, rather than attempt to know the thing in itself through reason or subjectivity in general, we can become aware of the thing in itself by transcending reason and subjectivity altogether. Insofar as philosophy itself performs its rational work from the standpoint of subjectivity (whether implicitly or explicitly), the thing in itself can be known only by completely transcending the standpoint of philosophy. In Nishitani's terms, the only way to know the thing in itself is by "breaking through self-consciousness". Like various other contributors to the present volume who retain an openness to Asian perspectives, Moss therefore finds echoes of the mystical resounding throughout Kant's theory of transcendental idealism, and nowhere more noticeably than in his theory of intuition.

3. References to Kant's Works and Other Editing Protocols

All chapters in this volume were edited for stylistic consistency covering a range of minor issues such as those relating to punctuation, use of quotation marks, various grammatical conventions, etc. Most of these conventions are too minor to merit mentioning here. But the main area covered by the editorial conventions imposed on each chapter was the citation of author sources. All authors were required to cite their sources in the main text as much as possible, following the Harvard method: the author's surname followed immediately by the year of publication (where this is deemed necessary); after a comma comes the relevant page number(s). The first occurrence of a citation is given in this way (though authors have the option of omitting the name where it has just been mentioned in the main text or omitting the year if only one work is cited by that author); any subsequent *consecutive* citations of the same source in the same paragraph cite only the page number. A few chapters have special features for referencing that are explained in an endnote. For example, all Kant quotes in Chapter 12 are from the third *Critique*, so no abbreviation is used; only section and page numbers are provided. In other chapters, citations from the third *Critique* normally also include the relevant section number, just prior to the Academy Edition volume and page number(s). In addition to the abbreviations specified below, a few chapters employ special abbreviations for frequently cited works other than those by Kant.

Readers may assume that, unless otherwise noted in an individual chapter, all English quotations from Kant's works cite the Cambridge Edition (Allison et al., 1992); in place of the author's surname and year of publication (e.g., in place of "Kant 1788" for the second *Critique*), an abbreviation will precede the page number(s) (e.g., *CPrR*). All such abbreviations used in this anthology are listed at the end of the present section of this Introduction. After specifying the relevant abbreviation, citations will provide the volume and page number(s) where the cited passage appears in the Berlin Academy Edition (*Akademie Ausgabe*, 1900–) of Kant's German works. The only exception is that, when citing Kant's *Critique of Pure Reason*, all authors follow the standard practice of citing the pagination of the original first ("A") and/or second ("B") editions; these are provided in the margins of nearly all translations, in place of the volume and page number(s) of the Academy Edition.

As with citations of other authors' works, only the page number(s) are given when the same work of Kant's is cited consecutively within the same paragraph. Any author who does not use the Cambridge Edition for a given work states this fact in an endnote and, if he or she uses any other published translation(s), the relevant additional publication(s) is/are listed in the References section that appears at the end of that chapter. Cambridge translations quoted in a given chapter are not included in the References list that comes at the end of that chapter, because all of the relevant bibliographical information is included later in this section.

The following list specifies, in alphabetical order by abbreviation, all works by Kant that are cited by authors in this volume. Following the abbreviation, each entry specifies Kant's German title, followed by the year of its original publication—or, if unpublished during Kant's lifetime, the date(s) when Kant is presumed to have written it (if known)—and the volume and page number(s) of its location in the Berlin Academy Edition of Kant's works. If at least one author quotes from the standard Cambridge Edition of Kant's works, then the full bibliographical details of that translation follow. Abbreviations with an asterisk (*) indicate a work that is quoted *only* from the translation indicated, which is not part of the Cambridge Edition.

A/B   1781 and 1787 editions of the *Critique of Pure Reason*. Text specific to the A edition is found in 4:1–252. The B edition, along with text common to both editions, is found in 3:1–552. (See *CPR*.)

APP   *Anthropologie in pragmatischer Hinsicht* (1798); 7:117–333. Trans. R.B. Louden as *Anthropology from a Pragmatic Point of View*. In: G. Zöller and R.B. Louden (eds.), *Anthropology, History, and Education*. Cambridge: Cambridge University Press, 2007, 227–429.

AQE   *Beantwortung der Frage: Was ist Aufklärung?* (1784); 8:33–42. Trans. M.J. Gregor as *An Answer to the Question: What*

Is Enlightenment? In: *Practical Philosophy*, ed. M.J. Gregor. Cambridge: Cambridge University Press, 1999, 11–22.

C   *Briefwechsel* (various years); Vols. 10–13. Trans. and ed. A. Zweig as *Correspondence*. Cambridge: Cambridge University Press, 1999.

CF   *Der Streit der Fakultäten* (1798); 7:1–115. Trans. M.J. Gregor and R. Anchor as *The Conflict of the Faculties*. In: A.W. Wood and G. Giovanni (eds.), *Religion and Rational Theology*. Cambridge: Cambridge University Press, 1996, 233–327.

CPJ   *Kritik der Urteilskraft* (1790); 5:165–485. Trans. P. Guyer and E. Matthews as *Critique of the Power of Judgment*, ed. P. Guyer. Cambridge: Cambridge University Press, 2000. GR indicates a General Remark within Kant's text.

CPR   *Kritik der reinen Vernunft* (1781/1787); Vol. 3 and 4:1–252. Trans. and ed. P. Guyer and A.W. Wood as *Critique of Pure Reason*. Cambridge: Cambridge University Press, 1998.

CPrR   *Kritik der Praktischen Vernunft* (1788); 5:1–163. Trans. M.J. Gregor as *Critique of Practical Reason*. In: *Practical Philosophy*, ed. M.J. Gregor. Cambridge: Cambridge University Press, 1999, 133–271.

DSS*   *Träume eines Geistersehers, erläutert durch Träume der Metaphysik.* (1766); 2:315–373. Trans. G.R. Johnson and G.A. Magee as *Dreams of a Spirit–Seer Elucidated through Dreams of Metaphysics*. In: *Kant on Swedenborg: Dreams of a Spirit–Seer and Other Writings*, ed. G.R. Johnson. West Chester, PA: Swedenborg Foundation, 2002, 1–63.

FI   *Erste Einleitung in die Kritik der Urteilskraft* (1790); 20:193–251. Trans. and ed. P. Guyer and E. Matthews as *First Introduction to the Critique of the Power of Judgment*. In: *Critique of the Power of Judgment*, ed. P. Guyer. Cambridge: Cambridge University Press, 2000, 1–51. (See *CPJ*.)

GMM   *Grundlegung zur Metaphysik der Sitten* (1785); 4:385–463. Trans. M.J. Gregor as *Groundwork of The Metaphysics of Morals*. In: *Practical Philosophy*, ed. M.J. Gregor. Cambridge: Cambridge University Press, 1999, 37–108.

GR   General Remark (see *CPJ*).

ID   *De Mundi Sensibilis atque Intelligibilis Forma et Principiis. Dissertatio pro Loco Professionis Log. et Metaph. Ordinariae Rite Sibi Vindicando quam Exigentibus Statutis Academicis Publice Tuebitur* (1770); 2:385–419. Trans. D. Walford with R. Meerbote as *On the Form and Principles of the Sensible and the Intelligible World [Inaugural Dissertation]*. In: *Theoretical Philosophy, 1755–1770*, ed. D. Walford. Cambridge: Cambridge University Press, 1992, 373–416.

JL   *Immanuel Kants Logik: Ein Handbuch zu Vorlesungen*, ed. G.B. *Jäsche* (1800); 9:1–150. Trans. J.M. Young as *The Jäsche Logic*. [*Immanuel Kant's Logic: A Manual for Lectures*]. In: *Lectures on Logic*, ed. J.M. Young. Cambridge: Cambridge University Press, 1992, 517–640.

KT*   *Über Kästners Abhandlungen* (2014; original publication date unknown); 20:410–423. Trans. and ed. C. Onof and D. Schulting as *On Kästner's Treatises*. In: *Kantian Review* 19(2), 305–313.

MFNS   *Metaphysische Anfangsgründe der Naturwissenschaft* (1786); 4:465–565. Trans. M. Friedman as *Metaphysical Foundations of Natural Science*. In: *Theoretical Philosophy, after 1781*, ed. H. Allison and P. Heath. Cambridge: Cambridge University Press, 2004, 171–270.

MMH   *Einige Bemerkungen zu Ludwig Heinrich Jakobs Prüfung der Mendelssohn'schen Morgenstunden* (1786). 8:149–155. Trans. G. Zöller as *Some Remarks on Ludwig Heinrich Jakob's Examination of Mendelssohn's Morning Hours*. In: *Anthropology, History, and Education*, ed. G. Zöller and R. Louden. Cambridge: Cambridge University Press, 2007, 176–181.

OD   *Über eine Entdeckung, nach der alle neue Kritik der reinen Vernunft durch eine ältere entbehrlich gemacht warden soll* (1790); 8:185–251. Trans. H. Allison as *On a Discovery whereby any New Critique of Pure Reason Is To Be Made Superfluous by an Older One*. In: *Theoretical Philosophy, after 1781*, ed. H. Allison and P. Heath. Cambridge: Cambridge University Press, 2004, 271–336.

PFM   *Prolegomena zu einer jeden künftigen Metaphysik, die als Wissenschft wird auftreten können* (1783); 4:253–383. Trans. G. Hatfield as *Prolegomena to any Future Metaphysics that Will Be Able To Come Forward as Science*. In: *Theoretical Philosophy, after 1781*, ed. H. Allison and P. Heath. Cambridge: Cambridge University Press, 2004, 29–169.

R   *Reflexionen* (various years); Vols. 14–19. Trans. C. Bowman, P. Guyer, and F. Rauscher as *Notes and Fragments*, ed. P. Guyer. Cambridge: Cambridge University Press, 2005.

VL   *Kant's Vorlesungen über Logik geschrieben von einer Gesellschaft Zuhörern* (1780–1782); 24:787–940. Trans. J.M. Young as *Vienna Logic: Kant's Lectures on Logic Written by a Society of Authors*. In: *Lectures on Logic*, ed. J.M. Young. Cambridge: Cambridge University Press, 1992, 249–377.

WOT   *Was heißt: Sic him Denken orientiren?* (1786); 8:131–147. Trans. A.W. Wood as *What Does it Mean to Orient Oneself in Thinking?* In: *Religion and Rational Theology*, ed. A.W. Wood and G. Giovanni. Cambridge: Cambridge University Press, 1996, 1–18.

4. Acknowledgments

The making of a successful academic conference, at least when the event is a relatively large one, is always a team effort. The second Kant in Asia International Conference was no exception to this generalization. The idea of focusing on a theme related to intuition was first proposed by my long-time friend, Guy Lown—probably the non-academic philosopher whose presence at academic events is best known by philosophers all around Hong Kong. The theme was considered and unanimously accepted by other members of the Programme Committee: aside from Guy and myself, the other active members were the three HKBU PhD students whom I was supervising at the time: Jonathan Johnson, Brandon Love, and Simon Sai-ming Wong. The committee members all deserve the highest praise, not only for their diligence in assisting with various organizational details prior to and during the conference itself, but also for each presenting a paper; revised versions of most of these now appear in this volume. Moreover, Simon, Brandon, and Jonathan led a team of seven undergraduates to carry out most of the onerous background work during the conference itself: Robert Yufeng Fei, Alice Yuxin Yang, Cherry Cheuk-yan Kwan, Shannon Yan Zhou, Carol ("Slowpoke") Tianyuan Lin, Lancelot Feiyuan Yang, and Tong Yang all deserve thanks for helping to make the conference run so smoothly.

Simon's tireless assistance over the several months prior to the conference was crucial in keeping track of participants' data; he also recommended the passage from the third *Critique* that became the theme sentence for the entire conference (quoted in §1, above). More recently, Brandon worked just as tirelessly in assisting me with various tasks related to the preparation of the revised conference papers for publication here. The latter assistance was made possible thanks to a Faculty Research Grant from Hong Kong Baptist University. (In 2016 the university had also provided a separate grant, to assist with running the conference.) An able and hard-working assistant, Brandon proactively noticed many errors as he performed the rather mechanical (and time-consuming) tasks of inputting my various formatting (and other editorial) changes onto the several iterations of each chapter and of compiling the index; in so doing, he caught many mistakes that I might have overlooked. I hasten to add, though, that all editing decisions were ultimately mine, so any grammatical errors or other stylistic infelicities that may remain in the book are my responsibility.

Various scholars and organizations gave background support for the conference and/or this publication. Members of the conference's International Organizing Committee offered encouragement during the pre-conference organizing stage: the late (and greatly missed) Claudia Bickmann, Jack Chun, Young Ahn Kang, Suet-kwan Lo, Eric Nelson,

T.K. Seung, Mario Wenning, and my HKBU colleague, Kwok-kui Wong. Although their roles in most cases were largely symbolic, their willingness to endorse the event in advance added credibility that surely contributed to the success of our grant application. The same is true for the various academic societies around the world that formally endorsed the conference: in addition to the (then) newly formed Hong Kong Kant Society (which co-sponsored the conference), other endorsing societies were the Kant-Gesellschaft, the North American Kant Society, the UK Kant Society, the Norwegian Kant Society, the Immanuel Kant Society of Ukraine, Sociedad de Estudios Kantianos en Lengua Española, and Societatea Kant din Romania. Naturally, the conference would never have happened, had it not been for the willingness of the 42 participating scholars to sacrifice part of their winter holiday in 2016 to come from all around the world and gather in Hong Kong to present and discuss their papers on Kant. The (roughly) 30 others who attended some or all of the sessions without presenting a paper also added greatly to the success.

I would surely be remiss were I not to express my sincere appreciation to Professor Chen Zhi, the former Acting Dean of the Faculty of Arts at Hong Kong Baptist University, for entrusting me with the task of organizing the faculty's final academic event in celebrating the university's 60th anniversary. He initially approached me, in a conversation we had in early 2016, with the request that I organize a sequel to the highly successful 2009 Kant in Asia conference (see note 1). After some consideration, I agreed, and when adequate funding was confirmed in mid-2016, through generous grants from both the university and the Jao Tsung-I Academy of Sinology, planning activities began in earnest. (A supplementary grant from the Faculty of Arts was also much appreciated, in order to cover the small unpaid balance that remained after all other grant funding had been spent.) Due in large part to the relatively shorter period of advance preparation time, this second conference ended up being slightly less than half the size of the first one (see note 2). Fortunately, according to reports by many of the participants, it was no less enjoyable and informative.

Both during the month or two immediately preceding the conference and for the month or two immediately preceding submission of the manuscript for this book, my wife (Yuen Ching Lok), my daughter (Grace, 9), and my son (Anthony, 3) had to tolerate my absence (or my being present but preoccupied) for far too many evenings and weekends. I owe them my deepest thanks for their kindness and understanding during those periods of labor, and for always welcoming me with loving arms when each day's work finally came to an end.

Stephen R. Palmquist
16 July 2018

Notes

1. The first Kant in Asia international conference took place in May 2009 at Hong Kong Baptist University; it featured three keynote speakers (Patricia Kitcher, Günter Wohlfart, and Chung-ying Cheng) and 94 submitted papers for presentation at concurrent sessions on the general theme "The Unity of Human Personhood". The conference proceedings (which can be viewed as the prequel to the present anthology) were published as Palmquist 2010, a tome of over 850 pages that included 67 chapters on a wide range of topics relating to Kant.
2. Perhaps due in large part to the more focused nature of the second conference's theme, the number of participants was smaller: the three keynote lectures, presented here as the opening chapters in Parts Two, Three, and Four, each had one designated respondent; these six invited speakers were supplemented by presentations of 37 submitted papers. The smaller size enabled us to avoid the use of concurrent sessions. Whereas approximately 150 people attended the first Kant in Asia conference, the overall attendance at the second conference was roughly 75. Incidentally, two of the three respondents to the keynote lectures did not present pre-written papers, so their contributions were not considered for the present anthology. The exception, Robert Clewis, prompted numerous specific replies from the corresponding keynote speaker; he therefore submitted a revised version of his paper, and their scholarly exchange is reflected in the endnotes and Appendix to Chapter 11.
3. Much more work remains to be done on this, as is evidenced by the essays included in Part IX of Palmquist 2010, most of which also deal with this same theme.
4. Along the lines suggested in several of these chapters, Palmquist 2000 (especially Chapters II, X, and XII) argues that Kant's Critical philosophy can itself be interpreted as providing the philosophical grounding for a genuinely mystical way of life. Noteworthy in this respect is that Kant mentions mysticism in several Reflections. For example, in *R*5637 (18:272–275), he distinguishes between "mystical intuition" and various other types of intuition; see also *R*6050 (18:435). Of course, he typically rejects the mystical form; but in *R*4228 (17:467) he *affirms* that "our intellectual intuitions of the free will do not agree with the laws of the *phaenomenorum*." See also *R*6611 (19:108), among others.
5. Due to limitations of space, only about half of the papers presented at the conference could be included in this anthology. One of the participants, Kiyoshi Himi, has placed his paper online, accessible at: www.korousa.com/K.H's%20 presentation%20in%20KIA2%20.pdf.
6. It is noteworthy here that Kant consistently uses "*Gegenstand*", not "*Objekt*", to refer to objects that appear to us through either inner *or outer* sense. While this may not detract from the legitimacy of Chun's claim that outer intuition puts us in touch with an independently existing *reality*, the fact that Kant typically reserves "*Objekt*" to refer to the object as it has been processed by means of the categories does at least suggest that the "reality" we "touch" through outer intuition is *empirical* reality, not the thing in itself.
7. An earlier version of this chapter was published in Chinese (see Zhouhuang 2017).
8. *Chin* (or *Qin*) is the name of the first dynasty of Imperial China (221–206 B.C.E.); it united the seven states that had been vying for power throughout the Warring States period (247–221 B.C.E.).

References

Allison, Henry E., Paul Guyer, and Allen Wood (eds.) (1992). *The Cambridge Edition of the Works of Immanuel Kant*. Cambridge: Cambridge University Press. For translations of individual works, see separate listing in Section 3, above.

Palmquist, Stephen R. (2010). *Cultivating Personhood: Kant and Asian Philosophy*. Berlin: Walter de Gruyter.

—— (2000). *Kant's Critical Religion: Volume Two of Kant's System of Perspectives*. Aldershot, UK: Ashgate, 2000.

Zhouhuang, Zhengmi (2017). 《从感性到理性的反转—康德崇高概念辨析》(Turn from Sensibility to Reason: Kant's Concept of the Sublime). 《世界哲学》(*World Philosophy*) 2, 67–76.

Part I

The Role of Intuition in Geometry and Transcendental Idealism

1 How Does Transcendental Idealism Overcome the Scandal of Philosophy?

Perspectives on Kant's *Objekt/Gegenstand* Distinction

Stephen R. Palmquist, Guy Lown, and Brandon Love

[I]f there perhaps occurs only one single word for a certain concept that, in one meaning already introduced, exactly suits this concept, and if it is of great importance to distinguish it from other related concepts, then it is advisable not to be prodigal with that word or use it merely as a synonym or an alternative in place of other words, but rather to preserve it carefully in its proper meaning.

(A312–313/B369)

1. Jacobi's Challenge to Transcendental Idealism's Account of Intuiting Objects

Kant's theory of transcendental idealism answers a twofold question: How is it possible for us to *intuit* particular objects, and what makes such intuition impossible for certain (metaphysical) types of object? While the other chapters in this book explore various aspects of Kant's theory of intuition, and the many controversies arising out of it, this opening chapter steps back from Kant's core question and asks: *What does Kant mean by "object"?* In the course of defending transcendental idealism, Kant introduces and discusses many different *types* of object, only some of which relate to intuition. Indeed, the question of whether or not a particular object is (or can be) intuited is crucial to the way we are permitted to talk about it. Given this widely accepted fact, we find it nothing short of astounding that interpreters have not devoted more attention to unpacking the question of whether Kant intended to distinguish between two words he uses, which are both normally translated as "object": namely, *Objekt*[1] and *Gegenstand*. While several valiant attempts have been made, as we shall see later in this section, each has been relatively brief and narrowly focused. But if widespread agreement is to be reached on the importance of such a distinction, in the manner Kant urges in the

4 Stephen R. Palmquist, Guy Lown, and Brandon Love

passage quoted above, the exposition needs to be comprehensive and its defense well-grounded in Kant's text. We therefore aim to begin the task of filling this lacuna by defending a way of understanding how these two terms shape and even determine Kant's theory of the object, in both its theoretical and its practical applications; this should prepare readers for a more nuanced assessment of the chapters that follow, all of which use the word "object" regularly. As we shall see, Kant's theory of the object is integrally bound up with his theory of how the peculiar features of human intuition (as limited to sensibility) make transcendental idealism the correct theoretical understanding of human cognition.

At A369, Kant famously defines "transcendental idealism" as a "doctrine" that requires us to regard "all appearances . . . as mere representations and not as things in themselves", for "space and time are only sensible forms of our intuition, but not determinations given for themselves or conditions of *Objekte* as things in themselves." Shortly before Kant published the second edition of the first *Critique*, F.H. Jacobi published *David Hume on Faith*, which included an appendix criticizing Kant's newfangled, "transcendental" version of idealism. Jacobi's discussion of Kant's position uses both "*Objekt*" and "*Gegenstand*" in ways that suggest he was aware of an implicit distinction between them. Most significantly, the oft-quoted claim that Jacobi makes at the climax of his criticism—typically misquoted as the claim that one cannot enter Kant's system without assuming the *thing in itself*, yet with this assumption one "cannot stay within his system" (Jacobi 1994, 228)—is actually not primarily (if at all) a claim about the thing in itself. Rather, Jacobi's actual challenge concerns Kant's assumption that what affects us through the process of intuition is a *Gegenstand*, which Jacobi takes Kant to regard as an object *within us*, not one that is external to the mind (228): "*without* that presupposition I could not enter into [Kant's] system, but *with* it I could not stay within it." Jacobi treats Kant's use of "*Gegenstand*" as referring *not* to objects outside the mind (and certainly not to the thing in itself), but to the mental *awareness* we must have of an object in order for us ever to cognize it objectively. Because *Gegenstände* are only in the mind, he argues, Kant's claim that they *affect* our sensibility makes no sense, unless Kant admits that transcendental idealism leaves no room for empirical realism.[2]

Jacobi's charge profoundly affected Kant. In response, he composed the Refutation of Idealism, the only entirely new section (other than the Preface) that Kant added to the second (1787) edition. (All other, *seemingly* new material, as Kant emphasizes at Bxxxixn, consisted of thoroughly rewritten versions of sections that also existed in 1781.) A fact that has gone curiously unnoticed in the literature, that the entire text of the Refutation employs *only* the term "*Gegenstand*", never "*Objekt*", therefore seems highly significant for our purposes. In §3, we will consider the implications of this fact and will argue that Kant had already demonstrated in the Deduction (in both the A and B editions) that *Objekte* are external to us; what remained to be argued (in response to Jacobi) was that, even if we limit our attention to *Gegenstände*, we can justify our belief that cognized objects are external (and thus legitimately defend a robust realism) without taking refuge in faith.

In §2, we examine textual evidence supporting our claim that Kant's two technical terms for "object" have quite distinct meanings. We show that our interpretation establishes a comprehensive framework for understanding not only how Kant thought he had resolved the scandal of philosophy (§3), but also (in §4) how certain key features of his practical philosophy relate to the theoretical. But first, let us briefly examine three previous, but less comprehensive attempts at distinguishing between *Objekt* and *Gegenstand*.

By far the predominant approach among Kant scholars is simply to avoid making any *Objekt/Gegenstand* distinction. However, three interpreters stand out as exceptions: Henry Allison, Rudolf Makkreel, and Howard Caygill. Allison distinguished the terms in 1983, though his view underwent a shift—in light of criticisms, especially from Béatrice Longuenesse—such that he had stopped using the distinction by 2004.[3]

According to Allison (1983, 135), an *Objekt* (at least in the B Deduction) is a "logical conception of an object (an object in *sensu logico*)." A *Gegenstand*, by contrast, is "a 'real' sense of object"—i.e., "an object in the sense of an actual entity or state of affairs (an object of possible experience)" (135). He relates objective validity to "*Objekt*" and objective reality to "*Gegenstand*". However, the problematic nature of this latter claim can readily be seen in the very paragraph from which Allison infers his "reciprocity thesis" (144), the thesis that "The essential move in the first part of the Deduction is the attempt to establish a reciprocal connection between the transcendental unity of apperception and the representation of objects." At B137, Kant explicitly relates objective validity to *Gegenstand*, rather than *Objekt*: "the unity of consciousness is that which alone constitutes the relation of representations to a *Gegenstand*, thus their objective validity."

The most relevant point for our understanding of the distinction (see §2) is Allison's claim that "*Objekt*" refers to an object "in *sensu logico*". Longuenesse (1998, 111n) points out the problem with this claim:[4] Allison is mistaken, because Kant's point concerning "*Objekt*" in the Deduction (though Longuenesse does not grant a distinction between the terms) is "a consideration of the logicodiscursive function of the understanding", while his point concerning *Gegenstand* is "a reevaluation, *in light of the first consideration*, of what we learned in the Transcendental Aesthetic about space and time, that is, about 'the manner in which things are given to us'" (70n). In revising his argument, Allison (2004, 44) says that Longuenesse convinced him to reject his initial distinction, since she showed that "the object at issue in the first part of the

Deduction is defined as the object of intuition as such and is therefore an *intuited* object rather than merely an object in the most general or logical sense." As a result, Allison (44) rejected "the extremely vague and potentially misleading notion of an object *in sensu logico*." More recently, Allison has confessed that he now sees "a certain randomness in Kant's use of these terms [*Objekt* and *Gegenstand*]", such that Allison has "ceased placing any weight on the terminology" (2015, 380n). Yet he still emphasizes (380n)—what will be crucial in our account, below— that Kant makes a distinction "between two conceptions of an object rather than between two kinds of object." This revised approach, along with Longuesse's criticism of Allison's earlier position, pose no problem to the position we will defend: even if the *Objekt* is not merely an object *in sensu logico*, abandoning this claim does not require abandoning the distinction altogether.

Makkreel (1990, 39–40) frames his discussion of the distinction in relation to Allison's. For Makkreel (40), "an *Objekt* need not be merely logical; it can be just as real as a *Gegenstand*." Still, Makkreel thinks Kant sometimes does view *Objekte* as merely logical. For Makkreel (41), "anything either merely thought or merely sensed would be an *Objekt* and becomes a *Gegenstand*—an object of experience—only through the mediation of the imagination. The difference between *Objekt* and *Gegenstand* is between an unmediated object and an object mediated by the schemata of the imagination." While Makkreel's interpretation of the distinction is more balanced, his view of "*Objekt*" as immediate depends on the notion of the object given in intuition. However, as we will see, Kant consistently uses "*Gegenstand*" for this aspect of the object. Makkreel refers to Kant's statement at B145 to claim that *Objekte* are given in intuition; however, Kant there says that the unity of apperception "combines and orders the material for cognition, the intuition, which must be given to it through the *Objekt*." On our reading, intuition occurs in *response* to the *Objekt*, but the material given in intuition is the *Gegenstand*. On this point, our reading is closer to that of Caygill.

Like both the early Allison and Makkreel, Caygill claims that "Kant's distinction between *Gegenstand* and *Objekt* is crucial to his transcendental philosophy, although never explicitly thematized" (2000, 305).[5] For Caygill, the two notions are intimately intertwined (305): "*Gegenstände* are objects of experience or appearances which conform to the limits of the understanding and intuition. . . . When objects [*Gegenstände*] of experience are made into objects *for* knowledge, they become *Objekte*."[6] Caygill's rationale for this view of the relationship (which seems to reverse Makkreel's) is that, while *Gegenstände* are appearances, *Objekte* are "that in the concept of which the manifold of a given intuition is *united*" (305, quoting B137). Caygill's interpretation of the distinction is correct, but does not go far enough. Moreover, although neglecting Kant's distinction altogether (as Longuenesse prefers) need not doom an interpretation to failure, we shall argue that taking on board the full extent of its complexities can serve not only to highlight certain contours of Kant's transcendental idealism that are otherwise easy to miss, but also to clarify various issues relating to his moral philosophy and to the overall coherence of his entire philosophical system.

2. Kant's Perspectival Use of *Objekt* and *Gegenstand*

The best way to detect the easily missed contours in Kant's transcendental idealism, while identifying strengths and weaknesses in the aforementioned interpretations, is to examine several key passages in which Kant states that an object can be viewed from two perspectives. He makes two different twofold distinctions, each with implications for the *Objekt/Gegenstand* distinction, and remains consistent in his use of these terms whenever he explicitly discusses these perspectival distinctions. One passage is in both versions; two others, Kant added in 1787. The first relates to the appearance/thing in itself distinction and the second to the phenomena/noumena distinction.[7]

In the first passage, Kant says an appearance "always has two sides" (A38/B55). We take this to refer to two *perspectives*, or ways of viewing appearances (cf. Palmquist 1986 and Allison 2015, 380). When the appearance is viewed from one perspective, "the *Objekt* is considered in itself (without regard to the way in which it is to be intuited, the constitution of which however must for that very reason always remain problematic)" (A38/B55). Viewed from the other perspective, "the form of the intuition of this *Gegenstand* is considered, which must not be sought in the *Gegenstand* in itself but in the subject to which it appears, but which nevertheless really and necessarily pertains to the representation of this *Gegenstand*" (A38/B55). If we regard an appearance *in itself* (i.e., without considering the way it is intuited), then we treat it as an *Objekt*; if, by contrast, we consider an appearance in relation to our mode of intuition (i.e., as it is for us), then we treat it as a *Gegenstand*. Kant adopts the latter perspective when he describes appearance as "The undetermined *Gegenstand* of an empirical intuition" (A20/B34) and the former perspective when he writes that appearances are "*Objekt[e]* of sensible intuition" (Bxxvi) and "empirical *Objekte*" (A46/B63).

This first distinction relates to the *empirical* object. We have seen that Kant speaks of the *Objekt* as "that in the concept of which the manifold of a given intuition is *united*" (B137). This claim confirms our consistent observation that in Kant's usage only *Gegenstände* are given in intuition;[8] *Gegenstände* in intuition are then united to form the empirical *Objekt* through the process of determination effected by the schematized categories (see A145–146/B185). When we view an appearance as an *Objekt*, we regard it as the unified empirical object (without considering our mode of intuition), whereas when we view it as a *Gegenstand*, we regard it as the material for forming an *Objekt*, given our mode of intuition. Because this way of making the distinction lines up well with the way both Longuenesse and Allison interpret the Deduction, we believe they have rejected the distinction prematurely.

Kant reiterates this first distinction throughout the B Preface, applying it not merely to the empirical object (which can be viewed as either appearance or thing in itself), but also to the phenomena/noumena distinction. Kant's main discussion of these latter notions comes in Chapter III of the Analytic of Principles, entitled "On the Ground of the Distinction of all *Gegenstände* in General into Phenomena and Noumena" (A235f/B294f). Throughout that chapter, Kant consistently portrays both notions as instances of *Gegenstände*. In 1781, he writes (A248–249):

> Appearances, to the extent that as *Gegenstände* they are thought in accordance with the unity of the categories, are called *phaenomena*. If, however, I suppose there to be things that are merely *Gegenstände* of the understanding and that, nevertheless, can be given to an intuition, although not to sensible intuition . . . then such things would be called noumena.

A phenomenon, then, is an appearance (a *Gegenstand* of intuition) that has been processed by the categories, whereas a noumenon is a *Gegenstand* that is merely thought, not given in sensible intuition. The key difference between these two types of *Gegenstand* is that the former is connected to an actual *Objekt* that we can experience through the senses, whereas the latter is not, at least as far as theoretical reason is concerned—a qualification whose full importance will emerge in §4. Kant restates these points in 1787 (B306):

> if we call certain *Gegenstände*, as appearances, beings of sense (*phaenomena*), because we distinguish the way in which we intuit them from their constitution in itself, then it already follows from our concept that to these we as it were oppose, as *Gegenstände* thought merely through the understanding, either other *Gegenstände* conceived in accordance with the latter constitution, even though we do not intuit it in them, or else other possible things, which are not *Objekte* of our senses at all, and call these beings of understanding (*noumena*).

Phenomena, therefore, are appearances (*Gegenstände* given in intuition) that have been determined by the categories, whereas noumena are *Gegenstände* that are merely thought and not intuited, because they have no connection to *Objekte* that we experience through *Gegenstände* given in intuition.

With these definitions in hand, we turn to two further distinctions Kant makes in the B Preface. First, he says that when pure reason goes

"beyond all boundaries of possible experience" (Bxviiin), we must consider "the same *Gegenstände* . . . from two different sides" (Bxviiin):
either "as *Gegenstände* of the senses and the understanding for experience", or as "*Gegenstände* that are merely thought at most for isolated
reason striving beyond the bounds of experience" (Bxviiin). As stated
in the Phenomena/Noumena chapter, we can consider the same *Gegenstände* as either phenomena or noumena. In explaining his rationale
for this distinction, Kant appeals to his practical philosophy, a move
whose legitimacy is guaranteed by the limits of theoretical cognition.
In culminating this discussion, he speaks of "the distinction between
things as *Gegenstände* of experience and the very same things as things
in themselves" (Bxxvii). Here, he gives the example of "the human
soul" (Bxxvii). Kant's distinction between the soul as phenomenon
(*Gegenstand* of experience) and as noumenon (a *Gegenstand* merely
of thought, which would be an *Objekt* viewed as thing in itself) allows
him to consider the soul in such a way "that its will is free and yet that
it is simultaneously subject to natural necessity" (Bxxvii).[9] He then
explains this same distinction in explicitly perspectival terms: "the
Objekt should be taken in *a twofold meaning*, namely as appearance
or as thing in itself" (Bxxvii).

As we shall see when we turn to Kant's practical philosophy in §4, this
distinction is fully in line with Kant's statement in *CPrR* (5:114):

> one and the same acting being as *appearance* (even to his own inner
> sense) has a causality in the world of sense that always conforms to
> the mechanism of nature, but with respect to the same event, insofar
> as the acting person regards himself at the same time as *noumenon*
> (as pure intelligence, in his existence that cannot be temporally deter-
> mined), he can contain a determining ground of that causality in
> accordance with the laws of nature which is itself free from all laws
> of nature.

One of the key factors in Kant's philosophical system that justifies this
twofold view of objects, whereby both *Gegenstände* and *Objekte* can be
either phenomenal *or* noumenal, is that practical reason provides us with
a direct awareness of a non-sensible *Objekt* that theoretical reason cannot reach: the highest good (see §4 for details).

Whereas Allison (who applied the *Objekt/Gegenstand* distinction
solely to the Deduction) regarded "*Objekt*" as Kant's term for an object
in the broadest sense, the above-quoted passages assign this status goes to
Gegenstände, not *Objekte*. Similarly, Kant writes (A290/B346):

> The highest concept with which one is accustomed to begin a tran-
> scendental philosophy is usually the division between the possible
> and the impossible. But since every division presupposes a concept

that is to be divided, a still higher one must be given, and this is the concept of a *Gegenstand* in general (taken problematically, leaving undecided whether it is something or nothing).

The highest concept in Kant's transcendental philosophy, therefore, is this concept of "*Gegenstand überhaupt*",[10] which grounds the modal distinction between possibility and impossibility. This, as we shall see in §3, is an insight without which Kant's strategy in the Refutation of Idealism cannot be fully understood. As we turn now to a consideration of that strategy, we must keep Kant's perspectival use of "*Objekt*" and "*Gegenstand*" firmly in mind: (1) viewed transcendentally, appearances are either *Gegenstände* (in us) or *Objekte* (outside us), depending on whether or not we take our mode of intuition into account; (2) viewed empirically, all *Gegenstände* are either phenomena or noumena, depending on whether they are given in sensible intuition, thereby constituting an empirical *Objekt*, or given merely in thought, thereby (allegedly) constituting an non-empirical *Objekt*; and (3) whereas phenomena are grounded in the *Objekt* through the processing of the categories, noumena stand in need of such a grounding being established by practical reason.

3. The Role of *Gegenstände* in the Refutation of Idealism

As we noted in §1, the Refutation of Idealism was Kant's response to Jacobi; as such, Kant's focus would obviously be on responding effectively to Jacobi's actual criticism. To reiterate: Jacobi rightly alleged that, in order to *enter* Kant's system we must assume that *Gegenstände*, as *represented* objects, are what affect the mind whenever we perceive something, yet he wrongly inferred that interpreting *Gegenstände* in this way makes it impossible to demonstrate that what we *believe* is experience of an external world really *is* an experience of something *outside* us. Jacobi's inference, if correct, would indeed cause anyone who is *not* a full-fledged idealist to be unable to remain in Kant's system. Jacobi thought anyone who holds Kant's view of the role of *Gegenstände* in intuition ought to come out of the closet and confess to being an out–and–out idealist. Now, armed with the nuanced, perspectival *Objekt/Gegenstand* distinction, introduced in §2, we can expose and resolve a previously unnoticed conundrum: as mentioned in §1, the word translated as "object" throughout the Refutation is *always* "*Gegenstand*", never "*Objekt*". This fact initially surprised us, for if Kant's purpose in writing the Refutation was to persuade his early critics that his special form of *transcendental* idealism actually allows for empirical realism, then we would expect him to focus on the reality of the empirical *Objekt* as existing *outside* us.

Instead of making any appeal to *Objekte*, Kant argues in the Refutation that, in order for us to become aware of our sense of "I", experience of *Gegenstände*—i.e., objects viewed as intuited appearances, precisely the feature of transcendental idealism Jacobi had found so intolerable—is *absolutely necessary*. The problem this poses, in short, is this: if Kant's argument in the Refutation is only that we must have representations of objects in order to gain any awareness of ourselves as a subject—given that Kant defines representations as "inner determinations of our mind" (A197/B242)—then how does this *not* make Kant an out–and–out idealist? Surely, it might seem, what Kant needs to establish is that these *Gegenstände* are and must be empirical *Objekte* in order for them to exist in our mind at all! Should not Kant have hammered home the externality of the empirical *Objekt* in this new Refutation? The aforementioned fact that Jacobi's actual criticism focused only on the status of *Gegenstände* is the reason Kant *had* to limit his attention to this term. The view of Kant's distinction that we have defended in §2 offers insight into how Kant could reach his intended goal *without* reference to *Objekte*.

In the pages of the Postulates of Empirical Thought that come just *before* the place where he inserted the new Refutation, Kant explicitly states that "the cognition of *Objekte*" requires a "synthesis" (of intuitions and concepts) that agrees with "the objective form of experience in general" (A220/B267). That form is what he had demonstrated to be space and time as forms of intuition (in the Aesthetic) and the categories as forms of conception (in the Deduction). Thus, he goes on to explain that if a concept "includes its own synthesis in it", then "it is held to be empty, and does not relate to any *Gegenstand*", because a concept (if it is empirical) must be synthesized with a *Gegenstand in intuition* in order to confirm its actuality. Even a "pure concept", he clarifies, attains objectivity only because and insofar as "its *Objekt* can be encountered only in [experience in general]" (A220/B267). He then asks a rhetorical question: "For whence will one derive the character of the possibility of a *Gegenstand* that is thought by means of a synthetic *a priori* concept, if not from the synthesis that constitutes the form of the empirical cognition of *Objekte*?" Kant takes the answer to be self-evident, given his argument in the foregoing sections of the *Critique*: only in experience do we meet *actual* (empirical) *Objekte*, so if we wish to know how specific *Gegenstände* that are *components* of a particular, cognized *Objekt* are *possible*, then we must look at the *formal conditions* that undergird our experience of empirical *Objekte*.

For the purposes of elucidating Kant's use of terms in the Refutation, the important point to note here is that Kant took the externality (or actuality) of *empirical* (cognized) *Objekte* to have been sufficiently established by his foregoing arguments in the Aesthetic and Deduction. The latter section's arguments in particular, being *conceptual* (i.e., being inextricably linked to the question of how the categories, through the activity of transcendental apperception, impart *unity* to empirical objects), were primarily about how the human mind modulates from being the (more or less) passive recipient of *Gegenstände* in intuition to being the active *cognizer* of external *Objekte*. As such, the actuality of that *Objekt* was not at issue for Kant at this point. Indeed, if Kant were merely to reiterate that argument in the Refutation, he would be begging the question posed by Jacobi's challenge, because Jacobi did not focus on the status of *Objekte* in Kant's theory. Jacobi recognized that Kant wanted *Objekte* to be external; he just did not think this would be possible, given the representational status of *Gegenstände*. So Kant's goal in the Refutation, in order to be effective, must be to show that his allegedly paradoxical view of the status of *Gegenstände* is actually itself a necessary requirement for us ever to become aware of the "I" of apperception, the very feature of the mind that, as the Deduction argues, is responsible for our awareness that the *Objekte* we experience actually are external to us. The details of that argument are well known, so our attention to that passage can remain at this general level. The key insight here is that the Refutation's strategy is not to prove we must have experience of *external objects* (whether *Objekte* or *Gegenstände*) in order for us ever to be aware of our own self–identity; rather, Kant argues that, whatever it may be that *impacts* our mind, it must do so in such a way that we gain representational awareness of it (i.e., it must be *given* to us in the *form* of a *Gegenstand*), otherwise the unity of apperception itself, the agency through which we *cognize Objekte* to be external, would be impossible.

Shortly after the end of the Refutation, when Kant resumes the text that had also been included in the first edition, we read (A234/B286) that the concern of the overall section of the *Critique* in which the Refutation appears—i.e., the Postulates of Empirical Thought—has been to demonstrate that the modal postulates

> add to the concept of a thing (the real), about which they do not otherwise say anything, the cognitive power whence it arises and has its seat, so that, if it is merely connected in the understanding with the formal conditions of experience, its *Gegenstand* is called possible; if it is in connection with perception (sensation, as the matter of the senses), and through this determined by means of the understanding, then the *Objekt* is actual; and if it is determined through the connection of perceptions in accordance with concepts, then the *Gegenstand* is called necessary.

Accordingly, intuitions are *possible* cognitions because we initially become aware of them as *Gegenstände* (i.e., initially they have the status of *appearances*, which are indeed problematic, precisely because they are only *possible* cognitions); *actual* cognitions are always of *Objekte*, because they are processed via the categories, thus confirming a real, empirical basis in *perception*; *necessary* cognitions arise only when we abstract from intuitions and regard *Objekte* as unified things (via the "I"), a process that takes us back to the level of *Gegenstände*, and leads human beings into the realm of the noumenal, where we think the abstract thoughts of metaphysics.

In a footnote to the B Preface (Bxxxixn), Kant describes the new Refutation of Idealism section as refutating "*psychological* idealism"; he claims it offers "a strict proof . . . of the objective reality of outer intuition." He famously continues:

> No matter how innocent idealism may be held to be as regards the essential ends of metaphysics (though in fact it is not so innocent), it always remains a scandal of philosophy and universal human reason that the existence of things outside us (from which we after all get the whole matter of our cognitions, even for our inner sense) should have to be assumed merely *on faith*, and that if it occurs to anyone to doubt it, we should be unable to answer him with a satisfactory proof.

This bold statement is normally taken as Kant's claim to have *overcome* the objections of Jacobi and other early critics (see e.g., Palmquist 1993, 391f). However, our study of Kant's *Objekt*/*Gegenstand* distinction suggests that something more subtle may be going on, given that Kant's new proof says nothing about the objective reality of *Objekte*, but explicitly focuses *only* on *Gegenstände*, the latter being what give rise to the threat of "psychological idealism". Unveiling this often-neglected contour of Kant's strategy suggests that here in the B Preface Kant may be wryly admitting to his reader—after having acknowledged a few pages earlier that, even without having the benefit of the Critical philosophy, "the scandal" of needing to rely on faith "sooner or later has to be noticed" (Bxxxiv)—that fully overcoming the scandal requires relocating the arena of "faith" (moving it from intuited *Gegenstände* to the noumenal [see Palmquist 1984]), rather than by straightforwardly replacing faith with apodictic certainty. With this in mind, we turn our attention now to the second *Critique*, where (as Kant states in *CPrR* 5:16) distinctions in the first *Critique* sometimes have to be *reversed*, if we are to understand morality aright.

4. *Objekt* and *Gegenstand* in the Second *Critique*: Toward a Comprehensive Distinction

In the third *Critique*'s Introduction, Kant concisely explains how the transition from theoretical to practical reason entails a subtle reversal in his use of the *Objekt*/*Gegenstand* distinction: "the concept of nature certainly makes its *Gegenstände* representable in intuition, but not as things in themselves, rather as appearances, while the concept of freedom in its *Objekt* makes a thing representable in itself but not in intuition" (*CPJ* 5:175). Here, Kant modifies the distinction as laid out in the first *Critique* (see §2, above), in line with the reversal of standpoint from theoretical to practical: *Gegenstände*, as objects of intuition that play a necessary role in the cognition of empirical *Objekte*, constitute what we can know about nature, from the standpoint of theoretical reason; the *Objekt* of freedom, by contrast, provides human beings with access to the noumenal (to the "in itself") in a way that enables us to overcome the limits of theoretical reason. Such overcoming, however, occurs through our access to *freedom*, which, as practical, is the focus of the second *Critique*; it therefore refers not primarily to *empirical Objekte* (as it did in *CPR*), but to the *Objekt* (which here also carries the sense of *goal* or *objective*) toward the realization of which all philosophizing ultimately aims.

We have already seen (in §2) a hint of the transition from theoretical to practical reason, in the form of Kant's phenomena/noumena distinction. Kant goes to great lengths to ensure that readers do not lose track of the notion that, while the use of practical reason is distinct from the use of theoretical (or speculative) reason, nonetheless these are still the workings of one and the same pure reason. For example, he says (*CPrR* 5:89): "practical reason has as its basis the same cognitive faculty as does speculative reason so far as both are *pure reason*." He even claims that "the concept of freedom", obviously central to his moral philosophy, "constitutes the *keystone* of the whole structure of a system of pure reason, even of speculative reason" (3).

If we are correct in assuming that Kant intended to distinguish sharply between "*Objekt*" and "*Gegenstand*", and that this distinction is as important to the second *Critique* as it is to the first, then it is no accident that Chapter II of the Analytic (in *CPrR*) is entitled: "On the Concept of a *Gegenstand* of Pure Practical Reason" (5:57). While his explanation of the role of *Gegenstände* in moral cognition is quite complex and therefore potentially confusing, the following passage provides one of the clearest and most explicit statements of the *Objekt*/*Gegenstand* distinction in Kant's entire corpus. He begins (57):

> By a concept of a *Gegenstand* of practical reason I understand the representation of an *Objekt* as an effect possible through freedom. To be a *Gegenstand* of practical cognition so understood signifies, therefore, only the relation of the will to the action by which it or its opposite would be made real, and to appraise whether or not something is a *Gegenstand* of *pure* practical reason is only to distinguish the possibility or impossibility of *willing* the action by which, if we had the ability to do so (and experience must judge about this), a certain *Objekt* would be made real.

In Kant's theoretical philosophy, *Gegenstände* given in intuition are taken up and determined by the categories, resulting in an empirical *Objekt* that we cognize as existing "outside us" (i.e., independently of our mind). Similarly, here in his practical philosophy, a *Gegenstand* (when employed properly) serves to bring about an *Objekt*. (Just what that *Objekt is* will become evident shortly.) Kant says the concept of a *Gegenstand* of practical reason is the representation of an *Objekt* as an effect of freedom. Such *Gegenstände* of practical cognition arise out of the relationship between the will and the action that is produced by the will. To determine whether something is a *Gegenstand* of pure practical reason is to determine the possibility (or impossibility) of willing an action that would bring about a desired *Objekt*. The *Objekt* is the effect of our willing, whereas the *Gegenstand* is the relationship between the will (as cause) and the effect of the will.

This brings us to one of the primary meanings of "*Objekt*" in Kant's practical philosophy—namely, *Objekt* as moral *goal* (or *objective*). In this instance, the goal of willing is to produce a certain effect, an *Objekt*, as the objective of one's choice in willing an action. Kant continues his explanation, offering different scenarios for the *Objekt/Gegenstand* relationship in willing an effect, as follows (*CPrR* 5:57–58):

> If the *Objekt* is taken as the determining ground of our faculty of desire, the *physical possibility* of it by the free use of our powers must precede our appraisal of whether it is a *Gegenstand* of practical reason or not. On the other hand, if the a priori law can be regarded as the determining ground of the action, and this, accordingly, can be regarded as determined by pure practical reason, then the judgment whether or not something is a *Gegenstand* of pure practical reason is quite independent of this comparison with our physical ability, and the question is only whether we could *will* an action which is directed to the existence of an *Objekt* if the object [literally, "if it"] were within our power; hence the *moral possibility* of the action must come first, since in this case the determining ground of the will is not the *Gegenstand* but the law of the will.

If a person regards the willed action (the *Objekt*) as the determining ground of the will, this would require considering whether achieving it is physically possible *before* we can ask whether it is a *Gegenstand* of practical reason. But if the moral law is the determining ground of the action, then the questions of physical possibility and whether the action is a *Gegenstand* of practical reason are mutually independent. In this latter case, the question is whether we could will an action that is aimed at bringing about an *Objekt* (i.e., at achieving a certain effect as the action's goal), if it is within our power. For an action to be free, the moral possibility must precede (and be independent of) the physical possibility. The determining ground is therefore the moral law instead of the *Gegenstand* (i.e., the relationship between the willing and its effect).

Putting the complexities of this passage aside, we can see that the effect of willing is not identical to the relationship between the will and the action. The former is the *Objekt* and the latter, the *Gegenstand*, of practical reason. Accordingly, Kant continues (*CPrR* 5:58): "The only *Objekte* of a practical reason are therefore those of the *good* and the *evil*. For by the first is understood a necessary *Gegenstand* of the faculty of desire, by the second, of the faculty of aversion, both, however, in accordance with a principle of reason." For practical reason, in other words, the sole *Objekte* are good and evil, the basis for principled moral choice. Good is a *Gegenstand* of the faculty of desire insofar as good is the relationship of the will to an action, the same applying for evil and the faculty of aversion. This means that the *proper* goal (*Objekt*) of practical reason is *bringing about good as the effect of the will*, good (as the *Gegenstand* of desire) consisting of the will's function as grounding the action, since moral goodness has its sole basis in the will.

Kant goes on to elucidate this point still further (*CPrR* 5:60):

> *Well-being* or *ill-being* always signifies only a reference to our state of *agreeableness* or *disagreeableness*, of gratification or pain, and if we desire or avoid an *Objekt* on this account we do so only insofar as it is referred to our sensibility . . . But *good* or *evil* always signifies a reference to the *will* insofar as it is determined by the *law of reason* to make something its *Objekt*; for, it is never determined directly by the *Objekt* and the representation of it, but is instead a faculty of making a rule of reason the motive of an action (by which an *Objekt* can become real).

Kant is saying that, if we merely desire or feel aversion toward an empirical *Objekt* (as a phenomenal effect), then we are always dealing only with matters of sensibility, rather than morality proper. Good and evil themselves, as genuine moral principles, always signify the relationship of the will to the moral law, the *goal* being to make a noumenal *Objekt* real. The will, when functioning morally, cannot be determined by the *Objekt*; rather, the will relates to the motive for performing an action, the *Objekt* being the effect of willing. This is simply the (familiar) claim that consequentialism cannot serve as the basis of morality, though the fine *contours* of his claim become more readily apparent when his *Objekt/Gegenstand* distinction is made explicit. Indeed, he goes on to clarify his understanding of moral good and evil still further, noting (61): "What we are to call good must be a *Gegenstand* of the faculty of desire in the judgment of every reasonable human being, and evil a *Gegenstand* of aversion in the eyes of everyone; hence for this appraisal reason is needed, in addition to sense." Good and evil therefore refer to how the will and the action are prioritized, not to the action's effect.

Previously, Kant had emphasized the importance of the order of priority even more clearly (*CPrR* 5:21):

> By "the matter of the faculty of desire" I understand a *Gegenstand* whose reality is desired. Now, when desire for this *Gegenstand* precedes the practical rule and is the condition of its becoming a principle, then I say (*first*) that this principle is in that case always empirical. For, the determining ground of choice is then the representation of an *Objekt* and that relation of the representation to the subject by which the faculty of desire is determined to realize the object [literally, "it"]. Such a relation to the subject, however, is called *pleasure* in the reality of the *Gegenstand*. This would therefore have to be presupposed as a condition of the possibility of the determination of choice. But it cannot be cognized a priori of any representation of a *Gegenstand*. . . . Hence in such a case the determining ground of choice must always be empirical, and so too must be the practical material principle that presupposes it as a condition.

Without making the *Objekt/Gegenstand* distinction, one might read Kant as claiming in this passage that the matter of the faculty of desire is an effect of an action; however, Kant's use of "*Gegenstand*" (rather than "*Objekt*") signals his concern for *prioritizing* between the will and the action. The matter of the faculty of desire is the desired relationship between the will and an action, not its effect. When we allow something empirical to determine our desire, we are not choosing to will freely. In this case, the determining ground of the choice is the empirical *Objekt*, and the relationship of the *Objekt* to the subject (this relationship being the *Gegenstand*). In moral cognition, the relationship of the *Objekt* to the subject is also pleasure in the reality of the *Gegenstand*. This pleasure cannot be cognized *a priori* for any representation of the relationship itself (the *Gegenstand*), no matter what the relationship may be; but the determining ground must be the moral law as *Objekt*.

If the foregoing were the full extent of the added insight we can gain into the contours of Kant's argument, by taking Kant's *Objekt/Gegenstand* distinction seriously, this would already justify a call to English-speaking Kant scholars around the world to make a concerted effort to search for a new way of translating one or the other of these terms, so that future English readers of Kant will be able to detect the nuances he built into his theory.[11] Yet, the potential insights this distinction contributes to a deeper understanding of Kant's philosophy do not stop here. The implications of Kant's distinction reach their apex once we discover that Kant identifies the ultimate *Objekt* of the practical philosophy (if not for metaphysics, and hence for all philosophizing whatsoever) as none other than the *highest good*. He consistently portrays "the promotion of the highest good" as "an a priori necessary *Objekt* of our will" (*CPrR* 5:114)—never as its *Gegenstand*. Thus, we read (122): "The production of the highest good in the world is a necessary *Objekt* of a will determined by the moral law."

While the vast majority of Kant's uses of "*Objekt*" and "*Gegenstand*" in *CPrR* fit the above description quite well, in a few passages he *appears* to use the wrong term. But in such cases, if we take his usage seriously, instead of simply assuming that he was being careless (or that his usage is merely random), then we stand to gain insights about the contours of his theory that would otherwise remain entirely hidden from the English reader's view. For example, in an earlier passage (5:109), Kant writes:

> though the highest good may be the whole *Gegenstand* of a pure practical reason, that is, of a pure will, it is not on that account to be taken as its *determining ground*, and the moral law alone must be viewed as the ground for making the highest good and its realization or promotion the *Objekt*.

The mere fact that Kant first uses "*Gegenstand*" and then changes to "*Objekt*" could, admittedly, be taken as evidence that the terms are interchangeable. But if, instead, we ask what Kant must mean in this passage, assuming he intentionally distinguished them, a significant insight emerges. Kant's point is, as usual, perspectival: even though from the perspective of our *feeling* about the highest good, we may experience it as not only *a Gegenstand* (a relation between our will and action), but as the sum total of all desires that practical reason regards as legitimate, only by attaching this feeling to the moral law do we succeed in making the highest good a genuine *Objekt* (goal), which we must pursue if we are to be fully rational.

We have shown that Kant's *Objekt/Gegenstand* distinction persists throughout his philosophical system, though its features change along with the system's perspectival shifts. In theoretical philosophy *Gegenstände* are given in intuition, as transcendentally ideal components of appearances, while in practical philosophy they are given in thought (through the concept of freedom), as representations of the relationship between moral actions and the will. Likewise, *Objekte* require categorial determination in order to be cognized empirically, thus barring us from access to noumena when viewed theoretically; yet they make the noumenal actual when viewed practically, as expressing the highest good.

While our defense of Kant's *Object/Gegenstand* distinction aims to be comprehensive, we fully recognize that this chapter has merely illuminated the contours of its implications for Kant's response to Jacobi: *Gegenstände* in intuition can be viewed as empirically real, despite the key role they play in Kant's transcendental *idealism*; and this robust realism requires Critical philosophers to shift the focus of faith from the phenomenal to the noumenal, thereby transforming faith from being a philosophical scandal for cognition to being the mantle that metaphysics proudly wears. A fully comprehensive defense of this distinction, however, will require a book-length work, where we will explain various important additional features, including: (1) mathematics, being grounded on *pure* intuition, involves non-empirical objects that are apodictically necessary;[12] (2) in contexts referring to the *subject*, Kant contrasts it with "*Objekt*", not "*Gegenstand*";[13] (3) the ideas of reason (God, freedom, and immortality) are *Gegenstände* (and thus merely possible) when viewed theoretically, yet are legitimately regarded as actual, as "*Objekte* of pure practical reason" (*CPrR* 5:5), when properly related to the highest good;[14] and (4) explaining Kant's denial of intellectual intuition in terms of the *Objekt/Gegenstand* distinction will provide a clear understanding of why the affirmations of practical philosophy are sufficient even though they do not amount to full-fledged intellectual intuition.

Our hope, then, is that in this first published attempt to defend the range of radical claims we believe can be made about Kant's highly neglected distinction, we have at least demonstrated that interpreters of Kant should henceforth make a point of inquiring whether Kant is using "*Objekt*" or "*Gegenstand*", especially when seeking to understand how his transcendental idealism relies on a complex theory of intuition. This chapter's introductory quote shows that Kant sought to avoid randomly using terms synonymously. Our comprehensive interpretation of his *Objekt/Gegenstand* distinction exonerates Kant from what would otherwise be a "prodigal" use of terminology. We aim "to preserve" Kant's words "carefully in [their] proper meaning", just as Kant himself says is "advisable" (A312–313/B369). Consistently applying the distinction renders some passages strange, but this may signal that the full depths of Kant's thought have not yet been plumbed, and the distinction may illuminate such strangeness rather than cause it (cf. Ertl 2013, 438–439). If we are to take Kant's thought seriously, we must take it on his own terms. In a word, Kant's application of his *Objekt/Gegenstand* distinction overcomes the scandal of philosophy by pointing the metaphysician's attention firmly and necessarily toward the moral standpoint, in order to ground the *Gegenstände* of our experiences as citizens of the phenomenal world in an *Objekt* that transcends the operations of our own mental capacities: the highest good.

Notes

1. Kant uses both "*Object*" and "*Objekt*" in various works. For consistency, and to avoid possible confusion with the English, "object", we always use "*Objekt*". Moreover, both "*Objekt*" and "*Gegenstand*" are spelled differently, depending on whether they are singular or plural and on what grammatical role they play in the sentence. To avoid perplexing English readers who may not be familiar with German grammar, we adopt the following

convention: when "object" or "objects" appears in a quote, we simply replace it with the German term (adjusting the English article, "a/an", if needed); whenever it is *singular*, we use either "*Objekt*" or "*Gegenstand*"; whenever it is *plural*, we use "*Objekte*" or "*Gegenstände*".

2. For an excellent account of this interpretation of Jacobi's challenge, see Karin de Boer (2014, 221–260), though she distinguishes between *Objekt* and *Gegenstand* only linguistically, not in meaning.

3. Two interpreters who explicitly follow Allison's 1983 distinction are Zammito (1992) and Kim (2015). Zammito ties the distinction to the scholastic *res/ens* distinction (1992, 362n; see also 54 and 72). Kim (2015, 129n) relates the distinction to two conceptions of the categorical imperative in *GMM*.

4. A detailed account of the Allison–Longuesese debate on this issue is irrelevant to our concern in this chapter, as it centers on how to interpret the Deduction. Indeed, Allison's *exclusive* focus on the Deduction may be what led him to adopt an untenable version of the distinction; as we will see in §2, the key features of the distinction relate as much (if not more) to Kant's theory of intuition as to his theory of the categories. For the debate itself, see Longuenesse (1998, 70, 110–111) and Allison (2012a, 35 and 2012b, 43–44).

5. Interestingly, Caygill does not acknowledge other versions of the distinction, yet Allison had not yet abandoned his position when Caygill advanced his alternative.

6. Caygill's brackets. By "knowledge", Caygill seems to mean "cognition". On this issue of the determination of objects, in relation to the *Objekt/Gegenstand* distinction, Makkreel's distinction is virtually the reverse of both ours and Caygill's.

7. Many interpreters treat these two distinctions as synonymous. For a detailed explanation of their different functions in Kant's theory, see Palmquist 1986. While we are broadly in agreement with systematic features of the interpretation presented there, that article did not distinguish between *Objekt* and *Gegenstand* and thus overlooked various nuances that would have given its interpretation further support and clarity. Moreover, Palmquist 1986 remained silent on how Kant's treatment of object–terms in the second *Critique* relates to that in the first.

8. In the process of examining every use of *Objekt* and *Gegenstand* in the first *Critique*, in order to classify them into different types of usage (a study the results of which we intend to publish later), we discovered that when Kant refers to an object being exhibited "in intuition", he consistently uses "*Gegenstand*". On the relatively few occasions where "*Objekt*" appears in such contexts, the statement is either counterfactual or else makes a claim that falls short of committing Kant to the view that an *Objekt* can be exhibited in intuition. For an excellent discussion of Kant's theory that objects are given in intuition, see Allais 2015, though she does not point out that Kant's concern here is exclusively with *Gegenstände*.

9. For an excellent discussion of the relationship between the phenomena/noumena and appearances/things in themselves, see Stang (2016, 182–183). He demonstrates that, while all things in themselves are noumena, not all noumena are things in themselves. This explains why Kant speaks of the soul as a thing in itself to illustrate the phenomena/noumena distinction.

10. While it may be tempting to interpret Kant's various references to an "object in general" as synonymous to his references to a "transcendental object", we regard these as distinct terms. On the latter, see Sherover (1982), who makes a valiant attempt to distinguish between Kant's use of "transcendental

Objekt" and "transcendental *Gegenstand*"; see also Love (2017, 203–204n and 193n). We plan to weigh in on this aspect of Kant's distinction in a subsequent publication.

11. For example, di Giovanni (2010, xxxvi), in translating Hegel, describes the project of translating *Gegenstand* and *Objekt* as "a translator's nightmare . . ." Yet, his explanation of the distinction is remarkably similar to the one we find in Kant. Interestingly, he uses "subject matter" as the standard translation for "*Gegenstand*".

12. For a detailed discussion of Kant's theory of pure intuition as it pertains to mathematics, but without relating it to the *Objekt/Gegenstand* distinction, see Palmquist 1987.

13. A statistical analysis of Kant's usage in *CPR* overwhelmingly supports this claim; in the few cases where "*Gegenstand*" occurs in the same context as "*Subjekt*", the two terms are not directly opposed. The reason for Kant's consistent use is not (merely) grammatical; rather, it is because transcendental apperception is the function whereby the subject (the "I") first enters Kant's system; *Gegenstände* in intuition come *before* that entry, whereas empirical *Objekte* assume the activity of the *Subjekt*.

14. Kant says (A798/B826): "The final aim" of speculative reason "concerns three *Gegenstände*: the freedom of the will, the immortality of the soul, and the existence of God." In *CPrR*, these become "*Objekte* of pure speculative reason" (5:134). The transition from the ideas as *Gegenstände* to *Objekte* is an essential feature of practical reason, in which "those concepts, otherwise problematic . . . for [speculative reason], are now declared assertorically to be concepts to which real *Objekte* belong, because practical reason unavoidably requires the existence of them for the possibility of its *Objekt*, the highest good" (134). Theoretical reason allows us to "grant *that there are such Gegenstände*, though it cannot determine them more closely and so cannot itself extend this cognition of the *Objekte* (which have now been given to it on practical grounds . . .)" (135). Kant continues: "for this increment . . . pure theoretical reason, for which all those ideas are . . . without *Objekte*, has to thank its practical capacity only." Practical reason has its own *Objekt*, the highest good, by which the *Gegenstände* of theoretical reason obtain objective reality as *Objekte*.

References

Allais, Lucy (2015). *Manifest Reality: Kant's Idealism and his Realism*. Oxford: Oxford University Press.

Allison, Henry E. (1983). *Kant's Transcendental Idealism: An Interpretation and Defense*. New Haven and London: Yale University Press.

—— (2004). *Kant's Transcendental Idealism: An Interpretation and Defense*, 2nd ed. New Haven and London: Yale University Press.

—— (2012a). Where Have all the Categories Gone? Reflections on Longuenesse's Reading of Kant's Transcendental Deduction. In: H. E. Allison (ed.), *Essays on Kant*. Oxford: Oxford University Press, 31–42.

—— (2012b). A Response to a Response: An Addendum to "Where Have all the Categories Gone?" In: H. E. Allison (ed.), *Essays on Kant*. Oxford: Oxford University Press, 43–48.

—— (2015). *Kant's Transcendental Deduction: An Analytical–Historical Commentary*. Oxford: Oxford University Press.

Caygill, Howard (2000). *A Kant Dictionary*. Oxford: Blackwell Publishers Ltd.

de Boer, Karin (2014). Kant's Multi-Layered Conception of Things in Themselves, Transcendental Objects, and Monads. In: *Kant-Studien* 105(2), 221–260.

di Giovanni, George (2010). Introduction. In: Trans. and ed. G. di Giovanni, *George Wilhelm Friedrich Hegel: The Science of Logic*. Cambridge: Cambridge University Press, xi–lxii.

Ertl, Wolfgang (2013). "Nothing but Representations"—A Suárezian Way out of the Mind? In: S. Bacin, A. Ferrarin, C. La Rocca, and M. Ruffing (eds.), *Kant und die Philosophie in weltbürgerlicher Absicht. Akten des XI. Internationalen Kant-Kongresses*, Vol. 4. Berlin: Walter de Gruyter, 429–440.

Jacobi, Friedrich Heinrich (1994). Trans. G. di Giovanni, David Hume on Faith, or Idealism and Realism, A Dialogue. In: *The Main Philosophical Writings and the Novel Allwill*. Montreal and Kingston: McGill–Queen's University Press, 253–338.

Kim, Halla (2015). *Kant and the Foundations of Morality*. Lanham: Lexington Books.

Longuenesse, Béatrice (1998). Trans. C. T. Wolfe, *Kant and the Capacity to Judge: Sensibility and Discursivity in the Transcendental Analytic of the Critique of Pure Reason*. Princeton, NJ and Oxford: Princeton University Press.

Love, Brandon (2017). Transcendental Philosophy in Scotus, Kant, and Deleuze: One Voice Expressing Difference. In: *Aretè* 2, 192–212.

Makkreel, Rudolf A. (1990). *Imagination and Interpretation in Kant: The Hermeneutical Import of the Critique of Judgment*. Chicago: The University of Chicago Press.

Palmquist, Stephen R. (1984). Faith as Kant's Key to the Justification of Transcendental Reflection. *The Heythrop Journal* 25(4), 442–455.

——— (1986). Six Perspectives on the Object in Kant's Theory of Knowledge. In: *Dialectica* 40(2), 121–151.

——— (1987). A Priori Knowledge in Perspective: (I) Mathematics, Method and Pure Intuition. In: *The Review of Metaphysics* 41(1), 3–22.

——— (1993). *Kant's System of Perspectives: An Architectonic Interpretation of the Critical Philosophy*. Lanham: University Press of America.

Sherover, Charles (1982). Two Kinds of Transcendental Objectivity: Their Differentiation. In: J.N. Mohanty and R. Shahan (eds.), *Essays on Kant's "Critique of Pure Reason"*. Norman: University of Oklahoma Press, 251–278.

Stang, Nicholas F. (2016). *Kant's Modal Metaphysics*. Oxford: Oxford University Press.

Zammito, John H. (1992). *The Genesis of Kant's Critique of Judgment*. Chicago: The University of Chicago Press.

2 Kant, Euclid, and the Formal Intuition of Space

Hoke Robinson and Dan Larkin

1. Introduction

What is space?[1] Even before his transcendental turn, Kant was interested in space, leaning first toward Leibniz and then toward Newton. But in the 1770 *Inaugural Dissertation* and especially with the 1781 *Critique of Pure Reason*, space played a central role in his philosophy. His transcendental epistemology was built on cognitions predicating a concept of an intuition, which latter was a singular representation of an individual object. But the individuality of this object (its identity) depended, not on Leibniz's infinite *complete concept* (which, as infinite, could only be known by God), but on its unique position in space (and time). Thus, to determine of two allegedly distinct objects, X and Y, whether they are to count as two different objects or as the same object, we needed to locate them (or it) in space and time.

Kant scholars have long argued over the nature of Kantian space. One of these disputes concerns a key assumption: for spatial determination, Kant reached back to Euclid (1956), the geometry for his day (and arguably the spirit for ours). But is this geometry still adequate for today's scientific knowledge, especially in astronomy, where space is typically assumed to be non-Euclidian? And what role does the faculty of intuition play in this assumption?

A recent proposal would provide a *diagrammatic* interpretation of Euclidian geometry, allegedly resolving difficulties seen in its use as a basis for Kantian space. This proposal has been criticized in Friedman (2012), relying on considerations similar to those supporting this chapter's conclusion; Friedman summarizes his own views in the process.[2] Though we find both his critique and his own interpretation for the most part convincing,[3] we argue that there is another way to justify Kant's use of Euclid, one which seems superior pedagogically—and perhaps in other ways as well.

2. Friedman on Kant and Euclid

Friedman (2012, 236) takes the view that the relation of Kant's space to Euclid is such that "the construction in pure [or formal] intuition of . . . [e.g.] a triangle . . . just *is* the Euclidian construction demonstrated in Proposition I.22"[4] of the *Elements*. Friedman quotes Kant's remark in the first *Critique* (A164/B205; the emphasis is ours, not Friedman's or Kant's): "I have here the mere function of the productive imagination, which can draw the lines greater or smaller, and thereby allow them to meet at any and all *arbitrary* angles." And again, quoting a passage from A140–141/B180 (emphasis ours), Friedman takes its core to be that "this 'rule of synthesis' appears to be nothing more nor less than the Euclidean construction of an *arbitrary* triangle, considered in the Axioms of Intuition as a 'mere [universal] function of the productive imagination'."

Friedman uses the term "arbitrary" and equivalents (e.g., "*gleichgül-tig*", "*willkürlich*") some ten times, sometimes in Kant quotes but often on his own. He sees (and we agree) that this is the key to propositions in geometry (and arithmetic as well) that can be true in this context, and known *a priori* to be true, without the involvement of empirical object-level concepts, and so also without the procedure of analysis through which analytic statements are known to be true: these propositions are thus *synthetic* and *a priori*.

Why they are known to be true *a priori* is clear enough: they exist in the first place by virtue of construction in pure intuition (on paper/blackboard, or only in imagination) according to certain rules, and the same rules must be followed in constructing every triangle (one constructed otherwise would not be a triangle at all). Why they are synthetic may be a little less obvious.

Let us consider the *rules* followed in this construction procedure. They are attributed to Euclid,[5] and though intimations of some aspects of his *Elements* can be found in predecessors such as Plato, we need only go a century or two earlier to find a time when certainly no specific set of explicit rules for geometrical construction such as we find in the *Elements* existed.

Then, did Euclid *invent* the construction rules of geometry, or did he *discover* them? The answer, we think, depends on their application. We can consider these rules alone, abstracting from the question of application, and if they are internally consistent (and perhaps even if they are not), we would say he invented them. If we then include consideration of their application, especially to aspects and features of the physical world that seem to have been present long before Euclid wrote the *Elements*, we would say he discovered them (similarly to our usage when we say Captain Cooke *discovered* a previously unknown island because we take the island to have existed before he discovered it).

We can compare Euclid's geometrical system, once again abstracting from its application, to certain games, such as chess, sudoku, and tic–tac–toe, which also came into existence at a certain time in human history and did not exist before then. Just as we follow Euclid and grant the validity of his proof of Kant's favorite example, that the sum of every triangle's internal angles is necessarily equivalent to two right angles (Euclid 1956, I:32), we can see a similar proof in the rules of chess, that a situation where the only pieces remaining on the board are the opposing kings necessarily amounts to a stalemate. We can also see that the player playing first in a game of tic–tac–toe, if he makes the right moves, cannot lose, and it ends for him at worst with a draw.

What this means is that if a proposition is necessarily true *within* the context of the constitutive rules of geometry, chess, or tic–tac–toe, the *rules themselves* that make it true were established at a certain time in human history; as a result, they themselves, and so the propositions depending on them, would have to be considered synthetic (as Kant used that term),[6] under abstraction from any possible application. (Of course it is just this application that makes geometry a condition of possibility of human experience of empirical objects, while the others are only the rules of games.)

Why is it that Kant is nearly alone in considering the propositions of arithmetic and geometry to be synthetic, while most thinkers agree with Hume and consider them analytic? The answer, we think, is that Hume and the others failed to make the distinction between propositions *within* the context of geometry (and arithmetic), and the propositions whose invention were outside of and *constitutive of* the context in question. Another example: it is analytic within the chess context that any single move by a bishop brings it from one square to another lying along the same diagonal as the starting square, though a potential move can be blocked by other pieces on the squares along that diagonal. But before chess rules were established—and so outside of and constitutive of that context—the proposition is synthetic. It amounts to a proposal to invent a game in which bishops have this property. The chess term "bishop" has no meaning without the rules applying to it.[7]

Within geometry (and arithmetic), similar considerations hold. The definitions given to begin Book I of the *Elements* are neither analytically true nor synthetically true *simpliciter*: They are analytically true (even trivially so) within the context of geometry (see *CPJ* 5:248, 251), but synthetically true outside it: they amount to a *proposal* to use the words in this way within the system of geometry, as the *Elements* was being written.

Still, there seems to be a problem. The word "triangle" seems to be a universal, applying to indefinitely many plane figures, those consisting of three noncolinear lines connected at their end points. In this way it seems to be like "dog", which applies to indefinitely many mammals with canine characteristics. But as Friedman (2012, 238n) points out, for Kant, triangles are figures that can be *constructed* following certain rules; this construction can occur within formal intuition by the productive imagination applying the rules. For example, we construct a line beginning with an arbitrary point and drawing a straight line from it an arbitrary distance. This line did not exist—even in the mind—until we drew it (A163/B203). It can be extended farther, as far as I want, but at any given time, it is only as long as I have drawn it so far. So the drawn line is not a universal; it is an individual. This holds for the rest of the triangle as well. Then the word "triangle" is a universal term (a concept) *within* the context of geometry applying to figures I construct (or can construct) by following the rules for triangle-construction. Each such figure is an individual, but I can form a geometrical concept which applies, within geometry, to all such individual figures so constructed or so constructible. The rules Euclid proposed to constitute the world (context) of geometry are neither universal nor individual to begin with, but once Euclid has invented and established them and we accept them, they may be used to construct individual triangles, and these, together with the *arbitrary* aspects of their construction, can serve the function of a concept (universal). (Natural concepts such as "dog" do not work this way: we find—discover—individuals; we do not construct or invent them.)

Dogs, of course, have a shape too, but not one we can construct in pure intuition, with an arbitrary starting-point, a line drawn in an arbitrary direction for an arbitrary distance, etc. And it is this very *arbitrary* aspect of the construction that stands in for the universality of an empirical concept.

3. Euclid and Relativity

Euclidian constructions require a straight-edge and a compass; no metric unit is involved (it is "arbitrary"), but there are circumstances in which standard units become necessary. Already in the eighteenth century the need for internationally recognized standard units of measurement was becoming obvious. In 1799, as the Napoleonic regime was replacing the Terror in France (and Kant was 75 years old), the BIPM (*Bureau International des Poids et Mesures*) set up in Sèvres outside Paris a depository for primary international measurement standards, and set up there platinum original master units with which all copies of the meter, kilogram, and second were required to conform.[8] Since then other standards have been added, and other embodiments and comparison techniques have been developed as greater precision has been required. But the point is the same: everyone using these metrics should employ identical master units, to prevent accidental and/or fraudulent inconsistencies.

There are other considerations which would seem to require a standard unit. The well-known Michelson–Morley experiment (1887) would seem to be such a case. It seemed to upend contemporary principles regarding light and its medium, and led to Albert Einstein's Special Theory of Relativity. Even more counterintuitive for the time was Einstein's subsequent General Theory of Relativity, which seemed to predict that a light ray passing near an object of sufficiently large mass would be deflected

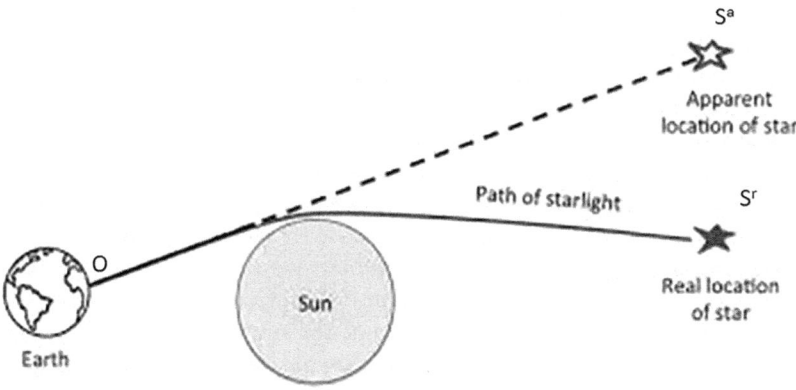

Figure 2.1 Eddington Eclipse Diagram[9]

toward the object, resulting in an apparent displacement of the observed object for an appropriately placed observer. Some observations seemingly correlating this prediction led to Eddington's famous 1919 experiment involving the deflection of light from the Hyades group of stars passing near the sun (observable during a full eclipse), resulting in the predicted displacement for an observer on earth. (See Figure 2.1.)

It would seem that the amount of deflection, the curvature, would vary according to the mass of the object and the light ray's distance from its center of gravity, so that if the sun were less massive or the light were passing it at a greater distance, the apparent deflection would be reduced accordingly; and if it were more massive and/or closer, deflection would be increased. Measurement of the amount of deflection would seem to require a standard unit of curvature akin to, and perhaps determined in relation to, the Euclidean straight-line meter; curved lines which are parts of circles can be compared with reference to the radius of the circle of which they are parts, and for all we know, mathematicians may be able to devise a method of reducing all curved lines to combinations of parts of circles. But if so, we would need to establish a standard unit of curvature.

Some interpretations of General Relativity consider that the deflected light ray should still be considered to follow a straight line, only now in a *space* which has been curved by the sun's gravity. But the notion of a curved space, while no doubt convenient for some purposes, is both counterintuitive and, as we shall argue, in systematic conflict with Kantian transcendental epistemology.

Many scholars hold that Kant is only being traditional in following Euclid, even that he never considered any other than Euclidian space.[10] Both views, we hold, are in error. Kant seems to have considered alternatives to Euclidean geometry in his pre-Critical period,[11] but had a good reason to base his Critical system on Euclidian space.

Take, for example, the Eddington experiment (see Figure 2.1). The assumption is that the sun's mass and position is responsible for the displacement of the Hyades stars' image for the observer on Earth. But the sun is an empirical object, and for Kant's transcendental epistemology, its intuition requires space (and time) for the determination of its identity. If the space used for this purpose is considered to be a curved space with the amount of the curvature determined by the sun's mass and position, the procedure would be impossibly circular: we would need to know the sun's position in order to know the amount of curvature of space, but need to know this curvature to determine the sun's position.

We take it that Kant was aware of this problem, and hence that the formal (or pure) intuition of space on which the spatial characteristics of empirical objects (such as the sun) are based must be neutral to the presence of any effect on space *itself*[12] of the presence of such empirical objects (which the terms "formal" and "pure" suggest). When Kant says "One can never represent to himself that there is no space, though one can very well think that there are no objects to be encountered in it" (A24f/B38f), it seems that the pure (formal) intuition of space would consist of a space empty of objects, a Euclidean matrix which would serve as the basis for the determination of the spatial characteristics from which empirical objects must derive their identity, their sameness to or difference from one another. The Eddington diagram in Figure 2.1 takes a Euclidean space as its background, and it is only against such a neutral background that the perceived location and the *real* location of the Hyades stars can be established and contrasted.

4. Conclusion

We take the above considerations to support the following: *Within* transcendental epistemology, *space* is not a thing at all (which the Kantian characterization "eternal and infinite un-thing"[13] makes clear). It is, together with time, part of the mechanism for establishing sameness or difference (i.e., identity) among humanly knowable physical (empirical) objects, and is not itself *physical* at all. Questions like, "How much does space weigh?" or "What color is it?" or "What is its shape?" are as unanswerable as the same questions about 5, or π, or lust, or contradiction: they embody *category mistakes*. (The shape question has been frequently asked seriously in the last century or so, though Kant makes clear that an answer would have to presuppose a second space in which ours is an object; and then the same question would arise again with regard to this second space, which would require a third, *ad infinitum* [see e.g., A24f/B39 and A430n/B458n].)

But when space, like time, substance or reciprocity, is taken as part of a system for working with our empirical world of singular and universal representations, with their objects' identity established by form, and their organization and articulation by content, it can be whatever works best. Calling a Euclidian curved line a straight one in a curved space makes impossibly circular the attempt to identify in the curved space the large massive object responsible for the Euclidian curve.

In short, for Kant's transcendental epistemology, space (with time) is responsible for our necessary determination of identity and difference of physical (empirical) things as the objects of our empirical representations. But this no more makes space and time themselves (see note 13, above) physical things than the important contribution that a welding robot on an automotive assembly line makes to the integrity of the products allows the robot itself to be considered an automobile.[14]

Notes

1. At A23/B37, Kant asks, "*Was sind nun Raum und Zeit?*" ("What, then, are space and time?"), of which one conjunct is the line cited.
2. Friedman 2012, 231–255. This article builds on the well-received Friedman 1992. For another approach, see Prauss 2015.
3. There are, however, problematic aspects, including: (1) the use in his abstract and paper text of the phrase "physical space", which seems to us like what Friedman in his note 7 refers to as an "oxymoron" (granted, in a different context); and (2) the description of what Friedman (2012, 242) calls "perspectival space". The latter passage also uses "line of sight" and refers to the point of view of the subject in a misleadingly narrow sense, in our view (though this is mitigated by his observation at 244.) He later (247) identifies perspectival space with metaphysical space, which he contrasts with geometrical space. We hope to deal with these problems in a later paper.
4. Friedman 2012, 236 (emphasis Friedman's). This construction appears as Proposition I.22 in Euclid (1956, 292f). Material in square brackets is an addition of the authors.
5. The general assumption has him flourishing around 300 B.C. in Alexandria; see Euclid 1956, 1–6 (Heath's Introduction).
6. For an interesting discussion of Kant's use of the term "synthesis", see Godlove 2009.
7. See A713f/B741f. For another example of the relative status of propositions within a context and of those constitutive of the context, see Carnap 1956.
8. We included "second" just to ensure the reader is paying attention. It is quite true, and in fact self-evident, that there can be no such thing as a standard platinum second. For the whole point of the platinum meter and kilogram is to be sure that those units do not change, whereas the second is the unit of time, and hence of change, and so some other way would be needed to establish a time unit.
9. This diagram follows Eddington (1920, 112), which is in the public domain.
10. See, however, §15 of Kant's *Inaugural Dissertation* (*ID* 2:404f), entitled On Space. L.W. Beck, who edited, translated, and commented on *ID* (in Beck 1992), suggests that Kant in *Lebendige Kräfte*, §10 (1:10f), had considered

that "various possible geometries" might apply to "bodies in space" (159n). He mentions in this connection a letter of May 5, 1761, in Euler's *Letters to a German Princess*, with which, Beck assumes, Kant would have been familiar. See also Godlove 2009, 788 (note 28).

11. In fact, in his very first publication. See note 10, above, *Leb. Kräfte*, §10 (1:10f).
12. Whether the notion of *space itself* is or can be rendered intelligible is beyond the scope of this chapter.
13. A39/B56: Taken as absolute, space and time would be *"zwei ewige und unendliche für sich bestehende Undinge"* ("two eternal and infinite self-subsisting non-entities"). Cf. Kant's use of *"Gedankendinge"* at A292/B348; see also *ID* 2:404f and *MMH* 8:153.
14. The authors would like to thank Sebastian Orlander for presenting an earlier version of this chapter to the second Kant in Asia conference in Hong Kong, when both authors were unexpectedly indisposed. We would also like to thank Ms. Stephanie Kinsler, of the University of Memphis Library Reference Department, for consultation on the copyright status of the Eddington diagram.

References

Beck, Lewis White (1992). *Trans. and ed. L.W. Beck, Kant's Latin Writings*, 2nd ed. New York: Peter Lang.

Carnap, Rudolf (1956). Empiricism, Semantics, and Ontology. In: *Meaning and Necessity*, 2nd ed. Chicago: University of Chicago Press, 205–221.

Eddington, Arthur Stanley (1920). *Space, Time, and Gravitation: An Outline of the General Theory of Relativity*. Cambridge: Cambridge University Press.

Euclid (1956). *Trans. and ed. T.L. Heath, Euclid: The Thirteen Books of the Elements*. New York: Dover Publications.

Friedman, Michael (1992). *Kant and the Exact Sciences*. Cambridge: Harvard University Press.

——— (2012). Kant on Geometry and Spatial Intuition. In: *Synthese* 186(1), 231–255.

Godlove, Terry (2009). Poincaré, Kant, and the Scope of Mathematical Intuition. In: *The Review of Metaphysics* 62(4), 779–801.

Prauss, Gerold (2015). *Die Einheit von Subjekt und Objekt: Kants Probleme mit den Sachen Selbst*. Freiburg and München: Verlag Karl Alber.

3 Geometrical Concepts and Formal Intuition

Xing Nan

1. Introduction

Kant famously claims that space is not only the form of all outer intuition, but itself a peculiar kind of intuition, which he calls "pure" or "formal" intuition.[1] This claim is indeed puzzling, for how could something be at the same time an intuition and a mere component or aspect of an intuition? Or does Kant mean by "space" different things in different contexts, so that space as a form of intuition is not the same as space as a formal intuition? In order to answer these questions, I shall first distinguish between four conceptions of space, then consider how they are related to Kant's notions of the forms of intuition and formal intuition. In particular, I shall concentrate on the question whether and how our spatial intuitions are dependent on geometrical concepts.

2. Four Conceptions of Space

Kant does not make any explicit distinction between different conceptions of space in the *Critique of Pure Reason* or indeed in any published work, but draws an important distinction between metaphysical and geometrical spaces in an unpublished text on Kästner's Treatises.[2] Kant writes (*KT* 20:419):

> Metaphysics must show how one can *have* the representation of space, geometry however teaches how one can *describe* a space, viz., exhibit one in the representation a priori (not by drawing). In the former, space is considered in the way it is *given*, before all determination of it in conformity with a certain concept of object. In the latter, one [i.e., a space] is *made*. In the former it is *original* and only one (unitary [*einig*]) space, in the latter it is *derived* and hence there are (many) spaces, of which the geometer however, in accord with the metaphysician, must admit as a consequence of the foundational representation of space, that they can only be thought as parts of the unitary original space.

This passage should be compared, first, with the Metaphysical Exposition of the Concept of Space.[3] In point (3) of the Metaphysical Exposition, Kant argues that "one can only represent a single [*einig*] space", that space is "essentially single", and that spaces in the plural are nothing but parts of the "single all-encompassing space" (A25/B39). From this, he concludes that space "is not a discursive or, as is said, general concept of the relations of things in general, but a pure intuition" (A24f/B39). Without considering the cogency of Kant's argument, there can be no doubt that what Kant means by original, metaphysical space in the passage quoted corresponds precisely to space as a pure intuition in the Metaphysical Exposition. Moreover, shortly after the passage quoted above, Kant claims that original space is represented as "infinite, in fact as infinitely given" (20:419). And in point (4) of the Metaphysical Exposition, Kant argues that space "is represented as an infinite *given* magnitude" (B40; cf. A25), which is also used to support his thesis that "the original representation of space is an a priori *intuition*, not a *concept*" (B40). Thus the equality of metaphysical space with space as an *a priori* intuition is further confirmed.

While the Metaphysical Exposition is unquestionably focused on metaphysical space, the Transcendental Exposition seems to be concerned with geometrical space. Kant writes (B40): "Geometry is a science that determines the properties of space synthetically and yet *a priori*. What then must the representation of space be for such a cognition of it to be possible?" Presumably, only the representation of geometrical space can make geometrical cognition possible. But what is a geometrical space? In the Transcendental Exposition, Kant's example of geometrical cognition is that space has only three dimensions (B41). He holds this to be an apodictic truth which is cognized through our pure spatial intuition. Since this proposition is about *space as such*, it seems that geometrical space is not something different from the single all-encompassing space. However, the majority of our geometrical knowledge is not about space as such, but about the figures in space. And our knowledge of, say, the properties of a triangle is possible not by virtue of a representation of the single all-encompassing space, but only by virtue of a representation of a triangle. When Kant says, in the passage quoted above, that in geometry there are many spaces, he must mean by geometrical spaces this or that particular triangle, circle, etc., all of which, of course, are parts of the all-encompassing space. It seems reasonable, therefore, to understand geometrical space exactly in this way, even if it might turn out to be incompatible with what Kant says in the Transcendental Exposition.

Geometrical spaces are particular parts of the single all-encompassing metaphysical space, and this part–whole relation is a peculiar one. Any particular drop of the water contained in my glass, for example, is a part of the water taken as a whole, but the existence of the former does not depend on the existence of the latter, nor do we need to know anything about the water as a whole in order to know something about the particular drop. The parts, in other words, are both metaphysically and epistemologically prior to the whole. By contrast, no part of the single all-encompassing space can have any independent existence from it, though perhaps it is not appropriate to talk about the existence of space at all. At any rate, we cannot know the geometrical properties of any particular figure without presupposing something about space as a whole, at least insofar as such knowledge is based on geometrical demonstration. Thus, in his comments on Kästner's Treatise, Kant writes (*KT* 20:420): "the geometer grounds the possibility of his task of increasing a space (of which there are many) to infinity on the original representation of a unitary, infinite, *subjectively given* space." Since the infinite extendibility of a straight line is stated by the second postulate of Euclidean geometry, on which geometrical proofs are based, properties about metaphysical space are always presupposed by our cognition of particular geometrical spaces. In short, the peculiarity of the part–whole relation concerning space consists in the fact that the whole is prior to the parts.

Despite the differences between geometrical spaces and metaphysical space, the former, like the latter, are also held to be objects of *a priori* intuition, "for from a mere concept no propositions can be drawn that go beyond the concept, which, however, happens in geometry" (B40f). On the other hand, it seems that the representation of geometrical spaces must presuppose geometrical *concepts*, for how could one represent a particular space as a triangle without knowing what "triangle" means? This point is well confirmed by the passage quoted above, where geometrical space is said to be "made", "derived", described by geometrical concepts, and determined "in conformity with a certain concept of object". If intuition and concept amount to a mutually exclusive division of our representations, as Kant often suggests (e.g., A19/B33 and A320/B377), then the status of our representation of geometrical spaces would be precarious. I shall return to this problem later.

Both metaphysical and geometrical spaces are pure intuitions, but space functions also as a form of intuition. Curiously, although it is a central thesis of Kant's transcendental idealism that space (and time) are nothing but sensible forms of intuition (see A369), I cannot find any lengthy discussion of this aspect of space (or time) in the *Critique*. Among his scattered discussion of space as the form of outer intuition, I think the following three points are especially worth noting. First, as the form of intuition, space is the "formal constitution [of the subject] for being affected by objects" (B41; cf. A26/B42; A267/B323). Second, "the mere form of outer sensible intuition, space, is not yet cognition at all; it only gives the manifold of intuition *a priori* for a possible cognition" (B137; cf. B154). Since Kant holds intuition to be a cognition, this means that space is not an intuition. Third, "pure space and pure time" are "the forms of intuit*ing*, but are not in themselves objects that are intuit*ed* (*ens* *imaginarium*)" (A291/B347, emphasis added; cf. A429/B457n). From the first and the third points, it seems not unreasonable to conclude that space as a form of intuition refers not to any representation, but simply to the *innate faculty ground* of our spatial representations.[4] This is the third conception of space in Kant, which, for the sake of brevity, might be called "space as faculty". This interpretation, however, is not so well supported by the second point concerning space as a form of intuition, which rather suggests another, fourth conception of space.

According to the fourth conception, "space" refers to the formal aspect of an *empirical* intuition, or the spatial property of a particular empirical object, such as the cuboid occupied by my copy of the *Critique*, or the space contained by my glass. Let us call space in this sense "empirical space". Like geometrical spaces, empirical spaces are also particular parts of a greater whole. And both geometrical and empirical spaces result from the actualization of space as faculty: "this very same formative synthesis by means of which we construct a triangle in imagination is entirely identical with that which we exercise in the apprehension of an appearance in order to make a concept of experience of it" (A224/B271, translation altered). But there are some important differences between these two conceptions. First, while geometrical spaces are always actively constructed, empirical spaces are passively perceived—indeed, they are the only kind of spaces that can be perceived. Second, and as a result of the first point, geometrical spaces always presuppose geometrical concepts, without which no geometrical construction would be possible. By contrast, empirical spaces do not depend on any *geometrical* concepts. For example, I may legitimately talk about the space now occupied by my body, without having any idea about how it should be characterized in geometrical terms. Third, although both geometrical spaces and empirical spaces are parts of a greater space, it seems that the part-whole relations in the two cases are different. Whereas our knowledge of particular geometrical spaces presupposes some assumptions about metaphysical space, it seems that our knowledge of particular empirical spaces does not depend on our knowledge of the entire physical space. For while only a few physicists can have some knowledge of the latter, everyone is capable of knowing some spatial properties of ordinary empirical objects.

To summarize: we have identified four conceptions of space, which might in turn be called metaphysical space, geometrical space, space as faculty, and empirical space. No other conceptions of space can be found, I think, in the *Critique*, though there are of course other aspects of space, which escape Kant's attention.[5] An object viewed from a particular angle, for example, appears to the observer as a particular image, which is roughly what phenomenologists call "profile" (*Abschattung*); and the spatial property of a profile is not necessarily the same as the spatial property of the object. Thus it seems that the spatial property of this image corresponds to none of those conceptions of space sketched above. However, Kant does not seem to have ever entertained this kind of space or spatial property. Indeed, the spatial property of a mere image belongs to what Kant would call "empirical ideality", while space for him is always "empirically real". Thus, although one may reasonably criticize Kant for his ignorance of the phenomenological space, it seems that one need not take other conceptions of space into account in order to understand Kant's doctrine of space and spatial intuition.

3. Interpreting Kant's (in)Famous Footnote

Although space belongs to the subject matter of the Transcendental Aesthetic, most recent controversies on Kant's doctrine of space are focused on a notoriously difficult footnote in the Transcendental Deduction of the B edition. The footnote reads (B160–161n):

> [1] Space, represented as *object* (as is really required in geometry), contains more than the mere form of intuition, namely the *comprehension* of the manifold given in accordance with the form of sensibility in an *intuitive* representation, so that the *form of intuition* merely gives the manifold, but the *formal intuition* gives unity of the representation. [2] In the Aesthetic I ascribed this unity merely to sensibility, only in order to note that it precedes all concepts, though to be sure it presupposes a synthesis, which does not belong to the senses but through which all concepts of space and time first become possible. [3] For since through it (as the understanding determines the sensibility) space or time are first *given* as intuitions, the unity of this a priori intuition belongs to space and time, and not to the concept of the understanding (§24).

Controversy begins already with the very intelligibility of this passage. Lorne Falkenstein claims, for example, that this passage "is so obscure that it can be made to serve the needs of any interpretation whatsoever" (1995, 91). He detects a quasi-contradiction in two claims involved in the passage: first, that the unity of formal intuition presupposes a synthesis through which all concepts of space and time first become possible; second, that this unity belongs to space and time, and not to the concept of the understanding. While most other commentators insist that this passage does make good sense, it is undeniable that there is a tension between the second and the third sentences. A satisfactory interpretation of this passage, then, requires a solution to this tension.

There are two main alternatives for such a solution: the unity of space is held to be the product of either sensibility or apperception. In recent literature, the former position is often called non-conceptualism, the latter conceptualism, in order to highlight the relevance of Kant's theoretical philosophy to contemporary discussions (see e.g., Onof and Schulting

2014 and 2015). As many commentators already note, however, these are not very good labels to characterize Kant's position, for it is far from unanimously agreed whether the Kantian distinction between sensibility and understanding/apperception corresponds precisely to the one between non-conceptual and conceptual content in contemporary discussions. In fact, according to one of the most influential interpretations of Kant, the unity of space (and time) results from the "pre-discursive" synthesis of the understanding or apperception, which is independent from any concept (see Waxman 1991, ch. 2; Longuenesse 1998, 72, cf. 63f; 2005, 69). Should this position be characterized as conceptualism or non-conceptualism? As it is difficult to answer such questions, we may use "intellectualism" and "sensibilism" to replace "conceptualism" and "non-conceptualism".[6] Formulated in these terms, the problem is whether Kant adopts an intellectualist view or a sensibilist view concerning the unity of space as a formal intuition.

In order to determine whether the unity of space as a formal intuition is yielded by the intellect/apperception or by sensibility, we have first of all to get clear about what space as a formal intuition actually refers to. Unfortunately, Kant never says explicitly what he means by it. While he attempts in the above-quoted footnote to distinguish between formal intuition and form of intuition, he treats them in at least one other passage as synonyms (cf. A429n/B457n). Thus, the meaning of "formal intuition" in our footnote can hardly be determined on textual evidence alone. Instead, we must see which conception of space makes best sense in the context of Kant's argument.

If we focus on the first sentence alone, it would be very natural to conclude that formal intuitions are nothing but geometrical spaces, which are "required in geometry" and which have a unity that is not possessed by the mere form of intuition—i.e., the unity yielded by geometrical concepts. This interpretation, however, seems to be incompatible with the second sentence, according to which the unity of formal intuition results from a synthesis through which all geometrical concepts first become possible. This implies that the unity of space as a formal intuition is yielded not by any concept, but rather by a *pre-conceptual* synthesis. Moreover, the third sentence says the unity of spatial intuition belongs to space itself, "not to the concept of the understanding". Since the pure concepts of the understanding or categories are the ground of all conceptual unity, it follows that the unity of spatial intuition must be non-conceptual, hence cannot be founded on any geometrical concept. As a result, it seems inappropriate to interpret the formal intuition of space as geometrical spaces.

The majority of recent interpreters, then, tend to take metaphysical space as the formal intuition of space. In contrast to geometrical spaces, metaphysical space possesses a particular kind of unity that is called by some commentators "unicity", which is further analyzed into "singularity", "mereological inversion", and "infinity" (Onof and Schulting 2015, 13–16). All these properties are attributed by Kant to space in the third and the fourth points of the Metaphysical Exposition of Space. Thus the unicity of space is obviously different from, and independent of, the unity yielded by any concept. The problem, however, is that it is unclear whether and how the unicity of metaphysical space "presupposes a synthesis", as indicated by the second sentence. We may note that Kant refers at the end of the footnote to §24, where he introduces the name "figurative synthesis" or "*synthesis speciosa*" for the "*synthesis* of the manifold of sensible intuition", which is to be contrasted with "*synthesis intellectualis*"—i.e., the synthesis "which would be thought in the mere *category* in regard to the manifold of an intuition in general" (B151). Obviously, if the unicity of metaphysical space does presuppose a synthesis, the latter must be the figurative synthesis. However, Kant also explicitly says that the product of the figurative synthesis is "*determinate intuition*" (B154), which may include both geometrical and empirical spaces, but by no means metaphysical space.[7] As a result, while interpreting formal intuition of space as metaphysical space makes good sense of the third sentence, it has some difficulties with what Kant claims in the second sentence.

Now it seems that neither of these two interpretations of the notion of formal intuition in Kant's footnote is fully satisfactory. Should we then accept Falkenstein's conclusion that the tension involved in this passage is insoluble? If one wants to be completely faithful to the letter of Kant's text, I'm afraid that the answer would be positive. But if our aim is rather to understand its spirit, I think that we can have a reasonably coherent picture of what Kant intends to convey here. In contrast to the majority of recent interpreters, I want to argue that what concerns Kant in this footnote has nothing to do with metaphysical space. My argument is based on three main grounds. First, the context of the Transcendental Deduction suggests that Kant's concern in the note cannot be metaphysical space, for the purpose of the Transcendental Deduction is to establish the possibility of experience in the sense of empirical cognition, but empirical cognition involves merely empirical space, not metaphysical space. In particular, although the argument of the passage to which this footnote is appended is not easy to understand, it has a clear conclusion, namely that "all synthesis, through which perception itself becomes possible, stands under the categories" (B161). The synthesis on which the possibility of perception is grounded is surely figurative synthesis, which, as we just noted, is responsible only for "determinate space", not for metaphysical space.

My second reason is that at the beginning of this footnote Kant unambiguously equates the formal intuition of space with space as *object*. But earlier in the B Deduction Kant writes: "in order to cognize something in space, e.g., a line, I must *draw* it, and thus synthetically bring about a determinate combination of the given manifold, so that the unity of this action is at the same time the unity of consciousness (in the concept of a line), and thereby is an object (a determinate space) first cognized" (B137f). Accordingly, only determinate space—i.e., geometrical or empirical space—can be regarded as an object. Moreover, in a later footnote of the *Critique* Kant indicates that space is "not a real object [*Gegenstand*] that can be outwardly intuited" (A429/B457n). As he explains in the next sentence, the space about which Kant talks here is the space "prior to all things determining (filling or bounding) it"—namely, the single, all-encompassing, metaphysical space which, like time, cannot be intuited or perceived in itself. Thus, although metaphysical space is also, in some sense, "required in geometry", the role it plays is not so much that of an object as that of the *background* or *horizon*. In other words, the interpretation of the formal intuition of space as metaphysical space is incompatible already with the first sentence.

Thirdly, although Kant persistently claims that metaphysical space is an intuition, this claim is in fact quite questionable. According to Kant, the two main criteria for intuition are *singularity* and *immediacy*. However, it is far from clear how the single, all-encompassing, metaphysical space can be given immediately. Indeed, later in the *Critique* Kant writes: "Now I always have the world–whole only in concept, but by no means (as a whole) in intuition" (A519/B547). If the world–whole cannot be given in intuition, it seems that metaphysical space as its form cannot be given in this way either. With regard to singularity, it is true that in the third and fourth points of the Metaphysical Exposition Kant successfully shows that space cannot be a universal concept. However, as we noted above, the singularity of metaphysical space is quite unique: it amounts to the unicity that does not belong to any ordinary intuition. This unicity is so peculiar that it makes it doubtful whether metaphysical space should be deemed as an intuitive representation. Although I cannot develop the point in detail here, I believe that singularity alone does not suffice to guarantee the intuitive nature of a representation, for there are obviously some singular representations that cannot fulfill the *epistemic* role Kant attributes to intuitions, such as that of God. It seems, then, that our representation of metaphysical space is neither a concept nor an intuition, but a *sui generis* one.[8]

4. Conclusion: Kant's Conceptualist Sensibilism

Now I think we have very strong reason for the interpretation of the formal intuition of space not as metaphysical space, but as determinate (i.e., geometrical or empirical) spaces. But since empirical spaces are not "required in geometry", it seems that the only alternative is geometrical spaces. However, this interpretation is challenged by a serious problem indicated above: the unity of such formal intuition "precedes all concepts". In order to find a solution to this problem, let us begin with a clearer understanding of what "conceptual unity" means. As I understand it, a conceptual unity is above all a unity by means of which its *marks (Merkmale)* are related. For example, the unity of the concept of gold implies that if something is gold, then it must be a yellow metal soluble only in *aqua regia*. Geometrical concepts, too, have their own unity, by means of which a circle, for example, is defined as the set of all points in a plane that are at a given distance from a given point. Thus, if a determinate space is determined through a geometrical concept, then it seems that its unity cannot precede all concepts.

This conclusion, however, is too premature. For I think it is possible within Kant's framework that one may use a geometrical concept to determine a particular space without involving the unity specific to that concept. This may sound paradoxical, but it is actually quite normal. For example, while many young children can use the concept of circle to characterize a plate, most of them have no knowledge of the *definition* of this concept. That is, they do not know that there is a point from which all the points at the edge of the plate are at the same distance. Furthermore, it is quite common for us to draw a plane figure arbitrarily on a piece of paper which we are unable to describe with geometrical concepts. We may give it the name "shape A", and, keeping this shape in mind, we may be able to know whether a new figure we encounter is of this shape or not; but we actually do not know any non-trivial property of such shape. By contrast, a geometer may possess certain general concepts which are applicable to this shape but are not available to us, and hence be able not only to determine a particular space with geometrical concepts, but also to know certain non-trivial properties of that space through the *unity* of such concepts. Indeed, this is an essential aspect of how mathematics helps in extending our knowledge of the material world: the latter is full of objects that can *prima facie* hardly be described through geometrical concepts, but the development of mathematics makes such description possible in more and more cases.

If it is legitimate to distinguish between mere geometrical concepts without unity and unified geometrical concepts (indeed, this distinction can also be made in regard to other concepts), then I think there is a way to solve the problem indicated above. For it becomes clear that we may use geometrical concepts to make a certain space determinate without attributing any *conceptual unity* to it. Every determinate space, *qua* particular space, possesses the *unity of an intuition* insofar as its spatial parts are coordinated into a whole. Such unity results, as I indicated above, from the figurative synthesis of the imagination, "through which all concepts of space and time first become possible." Admittedly, Kant holds that the (transcendental) imagination is somehow dependent upon the understanding (in Kant's words: as the understanding determines the sensibility). But the operations of the imagination are obviously prior to the proper operations of the latter, and do not invoke any pure concept of the understanding or category. As a result, the unity of the formal intuition of space, which is made possible by it, indeed "belongs to space and time, and not to the concept of the understanding".

Recognizing the difference between concepts without unity and unified concepts may also lead to a better appreciation of the distinction between sensibility and intellect. According to Kant's own explicit statements, this distinction is the same as the one between intuitions and concepts. However, from the account offered above it seems to follow that concepts without unity are not yet the product of the understanding or apperception, which is required only for the *unity* of geometrical concepts, as such unity can come about only by means of reflection in accordance with the *category* of quantity. If this is so, then the distinction between sensibility and understanding is better reflected in the one between intuitions and *categories* or *pure concepts of the understanding* than in the one between intuitions and concepts in general. Of course, this is a strong thesis that needs more detailed argument than what I offered here, but I think its plausibility is at least supported by the possibility of recognizing a particular shape A without being able to specify any non-trivial property of such shape. Moreover, this proposal also makes better sense of the connection between the second and the third sentences than other accounts: the third sentence is obviously intended as an explanation of the second, but in the former Kant explicitly speaks of "the concepts of understanding". Hence it is not implausible to interpret "concepts" in the second sentence as "concepts of understanding" or categories. In this way, there would be no conflict between the claim that the formal or determinate space must involve certain geometrical concepts and the claim that the unity possessed by such space is non-conceptual or, more precisely, non-categorial.

We are now in a position to answer the question raised at the beginning of the previous section: whether Kant's doctrine of formal intuition is intellectualist or sensibilist. Since the unity of the formal intuition of space is yielded by the figurative synthesis of the imagination, not by the intellectual synthesis of the understanding; and assuming imagination is part of sensibility, it should be concluded that his position is sensibilist. But since geometrical concepts are necessarily involved in the formal intuition of space, his position is at the same time conceptualist without being intellectualist. My interpretation thus stands in diametrical opposition to that proposed by Longuenesse and Waxman, according to whom Kant's position is intellectualist but non-conceptualist. Despite this, I believe that they would agree with me that the really interesting but also difficult question is about Kant's intricate conception of the (transcendental) imagination and its relationship to the senses and the apperception. But this question is too complicated to be adequately dealt with in this chapter.[9]

Notes

1. Similarly, Kant also claims that time is both the form of inner intuition and itself a pure or formal intuition. However, although he has a strong tendency to attribute exactly the same ontological and epistemic status to space and time, there are evidently some asymmetries between them. Most notably, while space is the object of a specific science, namely geometry, there is no such science of time. In this paper, I shall not deal with the problem of the asymmetry between space and time, but will confine myself to the examination of Kant's doctrine of space alone.

2. For background information about Kästner and Kant's text, see Onof and Schulting 2014, which is followed by a full translation of Kant's text by these authors, which appears as Kant 2014. Quotations from this text are taken from it with minor alterations.

3. See A22/B37–A25/B40. Although the content of Kant's discussions on space in the Transcendental Aesthetic remains largely unchanged in the A and B editions of the *Critique*, there are some significant differences between the ways he arranges the text. Most importantly, the headings Metaphysical Exposition and Transcendental Exposition appear in the B edition alone. My following observations are based on Kant's presentation in the B edition.

4. This view is urged by Waxman (1991, 95f). Waxman bases his interpretation mainly on a passage from *On a Discovery* (8:222), and we may add that this view is already explicitly endorsed in the *Inaugural Dissertation*, §4 and §13.

5. Tolley 2016 distinguishes between three kinds of representations of space in the *Critique*: the "originary intuition" of the single space, the conceptual metaphysical representation of it as object, and the geometrical space(s). In comparison to the distinction made above, Tolley ignores space as faculty and the difference between geometrical and empirical spaces, but stresses a conception of space that is totally absent in my account, namely space as an absolutely non-conceptual intuition, which is *simply given* to us and is not *thought* by us in any way. Tolley's view is shared by Falkenstein (1995, 63f). However, I think this interpretation of space as intuition is *ad hoc* and does not accord with Kant's general characterization of intuition, and I shall argue against it briefly at the end of the next section.

   Admittedly, Kant's expression "metaphysical exposition of the *concept* of space" (A22/B37) may be read as implying that the single, all-encompassing space he discusses there is the conceptual metaphysical representation of space, which is different from, and must presuppose, original space as intuition proper. But I tend to understand his use of the word "concept" here as non-technical, corresponding roughly to "idea" in early modern philosophy. For after all, what Kant endeavors to show in the Metaphysical Exposition is that our "concept" of the single, all-encompassing space is very different from conceptual representations proper.

6. These two terms are also used by McClear 2015. Messina uses the terms "the Synthesis Reading" and "the Brute Given Reading" to make roughly the same distinction.

7. This problem is fully recognized by Messina 2014. However, instead of rejecting the interpretation of formal intuition of space as metaphysical space, Messina claims that the unity of space is a "synthetic unity without synthesis" (23), a claim that is neither well supported by Kant's text—Messina makes just a single reference to a casual sentence in the *Critique of the Power of Judgment*—nor makes good sense in itself.

8. Melnick (1973, 11) and, following him, Allison (2004, 113), aptly call our representation of metaphysical space "pre-intuition", but they do not

thereby find Kant's claim that space is an intuition problematic. On the other hand, in *Metaphysical Foundations of Natural Science*, Kant takes "absolute space" as an *idea* in his technical sense (*MFNS* 4:559). Although I tend to equate metaphysical space with absolute space, I shall not further pursue this issue here.

9. I want to thank the participants of the Second Kant in Asia Conference for questions and comments, in particular Clinton Tolley, Lucy Allais, and Aileen Chenxuan Luo. Special thanks also to Steve Palmquist, whose extremely careful comments on the last draft saved me from enormous errors.

References

Allison, Henry E. (2004). *Kant's Transcendental Idealism. An Interpretation and Defense*, 2nd ed. New Haven: Yale University Press.

Falkenstein, Lorne (1995). *Kant's Intuitionism. A Commentary on the Transcendental Aesthetic*. Toronto: University of Toronto Press.

Kant, Immanuel (2014). Trans. and ed. C. Onof and D. Schulting, *On Kästner's Treatises*. In: *Kantian Review* 19(2), 305–313.

Longuenesse, Béatrice (1998). *Kant and the Capacity to Judge: Sensibility and Discursivity in the Transcendental Analytic of the "Critique of Pure Reason"*. Princeton, NJ: Princeton University Press.

——— (2005). *Kant on the Human Standpoint*. Cambridge: Cambridge University Press.

McClear, Colin (2015). Two Kinds of Unity in the Critique of Pure Reason. In: *Journal of the History of Philosophy* 53(1), 79–110.

Melnick, Arthur (1973). *Kant's Analogies of Experience*. Chicago: University of Chicago Press.

Messina, James (2014). Kant on the Unity of Space and the Synthetic Unity of Apperception. In: *Kant-Studien* 105(1), 5–40.

Onof, Christian and Dennis Schulting (2014). Kant, Kästner, and the Distinction between Metaphysical and Geometric Space. In: *Kantian Review* 19(2), 285–304.

——— (2015). Space as Form of Intuition and as Formal Intuition: On the Note to B160 in Kant's Critique of Pure Reason. In: *Philosophical Review* 124(1), 1–58.

Tolley, Clinton (2016). The Difference between Original, Metaphysical and Geometrical Representations of Space. In: D. Schulting (ed.), *Kantian Nonconceptualism*. London: Palgrave Macmillan, 257–286.

Waxman, Wayne (1991). *Kant's Model of the Mind*. Oxford: Oxford University Press.

4 Pure Intuitions and Pure Forms of Intuition in the Transcendental Aesthetic and Elsewhere

Gregg Osborne

1. Introduction

In the portion of his *Critique of Pure Reason* known as the Transcendental Aesthetic, Kant purports to establish a series of claims concerning our representations of space and time on the one hand and space and time themselves on the other. Among the most important are these:

1. Our *representations of* space and time are pure intuitions.
2. Space and time *themselves* are pure *forms of* intuition.
3. Space and time themselves are ideal rather than real in the transcendental sense.
4. Space and time themselves are nonetheless real rather than ideal in the empirical sense.

According to Kant, it seems clear, (1) entails (2), and (2) entails both (3) and (4). A full assessment of this whole argument would require detailed exploration of numerous issues, including his case in support of (1), the meanings of (3) and (4), the ground(s) of his move from (1) to (2), and the grounds of his moves from (2) to (3) and (2) to (4). Any detailed exploration of so many issues would vastly exceed the scope of this chapter. The focus here will thus be restricted to two closely related and equally crucial issues: the meaning of (1) and the meaning of (2). Kant may seem to make these clear at various points in the Aesthetic itself. As we shall soon see, however, the accounts of them he gives there are problematic. In the case of (1), the problems have to do with formulation and can be resolved on the basis of materials from outside the *Critique*. In the case of (2), however, the problems are more fundamental. Materials from outside the *Critique* are of great potential importance with respect to these problems, but more as grounds for an account of what he *could* and perhaps *should* have said in the Aesthetic than as tools to disentangle what he *does* in fact say there.

2. Pure Intuitions

What is the meaning of (1), first of all? The foundation for an answer may seem to be found in the Aesthetic at A20/B31: "I term all representations pure . . . in which nothing is to be encountered that belongs to sensation." The full meaning of (1), it may thus seem, is that our representations of space and time are intuitions and that they contain nothing that belongs to sensation.

Upon reflection, however, it does not seem like this can be its full meaning. In order to see why, let us note a process described by Kant just two pages later, at A22/B36: "In the transcendental aesthetic we will first isolate sensibility by separating off everything that the understanding thinks through its concepts, so that nothing but empirical intuition remains. Second, we will then detach everything that belongs to sensation, so that nothing remains except pure intuition". The result of this procedure, at least according to Kant, will be an intuition containing nothing that belongs to sensation.[1] Wouldn't such an intuition be derived from experience, however, and thus be empirical? Assuming that the answer is yes and that Kant takes "pure" to be opposed to "empirical", the mere fact that an intuition contains nothing that belongs to sensation cannot entail that it is pure.[2] Another condition will have to be met, a condition having to do with *why* the intuition contains nothing that belongs to sensation.

The nature of that other condition becomes at least verbally clear in a sentence concerning our representation of space at B41: "But this intuition must be encountered in us *a priori*, i.e., prior to all perception of an object, thus it must be pure, not empirical intuition." Perception of an object involves sensation, of course, and so it now seems that the true meaning of (1) must be that our representations of space and time are intuitions and that they are in us *prior to all sensation*. This being the case, they indeed contain nothing that belongs to sensation, but the mere fact that they contain nothing that belongs to sensation is not what makes them pure.

In order to move from mere verbal clarity to genuine clarity, however, we need to know what Kant means here by "prior". The most obvious sense would be temporal, but he cannot mean this term in such a sense. If he did, after all, (1) would contradict his own emphatic statements from both before and after the *Critique*. In the Corollary to §15 of his *Inaugural Dissertation* (ID 2:400), for example, he first argues that our representations of time and space are pure intuitions but then insists that they arise *in response to* sensations:

> Finally, the question arises for everyone . . . whether each of these concepts [representations] is innate or acquired. The latter view . . . already seems to have been refuted by what has been demonstrated . . . But each of these concepts [representations] has . . . been acquired, not . . . by abstracting from the sensing of objects . . . but from the very action of the mind, which coordinates what is sensed by it . . . For sensations, while exciting the action of the mind, do not enter into and become part of the intuition. Nor is there anything

innate here except the law of the mind, according to which it joins together in a fixed manner the sense-impressions made by the presence of an object.

Kant repeats the gist of this insistence in a rather ill-tempered polemic from 1790 entitled *On a Discovery whereby any New Critique of Pure Reason Is to Be Made Superfluous by an Older One*. He also explicitly confirms there (*OD* 8:312) that this represents the view of the *Critique*:

> The *Critique* admits no innate *representations*. One and all . . . it considers them as acquired . . . According to the *Critique*, there are, *in the first place*, the forms of things in space and time, *second*, the synthetic unity of the manifold in concepts; for neither of these does our cognitive faculty get from the objects as given . . . rather it brings them about *a priori* and out of itself. There must indeed by a ground for it in the subject, however, which makes it possible that these representations can arise in this and no other manner . . . Only this . . . ground, e.g. of the possibility of an intuition of space, is innate, not the spatial representation itself. For impressions would always be required in order to determine the cognitive faculty to the representation of an object . . . Thus arises the formal intuition of space.

In the sentence concerning our representation of space from B41, therefore, Kant cannot mean "prior" in a temporal sense. He can only mean it in some sort of logical or conceptual sense. What exactly *is* that logical or conceptual sense, however? What can and does he mean by the claim that our intuition of space is in us "prior" to all sensation?

What he must mean, it seems clear, is that this intuition does not *depend on* sensations. At least at face value, however, even *this* is hard to square with the passages just cited, from before and after the *Critique*. If we did not have any sensations, Kant makes clear in both of those passages, we would not have this intuition (or that of time either). In at least one major respect, he thus clearly maintains, this intuition *does* depend on sensations. His considered position, it thus finally seems, must be that there is a second and at least equally major respect in which it does not.

In order to determine what this respect is, let us note some details of the first of the two passages just cited, namely that from the *Inaugural Dissertation*. Our representations of space and time have indeed been acquired, he insists in that passage, but not by abstracting from the sensing of objects. They have rather been acquired from the very action of the mind, which coordinates what is sensed by it. There is an innate law of the mind, he further maintains, according to which it joins together in a fixed manner the sense impressions made by the presence of the object. *At least with respect to their nature*, this entails, our representations of space and time do not depend on sensations. They would not exist at all without sensations, and thus depend on them with respect to their *existence*, but do not depend on them with respect to their *nature*. With respect to their *nature*, they depend entirely upon the action of the mind in its coordination of what is sensed by it, and thus on the innate law of the mind according to which this takes place. Unlike our representations of space and time, moreover, this innate law of the mind does not depend on sensation *at all*, even with respect to its existence. With respect to their *nature*, therefore, our representations of space and time depend entirely on something that does not depend on sensation *at all*.

The precise meaning of (1), it therefore turns out, can only be that our representations of space and time are intuitions and that, with respect to their nature (though not their existence), they do not depend on sensations (or on anything else—such as empirical intuition—in which sensations are contained). This being the case, it makes sense to deny (as Kant does in the passage from *ID*, cited above) that sensations enter into and become part of them, and thus to imply (as Kant does in the *Critique*, at A20/B34) that they contain nothing that belongs to sensation. At least in and of itself, however, the fact that they contain nothing that belongs to sensation is not *why* they are pure. The reason *why* they are pure is that they do not depend on sensations (or anything else that is empirical) with respect to their nature. Kant's claim at B41 of the *Critique*, that they are in us prior to all sensation, is at least potentially misleading and remains far from fully clear even when we grasp that "prior" cannot be meant in a temporal sense. With the help of passages from outside of the *Critique*, however, we can make sense of that claim.

3. Pure Forms of Intuition

Let us now consider (2), the claim that space and time *themselves* are pure *forms of* intuition. What does Kant mean by this claim? The basis for an answer may appear to be found in the following passage, which is located in the third and fourth paragraphs of the Aesthetic in both editions of the *Critique* (A20/B34–35):

> . . . that which allows the manifold of appearance to be ordered in certain relations I call the *form* of appearance. Since that in which sensations can alone be ordered . . . cannot itself be sensation, the matter of appearance is given only *a posteriori*, but its form must lie all ready for it in the mind *a priori*.
>
> I call all representations pure . . . in which nothing is to be encountered that belongs to sensation. Accordingly, the pure form of sensible intuitions in general is to be encountered in the mind *a priori*, wherein all the manifold of appearance is intuited in certain relations. This pure form of sensibility is also called pure intuition.

This apparent basis is disconcerting. According to it, the meaning of the claim that space and time *themselves* are pure *forms of* intuition (or appearance or sensibility) is that space and time themselves are pure intuitions in which sensations can alone be ordered. Such a claim is liable to make an attentive reader's head spin. An *intuition* must be *of* something, she may well be convinced. An intuition must have an intentional object, she may in other words hold. For any reader who holds this, the set of claims to which Kant is now committed leads straight into an abyss. According to this set of claims, after all, our representations of space and time are pure intuitions, space and time themselves are pure *forms of* intuition, and space and time themselves are pure intuitions. What this set implies for any reader who holds that an intuition must be *of* something is that the intentional objects of our pure intuitions of space and time are themselves pure intuitions. If this is really the case, however, what are the intentional objects of this second pair of pure intuitions— i.e., the pure intuitions that serve as the intentional objects of our pure intuitions of space and time?

Given the set of claims in question, Kant is faced with the prospect of a problematic regress. In order to avoid it, he could either (a) reject the contention that an intuition must have an intentional object, or (b) give up the claim that pure forms of intuition are themselves pure intuitions. It seems hard to believe that he would (at least upon careful consideration) do (a). The claim that an intuition must be *of* something, and thus have an intentional object, seems overwhelmingly strong and quite possibly analytic. If he were to do (b), however, he would need to revise or withdraw numerous claims from both the *Critique* and *Prolegomena*. The following sentence from A27/B43 would stand in need of emendation, for example: "The constant form of this receptivity, which we call sensibility, is a necessary condition of all the relations within which objects can be intuited as outside us, and, if one abstracts from these objects, it is a pure intuition." So would this passage from A42/B59–60:

> What may be the case with objects in themselves and abstracted from all . . . receptivity of our sensibility remains entirely unknown to us. We are acquainted with nothing except our way of perceiving them . . . Space and time are its pure forms, sensation in general its matter. We can cognize only the former *a priori* . . . and they [space and time] are therefore called pure intuitions.[3]

If Kant were to do (b), moreover, he would need to rebuild his account of a pure form of intuition. The relevant remains of his account at A20/ B34–35 would merely say that such a form lies in the mind *a priori* and that it is that in which sensations can alone be ordered. What could such a thing possibly be, if not an intuition? In the absence of an answer to this question, Kant would be in much the same boat as Locke, who invokes a mere "something, I know not what" as the support of qualities that cannot subsist by themselves. If Kant were to do (b), therefore, he would need to explain what it means to say that something is a pure form of intuition in a way that was robust but did not equate such a form with a pure intuition. He does not do so in the Aesthetic or in any other portion of the *Critique*. At the very least, however, he might be held to supply materials that would allow him to do so in his *Inaugural Dissertation*.

In §4 of that work, Kant writes at length about the form in and/or of a sensible representation. In the course of doing so, he makes claims that reappear in the passage from A20/B34–35 of the *Critique* cited above. Having distinguished between the matter and form of a sensible representation, for example, he identifies the matter with sensation and insists that objects do not strike the senses in virtue of their form. In §14 and §15 of *ID*, moreover, he argues that our "ideas" or "concepts" (i.e., representations) of time and space are pure intuitions, concludes on this basis that neither time nor space is something objective and real, and emphasizes that both and/or the "concepts" of both are nonetheless in the highest degree true. He also says in §14 that time is a pure intuition and in §15 that the "concept" of space contains within itself the very form of all sensible intuition. Given such numerous similarities (of which this list is merely partial), it seems safe to suppose that the form in and/or of a sensible representation discussed in 1770 and the form(s) of intuition (or appearance or sensibility) discussed eleven (and again seventeen) years later in the *Critique* are supposed to be equivalent.

In the context of an attempt to develop an account of (2) that is robust but not faced with the prospect of a problematic regress, therefore, Kant's discussion of the form in and/or of a sensible representation in §4 of that earlier work may be of great help. Here is that discussion in full (*ID* 2:292–293):

> In a representation of sense, there is, first of all, something you might call the *matter*, namely the *sensation*, and there is also something which may be called the *form*, the *aspect* namely of sensible things which arises according as the various things which affect the senses are coordinated by a certain natural law of the mind. Moreover, just as the sensation which constitutes the *matter* of a sensible representation is, indeed, evidence for the presence of something sensible, though in respect of its quality it is dependent upon the nature of the subject in so far as the latter is capable of modification by the object in question, so also the *form* of the same representation is undoubtedly evidence of a certain reference or relation in what is sensed, though properly speaking it is not an outline or any kind of schema of the object, but only a certain law, which is inherent in the mind and by means of which it coordinates for itself what is sensed

from the presence of the object. For objects do not strike the senses in virtue of their form or aspect. Accordingly, if the various factors in an object which affect the sense are to coalesce into some representational whole there is needed an internal principle of the mind, in virtue of which those various factors may be clothed with a certain aspect, in accordance with stable and innate laws.

In the first sentence of this passage, Kant equates the form in (and/or of) a sensible representation with the *aspect* of sensible things which arises according as the various things which affect the senses are coordinated by a certain natural law of the mind. In the very next sentence, however, he equates it with a certain *law*, which is inherent in the mind and by means of which it coordinates for itself that which is sensed from the presence of the object. In the sentence after that, he equates the form of objects which strike the senses (as opposed, perhaps, to sensible representations of those objects) with their *aspect*, while in the fourth and final sentence he speaks again of a certain *aspect*, with which the various factors in an object which affect the sense may be clothed, in accordance with stable and innate laws.

In the course of this passage, in short, Kant explicitly identifies the form in and/or of a sensible representation both with the aspect of sensible things which arises according as the various things which affect the senses are coordinated by a certain natural law of the mind and with that very law itself, which is described as inherent and later said (at least by implication) to be stable and innate. An aspect of a sensible representation is not a law and a law (or set of laws) of the sort described here is not an aspect of the sort in question. Which of them is really the form in and/ or of a sensible representation, therefore: the aspect or the law?

At least in this passage, the balance of evidence favors the aspect. In the second sentence, after all, Kant asserts that the form of a sensible representation is undoubtedly evidence of a certain reference or relation in what is sensed. Even though Kant equates the form with the law later in this very sentence, it is difficult to see how the law could be described as such evidence. It is far less difficult to see how an aspect of the sort in question could be so described, however. In the third sentence, moreover, Kant identifies the form of objects that strike the senses with their aspect, which might be taken to suggest a more general equation on his part of "form" and "aspect".

What all of this might suggest to a reader nonplussed by the claim that a pure form of intuition is a pure intuition is that Kant would be better off with the assertion that a pure form of intuition is an *aspect* of the sort described in §4 of his *Inaugural Dissertation*. Such an assertion would not be subject to any prospect of a problematic regress, since such an aspect could be an intentional object but would not need an intentional object of its own. The real content of (2), such an assertion would entail, is that space and time themselves lie in the mind *a priori* and that they (and/or spatiality and temporality) are aspects of sensible things that arise as various things which affect the senses are coordinated by certain natural laws of the mind. The real content of (2), in other words, would be that space and time themselves lie in the mind *a priori* and that they are aspects with which various factors in objects which affect the sense are clothed in accordance with stable and innate laws of the mind.

This basic account would still give rise to questions and thus stand in need of refinement. The claim that these aspects lie in the mind *a priori* would have to mean that they are in us prior to sensation, at least in a logical or conceptual sense, and thus that they do not depend on sensations. How could this be if they arise according as various things which affect the senses are coordinated by a certain natural law of the mind? Doesn't this entail that they arise *in response to* sensations, in which case they would not exist in the absence of sensations and would therefore depend on them?

At least in principle, there would be two different ways in which these questions could be answered. On the first, we would distinguish once again between existence and nature. In this way, we would take the claim that a pure form of intuition lies in the mind *a priori* to mean that the relevant aspect of sensible things does not depend on sensations with respect to its nature even if (or though) it *does* rely on them with respect to its existence. On the second, we could point to Kant's explicit identification of the form of a sensible representation not only with the aspect of sensible things which arises according as various things that affect the senses are coordinated by a certain law of the mind, but also with that very law itself. Given that he does this, we could maintain, he really means the *law* rather than the *aspect* when he says that a pure form of intuition lies in the mind *a priori*. This being the case, we could observe that he is entitled to deny that there is any respect at all in which a form of intuition depends on sensations. On the first of these ways, "form of intuition", "space", and "time" would each have a single referent but we would have to appeal to a distinction between their existence and their nature in order to make sense of the claim that they lie in the mind *a priori*. On the second of these ways, those terms would each have different referents (either an aspect or a law) in different contexts but there would be no need to appeal to a distinction between their existence and their nature in the context of the claim that they lie in the mind *a priori*.

For the sake of symmetry between (1) and (2), we might well favor the first of these ways. No matter which of them we favored, however, we could make sense of Kant's description at A20/B34 of a form of intuition (or appearance or sensibility) as that in which alone sensations can be ordered. The meaning of this description on both of these ways would be that whatever is given by means of sensations is ordered in terms of the relevant aspect. No matter which of these ways we favored, moreover, we could also make sense of Kant's claim that space lies in the mind *a priori* but is nonetheless three dimensional and infinite. On the first of them, this would mean that space (or spatiality) is an aspect of things that arises according as various things which affect the senses are coordinated by a certain natural law of the mind, that with respect to its nature this aspect does not depend on sensations, and that whatever is intuited in terms of this aspect is intuited as having location in something three dimensional and boundless. On the second of them, this would mean that a certain natural law of the mind according to which things which affect the senses are coordinated does not depend in any respect upon sensations, that the coordination of those things by that law gives rise to an aspect of those things that with respect to its nature does not depend upon sensations, and that whatever is intuited in terms of this aspect is intuited as having location in something three dimensional and boundless. On this second way, we might think it best to distinguish in an explicit manner between the possible referents of the term "space", perhaps by means of "space$_L$" and "space$_A$", where the subscripts refer to "law" and "aspect", respectively.

4. Conclusion

The focus of this chapter has been restricted to the meanings of (1) and (2). The meaning of the former, we have determined, is that our representations of space and time are intuitions and that with respect to their nature they do not depend on sensations. The meaning of the latter, I have argued, would best be amended so as to avoid the prospect of a problematic regress. Instead of stating that space and time themselves are pure intuitions in which sensations can alone be ordered, Kant's position should be that space and time themselves (and/or spatiality and temporality themselves) are aspects of sensible things which arise according as the various things which affect the senses are coordinated by a certain natural law of the mind and that with respect to their nature they do not depend on sensations.[4] Even if this chapter is right on both of these counts, much remains to be done for the purpose of a full assessment of the argument in which the relevant claims arise. As mentioned in the introduction, such an assessment would require detailed exploration of Kant's case in support of (1), the meanings of both (3) and (4), the ground(s) of Kant's move from (1) to (2), and the grounds of his moves from (2) to (3) and (2) to (4). If my argument is right with respect to the meanings of (1) and (2), however, the basis for such exploration should now be more solid.

Notes

1. According to Berkeley, of course, the result of this process would be nothing at all—i.e., no representation at all.
2. As we shall see in a passage from B41 about to be cited, Kant *does* in fact take "pure" to be opposed to "empirical".

3. If anything, Kant doubles down in the *Prolegomena* on the claim that space
   and time themselves are pure intuitions. Perhaps the most striking instances
   are contained in §11 of that work. At the same time, he sometimes writes even
   there as though there is a distinction between space and time themselves on
   the one hand and our intuitions of them on the other. In §9, for example, he
   speaks of what a pure intuition must "contain". In §8, moreover, he observes
   that an intuition is a representation of the sort that would depend immediately
   on the presence of an object, which seems to entail that an intuition must be
   of something, and thus have an intentional object.
4. This account of the relevant conclusion assumes that we would opt for symmetry between (1) and (2) and thus for the first of the two ways in which we
   might explain Kant's claim that space and time themselves (as well as spatiality and temporality themselves) lie in the mind *a priori*.

5 Intuition and Existence

How Intuition Helps Construct and Disrupt Transcendental Idealism[1]

Jack Chun

1. Introduction: Intuition and Extra-Conceptual Existence

The duality of concept and intuition in the explanation of the possibility of cognition is one[2] of the hallmarks of Kant's transcendental reflection (A261/B317).[3] Intuition is famously blind without concepts (A51/B75). But it has a special function that a concept could never match: it can directly give us *raw contact with reality*, though the forms of intuition, space and time, delimit *a priori* the reality knowable to us. For Kant, it is intuition and nothing else that nails us down to the world of existence that lies beyond the mere circle of concepts. *Existence*, as different and distinguishable from *being* a concept, I call *extra-conceptual* existence. The questions I examine below concern how Kant constructs his superstructure (A319/B376) of transcendental idealism with intuition and, more importantly, whether he can ever break out of the circle of concepts through intuition, whereby *the world of extra-conceptual existence is actually reached in such a way that the objective reality of what is intuited can be established*. I will argue that intuition, given its assigned functions, paradoxically helps construct and disrupt Kant's transcendental idealism.

2. Forms of Intuition Abstracted: Transcendental Aesthetic

Let us start with the forms of intuition Kant expounds "as the subjective constitution of our mind" (A23/B38) in the Transcendental Aesthetic. I will focus on space as the form of outer intuition in this section and examine its relationship with time in the next section.

The closest way for us to get in touch with the existence of anything in particular, according to Kant, is through nothing but intuition. He claims that objects are *immediately given* to us in intuition, "from which all thought gains its material" (A19/B33). The immediate given-ness of an empirical object is *stipulated* by Kant as explicable only in terms of the receptivity of our sensibility, through which we are "affected" by it.

Insofar as a spatial object is concerned, the subject is *given* it in intuition when it is *presented* to the consciousness from an empirical source other than the subject's own consciousness. Kant refers to this sort of source as the matter of the spatial object (A20/B34). He further explains the "matter (the physical element) or content" of the intuition as "signifying something which is met with in space and time and which therefore contains an existent [*Dasein*] corresponding to sensation" (A723/B751). Kant expounds the intuition's *immediacy* in terms of the sameness of the forms in which the object exists and in which it is given to us in intuition. Supposedly, the forms introduce no mediacy between the object and our intuition.

Kant addresses two questions that further articulate the idea of the immediate given-ness of objects. First, it concerns how our intuition and the object are argued to have the same necessary forms. Second, it expounds why space is originally related to intuition and only derivatively to concepts. To address the first question, Kant's strategy is twofold. First, he argues from abstraction. He notes that, by *isolating* sensibility from concepts and *separating* sensation from sensibility, "nothing may remain save pure intuition and the mere form of appearances" (A22/B36). This method of isolation and separation in considering a particular aspect of experience is typical of Kant's transcendental reflection. In refining the notion of "pure intuition", for instance, he goes on to claim: "objects can be intuited as outside us; if we abstract from these objects, it is a pure intuition, and bears the name of space" (A27/B43).

This method of abstraction, however, prompts the question how one may understand the status of the *residue* of the analysis. For instance, a thing *considered* as it is in itself—i.e., in abstraction from the sensible forms of experience (space and time)—is a case in point. This sort of abstraction has led to the debate between the two-aspect and two-world interpretations of the thing considered as in itself.[4] On this score, one needs to be cautious in interpreting Kant's abstractive regression to intuition and its forms. His first move of isolating intuition from concepts has also engendered the recent debate on the question whether or not intuition, despite its overt concept-blindness, might still properly function cognitively as a standalone feature of sensibility, accessible from within the subject's consciousness: this has led to so-called Kantian non-conceptualism on the pro side of the debate.[5] To anticipate what follows: we shall see that Kant meets with problems in explicating the residue of this sort of abstractive analysis when pushed to the limit of inquiry, particularly regarding the explanation of the objective reality of what is intuited by us when it is *isolated from the forms of intuition.*

Now, for the second strand of his twofold argument for the necessary forms of objects and intuition, Kant asserts that "space comprehends all things that appear to us as external" (A27/B43), and without space, we could not conceive of anything as outside us. Spatiality is the necessary *form of objects* to be presented (given) to our consciousness as empirically "outside us". In addition, Kant asserts that we could not even conceive how the synthetic *a priori* judgments in mathematics, and geometry in particular, are possible without assuming space as the *form of intuition*; through it we conduct mathematical activities and construct geometrical objects in our mind, these objects as such being called pure intuitions. Kant contends that, since we have to assume space in this necessary manner and know about it *a priori*, we must see it as the *necessary form both of our outer intuition and of the object "outside us"*.

Nonetheless, one might object that, by this type of abstraction and necessity of assumption, Kant at most shows that space can be chosen to be *definitive* of what is selectively considered as necessary for a certain aspect of experience—in this case, the experience of the external world and mathematical construction. But this might appear theoretically arbitrary in terms of the choices to be abstracted *away*.[6] In this connection, interestingly enough, Kant's criticism of Leibniz in the Amphiboly of Concepts of Reflection might reflect, indirectly, the fact that the Leibnizian, for one, would dispute with Kant on what should and should not be abstracted away without distorting the way we understand the genuine nature of reality.

At this point, Kant's argument for space as intrinsically related to *intuition* becomes very crucial. For it is this strategy that allows Kant to construct his superstructure with an anchor directly fixed to the territory of extra-conceptual existence. Kant's explanation is this: our representation of "[s]pace is not a discursive or, as we say, general concept of relations of things in general, but a pure intuition" (A24/B39). Here one needs to note that concepts, for Kant, serve as spontaneous rules of combination in our judgment (A126). They can be used to describe the general features of possible objects. However, concepts alone cannot fix the referent because, theoretically speaking, either none or more than one of the objects might answer the descriptive content of the concepts. Only the concept-blind intuition can fix the particular referent directly through the immediate given-ness of the object to us.

But how is the special function of intuition connected with our experience of space? Kant's ultimate rationale, which is pivotal to the entire transcendental architectonic, is that space is a *singularity*. It will be seen below how this thesis is required for the arguments of the Refutation of Idealism. Here the point to note is Kant's claim that "we can represent to ourselves only *one space*; and if we speak of diverse spaces, we mean thereby only parts of *one and the same unique space*" (A25/B39, emphasis added). The oneness or singularity of space is the decisive reason for Kant to identify intuition as solely responsible for forming our primary relation with the spatial order out there. For whatever spatial region we pick out from experience, it has to be from one and the same space. Being *singular* in dimension, space is a special case of a *particular*: special in the sense that "[s]pace is represented as an infinite *given* magnitude" (A25/B40), where infinitude means "limitlessness" (A25). Kant further explains in the Antinomy that space, as a condition of our outer experience, should not be considered as given to us complete in itself (A500/B529). The vastness of the singularity of space is thus defined by the possible indefinite progression we can make within it. Given this special sense of the singularity of space, the subject's relationship with any space is always on a one–on–one basis, referentially fixed only to one particular: the Space of the spaces within it (B40). This sort of relationship with the referentially fixed particular can be fulfilled, according to Kant, only through intuition. Concepts can be used only secondarily to delimit any spatial region within the one space: "Space is essentially one; the manifold in it, and therefore the general concept of spaces, depends solely on [the introduction of] limitations" (A25/B39).

In this sort of form-abstraction regarding space, Kant hastens to draw up the transcendental implications: space is empirically real but transcendentally ideal (A26/B42). Kant does not provide any further substantial arguments in support of such implications in the Transcendental Aesthetic, which he at any rate considers as inconclusive "expositions" (A23/B38 and A729/B757). In this regard, I will explore below three of the questions Kant addresses in other parts of the *Critique*. First, in what *existential* sense are spatial objects claimed to be real? Second, what is Kant's justification for our epistemic access to spatial objects *out there*? Finally, why does Kant argue for the transcendental object as the ground of the objects of our empirical intuition?

3. Empirical Intuitions Interconnected: Refutation of Idealism

In the Refutation, Kant aims to argue that the "consciousness of my own existence proves the existence of objects in space outside me" (B275). He begins his argument with the statement that "I am conscious of my own existence as determined in time. All determination of time presupposes something *permanent* in perception" (B275). This statement echoes the First Analogy, in which he already argued that time-determinations in experience require the permanent (framework of reference). But unlike the First Analogy, the Refutation emphasizes the actual existence of spatial objects for the possibility of empirical consciousness in time. How does intuition come into play in this argument?

Kant explains that, although the presence of the *representation* "I am" "immediately includes in itself the existence of a subject" (B277), empirical consciousness of oneself requires something more than a mere thought. It requires *intuition*: "For this we require, in addition to the thought of something existing, also intuition, and in this case inner intuition." Inner intuition is required because "consciousness in time is necessarily bound

up with consciousness of the possibility of this time-determination"
(B276). Time being the form of inner intuition, time-determination is
therefore a matter of inner intuition to begin with.

Given this consideration, Kant asks whether the correlate of the permanent for time can ever be located within the realm of inner intuition.
His answer is negative: *"But this permanent cannot be an intuition in
me"* (Bxxxix). His point is that, instead of providing us with something
that we can perceive as the unchangeable (permanent), inner intuitions
in their successive order are changes themselves and, therefore, presuppose something else as the permanent that can explain their changes.
Kant contends that only the spatial order could fulfill the permanency
requirement. He claims, "perception of this permanent is possible only
through a *thing* outside me and not through the mere *representation* of a
thing outside me. . . . In other words, the consciousness of my *existence*
is at the same time an immediate consciousness of the *existence* of other
things outside me" (B275–276, emphasis on "existence" added). Kant's
argument in effect trades on intuition as the medium through which
objects of outer intuition are existentially presupposed as "the permanent
in perception" by that of those of inner intuition. In other words, since
the question concerns not a mere thought but the *intuition* of the actual
existence of oneself in time, the identified spatial correlate for the permanent is argued to be one which *obtains in reality*. Inner consciousness in
time presupposes the existence of spatial objects in general.

In the Refutation, Kant does not proceed any further to show how
exactly the realm of spatial objects can serve as the necessary correlate of
the permanent framework of time. Even if one connects the Refutation
with the First Analogy, where the permanent refers to substance, one
may still ask how the actual existence of *spatial* objects is related to the
possible *time*-determinations. At this juncture, one sees the importance
of the Transcendental Aesthetic. There Kant holds, as noted in the previous section, that the universal spatial order is "an infinite *given* magnitude" (A25/B41), and "space comprehends all things that appear to
us as external" (A27/B43). The infinite quantum of space is a *singular*
order of outer objects and in this sense its singular *oneness* (with the
permanency of matter therein) is *unchangeable*. One cannot change its
quantum any more than one can change that of, for instance, an infinite numerical sequence. In short, Kant *externalizes* the permanent
(= unchangeable) framework required for the *internal* consciousness of
time-determinations to the *actual existence* of the unitary spatial order
out there. All this concerns intuition, which, on Kant's account, has the
very special function of relating us to the extra-conceptual existence of
objects immediately.

Here one might still ask why the same sort of *presupposed* singularity of the temporal order (A31/B47) cannot serve the required purpose?
Kant's reply is essentially epistemic: the *actualized* possibility of our

empirical consciousness in time demands the *perceptible* singular frame-work as the background against which the concerned *performative* of time-determinations can be carried out. For anything to be the correlate of the concerned permanent, being singular and permanent is not adequate. It requires perceptivity (B274). The singular (but invisible) dimension of time as such cannot be perceived (i.e., identified and reidentified as the same framework of reference) for that special purpose. Only space can.

This Kantian line of reasoning, however, would face an even more chal-lenging question. From the epistemic *need* to consider the spatial order *as* real in order to account for possible time-determinations, can Kant really demonstrate the extra-conceptual *existence* of spatial objects as such? Ever since Stroud (1969), the typical objection to Kant can be formulated this way: in the Refutation, one could at most prove the necessity of the *presupposition* of our *belief* in the existence of the spatial world. *That* we have to *believe* in it certainly does not mean *that* it *does* exist. The two *that*-clauses, one concerning the propositional attitude and the other concerning the existential question, are logically independent from each other. To see how this sort of skeptical challenge can be met by Kant, one needs to turn to the Transcendental Deduction.

4. Manifold of Intuition Unified: Transcendental Deduction

To address the skeptical challenge, it is important to unravel the assump-tions behind it. They concern two sets of apparently unbridgeable gaps between the objects of inner and outer intuition. They are the ontological and the epistemic gaps. Ontologically speaking, one might claim that the existence of the objects of the inner and the outer realms are so disparate and distinct from each other that the existence of one realm could have no *existential implication* whatever for that of the other. That is, even given the existence of the inner realm, coupled with our necessary *belief* in the existence of spatial objects, the outer realm might still not exist. This is the ontological gap. On the other hand, epistemically speaking, even if it is conceded that both the inner and the outer realms of objects exist, the ontological disparity between them still robs us of the justifica-tion for having the same sort of epistemic access to them. Granted that we have knowledge and are certain about the existence of the objects of the inner realm, it would still be unclear how we might ever have epis-temic access to or indeed any certainty about objects of the outer realm, whose ontological identity is presumably so different from that of those of the inner realm. This lack of certainty due to the epistemic gap, which is criticized by Kant as a "scandal" (Bxxxixn), is indeed a consequence of the ontological gap.

For the sake of brevity, I will sketch what I think to be the core argu-ment of the Transcendental Deduction and show how it might confront the skeptical challenge. The core argument starts with the transcendental unity of apperception (A108 and B139), which is seen as the necessary ground of any possible experience that one is able to attribute to oneself as of one's own (B131). To account for the *possibility* of the transcendental unity of apperception, Kant argues that it has to be grounded on some synthetic unity—synthetic because it concerns the synthesis of the "data of experience" (A267/B323) into a coherent unity constitutive of the same subjecthood across time—data which would otherwise be truncated and chaotic, leading to the possible *fragmentation of subjecthood in time*.[7] Kant argues that this synthetic unity is found in the correlate of the concept of objecthood in general: "Concepts of objects in general thus underlie all empirical knowledge as its *a priori* conditions" (A93/B126). This concept of objecthood, through the productive synthesis of imagination (A118 and B152), is argued to make possible the concerned synthesis, and specifically the synthetic unity of apperception, grounding the possibility of the self-ascription, "I think", to the same subject across time, this being considered as the necessary condition for any type of consciousness that is to be counted as human.

The unifying function of the concept of objecthood is also requisite for the manifold of intuition, *inner* and *outer*, to be given *us* as an *object*. The manifold of intuition would be "for us as good as nothing" (A111) were it not synthetically unified in the concept of objecthood in general as well. Kant claims (A116–117, emphasis added), "Since this unity of the manifold *in one subject* is synthetic, pure apperception supplies a principle of the synthetic unity of the manifold in all possible intuitions." In this way, the unity of subjecthood would have a *necessary* ripple effect on how the manifold of intuition can be coherently taken up in the unitary consciousness. Although Kant directly speaks of the unities of space and time in abstraction from concepts in the Transcendental Aesthetic, one thing is made clear in the Deduction: nothing can be claimed to be part of the experience of *one and the same subject* unless and until the otherwise "haphazard" (A104) manifold of intuition is synthetically unified in the same subjecthood. And it cannot be so unified unless it is synthesized through the general concept of objecthood as well. Only under this condition of conceptual unity can the manifold of intuition be more than "nothing" and successively figure into the subject's consciousness.[8] As a result, both subjecthood and objecthood, as two sides of the same coin, simultaneously demand the application of the concept of an object in general, which Kant calls the category in the general sense.

But in what sense are both the inner and the outer realms of objects grounded in the concept of objecthood in general? From the transcendental perspective, the ontological gap between the two realms is supposedly demolished in the Deduction because *the concept of objecthood in general, spontaneously construed by us, is constitutive of the very ontological identity of the objects of both realms*, insofar as "the human standpoint"

(A26/B42) is concerned. Whatever conditions are necessary and sufficient for the essential ontological identity of the object *qua* object of one realm (inner or outer) would in this case also be necessary and sufficient for that of the object *qua* object of the other realm. Ontologically speaking, the two realms, which are different at the empirical level, are now *constitutively* unified in the very concept of objecthood as of the same ontological type at the transcendental level. The specific identity ("the physical element or content") of an empirical object, which is contingent and knowable *a posteriori*, will then be discerned through the empirical experience one happens to have.

Once the ontological gap is eliminated at the transcendental level, the question about the epistemic access and certainty may well be answered. Now, given the same type of ontological identity of inner and outer objects at the transcendental level, *prima facie* there is no reason why the subject could not have the same epistemic access to both realms. For the objects of inner and outer realms are on this account indistinguishable from each other at the transcendental level so far as their general ontological status is concerned. Having the epistemic access to one realm in this case would already serve as a *sufficient* justification for one to have the same type of access to the other realm. It would be difficult, if not simply impossible, for the skeptic now to maintain that, while one has a legitimate access to and certainty about one realm (the inner), one is never entitled to the same sort of access or certainty regarding the other realm (the outer).

In this way, the Deduction demonstrates the identical status of the *knowability* of the objects of *both inner and outer intuition* at the transcendental level through the construction of their ontological identities. The unbridgeable gap alleged by the skeptic between the two realms is thus demolished.[9] In the Refutation, Kant then further addresses the question of how the actual existence of the objects of outer intuition in general is not only knowable to us but also *presupposed* and *immediately known* by us in empirical consciousness. The Refutation *cum* the Deduction are Kant's most powerful transcendental arguments against the most treacherous skeptical challenge.

5. Conclusion: Disruptions From the Irreducible *Transcendental Package*

No doubt, the feasibility of the Kantian overarching superstructure, however elaborate, ultimately boils down to the question whether it can be coherently connected with extra-conceptual reality in the way Kant aims. Or else it would be no more than "a dream" (A492/B521). To reach out to reality as such is the unique function of intuition. However, instead of simply anchoring the superstructure to empirical reality, which he defines as "being (in time)" (A143/B182), Kant introduces the transcendental object as the "transcendental ground" of empirical objects (A274/B334). He asserts of the transcendental object (A252/B309): "Unless, therefore, we are to move constantly in a circle, the word appearance must be recognized as already indicating a relation to something, the immediate representation of which is . . . something in itself, that is, an object independent of sensibility." Why does Kant find it necessary to introduce the transcendental object as the "non-empirical" (A109) ground of empirical objects?

Now, when the *forms* of the *existing* objects of experience are all abstracted *away*, would it not follow, as a linguistic inference, that only the form*less* reality or being (= x), in contrast with being (*in time*), remains in existence? But this *linguistic* consideration cannot be Kant's *philosophical* reason, although sometimes he takes advantage of this linguistic fluidity in the *Critique*.[10] Kant is fully aware of the logically possible implications for his form-abstraction. He critically notes that, so far as the transcendental object is concerned, it remains to be decided (A288/B344, numbers added):

1. whether it is to be met within us or outside us,
2. whether it would be at once removed with the cessation of sensibility, or
3. whether in the absence of sensibility it would still remain.

The point to note is that the form-abstraction by itself is neutral to the question whether one is committed to the transcendental object. Option (2) points out the possibility of the removal of the transcendental object when the forms of the object of intuition are abstracted away. Kant is clearly alert to this possibility.[11] Nonetheless, he opts for a positive answer to option (3) as his transcendental position: the transcendental object remains in existence in the absence of sensibility.

To unravel Kant's reasons, one might start with two important claims he makes on the transcendental object. First, the transcendental object is considered as "given in itself prior to all experience . . . merely in order to have something corresponding to sensibility viewed as a receptivity" (A494/B523), and second, "[t]his transcendental object cannot be separated from the sense data, for nothing is then left through which it might be thought" (A250). It is clear that, for Kant, the concept of the transcendental object, *so far as the conditions of the possibility of our knowledge are concerned*, comes as a package of concepts with the receptivity of our sensibility as two sides of the same transcendental explanation. These two sides I shall call the *transcendental package*, which will be seen below as being *irreducible*.

In claiming that *the transcendental object is given in itself prior to all experience*, Kant in effect holds that there is something in general whose *existence* does not depend on human knowledge. And he finds the transcendental package "indispensably required" (A393) because, to his mind, we need something *existent* and *distinguishable* from "the subjective constitution of our mind" in order to make our experience *objectively valid*—i.e., something *other than* what, as the Copernican revolution would suggest, we *subjectively* (= as the subject) "put into" it (Bxviii). Only by upholding the existence of the transcendental object, *completely* in abstraction from the forms of experience, Kant argues, could one justify the *objective reality* of our experience (A109): that is, there should be something in the world of extra-conceptual existence independent of the subject's consciousness, and it is *given in itself* and *intuitable* to the subject, making our experience possible. Note that the *empirical matter* in the spatial realm is already something whose existence is dependent *in form* on our possible experience. As such, matter does not qualify to be something *completely* independent of the forms of our experience. For Kant, the *radical distinguishability* between the subject and the object could be established only if the transcendental object presumably underlying the spatial objects is accepted, whereby the objective reality of what is intuited by us is ultimately justified. The entire transcendental superstructure is then hooked up to "something in general = x" (A104), whose existence is considered as given in itself and whose nature in itself, as a result, is unknowable to us.

Could there be anything whose nature in itself is unknowable to us and yet whose existence can justifiably be affirmed by us? There are two possible interpretations of Kant's position,[12] if one attempts to open up the transcendental package (where the transcendental object stands against the human faculties) as an answer to the question. On the first interpretation, Kant *presupposes* the transcendental object *implicitly* as the *starting point* of transcendental idealism—implicitly, because it does not fully reveal itself as *already* assumed until and unless he is engaged in the second step of his argument, concerning the explanation of the nature of the subjective constitution of our mind, in particular about the forms and content of intuition. When the assumption of the transcendental object is stated in its simplest form (that *something in general is*), it is indeed a very minimal assumption to start with, pending of course the further articulation of how that something figures into the account of experience. According to this interpretation, the *Critique* would be Kant's account of our possible experience identified as the confrontation between the human faculties and reality *given in itself*. What might appear controversial, nevertheless, is whether Kant could explicate how objects of experience are existentially *grounded* on the transcendental object. To this question, the first interpretation could not provide an adequate answer, because it is based on an unargued assumption, no matter how innocuous the idea of the existence of something in general may be.

The second interpretation is similar to the first, except for the *sequence* of the steps Kant might take. According to this interpretation, Kant starts *not* with the existence of the transcendental object but with our pre-theoretical conception of experience. He then constructs its structure by abstracting regressively from the experience through the forms and content of intuition, to the forms of understanding and finally to the extra-conceptual existence of the transcendental object. No doubt, this is exactly the interpretation adopted here. But, obviously, Kant could not sustain his position merely by taking this second route, on pain of the possibility of option (2) noted above: namely the transcendental object might well be removed in the absence of sensibility if the regressive method is followed through. Kant is alert to this possibility. To close off option (2), he has to take the route of the first interpretation as well. And the first route, however innocuous, depends on the second route as its *explicative* justification up to a point. A proper conclusion is that the *Critique* is the product of the dynamic confluence of these two different but at the same time complementary routes, culminating in different ways at the transcendental object that conditions our sensibility as receptivity, which in turn makes possible the objective reality of the objects of our intuition at the transcendental level.

Nonetheless, if one goes deeper into Kant's superstructure, one may see how disruptions arise, even assuming that the confluence interpretation is to be entertained at all. Now, apart from the objects of outer intuition, Kant applies the transcendental–empirical distinction to those of inner intuition as well. He notes that, in intuiting oneself through inner intuition, one is known to oneself as an appearance and not a thing in itself. Underlying the intuited subject would also be the transcendental object, which serves as the ground of its existence (A380). A pertinent question is whether there is any distinction between the transcendental objects grounding the subject and the object respectively. Kant's answer is negative. He holds that the transcendental object, considered merely as something in general, is "always one and the same" for all of the objects of experience, inner and outer (A109 and A380).

Kant's answer here sheds light on the question of option (1) above, concerning whether the transcendental object is met with in us (in empirical consciousness) or outside us (in space). Obviously by now, it is met within us *and* outside us, in the sense that it grounds both realms. Yet, disruptions are occasioned when one sees that the grounding of both realms is *one and the same transcendental object*. For this would undermine Kant's attempt to justify the *objective reality* of our experience of spatial objects as external to us, based on the supposed radical distinguishability and confrontation between the subject and the object—that is, between the human faculties and the transcendental object that grounds the spatial objects. If the transcendental objects grounding the human faculties and spatial objects are one and the same, the intended confrontation and radical distinguishability between the subject and the object would collapse at the transcendental level. The transcendental object would confront itself. This would nullify the type of objective reality Kant is so keen in setting up through regressive abstraction to the transcendental object in relation to the special function of intuition that belongs to the human faculties.

Nevertheless, Kant's possible rejoinder is that, from the perspective of theoretical reason, the criticism advanced above would already involve too much speculation to be allowed within the scope of our knowledge. There is a reason why Kant emphasizes so much that, in speaking of the transcendental object as a condition of our empirical knowledge, one has to connect it with "sense data" (A250); or else one's talk is "empty" (A155/B194), as concepts without intuition are empty (A51/B75). This is the "critical reminder" (A30/B45) Kant would invoke on the way the transcendental package is supposed to be interpreted. That is, *there is no way to fully unpack the transcendental package without violating the limits and scope of human knowledge.* One has to consider the transcendental package as *irreducible*, so far as the possibility of our *cognition* is concerned. The *existence* of the transcendental object as such, therefore, could not be meaningfully considered without regard to the presence of our sense experience. Thus, the statement that the transcendental object confronts itself is already a sign of trespassing the limits of our knowledge, forbidden by theoretical reason.

Last but not least, if one further considers the practical use of reason, there is a case for clarifying how one might proceed with the transcendental or non-empirical realm, including the transcendental object. All in all, one might see the instability engendered by the special function of intuition in the transcendental package as disruptive but not necessarily destructive. This and other disruptions, however, would keep on rocking the superstructure of transcendental idealism. For it is the inborn nature of our speculative reason that, on Kant's account, it always pushes our knowledge claims beyond the bounds of sensibility in order to catch a glimpse of the transcendent realm. The job of the *Critique* is to curb the pretentions of sensibility (A255/B311) and keep fighting against exactly this sort of incessant "restlessness of reason" (A757/B785), here and there, now and then.

Notes

1. I would like to thank Stephen Palmquist, Julian von Will, Clinton Tolley, and Ole Döring for their help with the present version. Since parts of this paper have been developed from my previous writing, I would also like to thank Margaret Morrison, Gordon Nagel, Robert Imlay, and Ralf Meerbote for their kindest support as well.
2. Nagel (1983) points out that the tripartite division of faculties should not be overlooked—namely sensibility, understanding, and reason. And Heidegger (1997) would add imagination as the indispensable, if not the most important, faculty in the *Critique*.

3. The A/B pagination, which refers to the first and the second editions of *Kant's Critique of Pure Reason*, and the English translation follow Norman Kemp Smith in Kant (1781/1787).
4. Among others, the two-aspect exponents include Prauss (1974) and Allison (2004) and the two-world exponents Adickes (1924) and Strawson (1966).
5. Kantian non-conceptualism is typically traced back to Evans (1982), though it is Hanna (2005) who kindles the Kantian interpreters' interests. Schulting (2016) is a further recent significant development.
6. For instance, Strawson (1959) argues for a possible conception of the no-space world where the distinction between the subjective and the objective is construed purely on the different patterns of sounds without appealing to any spatial objects.
7. "Subjecthood" here refers to the identity of the subject qua subject.
8. In this connection, the recent concession made by the Kantian non-conceptualist, Allais, from her strong 2015 position to the "modest" position (2016, 25), would still be too strong a position if the requisite unity of subjecthood (and not only of intuition) is properly addressed.
9. My reconstruction is different from that of Strawson (1966), who argues that the Deduction fails to fulfill its objective, interpreted as a proof of the *existence* of outer objects, and also from that of Allison (2004 and 2015), who argues that it merely concerns the applicability of the categories to logical and inner objects only, excluding outer objects, and therefore amounts only to a "qualified success" (2015, 452). The interpretation presently advanced presents a third alternative, which I think is closer to Kant's intention in the Deduction.
10. Bennett (1966) seems misguided when he criticizes Kant for adopting this sort of linguistic inference as a philosophical argument. Interestingly, Langton (1998) argues that this type of linguistic inference makes sense as a consequence of a relational account of empirical knowledge. But this would still render the linguistic inference impotent as an argument in its own right.
11. Option 2 can be adapted, for instance, by phenomenalism.
12. These two possible routes are associated by Henrich (2003) with what he calls Kant's pre-Critical mysticism (the descent from the non-empirical) and his Critical, systematic approach (the ascent from the empirical). Henrich argues that in the *Critique* Kant is clean enough from the allure of mysticism. But in the remainder of this chapter I will argue that the *Critique* is a mixture of the mystical and the post-mystical approaches at the fundamental level.

References

Adickes, Erich (1924). *Kant und das Ding an sich*. Berlin: Pan.
Allais, Lucy (2015). *Manifest Reality: Kant's Idealism and His Realism*. Oxford: Oxford University Press.
———— (2016). Conceptualism and Nonconceptualism in Kant: A Survey of the Recent Debate. In: D. Schulting (ed.), *Kantian Nonconceptualism*. London: Palgrave Macmillan, 1–25.
Allison, Henry (2004). *Kant's Transcendental Idealism: An Interpretation and Defense*, 2nd ed. New Haven and London: Yale University Press.
———— (2015). *Kant's Transcendental Deduction: An Analytical–Historical Commentary*. Oxford: Oxford University Press.
Bennett, Johnathan (1966). *Kant's Analytic*. Cambridge: Cambridge University Press.

Evans, Gareth (1982). *The Varieties of Reference*. Oxford: Oxford University Press.

Hanna, Robert (2005). Kant and Nonconceptual Content. In: *European Journal of Philosophy* 13(2), 247–290.

Heidegger, Martin (1997). Trans. R. Taft, *Kant and the Problem of Metaphysics*, 5th ed. Bloomington and Indianapolis: Indiana University Press.

Henrich, Dieter (2003). Ed. D. S. Pacini, *Between Kant and Hegel: Lectures on German Idealism*. Cambridge: Harvard University Press.

Kant, Immanuel (1781/1787). Trans. Norman Kemp Smith, *Immanuel Kant's Critique of Pure Reason*. London: Macmillan, 1929.

Langton, Rae (1998). *Kant's Humility: Our ignorance of Things in Themselves*. Oxford: Oxford University Press.

Nagel, Gordon (1983). *The Structure of Experience*. Chicago: Chicago University Press.

Prauss, Gerold (1974). *Kant und das Problem der Dinge an sich*. Bonn: Bouvier.

Schulting, Dennis (2016). *Kantian Nonconceptualism*. London: Palgrave Macmillan.

Strawson, P. F. (1959). *Individuals*. London and New York: Methuen.

——— (1966). *The Bounds of Sense: An Essay on Kant's Critique of Pure Reason*. London and New York: Routledge.

Stroud, Barry (1969). Transcendental Arguments. In: T. Penelhum and J. J. MacIntosh (eds.), *The First Critique: Reflections on Kant's Critique of Pure Reason*. Belmont, CA: Wadsworth Publishing Company, 54–70.

Part II

The Function and Status of Intuition in Human Cognition

6 The Given in Theoretical and Practical Cognition
Intuition and the Moral Law

Lucy Allais

1. Introduction

Cognition (*Erkenntnis*) is a central notion in Kant's Critical philosophy. The *Critique of Pure Reason* is addressed to the question of how cognition of synthetic *a priori* propositions is possible and is also centrally concerned with the conditions of empirical cognition. Kant famously argues that we cannot have cognition of things as they are in themselves, and also that we cannot have cognition of what he calls supersensible objects, which includes God, our souls, and our freedom. He then also argues, in the *Critique of Practical Reason* and other places, that we *can* have cognition of freedom through practical reason, as well as grounds for belief in God and the immortality of our souls.

To understand these positions we clearly need to know what he means by *cognition*. For a long time, English language translations of Kant's work translated *Erkenntnis* as knowledge, rather than cognition, and did not pay much attention to the difference between knowledge and cognition in Kant's system. This may not simply be a problem of translation; in their recent paper on "Cognition and Knowledge in Kant's system", Eric Watkins and Marcus Willaschek argue that much *German* language scholarship on Kant has also used "*Wissen*" and "*Erkenntnis*" interchangeably (Willaschek and Watkins 2017, 2). Recently this situation has changed, with a lot of attention being paid to the significant differences between these two notions. Arguably, this makes a significant difference to how one understands Kant's central concerns in the first *Critique* as well as his account of what practical reason adds.

Willaschek and Watkins argue that not distinguishing knowledge and cognition in Kant "is at best misleading and at worst a serious mistake that can prevent one from understanding the subject matter, goal, and overall argument of the *Critique of Pure Reason*" (Willaschek and Watkins 2017, 2). I have made similar points in my recent book, *Manifest Reality* (2015), where I argue that paying attention to Kant's concern with cognition and its conditions is crucial for properly understanding his transcendental idealism. My focus in that work is on theoretical cognition. In particular, I argue that properly understanding the role of *intuition* in theoretical cognition is crucial for understanding both the nature of transcendental idealism as well as Kant's argument for this position. In this paper, my aim is to extend this account to reflect on Kant's account of practical cognition. The *Critique of Pure Reason* holds that intuition is a crucial ingredient without which we cannot have cognition,[1] yet Kant allows that we can have practical cognition without intuition. Both theoretical and practical cognition have concepts, the other central ingredient in theoretical cognition, so in practical reason something must take the place of intuition. My aim in this paper is to reflect on the role of intuition in theoretical cognition to see if this helps us understand what plays this role in practical cognition, where intuition is lacking.

I will first say something briefly about the significance of distinguishing between cognition and knowledge. Then I will present my account of intuition and the role it plays in theoretical cognition. I then extend this to look at practical cognition, and will attempt to examine, in both directions, how Kant's account of practical cognition might inform how we understand theoretical cognition, and vice versa. Finally, I speculatively connect this discussion to one famous criticism of Kant by Mou Zongsan.

2. Cognition and Knowledge

Watkins and Willaschek argue that "cognition, in the basic kind of case, is a mental state through which we are aware of the existence and (some of the) general features of objects" (Willaschek and Watkins 2017, 2–3).[2] They say it is a kind of conscious representation of an object, that it need not be a propositional attitude, that it need not involve assent and need not involve epistemic justification. Further, they point out that it sometimes seems that Kant allows that cognitions, unlike knowledge, can be false. While questions about the conditions of knowledge often concern justification, they argue, in contrast to this, that Kant's concern with cognition is with how it is possible for us represent particular objects and their determinate features and to be directly aware of them (19). Similarly, Karl Schafer (forthcoming, 7) argues that

> a representation counts as a cognition for Kant not primarily because it is better warranted or justified than other representations, but rather because it possesses certain distinctive representational features that mark it off from other sorts of representations. Thus, when Kant claims that we cannot achieve cognition of things–in–themselves, this is not primarily a claim about the limits of our ability to make judgments in a justified or warranted fashion. Rather, it is, first and foremost, a claim about the representational limitations

of our faculties—namely, that there is *an* important sense in which we cannot even successfully represent to ourselves the nature of things in themselves.

An important point here, which follows from both of these accounts, is that unlike knowledge, cognition may not require justification or warrant. There are a number of interesting things that follow from this. For example, Watkins and Willaschek argue that Kant's famous claim is that we cannot *cognize* things in themselves and *not* that we cannot have *knowledge* of them; they suggest that this allows as a possibility that we may have some knowledge of things we cannot cognize. Schafer denies this, seeing cognition as the broader class and saying that we can have knowledge only of objects we can cognize.

In my book (Allais 2015) I argue that the claim that cognition does not require justification or warrant makes a crucial difference to understanding Kant's central question of how synthetic *a priori* propositions are possible, as well as for understanding the role transcendental idealism plays in the answer to this question. If we see this question as concerned with knowledge (and therefore with justification) we will understand Kant's question as asking how it is possible for us to justify or establish synthetic *a priori* propositions. If we then see transcendental idealism as part of the answer to the question of how synthetic *a priori* knowledge is possible, we will be liable to think that Kant's answer is that we are able to justify synthetic *a priori* propositions because our minds make them true, so having insight into them is simply a matter of having insight into a feature of our minds. Simply and roughly put the idea would be: we have insight into our own minds; if certain synthetic *a priori* claims about the world really just reflect our minds, we can explain having insight into them; so, postulating transcendental idealism (certain fundamental synthetic *a priori* claims reflecting our minds and not the mind-independent world) explains our having knowledge of synthetic *a priori* claims. Add to this that we do in fact have knowledge of synthetic *a priori* claims in geometry, and it might look like we have an argument for transcendental idealism.

I have argued that there are a number of problems with this reading. It assumes that we have transparent insight into our minds. It fails to distinguish between the different ways, in Kant's account, different kinds of synthetic *a priori* propositions are justified: Kant has a different explanation of how we justify or establish synthetic *a priori* claims in mathematics (through construction in pure intuition) from how we do this in metaphysics (through transcendental arguments showing them to be conditions of the possibility of empirical cognition). Further, this reading attributes to Kant a very weak argument for transcendental idealism, which would not establish what he needs it to. Kant opens the *Critique* asserting that we have cognition of synthetic *a priori* claims in mathematics and asking how this is possible, but regarding such claims in metaphysics as very much in doubt. If he then goes on to postulate that the explanation of our capacity for insight into synthetic *a priori* geometrical claims is that our minds "shape" objects in such a way as to make these claims come out as true, and then takes this to establish transcendental idealism—the dependence of objects on our minds—he would still have no grounds for concluding that our minds shape objects in such a way as to make metaphysical synthetic *a priori* claims come out as true.

Rather than seeing Kant's asking how cognition of synthetic *a priori* propositions is possible as a question about how it is possible for us to *justify* such propositions, I argue that his central concern is with how it is possible for such propositions to concern objects that are given to us. This is a concern with how it is possible for our judgments to succeed in referring to objects, or to succeed in connecting with the world. Kant says that cognition requires both concepts and intuitions, that concepts enable us to *think* objects and intuitions *give* us objects. Without given objects we have a mere play of concepts, which does not manage to actually connect to a world, and with respect to which we do not even know if the objects the concepts represent are really possible. In my view, Kant holds that the way in which we are given objects that are independent of us is through their affecting our senses. This immediately shows why there is a problem understanding how cognition of synthetic *a priori* propositions can be possible for us: since such propositions are *a priori*, they will not involve anything affecting our senses; for them to be *cognition* they must concern objects that are (or can be) given to us, but objects that are independent of us are given to us by affecting our senses. It looks like such propositions will fail to connect to or properly be about objects. Thus, before we get into questions about how to establish or justify such propositions, we have a prior question about how it is even possible to make *a priori* claims that connect to or are properly about objects. Kant's primary answer to his question is to appeal to the idea of *a priori* intuition. This fits the bill because it enables us to see how synthetic *a priori* geometrical propositions could have objects (something given to us) because *a priori* intuition gives us something (it is intuition) but does this *a priori*.

3. The Role of Intuition in Theoretical Cognition

To understand this account of synthetic *a priori* cognition we need to understand what is meant by the claim that intuitions *give* us objects, and we need an account of the kind of representations intuitions are that explains how they are able to do this. Kant says that intuitions are singular and immediate representations that give us objects. As I read this, intuitions are representations that give us acquaintance with (present us with) perceptual particulars. They present us with things that are given as one (single) and they present these things immediately. This is how they give us objects: they give us direct acquaintance with objects. I understand by "perceptual particulars" things that are present in consciousness that can be picked out or attended to, so are presented as bounded, as distinct from other things, and as spatially related and located.

There are two central parts of my reading that are controversial. First, many scholars read Kant as saying that we could not be consciously presented with anything as singular or particular—as a distinct thing—without concepts or at least without conceptually governed synthesis. They do not think it would be possible to be presented with distinct *perceptual particulars* without this. In my view, by contrast, intuitions do not depend on concepts to play their role of being singular and immediate representations that give us objects. Second, on my view, when we have an intuition, the object that the intuition represents is actually present to consciousness. So, a hallucination of an object would not be an outer intuition, because we would not be immediately presented with, or in direct mental contact with, an object outside us. This holds even if a hallucination of an object would be subjectively indistinguishable from an intuition of that object. I will say a bit to motivate both these two parts of my view.

The alternative view—the idea that intuitions cannot present us with objects (perceptual particulars) without concepts or at least without synthesis—is primarily based on Kant's many claims in the Deduction that conceptually governed synthesis is needed to give thought "relation to an object", and that without this thought lacks an object and we would have merely "unruly heaps" and cognition would not be organized and connected. We would have merely a "swarm" of appearances, which "would belong to no experience, and would consequently be without an object, and would be nothing but a blind play of representations, i.e., less than a dream" (A112). These kinds of claims are taken by many commentators to mean that we do not have distinct things presented to consciousness without concepts; we simply have a blooming buzzing confusion of sensations. The thought would be either that intuitions are something like sensations (so are not representations that present us with particular objects) and it is synthesis governed by concepts that produces representations of particular objects, or that intuitions are more than just sensations and do give us particular objects but that they depend on concepts for this. I call the latter view conceptualism about intuition. In my view neither of these options can be sustained as interpretations of the text.

Against the first option, it is very clear that Kant distinguishes between sensations and intuitions and says that it is intuitions, not sensations, that give us objects. Further, he says that intuitions are singular representations that give us objects. There are also many problems with the second option. Kant emphasizes throughout the *Critique* the claim that intuitions and concepts are entirely distinct representations that make distinct and essential contributions to knowledge. Making intuitions dependent on concepts to play their role in cognition is not consistent with this. Further, at the beginning of the Deduction, the very section taken to support conceptualism about intuition, Kant explicitly *denies* that intuitions depend on concepts. He says that "[t]he categories of the understanding, on the contrary, *do not* represent the conditions under which objects are given in intuition at all, hence objects *can* indeed appear to us without necessarily having to be related to functions of the understanding", and that even if objects were so constituted that they were not in accordance with the functions of the understanding (a possibility he is going to argue against) "[a]ppearances would nonetheless offer objects to our intuition, for *intuition by no means requires the functions of thinking*" (A89–90/B122–123, my emphasis).

What about the sections in the Deduction where Kant says that conceptually governed synthesis is needed for thought to have relation to an object? I hold that his concern here is not with conscious presentation of a perceptual particular. After all, "relation to an object" clearly must be something different from being "given" an object. In my view, relation to an object is something that a concept can lack, and something a concept has when it succeeds in being referential or possibly referential. Having perceptual presentation of a particular is something different from having a successfully referring thought. To say that without the categories we would have unruly heaps and swarms of appearances is not to claim that we would have merely a mass of sensations; after all, what we would have swarms of is *appearances*. Rather, the claim is that the singular things presented to us would not be ordered, organized and grouped in the way needed for *cognition* (which is what Kant means by "experience").

In my view, synthesis does not *produce* intuitions, rather it is something done *to* intuitions, to make cognition possible. Kant talks about synthesizing the manifold of intuitions and the manifold in an intuition; both these locutions assume intuitions that are being synthesized. Kant talks about this synthesis as producing unity, which leads commentators to think that we could not have distinct perceptual particulars without it, because we would not have a representation of anything unified. However, his account of human cognition in fact includes two different ways of representing unity, aesthetic unity and intellectual unity. Aesthetic unity involves representing something as a whole or unicity (oneness) prior to representing its parts, and therefore cannot depend on synthesis, which is a running through and combining of parts. Central arguments in the Transcendental Aesthetic depend on this unity not requiring concepts. In contrast to intuitional or aesthetic unity which simply presents a singular thing, conceptually governed synthesis enables us to represent something as a unified complex of parts or a unified complex of properties: to unify the manifold in an intuition. Rather than showing that we cannot represent something as unified in any way without conceptually governed synthesis, this in fact shows that without synthesis we can only be presented with things as singular and particular, and cannot grasp them as complexes.

Thus, I conclude that intuitions are representations that present us with distinct perceptual particulars (they are singular), and that they are immediate in the sense that, unlike with concepts, having an intuition involves the object of the intuition being present to consciousness. This is how they give us objects. And this is how they ensure that we have *cognition*: that our concepts are actually related to objects, and not a mere play.

In further support of this reading of intuition, it explains how Kant's argument for transcendental idealism goes through at exactly the point he presents it as going through, without attributing to him the weak argument presented above. All we need to add to the things he explicitly says is the (not very controversial) thought that Kant holds that the way in which we are immediately presented with things that are independent of us is through being affected by them. He argues that our representations of space and time are *a priori* and are intuitions. This means that what they represent (space and time) is immediately present to us independent of anything affecting us. But if things independent of us can get to be directly present to us only by affecting us, it follows that what our representations of space and time present us with is not something independent of us.

On my account, being "given" an object involves it being directly present to consciousness. Watkins and Willaschek understand givenness as an object's being "made available to the mind so that one can be aware of its existence and at least some of its features" (Willaschek and Watkins 2017, 6) and they argue that givenness need not require actual presence to mind, since Kant allows us to be given mathematical objects and empirical objects which we do not actually perceive, like magnetic matter, which he says we could perceive if our senses were finer. Similarly, Schafer (forthcoming) and Stefanie Grüne (2017) argue that what the givenness of intuition provides is merely the real possibility of an object, so need not involve its actual presence. In my view neither of Watkins' and Willaschek's examples counts against the idea that givenness involves actual presence. Mathematical objects, as I understand Kant, *are* actually present to the mind when we perform constructions in pure intuition; mathematical objects are constructions in pure intuition (or, if one prefers not to say that mathematics has objects, one could say simply that mathematics concerns or is about constructions in pure intuition, where pure intuition is given). In terms of their second example, Kant does not hold that magnetic matter is given to us, but that it *could* be given in an empirical intuition if our senses were finer. Thus, the example does not count against seeing "givenness" as involving objects being directly presented to consciousness, but rather against the idea that we can cognize only what is actually given. Kant holds (as I understand him) that our cognition is limited to objects which are actually given to us *or* which could possibly be given in intuition and are causally connected to something actually given.

4. The Given in Practical Cognition: The Moral Law

I have given an account of what intuition is and of the role it plays in theoretical cognition: it ensures that our concepts are actually connected to objects in a world. I now turn to practical cognition. On the face of it, there are a number of ways we might understand a distinction between practical and theoretical cognition. One might have thought that a main difference between them is that they give different kinds of justification or grounds for claims; this would mean that practical cognition gives practical grounds for believing claims which could not be established theoretically. However, we have already seen reason to think that Kant's central concern with cognition is not (as it would be with knowledge) a concern with justification or grounds for establishing claims. I therefore suggest that we should expect the difference between practical and theoretical cognition to concern either their having different kinds of objects, or their giving us access to the objects of cognition in a different way, or some difference in the kind of content with which they can represent the objects of cognition. As we have seen, commentators have emphasized two aspects of cognition: its involving awareness of the *existence* of the object of cognition and its giving us some determinate content about the object of cognition. We now need to see how this can occur with respect to practical cognition.

In the *Critique of Practical Reason*, Kant says that we have immediate access to the moral law and that this enables us to know freedom *a priori*, because freedom is a condition of the moral law (*CPrR* 5:3): a rational agent "judges, therefore, that he can do something because he is aware that he ought to do it and cognizes freedom within him, which, without the moral law, would have remained unknown to him" (30). He says that the ideas of God and immortality are *not* conditions of the moral law, so we cannot say that we cognize and have insight into them, even with respect to their possibility (4), but we do have practical grounds for assuming their possibility (4). He says that practical reason furnishes reality to a supersensible object of the category of causation (namely, to freedom), and hence establishes by means of a fact what could only be thought in speculative reason (6). The fact in question is our awareness of the moral law. He says (31):

> Consciousness of this fundamental law may be called a fact of reason because one cannot reason it out from antecedent data of reason, for

example, from consciousness of freedom (since this is not antecedently given to us) and because it instead forces itself upon us of itself as a synthetic a priori proposition that is not based on any intuition, either pure or empirical . . .

One of our questions about practical cognition was whether it involves access to a different kind of object from the sensible objects we cognize theoretically: a supersensible object. In my view, these passages count against understanding practical cognition in this way. There are at least three different kinds of supersensible things which we might think are accessed in our practical cognition of freedom: a supersensible kind of causality, our supersensible selves, and a non-empirical kind of truth—a kind of truth that is not an empirical claim about how the world is, but rather a truth about what we ought to do. Of these, Kant in fact says that the first two are *not* given to us, and the only thing he thinks we have immediate access to is the moral law. In other words, practical cognition does *not* involve immediate access to freedom or our supersensible selves.

The moral law is not an "object" except in the very general sense in which the object of a thought is whatever it is that thought is directed to. Kant frequently means something more specific by "object"—a spatio-temporal, causally unified thing; in this sense, our awareness of the moral law is clearly not awareness of an object. He says: "However, in order to avoid misinterpretation in regarding this law as *given*, it must be noted carefully that it is not an empirical fact but the sole fact of pure reason which, by it, announces itself as originally lawgiving" (*CPrR* 5:31). The moral law is given, but this does not mean that what is given is some kind of empirical claim about the way the world is. However, the moral law is also not a supersensible object in the sense in which monads, the soul, or God could be supersensible objects: it is a claim about how we ought to act. Thus, it is the moral law that plays the role in practical cognition analogous to that played by intuition in theoretical cognition, in being something immediately given to us,[3] but what is given to us is not a sensible or a supersensible object, but our awareness of what ought to be done (or ought not to be done). The moral law gives us access to something supersensible or nonsensible, but not to a supersensible object.

Kant is clear that it is not freedom but rather "the *moral law* of which we become immediately conscious (as soon as we draw up maxims of our will for ourselves)" (*CPrR* 5:29).[4] In contrast, he says that we cannot be immediately conscious of freedom. However, Kant does think that practical cognition can establish the actuality of freedom, and in this sense does give us awareness of the existence of something supersensible or nonsensible—a nonsensible kind of causality. With respect to freedom, Kant thinks that our access to the moral law establishes not just its real possibility but its actuality. However, we have seen that it does not do this by presenting us with (or "giving" us) the causality of freedom, but rather by presenting us with the moral law. This enables us to know the actuality of freedom because (Kant thinks) freedom and the moral law reciprocally imply each other and the moral law is actual (29, 47).

While the moral law establishes the reality of freedom, it may be that it is best thought of as establishing merely the *real possibility* of God and our immortal souls. Kant says that the concept of freedom alone provides "extension in the field of the supersensible . . . whereas the others merely indicate the vacant place for possible beings of the understanding" (*CPrR* 5:103–104). Real possibility is part of what Kant means by objective reality.[5] So far as theoretical cognition is concerned we are not able to determine whether God and the soul are more than merely logically possible, which means that these concepts lack what Kant calls "objective reality". However, practical cognition expands on this and shows us that we are committed to thinking of them as really possible because they are conditions of something practical reason commits us to: realizing the highest good. He says: "nothing further is accomplished in this by practical reason than that those concepts are real and really have their (possible) objects" (134) and that "they receive objective reality through an apodictic practical law, as necessary conditions of the possibility of what it commands us *to make an object*, that is, we are instructed by it that *they have objects*, although we are not able to show how their concept refers to an object, and this is not yet cognition *of these objects*" (135).

I have argued so far that the moral law is the practical correlate of intuition in theoretical cognition, as something that is given to us. With respect to theoretical cognition we saw a dispute as to whether the role of intuition in giving us objects required actual presence to consciousness, or merely some awareness of the existence of the object that does not involve this. As we have seen, Watkins and Willaschek hold that the givenness of intuition need not involve the actual presence of an object, and Schafer and Grüne argue, similarly, that what we need intuition for is to guarantee the real possibility of the objects of cognition,[6] and not their actuality, and therefore that intuition need not involve the actual presence of the objects of intuition to consciousness. On the face of it, it might be thought that Kant's account of practical cognition supports this, since what is added in the cases of God and the soul are merely the real possibility of the objects of these concepts. However, it seems to me, by contrast, that Kant's account of practical cognition in fact supports my reading of intuition as involving actual presence to consciousness. This is because although practical cognition may involve only real possibility, and although it establishes the actuality of something that is not immediately given (freedom), what plays the role analogous to intuition in practical cognition is the moral law, and this *is* immediately given and present to consciousness.

5. The Content of Practical Cognition

Our original question with respect to practical cognition was whether it involves access to a different kind of object, a different kind of access to the objects of cognition, or presents its objects with a different kind of representational content. I have argued that practical cognition does not involve access to either sensible or supersensible objects, though it involves being given something non-empirical (non-sensible): the moral law. With respect to theoretical cognition, commentators argue that in addition to demonstrating the actuality or real possibility of the objects of cognition, intuition contributes determinate content that is necessary for cognition. So the next thing to look at is what kind of determinate content is added by practical cognition. There are two parts of Kant's account that I want to note here. First, he does not think practical cognition is able to add determinate contentful representation of the self as a soul or of God. Second, with respect to the content that practical cognition adds to our understanding of freedom, it does not give us a different kind of contentful representations of the supersensible (of the metaphysics of the causality of freedom), but rather adds different (practical) content to the way we understand freedom. In other words, our practical cognition of freedom does add determinate content to our understanding of freedom but does not give us any understanding of how the causality of freedom works as a causal power.

Against these points, it might be thought that practical reason gives us some kind of cognition of our supersensible selves. Kain says that the fact of reason provides "an example of a supersensible object (myself as *causa noumenon*) whose real possibility and actuality we practically cognize" (Kain 2010, 227). This seems to me misleading, since we do not have immediate access to ourselves as supersensible objects, and the only contentful representation of our supersensible selves that is added is our freedom, where this involves seeing ourselves as being under the moral law, not seeing ourselves as noumenal objects. Kant says (*CPrR* 5:42) that the fact of reason

> is inseparably connected with, and indeed identical with, consciousness of freedom of the will, whereby the will of a rational being that, as belonging to the sensible world, cognizes itself as, like other efficient causes, necessarily subject to laws of causality, yet in the practical is also conscious of itself on another side, namely as a being in itself, conscious of its existence as determinable in an intelligible order of things—conscious of this not, indeed, by a special intuition of itself but according to certain dynamic laws that can determine its causality in the sensible world . . .

The way we are aware of ourselves as supersensible involves simply our being part of a determinable order that falls under the moral law.[7]

Our awareness of ourselves as free involves awareness of our wills as subject to laws of causality, but this is not a metaphysical awareness of supersensible causal laws, but rather of the moral law, as a commitment of practical reason. Our only positive characterization of the causality of freedom involves seeing ourselves as committed to acting in ways that are constrained by the moral law. He says (*CPrR* 5:43) that the moral law

> provides a fact absolutely inexplicable from any data of the sensible world and from the whole compass of our theoretical use of reason, a fact that points to a pure world of the understanding and, indeed, even *determines* it *positively* and lets us cognize something of it, namely a law.

Again, the determinate content added—what we cognize positively—is merely the moral law. Not only do we not add determinate contentful representations of the self as soul, we also do not add insight into how the causality of freedom works.

> Kant says (*CPrR* 5:48) that the moral law adds a positive determination to a causality thought only negatively, the possibility of which was incomprehensible to speculative reason, which was nevertheless forced to assume it; it adds, namely, the concept of a reason determining the will immediately (by the condition of a universal lawful form of its maxims), and thus is able for the first time to give objective though only practical reality to reason . . .

The positive content that is added is not a further understanding of freedom as a causal capacity: "how freedom is even possible and how this kind of causality has to be represented theoretically and positively is not thereby seen; that there is such a causality is only postulated by the moral law and for the sake of it" (133).[8]

In my view, this relates interestingly to central threads in the contemporary debate about freedom of the will. A leading stream of contemporary compatibilism about free will understands freedom in terms of what is called "reasons responsiveness": our capacity to respond to reasons. A central objection contemporary compatibilists make to agent causal, libertarian, incompatibilist notions of freedom is that since these accounts hold that an agent could have had the same reasons for action yet acted differently, it seems that they are unable to give any rational explanation of why the agent chose as they did. In contrast, compatibilists can appeal to the stronger reasons as playing a causal role. Kant, as I understand him, thinks that there is something right and something wrong with both these positions. Compatibilists are right to think that agent causal accounts of freedom fail to give any metaphysical account of how the causality of freedom works: it is not possible for us, Kant thinks, to give such an account. Further, compatibilists are right to think that the only positive account of freedom we can give is in terms of reasons responsiveness or practical reason. However, they are wrong to think that reasons explanations are any kind of causal explanation, but also wrong to think that reasons explanations do not depend for their possibility on a kind of causality that is different to the causality of nature.[9] Kant's distinction between practical and theoretical cognition seems to me to be helpful here and in fact diagnostic (as he thinks it is) of why our thought gets stuck around the free will problem. The problem is that our cognition of freedom is limited to practical cognition, but we want to understand it theoretically; both contemporary compatibilists and agent causal libertarians attempt to characterize freedom as a metaphysical causal capacity, but this is something that cannot be done.

Kant thinks that not being determined (not being caused by the causality of nature) is not enough to get us freedom, and he thinks that we need to understand the spontaneous causality of freedom both as different from the causality of nature and as *causality* (not mere randomness or lack of determination).[10] The way he thinks we can give this conception positive content is through the idea of a capacity to initiate actions in ways that are governed by higher order rational principles, and, in particular, higher order rational principles that rational agents are committed to independently of their particular projects, goals, and desires (and in virtue of thinking of themselves as acting for reasons). We can only positively characterize freedom in terms of a capacity to initiate actions in ways that are committed to seeing the humanity of others as a constraint on what counts as a reason for action (the moral law).

6. Intellectual Intuition and Mou Zongsan

In this final section, I attempt to relate the account I have given of practical cognition to one of Mou Zongsan's famous criticisms of Kant: his argument that Kant was wrong to deny humans intellectual intuition.[11] Nick Bunnin says that "In *Phenomena and Noumena* Mou Zongsan held that 'if it is true that human beings cannot have intellectual intuition, then the whole of Chinese philosophy must collapse completely, and the thousands years of effort must be in vain.' It is just an illusion" (Bunnin 2008, 613; see also Xie 2010). Different things could be meant by intellectual intuition; some understand it as cognition that is infallible or complete, and therefore see the criticism as concerning whether or not this is possible for us. Some commentators have looked at Mou's critique in relation to whether we have something like intellectual intuition in theoretical cognition. In my view, we may understand Mou's point better if we rather look to practical cognition, because Kant's account of practical cognition involves something like intellectual intuition in one crucial respect: whereas a sensible intuition has to be given its materials from outside, this is not true of intellectual intuition. Rather, with respect to intellectual intuition, the cognizing subject in some sense makes or is responsible for the object accessed; the object is actualized by the subject that accesses it. Kant says something close to this about the moral law. Rather than being concerned with objects given to it from outside, he says that practical reason has to do with its own ability to make the objects of cognition real (*CPrR* 5:89).[12] Likewise, he says (46):

> The moral law is not concerned with cognition of the constitution of objects that may be given to reason from elsewhere but rather a cognition insofar as it can itself become the ground of the existence of objects and insofar as reason, by this cognition, has causality in a rational being, that is, pure reason, which can be regarded as a faculty immediately determining the will.

Later (66), he adds that,

> since all precepts of pure practical reason have to do only with the *determination of the will*, not with the natural conditions (of practical ability) for *carrying out its purpose*, the practical a priori concepts in relation to the supreme principle of freedom at once become cognitions and do not have to wait for intuitions in order to receive meaning; and this happens for the noteworthy reason that they themselves produce the reality of that to which they refer (the disposition of the will), which is not the business of theoretical concepts.[13]

Thus, insofar as practical cognition makes its object real rather than being given an object that exists independently of it, it seems to have a central characteristic of intellectual intuition, which may provide a way of vindicating Mou Zongsan's claim that humans have intellectual intuition.

Against the view I am suggesting, Schafer argues that seeing practical cognition as "maker's knowledge" (cognition that is in touch with its object because it actualizes its object) cannot be a general account of practical cognition in Kant, because it would not include cognition of God. However, it is not clear that Kant really allows *cognition* of God.[14] He says (*CPrR* 5:70) that

> of all the intelligible absolutely nothing is cognized except freedom (by means of the moral law), and even this only insofar as it is a presupposition inseparable from that law; and since, moreover, all intelligible objects to which reason might lead us under the guidance of that law have in turn no reality for us except on behalf of that law and of the use of pure practical reason . . .

Thus, I think we can understand practical cognition as involving something like intellectual intuition, in the sense of maker's knowledge.

There is a further point in which I think we can find agreement here between Kant and Mou Zongsan. Some commentators focus on Mou's objections to Kant on intellectual intuition with respect to knowledge of things in themselves. For example, Wing-cheuk Chan says that Mou Zongsan argues that Kant's denial of intellectual intuition to humans, with its corresponding denial that humans are capable of intuitive knowledge of things in themselves, makes "thing–in–itself" a limiting concept, which means that the distinction between phenomena and noumena can never be evidently justified (Chan 2006, 127). However, he also points out that "[m]ainly along the Confucian line, Mou Zongsan's transformation starts with an identification of intellectual intuition with moral activity" (130). This seems to me to support thinking that a central way in which Mou Zongsan holds that Kant's account should include intellectual intuition is precisely with respect to practical cognition, our cognition of value, which is where I have argued Kant *does* in fact have something like intellectual intuition. Bunnin argues that Mou Zongsan criticizes Kant for not allowing a moral metaphysics, and that he sees the point of this as demanding that "human beings have intellectual intuition so that we can see things that we know, including ourselves, as having moral value" (Bunnin 2008, 620). If a moral metaphysics is an account of values as objects existing in empirical reality or objects existing in supersensible reality, it is true that Kant's account does not include it. But if it is an account of ourselves as having moral value and recognizing the requirements of practical reason, then it seems to me that Kant's account does include it.

As we have seen, Watkins and Willaschek hold that cognition, for Kant, involves awareness of the existence and some of the basic features of objects. In the case of practical cognition, we have seen that we do not cognize the self as a noumenal object, and what we have awareness of is not in an obvious sense an object. Further, the determinate content that is added does not give us further insight into ourselves as noumenal objects, but rather gives us insight into something else, a world of moral value. However, we do, through our awareness of the moral law, have awareness that our freedom is actual, and we do add some determinate understanding of it.

I have argued that Kant's account of cognition centrally involves the object of cognition being given to us. In theoretical cognition, it is sensible intuition that plays the role of giving us access to the objects of cognition, and our cognition is limited to things which can be presented to us in empirical intuition. Practical cognition also involves something immediately given to us (the moral law); unlike sensible empirical intuition which gives us things passively, our access to the moral law is access to something our wills determine, and therefore more like maker's knowledge, or the intellectual intuition Mou Zongsan finds lacking in Kant.

Notes

1. Kant sometimes uses the term "cognition" more broadly, in such a way that he calls either intuitions or concepts cognitions, but in the first *Critique* his central use is that cognition requires both intuitions and concepts.
2. Similarly, Patrick Kain (2010, 213) says that cognition is "an objective perception or representation that refers to an object."
3. As Kain (2010, 220) puts it, "[w]e are immediately confronted with a determinate constraint on our action or constraint to action."
4. He says (*CPrR* 5:30): "how is consciousness of that moral law possible? We can become aware of pure practical laws just as we are aware of pure theoretical principles, by attending to the necessity with which reason prescribes them to us and to the setting aside of all empirical conditions to which reason directs us."
5. He says that the postulates (*CPrR* 5:132): "are not theoretical dogmas but *presuppositions* having a necessary practical reference and thus, although they do not indeed extend speculative cognition, they give objective reality to the ideas of speculative reason in *general* (by means of their reference to what is practical) and justify its holding concepts even the possibility of which it could not otherwise presume to affirm."
6. On Schafer's account what intuition gives us is the real possibility and determinacy of its object (Schafer forthcoming, 12).
7. Similarly, at 5:105–106 he says that, "with respect to *our own* subject inasmuch as we cognize ourselves *on the one side* as intelligible beings determined by the moral law (by virtue of freedom), and *on the other side* as active in the sensible world in accordance with this determination. The concept of freedom alone allows us to find the unconditioned and intelligible for the conditioned and sensible without going outside ourselves. For, it is our reason itself which by means of the supreme and unconditional practical law cognizes itself and the being that is conscious of this law (our own person) as belonging to the pure world of understanding and even determines the way in which, as such, it can be active." What is unconditioned and intelligible here is the moral law, not a supersensible object.
8. And at 5:72 he says that "how a law can be of itself and immediately a determining ground of the will (though this is what is essential in all morality) is for human reason an insoluble problem and identical with that of how a free will is possible."
9. Kant says (*CPrR* 5:94): "there are many who believe that they can nevertheless explain this freedom in accordance with empirical principles, like any other natural ability, and regard it as a *psychological* property, the explanation of which simply requires a more exact investigation of *nature of the soul* and of the incentives of the will, and not as a *transcendental* predicate of the causality of a being that belongs to the sensible world (although this is all that is really at issue here); and they thus deprive us of the grand disclosure brought to us through practical reason by means of the moral law, the disclosure, namely of an intelligible world through realization of the otherwise transcendent concept of freedom, and with this deprive us of the moral law itself, which admits absolutely no empirical determining ground."
10. This is one reason Kant's account of free will would not, in my view, be affected by allowing that the fundamental laws could be irreducibly probabilistic.
11. Unfortunately, his main works are not available in English, so I have taken what I know about his work from other peoples' papers and his lectures.

12. He says (*CPrR* 5:89): "Practical reason, on the contrary, since it does not have to do with objects for the sake of *cognizing* them but with its own ability *to make them real* (conformably with cognition of them), this is, with a *will* that is a causality inasmuch as reason contains its determining ground; since, accordingly, it does not have to provide an object of intuition but, as practical reason, *only a law* for such an object (because the concept of causality always contains reference to a law that determines the existence of a manifold in relation to one another); it follows that a critique of the Analytic of reason, insofar as it is to be a practical reason (and this is the real problem), must begin from the *possibility of practical principles* a priori."

13. He says that the concept of an object of practical reason is the representation of an object as an effect possible through freedom (*CPrR* 5:57) and adds: "To be an object of practical cognition so understood signifies, therefore, only the relation of the will to the action by which it or its opposite would be made real, and to appraise whether or not something is an object of *pure* practical reason is only to distinguish the possibility or impossibility of *willing* the action by which, if we had the ability to do so (and experience must judge about this), a certain object would be made real."

14. Following Watkins and Willaschek's reading of the relation between cognition and knowledge, this may allow for a proof of the existence of God, as well as grounds for believing in God; what is excluded is cognition of God.

References

Allais, Lucy (2015). *Manifest Reality: Kant's Idealism and His Realism*. Oxford: Oxford University Press.

Bunnin, Nicholas (2008). God's Knowledge and Ours: Kant and Mou Zongsan on Intellectual Intuition. In: *Journal of Chinese Philosophy* 35(4), 613–624.

Chan, Wing-cheuk (2006). Mou Zongsan's Transformation of Kant's Philosophy. In: *Journal of Chinese Philosophy* 33(1), 125–139.

Grüne, Stefanie (2017). Givenness, Objective Reality, and A Priori Intuitions. In: *Journal of the History of Philosophy*, 55(1), 113–130.

Kain, Patrick (2010). Practical Cognition, Intuition, and the Fact of Reason. In: B. Lipscomb and J. Krueger (eds.), *Kant's Moral Metaphysics: God, Freedom and Immortality*. Berlin: Walter de Gruyter, 211–230.

Schafer, Karl (forthcoming). Kant's Conception of Intuition and our Knowledge of Things–In–Themselves. In: K. Schafer and N. Stang (eds.), *The Sensible and Intelligible Worlds*. Oxford: Oxford University Press. Page references cite unpublished manuscript.

Willaschek, Marcus, and Eric Watkins (2017). Kant on Cognition and Knowledge. In: *Synthese* DOI: 10.1007/s11229-017-1624-4.

Xie, Sammy Xia-ling (2010). On Kant's Duality of Human Beings. In: S. Palmquist (ed.), *Cultivating Personhood: Kant and Asian Philosophy*. Berlin: Walter de Gruyter.

7 Intuitions Under the Asymmetric Structure of the Subject–Object Relation— A Conceptualist Reading Based on the B Deduction

Xi Chen

1. Two Non-Conceptualist Arguments

Among all topics in the debates between conceptualism and non-conceptualism, there are two questions significant for the successful interpretation of Kant's transcendental deduction. The first one is whether there are sensory perceptions of the objects without any involvement of concepts. The other question is concerned with how to understand the cognition of animals.

Now to the first question. Whether there are non-conceptual representations of objects is the central difference between conceptualism and non-conceptualism. The non-conceptualist believes that there are sensory perceptions of objects without the involvement of any concepts, including pure concepts *a priori*—that is to say, the categories—and empirical concepts. It is clear that the existence of non-conceptual representations would cause serious difficulty for the transcendental deduction. The conformity of all the representations to the categories would be called into question. Robert Hanna (2011, 402) calls it the gap in the B Deduction:

> The Gap in the B Deduction is that the B Deduction is sound only if Conceptualism is true, but Conceptualism is arguably false and Kant himself is a non-conceptualist. If Kant is a non-conceptualist and Kant's Non-Conceptualism is true, then there are actual or possible "rogue objects" of human experience—or what Timothy Williamson calls "elusive objects"—that either contingently or necessarily do not fall under any concepts, whatsoever, including the Categories.

In this case, the transcendental deduction would be a failure. To make non-conceptualism and the transcendental deduction compatible with each other, the application of the categories should be restrained to some special kind of intuitions—that is, intuitions with some "special kind of unity" (Allais 2011, 105). Or as stated in a recent paper, "categorical [*sic*] synthesis is not necessary for empirical intuition per se, but only for the representation of a special class of relations among such intuitions"

(Golob 2016, 380). These restraints try to draw a line between conceptual and non-conceptual representations. However, from my point of view, they are not solving the problem but just easing the tension between non-conceptual representations and the application of the categories to them. As a result, I do not think there could be a compatible relation between the existence of non-conceptual representations of objects and the objective validity of the categories. It is true that if we want to prove the application of the categories to all representations, we have to find a sound conceptualist reading of Kant to explain how concepts get involved in sensory intuitions. This is the first challenge for conceptualism.

The other difficulty that conceptualism faces is how to understand the cognition of non-human animals. Conceptualism tells us that our conceptual capacities determine human cognition and in this way all the perceptions of our cognition. Meanwhile, non-human animals are thought to be lacking the possession of concepts, but they still have some perceptual cognitions. As Robert Hanna puts it, they are "capable of non-conceptual cognition with non-conceptual content" (2008, 43), which means that non-conceptual representations of objects are possible. If conceptualism still wants to make the claim on its thesis, a proper explanation of animal cognitions should be given, and especially its difference from the rule-governed activities of human cognition has to be clarified. This is the second challenge for conceptualism.

2. The Symmetric Structure of the Subject–Object Relation in the A Deduction

The asymmetric structure of the subject–object relation can be defined through the clarification of the symmetric structure in the A Deduction. To say the relation between the subject and the object of cognition is symmetric means that there is a subject–in–itself as the substratum of the representations of "I". (Kant writes in A350, "we have no acquaintance with the subject–in–itself that grounds this I as a substratum".) It is similar to the thing–in–itself and should be unknowable to us. However, since I have special access to myself as the subject of cognition, unlike the thing–in–itself as the object of my cognition, I still can have some clues to this subject. Compared to this model, the subject–object relation in the B Deduction is asymmetric because the subject of cognition becomes pure activity (*reine Aktivität*), and there is no substratum, like the subject–in–itself, to ground the representations of "I", the subject of cognition. The subject, therefore, cannot be understood as any object at all. In this way, the subject of cognition and the objects that I am cognizing are essentially distinct from each other in the B Deduction.

In Kant's writings from the pre-Critical period, apperception is defined as "perception of oneself as a thinking subject in general" (*R*4674, 17:647). As Wolfgang Carl reads it (1989, 12), "apperception doesn't give us any special kind of perception, but it defines a certain manner of having them—namely, as perceptions of which we are conscious and which all belong to one common subject." The unity of the subject is the pre-condition of apperception, namely the pre-condition of the consciousness of such unity. The unity of the subject refers to a unitary subject, that is to say, a thinking subject in general, as its ontological foundation. Furthermore, Kant tells us that "the condition of any apperception is the unity of a thinking subject. From that comes the connection (of the manifold) according to a rule" (*R4675*, 17:651). It seems that Kant takes the unity of the subject itself as the reason for the rule-governed connection between the representations. The representations "have a unity just by belonging to a 'unitary' subject" (Carl 1989, 15).

It is clear that Kant's early arguments based on the unitary subject have been abandoned in the 1780s. As Carl puts it (1989, 19), "instead of founding apperception on the unity of a self taken as a mental substance, he developed the theory of synthetic unity of apperception, which takes account of the cooperation of basic cognitive faculties." We can see this change in the A Deduction. However, one serious problem arises with this change. The claim that all representations belong to the same "I", namely to the subject of cognition, cannot spontaneously lead to the correlation or the conceptual synthesis of the representations themselves. As we have seen, in the early drafts of the Deduction the thinking subject plays a foundational role, as the reason for the rule-governed connection of representations. Since the foundation is supposed to be removed, Kant has to argue for the necessary correlation of the representation in another way and explain its relation to the synthetic unity of apperception. Therefore, we see that the notion of the transcendental object is introduced into the A Deduction. It seems to have solved the problem in a new way. Unfortunately, if we examine the arguments concerning the transcendental object carefully, we will find that these arguments still refer to the subject–in–itself, but in an indirect way.

Roughly speaking, the transcendental object guarantees the necessary relation between representations and connects them to transcendental apperception at the same time. The first step is to claim that all perceptions are necessarily related to objects—that is, all representations have their objects. Then, all objects of representations stand in relation to the abstract object "as something in general = X" (A104), understood as the transcendental object. How objects of cognition are related to the transcendental object is not thoroughly clear, but it is sure that "our thought of the relation of all cognition to its object carries something of necessity with it" (A104). Kant explains it as follows (A104–105):

> since namely the latter [i.e., "something of necessity"] is regarded as that which is opposed to our cognitions being determined at pleasure or arbitrarily rather than being determined *a priori*, since insofar as

they are to relate to an object our cognitions must also necessarily agree with each other in relation to it, i.e., they must have that unity that constitutes the concept of an object.

As shown in this passage, through the notion of the transcendental object, representations obtain unity and are necessarily connected to each other in a certain way. At this point, the transcendental object rules out the possibility that the representations taken into our consciousness are totally unrelated to each other. Since the transcendental object is related to objects and the latter are necessarily composed of representations, this can be the sufficient condition of the fact that representations are related to each other in a certain way.

From my point of view, the way the transcendental object represents necessity implies its relation to a subject as the subject–in–itself. First, the transcendental object reveals that the transcendental subject stands behind or beyond the sphere of subjective representations. Kant makes a sharp distinction between merely subjective states and objective experience. The former is regarded as being arbitrary and lacking necessity. As one of the subjective conditions of cognition, the transcendental object has a characteristic that subjective states do not have, and this is one of the conditions which allows those subjective states to become an objective experience. Therefore, the source that enables it to do this can be neither in nor among those subjective states. It points to the subject–in–itself, the substratum of the "I".

Second, the way the transcendental object represents necessity, as well as objectivity, suggests that the subject–in–itself is similar to the thing–in–itself, or external objects. For those who believe that external objects are the basis of the objectivity of our knowledge, the most important thing for representations to be objective is their accordance with the objective source, namely the objects outside us. Objectivity is the innate attribute of objects outside us, and we have it by referring to external objects, instead of by constructing it. If we look at the theory of the transcendental object in the A Deduction, we will see that the way it represents objectivity in forming our knowledge is similar. Being related to the transcendental object and therefore having the further reference to numerical identity, subjective representations have necessity as well as objectivity. Again, it is not constructed but gained from some source, and this time, it is the subject–in–itself. The subject–in–itself should have absolute objectivity, otherwise numerical identity could not be "the purest objective unity", and the numerical unity of apperception could not be what "grounds all concepts a priori" (A107) either. The way Kant deals with objectivity is similar to those who believe in external objects. The real difference between them is in identifying which one is the source of objectivity, external objects (the thing–in–itself) or the subject–in–itself. Obviously, Kant does not think that we can turn to the thing–in–itself for objectivity, for it is unknowable. Instead, we only have representations and may refer to the subject–in–itself as the source of objectivity.

In this way, we see that the subject–in–itself might stand behind the arguments concerning the transcendental object in the A Deduction. The transcendental object is supposed to solve the problem caused by removing the unitary subject. With the subject–in–itself hiding between the lines of the arguments, the transcendental object, as well as numerical identity, provides an incomplete solution. It is incomplete because it leads to some other problems. One of those problems is: it leaves room for the non-conceptualist reading of Kant's theory of cognition and precisely for non-conceptual perception of objects. Since numerical identity grounds the concepts *a priori* and at the same time refers to the subject–in–itself as its foundation, the importance of the concepts *a priori* will be limited. Transcendental apperception is the necessary condition of the application of the categories, but the latter is not necessarily required by the former. This means that mental activities without any concepts are allowed within the A Deduction and, in other words, non-conceptual representations are possible. Furthermore, if the subject–in–itself as the foundation of the subject of cognition can be seen as an object in the way it grounds the objectivity of our knowledge, then it is reasonable to suppose that there are some perceptions received from the objects before any involvement of the concepts *a priori*. It also means that non-conceptual representations of objects are possible within the context of the A Deduction. Later, in the B Deduction, as the subject of cognition becomes pure activity, such possibility will be ruled out.

3. The Asymmetric Structure of the Subject–Object Relation in the B Deduction

If the subject–in–itself can be understood as something similar to the object/thing–in–itself, then pure activity is totally different from all objects. It is in this sense that the subject–object relation has an asymmetric structure. The transcendental object does not play any important role in the B Deduction, which implies that Kant thoroughly abandons any substratum of the subject of cognition. Instead, the B Deduction starts with combination in general and Kant claims that "among all representations combination is the only one that is not given through objects but can be executed only by the subject itself, since it is an act of its self-activity" (B130).

Pure activity can be seen as the potential to combine the representations and the activities which take place in our cognition as its reality. The crucial difference between the subject–in–itself and pure activity is the way the subject of cognition identifies with itself. Roughly speaking, the subject of cognition can turn to the subject–in–itself every time to identify with it, while for pure activity, there is no such reference. The identification of the subject of cognition has to be done in another way. In my opinion, this is the reason the original synthetic unity of apperception becomes one of the central arguments and why "I think" occurs in the B Deduction. The synthetic unity of apperception can be seen as the framework of pure activity and defines how the subject as pure activity acts. All activities of the subject of cognition are determined in the judgment under the synthetic unity of apperception.

Earlier in the A Deduction, as I have discussed in the previous section, numerical identity has the subject–in–itself as its foundation. Although it is the necessary condition of our cognition, it is not the necessary condition of the subject of cognition. Instead, the subject of cognition has the subject–in–itself as its foundation and the latter is also the reason for numerical identity.[1] As a result, the threefold synthesis can be discussed first and transcendental apperception is mentioned at the end of the reasoning sequence. The regressive progress is possible because the subject of cognition possesses all these cognitive capacities and it is the sufficient condition for each of them. However, in the B Deduction, if the argument had not begun with the synthetic unity of transcendental apperception, it would have been difficult to understand how the subject of cognition is activated, for without the synthetic unity of apperception, there cannot be any cognitive activities. Transcendental apperception is the necessary condition of the activities and therefore also the necessary condition of the subject of cognition. Then, it would be meaningless to talk about other capacities before clarifying the necessary condition of the subject of cognition. As a result, we see Kant writes the following sentence at the beginning of §16 (B131–132): "The *I think* must *be able* to accompany all my representations; for otherwise something would be represented in me that could not be thought at all, which is as much as to say that the representation would either be impossible or else at least would be nothing for me."

The part of the sentence before the semicolon describes the synthetic unity of apperception in another way, by saying that all my representations should be taken into one consciousness. The word "otherwise" leads to the argument for the synthetic unity of apperception, as the necessary condition of our cognition. The second clause gives an argument similar to the synthesis of recognition in the A Deduction. "Something would be represented in me" can be read as the synthesis of apprehension and the synthesis of reproduction. As Kant says at A103: "Without consciousness that that which we think is the very same as what we thought a moment before, all reproduction in the series of representations would be in vain." The consciousness which unifies the manifold into one representation is the concept (A103), and the concept has a transcendental condition as its ground: that is, transcendental apperception as well as numerical identity (A106–107). Until now, it seems Kant's argument is not significantly different from the argument in the A Deduction.

Kant then tells us two possible consequences: if the I think did not accompany our representations, "the representation would either be impossible or else at least would be nothing for me" (B 132). In my opinion, we come here to something new, though Kant claims that these consequences are "as much as" what is given in the second clause. I shall examine the second consequence first. It is similar to what is given in the second clause. For the representation being nothing for me could be understood to mean that the representation could be represented in me but could not be thought at all. (Or perhaps, it means that the representation which is not taken up into my consciousness but into some other's could be possible for others but not for me.) But it can still imply that the subject of cognition would be impossible if there were no synthetic unity of apperception. By the phrase "at least", Kant clearly means that the second consequence is only the minimum. Turning back to the first consequence, we find that Kant seems to have made a stronger claim. If there is no synthetic unity of apperception, then there would be no representation at all. The fact that such a strong claim can be made suggests not only that the synthetic unity of apperception is a necessary condition of the subject of cognition, but also that the subject of cognition can only be pure activity, not any object. There are two reasons for this suggestion.

First, if the subject of cognition were taken as the object, then it would always be possible that there could be some intuitions without the application of concepts. It is true that transcendental apperception is the necessary condition of apprehension, reproduction, and recognition. Without it, the other functions would be impossible. However, sensibility and the understanding—that is, the capacity to have something given in our intuition and the capacity to combine the given according to concepts—are possessed by the subject independently, if the subject is understood as an object. Furthermore, if the subject is understood in this way, the cognitive activities are only attributes of the subject. It is possible that there would be no cognitive activities at all if the subject were not activated at all. Such possibilities cannot be thoroughly ruled out if the subject of cognition is understood as an object. It is then reasonable to say that, since Kant makes such a strong claim here in §16, it is unsuitable to interpret the subject of cognition in the B Deduction as an object.

Second, numerical identity should have played a central role in the transcendental deduction, as long as the subject of cognition has the subject–in–itself as its foundation. Numerical identity represents the way objectivity is granted by the subject–in–itself. Actually, as long as the subject is understood as an object, no matter what kind of object it is, a metaphysical one or a logical one, the transcendental deduction has turned to numerical identity for the purest objectivity. However, we see that numerical identity is removed from the main arguments of the B Deduction. Certainly, consciousness always has to be identified with itself, and this time, it no longer stands at the end of a line of regressive arguments as the most important transcendental ground. The B Deduction has to start with combination and the synthetic unity of apperception, to prove initially the identification of consciousness itself. Furthermore, that the I think must be able to accompany all my representations has a more complicated framework, which contains not only the identification of the subject of cognition but also the manifold and the combination between self-consciousness and the representations. In my opinion, the complicated framework of the synthetic unity of apperception implies pure activity.

Kant has emphasized time and time again that the unity of transcendental apperception is first synthetic, and then analytic. The notion "synthetic" means combination. Combination is an activity or the result of an activity. In this way we can see that activity is implied in the synthetic unity of apperception. In fact, the synthetic unity of apperception is the framework of pure activity, the way the subject as pure activity exists and operates. Without the synthetic unity of apperception, there would not be any activities at all, and therefore no pure activity. Therefore, Kant has to begin his arguments with the synthetic unity of apperception in the B Deduction and we can see that the subject of cognition can only be pure activity.

Besides, there is more evidence to prove that the subject of cognition is pure activity. As Kant writes, shortly after the "I think" sentences (B132): "Thus all manifold of intuition has a necessary relation to the I think in the same subject in which this manifold is to be encountered. But this representation is an act of spontaneity." This passage tells us that spontaneity is also connected with the synthetic unity of apperception, which also indicates the subject as pure activity. It is hard to explain how spontaneity is necessarily bound up with any object; instead, it is sound to think that activity has spontaneity. With spontaneity, the lack of motivation for the subject of cognition to activate itself in the A Deduction is solved. The subject as pure activity has the synthetic unity of apperception as its framework and highest principle. The spontaneity bound up with the representation "I think", namely with the synthetic unity of apperception, guarantees the necessity of the reality of pure activity. The possibility that the subject does not activate itself at all has been excluded. Actually, the definition of the synthetic unity of apperception does not change much from the A Deduction to the B Deduction. The real development concerns Kant's conception of the subject. Because the subject of cognition cannot be seen as an object, the similar arguments regarding transcendental apperception are assigned a different importance in the Deductions.

Now we turn to the judgment where the identification of the activities— that is to say, the combination in our cognition—is finally achieved. We should notice that the activities are variable and their identification will be totally different from that of an object. Rather than referring to some persisting substratum, the key to identification now lies in the rules of combination. Representations are combined not randomly but according to rules. If the subject is conscious of using identical rules in combining representations, then the activities which involved the same rules can be identified. This means that a unity of concepts is required by the identification of the combining activities of the subject, and therefore also by self-consciousness. Only when a unity of concepts is recognized, can the activities as the reality of pure activity be identified. For they are combining according to identical concepts (rules). To be conscious of applying identical rules in combining representations, the activities of combining representations according to identical rules can be identified with themselves, and in the same way, the subject of cognition is identified with itself. The presupposition of the identification of activities is then also the condition of the possibility of the subject of cognition.

Up to this point, I do not think there is a big difference between the A and B Deductions. If concepts are understood as rules for combination and judgment is "nothing other than the way to bring given cognitions to the objective unity of apperception" (B141), then this means that judgment also involves combination. Judgment can be conducted only by following rules of combination—namely, concepts. On the other side, concepts function as rules for combination in judgment. It seems that the logical relation between them does not change from the A Deduction to the B Deduction. The essence of the arguments remains the same.

The theory of judgment is required to construct objectivity when the subject of cognition becomes pure activity. The identity of the subject and objectivity construct each other through the synthetic unity of apperception. That is (B136–137): "all the manifold of intuition stand under conditions of the original synthetic unity of apperception . . . [for] they must be capable of being combined in one consciousness." However, it is still hard to see how objectivity is constructed by combining representations in one consciousness only from the synthetic unity of apperception. The synthetic unity of apperception as the first principle and the framework formulates cognition in a general way in order to find out how objectivity is constructed concretely; the theory of judgment has to be introduced into the arguments to prove the objective validity of the categories. Indeed, since the aim of the transcendental deduction is to prove the conformity of representations to the categories and with the arguments of the synthetic unity of apperception, there is little reference to the application of concepts. Now, the question is: how is the objectivity of cognition concretely constructed in every judgment?

To say that the synthetic unity of apperception constructs objectivity in a general way while judgment does so in a concrete way is not accurate. It is true that the synthetic unity of apperception underlies every combination of representations and therefore also underlies every judgment. For judgment is nothing other than the way to bring given cognitions to the objective unity of apperception. But this is only one side of the claim. The other side is that the objectivity of cognition is partly constructed by referring to universality at this stage, before judgment is introduced into the discussion. Objectivity consists of necessity and identity. If cognition can be necessarily identified with itself, then we say it is objective. It should be noticed that when Kant discusses the synthetic unity of apperception, he refers quite often to *all* representations, which seems to imply universality. For example, the I think must be able to accompany all my representations (B131); "the representation I think, which must be able to accompany all others and which in all consciousness is one and the same" (B132); and so on. There is a manifold *a priori* implied in the expression of "all" my representations. Since the subject stands against all representations, it remains identical. The unity of the subject, like the unity of consciousness, is universal. This kind of universality is then related to necessity, because for all representations, the subject is identical. The first part of objectivity is then constructed by the synthetic unity of apperception, or strictly speaking, the first part of the construction of objectivity by the synthetic unity of apperception is explicated.

For the full construction of the objectivity of cognition, as well as the objective validity of the categories, we now need the identity of objects. Until now, we have the identity of the subject and the necessity underlying representations. Because the necessity that we have from the synthetic unity of apperception lies under all representations without differences, no objects can be made from merely undifferentiated necessity. Objects need internal unity as well as to be differentiated from other objects. The subject must combine representations according to concepts, which brings differences into the representations. The application of concepts outlines objects against the whole of the undifferentiated representations belonging to one consciousness. Henceforth, the correlation between the unity of concepts and the identification of the subject starts to play a role. The identification of objects is accomplished, and the objectivity of cognition is fully constructed. I think it is in this sense that Kant claims (B141–142): "That is the aim of the copula *is* in them: to distinguish the objective unity of given representations from the subjective. For this word designates the relation of the representations to the original apperception and its necessary unity, even if the judgment itself is empirical."

Kant's theory of judgment in the B Deduction emphasizes activity, which agrees with the subject as pure activity and with his emphasis on the synthetic unity of apperception. Combination as an act is reinforced through the idea of judgment. It is true that activities are already involved in the discussion of concepts in the A Deduction. For example, Kant describes concepts as the consciousness that "unifies the manifold that has been successively intuited, and then also reproduced, into one representation" (A103). The word "unifies" implies combining activity. However, the whole discussion of recognition in concepts is focused on searching for the transcendental condition which grounds the necessity of the synthesis of recognition as well as reproduction and apprehension. For this sake, those notions, such as the transcendental object, apperception, and concepts, are only concerned with their logical relations, instead of with activities which bring them together. Kant himself also admits that it is hard to see how consciousness—namely, the concept—acts as a mental activity (A103): "This consciousness may often only be weak, so that we connect it with the generation of the representation only in the effect, but not in the act itself." The theory of judgment shows more clearly the consciousness in the act itself. The notion of combination/activity is emphasized in the B Deduction.

Now, we see that in judgment, the synthetic unity of apperception and the application of the categories connect to each other with the word "is" and construct objective knowledge. Although I have to analyze them separately, it does not mean both of them function independently. Judgment can be made only under the synthetic unity of apperception and the supreme principle of the synthetic unity of apperception implies judgment. The subject as pure activity can only combine representations according to concepts. As long as they are conducting activities—namely, combining—the application of concepts is involved, and the objectivity of knowledge, as well as the objective validity of the categories, is constructed and achieved in the judgment.

4. Refutation of the Non-Conceptualist Reading of Kant's Theory of Cognition

Based on the discussion in the previous section, we find that there is no room left for non-conceptual representations of objects. The subject of cognition becomes pure activity and its activity is combination according to rules. The unity of the rules is required by the identity of the subject and the construction of the objectivity of knowledge. This means that the involvement of concepts is a necessary and inseparable condition of our cognition, without which cognitive activity could not happen. This might lead to the consequence that intuition, as well as sensory perception, has a lower status in such an asymmetric structure of the subject–object relation. Under a symmetric structure, it might still be possible that single pieces of representation have some corresponding relation with their source or with objects. However, under the asymmetric structure, the activity of combination is logically prior to intuition, and all representations of objects are possible only when the mind's combination happens; therefore, they cannot avoid the involvement of concepts. In this way, I think there is no gap in the B Deduction and no such thing as the elusive objects discussed by Robert Hanna.[2]

Concerning the cognition of animals, I do not agree with Hanna that such cognition can be used as evidence that there is non-conceptual cognition with non-conceptual content. I think what animals have is not non-conceptual perception, as non-conceptualists want to claim. Animals can follow some rule-governed connectedness. The real difference between the cognition of human beings and of animals is that animals do not have a correlation between the identity of the subject and consciousness of using identical concepts, as I have discussed above with regard to human cognition. Animals can, therefore, have rule-governed connections only at random. It is reasonable to assume that this kind of acts could possibly not happen at all for some animals. For this reason, animals cannot finally form their rule-governed connectedness into real cognition, like that of human beings. Their rule-governed actions cannot be used to construct an argument for non-conceptualism.

Notes

1. The problem in the A Deduction is similar to the one Wolfgang Carl has found in the early drafts of the Deduction before 1781. Carl (1989) notices that the unity of the thinking subject underlies the apperception/consciousness of an identified self.
2. As we saw in §1, Hanna (2011, 402) writes: "If Kant is a non-conceptualist and Kant's Non-Conceptualism is true, then there are actual or possible 'rogue objects' of human experience—or what Timothy Williamson calls 'elusive objects'—that either contingently or necessarily do not fall under any concepts whatsoever, including the Categories."

References

Allais, Lucy (2011). Transcendental Idealism and the Transcendental Deduction. In: D. Schulting and J. Verburgt (eds.), *Kant's Idealism*. London: Springer, 91–108.

Carl, Wolfgang (1989). Kant's First Drafts of the Deduction of the Categories. In: E. Förster (ed.), *Kant's Transcendental Deductions: The Three Critiques and the Opus Postumum*. Stanford: Stanford University Press, 12–15.

Golob, Sacha (2016). Kant as Both Conceptualist and Non-conceptualist. In: *Kantian Review* 21(3), 367–391.

Hanna, Robert (2008). Kantian Non-Conceptualism. In: *Philosophical Studies: An International Journal for Philosophy in the Analytic Tradition* 137(1), 41–64.

——— (2011). Kant's Non-conceptualism, Rogue Objects, and the Gap in the B Deduction. In: *International Journal of Philosophical Studies* 19(3), 399–415.

8 Non-Conceptual Content of Intuition and Perception

Jieyao Hu

1. Introduction

There has been a lively debate over whether or not, according to Kant, non-conceptual content in intuition is possible. In this chapter, I defend a non-conceptual reading of Kant's theory of intuition and argue that merely through sensibility the object of intuition is able to be presented to mind, while denying that the non-conceptual claim may lead to unnecessary difficulties in the theory of cognition. However, it is also worth noting that even inside the non-conceptualist camp there are two distinct views on what should be considered as something non-conceptual. Roughly speaking, the non-conceptualist camp can be divided into two groups, one holding that there is non-conceptual intentional content of intuition,[1] the other denying the existence of any non-conceptual content, holding that only the perceptual state is non-conceptual.[2] The former view can also be called a representational account of intuition, the later a relational one. The second aim of this chapter is to defend the "content view", or the representational account of intuition, by arguing that this account is more faithful to Kant. The third aim is to clarify the subtle distinction between intuition and perception in a Kantian context, since what has been recently mainly discussed by philosophers is perception or perceptual experience, rather than intuition itself. It seems that many commentators identify intuition with perception, but by so doing they neglect the difference between these two terms. Once a clear distinction between intuition and perception is made, a better response to the conceptual/non-conceptual debate emerges.

2. Why Is a Non-Conceptual Reading Right?

It is widely agreed that according to Kant the two fundamental mental capacities, namely understanding and sensibility, are by no means reducible to each other. It is also clear that they contribute to cognition in different ways, respectively. If we accept this fundamental distinction between mental capacities, this leaves much less room for a conceptual reading of Kant. Three arguments for a non-conceptual reading will be provided in turn.

2.1 Different Roles of Understanding and Sensibility in Cognition

By pointing out that the task of sensibility is to receive representations, while that of understanding is to bring forth representations itself, Kant explicitly states that both understanding and sensibility contribute to human cognition, (A51/B75): "If we wish to call the receptivity [*Rezeptivität*] of our mind to receive [*empfangen*] representations, so far as it is in some way affected [*affiziert*], sensibility, then in contrast the faculty of bringing forth representations itself, or the spontaneity of knowledge, is the understanding."

Although even conceptualists won't deny that through sensibility the mind receives representations, they deny that objects can be given merely through sensibility. Conceptualists insist that, not until the manifold in intuition has been synthesized by understanding could an object in a full-blown Kantian sense be presented to mind.[3] The most common response to the synthesis issue is to distinguish synthesis in intuition from synthesis in judgment, and further to attribute synthesis in intuition merely to the function of imagination.[4] Here, however, I will adopt another approach to the roles of sensibility and understanding, which depends on the fact that human cognitions are finite cognitions, since our spontaneity is finite. By contrasting human cognition with the cognition of an infinite being, we may find that the distinction between human being as finite being and infinite being is that an infinite being has absolute spontaneity, which human minds don't have. Having absolute spontaneity means that an infinite being can produce an object merely by bringing forth a representation of it. And since human spontaneity as partial spontaneity could not create the existence of an object simply by virtue of bringing forth a representation of it, the complement of human cognition must rest upon our sensibility, which serves to provide the mind with representations of objects by affecting them. In other words, because of our finite spontaneity, the representations of objects can only be given through sensibility, instead of being created by understanding.

2.2 Intuition and Concept Relate to Objects in Different Manners

Regarding their relation to objects, Kant draws a precise distinction in the type of relation that intuition and concept bear to their object, respectively. A concept relates to its object in a mediate manner, whereas an intuition possesses an immediate relation to its object. In other words, a concept can still be conceived if the corresponding empirical object is absent, while an empirical intuition is impossible when no corresponding empirical object is present. That means an empirical intuition is object-dependent, whereas a concept's being conceivable is object-independent. As Kant puts it (A19/B33): "In whatever way and through whatever means a cognition may relate to objects, that through which it relates immediately to them, and at which all thought as a means is directed as an end, is intuition."

Apart from their bearing different relations to objects, intuition and concept are themselves different representations in kind as well. Intuitions are singular representations, as Kant says that intuition "refers immediately to the object and is singular" (A320/B377), while concepts are general, containing certain marks which are common to several representations.

The distinct nature of intuition and concept, as shown, indicates that these two types of representations are irreducible to each other. Accordingly, it may be plausible to conclude that merely to have an intuition does not involve our conceptual capacities, since the mediate relation of concept and object can by no means be part of an immediate relation of intuition and its object. Therefore, a general representation could not make a singular one possible.

2.3 Demonstrative Concepts

Some conceptualists deny that only intuitions can relate to objects immediately by pointing out that demonstrative concepts are in an immediate relation to objects as well. In particular, Sellars argues that to intuit an object is in fact to "represent a 'this'" (1968, 4). In other words, demonstrative concepts are the minimal conceptualization involved in the process of intuiting.

Sellars' argument seems to be convincing at first sight, but if we further examine his argument, we can find it may not be as convincing as it appears to be. The first thing I would like to point out is that Sellars obviously confuses the mind's having an intuition of a cup and the mind's making a judgment, "this is a cup." The former is something relating to a certain perceiver, whereas the latter is an objective assertion. These two things indicate two completely different cognitive stages, and critically, a subject without the capacity to make an objective judgment can still intuit or perceive a particular. Furthermore, my second criticism concerns the priority question. The need to employ a demonstrative concept indicates that some relevant experience is there to be referred to. Thus, logically speaking, the existence of relevant experience is prior to the adoption of a demonstrative concept that refers to it. That is to say, it is not that the employment of a demonstrative concept makes relevant experience possible; rather, the existence of relevant experience makes the application of the demonstrative concept conceivable.

Thus far, I have provided three arguments to defend a non-conceptual standpoint, and those arguments demonstrate that a non-conceptual reading of Kant might be more faithful to Kant than a conceptual reading might be.

3. Is There Representational Content in Intuition?

Not all non-conceptualists insist on the same kind of account of intuition. Roughly speaking, their accounts can be divided into two kinds: representational accounts and relational accounts. Philosophers holding the representational standpoint argue that there is representational content or intentional content in intuition, while relationalists defend a direct realist account of intuition. The central difference between these two views hinges on whether a further intermediate mental activity is required for us to achieve an intuition, or, in other words, whether the representation of an object is exactly the same as how it appears to us. I tend to put Kant in a position closer to the representational standpoint, which claims that the representation of an object is not simply identical with how it appears to us. I concede that some people may criticize the representational point of view by claiming that such a "content view" may lead us back to a conceptual interpretation of intuition, and therefore the "content view" is not at all compatible with the non-conceptual claim. However, this criticism is unfair, for it presupposes a very strong version of "content", which takes the content of perceptual experience to be the truth-condition of the content of a relevant belief or judgment and further claims that the content of perceptual experience consists in a similar conceptual structure as that of a belief.[5]

This claim–too–much view, however, is not one that Kant would agree with. Rather, as Clinton Tolley suggests in a recent article (Tolley 2014), Kant insists on a much more moderate version of content, which he mentions several times in the first *Critique*: for example, "General logic abstracts from all content of cognition, i.e., from any relation of it to the object" (B79); and (B87) "No cognition can contradict [the transcendental analytic] without it at once losing all content, i.e., all relation to an object." From such passages we can see that Kant defines the content of cognition as the relation to an object; or, more precisely, it is how we representationally relate to an object. Essentially, the representational relation to an object involves two aspects: one is how the object appears to us; the other is how we represent an object in one representation. Rather than confusing one aspect with another, I shall draw a distinction between them.

Concerning the question about how an object appears to us, both Lucy Allais (2009) and Clinton Tolley (2013) have pointed out that an object can be presented to the mind only in a mind-dependent way. That is to say, objects can appear to minds only as mind-dependent appearances.

However, this describes only how the manifold of intuition runs through appearances, not yet explaining the taking together (*Zusammennehmung*) of the manifoldness into one representation. I shall try to prove that a rudimentary mental activity is involved in the taking together process, and that is what makes the representational content of an object not exactly identical with how the object appears to us.

Kant formulates his position in the A Deduction as follows (A99): "Every intuition contains a manifold in itself, which however would not be represented as such if the mind did not distinguish the time in the succession of impressions on one another; for as contained in one moment no representation can ever be anything other than absolute unity." Kant here reminds us that, not until the mind completes its minimal mission—namely, distinguishing the time in the succession of impressions on one another—can a representation be regarded as such a representation. In other words, we are not able to receive a representation as containing absolute unity unless our minds are able to differentiate one moment from another. This basic mental activity, or "synthesis of apprehension", as Kant names it, is necessarily required for us to obtain a genuine representation.

Again, does this "content view" in a minimal sense still lead us to the pitfall of conceptualism? The answer is no, for synthesizing is not conceptualizing. Although it is still a controversial issue, Kant indeed distinguishes lower-level synthesis from higher-level synthesis and further claims that only lower-level synthesis is required in synthesizing the manifold in intuition. What is more, this minimal representational account of content can be applied to the case of infants as well, whose inner sense is also subjected to time as its form. That means, by differentiating the time in a succession of appearances, one after another, a blind intuition can also be obtained in an infant's mind.

4. Perception and Intuition

In *Jäsche Logik* there is an interesting example of a "savage" who sees a house but does not know that it is a house (*JL* 9:33):

> [H]e admittedly has before him in his representation the very same object as someone else who is acquainted with it determinately as a dwelling established for men. But as to form, this cognition of one and the same object is different in the two. With one it is mere intuition, with the other it is intuition and concept at the same time.

Clearly, the concept here refers to an empirical concept, not an *a priori* concept. What I want to point out is that this paragraph actually tells us something about the perception of a house rather than a cognition of it, for all that the savage and the civil man have done is to receive a representation through their eyes. What is different, however, is what they eventually perceive through their seeing. In other words, what is different is what they are eventually aware of. The savage might notice all the details of the house as particulars and receive almost the same picture as the civil man has, and the civil man is likely to notice all the details as well, but those are not important to him, because he is really aware of a general empirical concept, or the meaning behind this particular concept. This is why Kant says that one representation conveys mere intuition, whereas the other conveys intuition and concept at the same time. Although I admit that this account of perception seems difficult to reconcile with how Kant himself defines perception in the first *Critique*, I will try to show later that Kant's own definition of perception shares some similarities with the account here.

As is well-known, two common definitions Kant gives to perception are: (a) perception (*Wahrnehmung*) is empirical intuition with consciousness; and (b) perception is a representation companied by sensation (B147–148). These definitions together signify two essential features of perception: (a) perception is connected with consciousness, and (b) a perception is a representation received through the senses. By pointing out the first feature, Kant seems to identify perception with empirical intuition. However, his emphasis on the second feature shows us the distinction between them: perception is connected with consciousness, while intuition is not, or at least whether or not it is connected with consciousness is not important to empirical intuition. So let us focus on the distinction between these two terms. By emphasizing the connection of perception and consciousness, Kant is not only saying that perception is what we are conscious of, but he is also indicating that perception is a subjective status, which means rather than relating to an object, perception relates merely to the subject. This point is both fair and unfair. It is fair because perception indeed concerns more about the status of the subject than the objective relation between objects or between objects and their properties, which means that the object we obtain through perception is merely an undetermined object that has not been determined by pure concepts yet. Thus, perception alone does not enable us to have an objective cognition of an object. Nevertheless, it is unfair because perception has a subjective status connecting objects or certain properties of objects and subjects, and actually Kant even explicitly indicates in *Prolegomena* that "judgment of perception" (*Wahrnehmungsurteil*) plays a mediating role in the transition from intuition to experience (*PFM* 4:300–301). It seems contradictory, however, that on one hand perception has been degraded to a rather low epistemic position since it is merely something subjective, but that on the other hand, it plays a mediating role between intuition and experience inasmuch as Kant regards both as objective representations. How can this make sense?

I account for it in terms of the relation between perception and the perceiving subject and further argue that the subjective character of perception functions as a mediating stage between intuition and experience. Admittedly, by perceiving we are being made directly aware of an object through the senses, but what we should pay attention to is that being aware of an object differs from merely having an intuition of it. In the "an intuition's being aware of" case, we presuppose a perceiver before the perception takes place, and this implies that such a perception is by no means a random one; rather, it must serve some cognitive purpose for the perceiver. As a rational being, the first and most significant purpose for perceiving is to cognize the object presented to us by applying pure concepts to it. In other words, we are allowed to make a judgment about an object by applying pure concepts to it for the purpose of cognizing it in the process of perceiving. If this account is plausible, then what we can further infer from it is not only that perception is a mediate stage between intuition and experience, but also that perception enables the conceptual capacities to start to function.

With the above analysis in mind, we can see why it is possible that perception plays a mediating role. More supports can also be found in Kant to defend perception's mediatory status. One support would be that, by distinguishing different kinds of representations in his logic lectures, Kant shows a "progressive" procedure of cognizing an object. In this progression, our mental representations develop from mere representation to perception (to represent something with consciousness), to cognition (to cognize something through the understanding by means of concepts), and finally, to those representations which depend on reason (see *JL* 9:64–65). Only through perception, as the middle step that connects mere representations with consciousness, can the cognition of an object be achieved.

What is more, Kant also considers perception as the necessary condition for experience. As Kant says in the Analogies of Experience (B219), "experience is a cognition of objects through perception. . . . [E]xperience is thus possible only through a representation of the necessary connection of the perceptions." This statement implies that through the necessary connection of perceptions experience is produced, which indicates that perceptions play a mediating role in forming experience. Given the distinction between intuition and perception, what most conceptualists are concerned about might be perception instead of intuition in Kant's terminology. With the clarification between these two terms in mind, we can see that concepts are necessarily involved in perception, but not in intuition.

5. Conclusion

By clarifying the contribution of sensibility to cognitions, I have argued that through intuition alone an object can be presented to mind, which supports a non-conceptualist reading of Kant. However, according to Kant, an object's being presented to the mind involves certain minimal mental processing, which makes content non-conceptualism more faithful to Kant than mere state non-conceptualism. Since the confusion of intuition and perception in Kant's terminology might have led to this conceptual/non-conceptual debate, I distinguish perception from intuition by virtue of pointing out that, as an empirical representation that is connected with consciousness, perception serves the cognitive purpose of the perceiver, which purpose intuition does not necessarily serve. What is more, the mediating role between intuition and experience that Kant assigns to perception also explicitly requires this distinction between intuition and perception.

Notes

1. Robert Hanna argues that Kant not only defends the existence of the non-conceptual content in intuition, but also offers a fundamental explanation of it. See Hanna (2005, 2008, 2011).
2. When Anil Gomes (2014) drew the distinction between conceptualism and non-conceptualism by insisting that the former holds a representational point of view while the later holds a relational view, he might have oversimplified or even misunderstood their differences. Since even among non-conceptualists, there are representatives of both the representational view or "content view" and representatives of the "state view". See Colin McLear (2016).
3. Hannah Ginsborg (1997) identifies synthesis in intuition with synthesis in judgment by virtue of claiming that synthesis can only follow the rules of understanding. Also see Ginsborg (2008, 2011).
4. Similar arguments can be found in Allais (2009) and Hanna (2005).
5. McDowell (1994) articulates this "content view" in *Mind and World*.

References

Allais, Lucy (2009). Kant, Non-Conceptual Content and the Representation of Space. In: *Journal of the History of Philosophy* 47(3), 383–413.

Ginsborg, Hannah (1997). Lawfulness without a Law: Kant on the Free Play of Imagination and Understanding. In: *Philosophical Topics* 25(1), 37–81.

——— (2008). Was Kant a Nonconceptualist? In: *Philosophical Studies* 137(1), 65–77.

——— (2011). Primitive Normativity and Skepticism about Rules. In: *Journal of Philosophy* 108(5), 227–254.

Gomes, Anil (2014). Kant on Perception: Näive Realism, Non-conceptualism, and the B-Deduction. In: *The Philosophical Quarterly* 64(254), 1–19.

Hanna, Robert (2005). Kant and Nonconceptual content. In: *European Journal of Philosophy* 13, 247–290.

——— (2008). Kantian Non-Conceptualism. In: *Philosophical Studies* 137, 41–64.

——— (2011). Kant's Non-Conceptualism, Rogue Objects, and the Gap in the B Deduction. In: *International Journal of Philosophical Studies* 19, 399–415.

McDowell, John (1994). *Mind and World*. Cambridge: Harvard University Press.

McLear, Colin (2016). Kant on Perceptual Content. In: *Mind* 125(497), 95–143.

Sellars, Wilfrid (1968). *Science and Metaphysics*. New York: Routledge and Kegan Paul.

Tolley, Clinton (2013). The Non-Conceptuality of the Content of Intuitions: A New Approach. In: *Kantian Review* 18(1), 107–136.

—— (2014). Kant on the Content of Cognition. In: *European Journal of Philosophy* 22(2), 200–228.

9   Kant on Schematizing

Drawing the Line in Inner Intuition[1]

Sebastian Orlander

1. Introduction

Kant's theory of schematism presents a number of difficulties for interpretation. On the one hand, there is the systematic difficulty of explaining
why a "third thing"—i.e., the schema—is supposed to mediate between
sensibility and understanding. On the other hand, there is the interpretive
problem of understanding what schemata are, specifically as "transcendental time-determinations", such that they can perform this mediating
task. Many commentators have broached these interconnected problems
(e.g., Allison 2004; Gardner 1999; Guyer 1987; Heidegger 1929/1997;
Longuenesse 1998; O'Shea 2012), but the theory still remains an interpretive problem.

In this chapter, I offer partial clarification to the second problem, while
considering the first problem with reference to recent controversies over
the question of conceptualist and non-conceptualist readings of Kant.
Most of the debate is centered on detailed exegeses of the Transcendental
Deduction, to determine which passage states the overall scope of Kant's
theory of content in relation to his *Kategorienlehre*. While any resolution
of this debate would need to resolve the arguments of the Deduction,
I argue here that the Schematism chapter ought to be considered as well.
In doing this, I closely follow Kant's proposal to understand the schema
of quantity as "number" (A142/B182). I will focus on passages from the
Schematism chapter, as well as others closely adjacent thereto—i.e., the
Transcendental Deduction (A and B editions) and the Axioms of Intuition.
With these latter passages, I draw on the example of "drawing a line" to
shed light on why the process of schematization is a process of determining intuition in inner sense. Throughout, I will develop a phenomenological reading of schematization as transcendental time-determination,
which will hopefully clarify some parameters of the debate on conceptualism and non-conceptualism in Kant.

Rather than attempting to settle the debate, my goal here is merely to
determine the significance of the Schematism chapter for the debate as

a whole. The justification for my approach lies in the opening lines of Kant's Schematism chapter (A137/B176):

> Whenever an object is subsumed under a concept, the representation of the object must be *homogeneous* with the concept; i.e. the concept must contain what is represented in the object that is to be subsumed under it. For this is precisely what we mean by the expression that an object is contained *under* a concept.[2]

Now, while this claim may remind us of certain aspects of conceptualism,[3] Kant immediately points out that the subsumption of a particular under a universal in the case of the categories of understanding is wholly distinct because of a missing feature with regards to how the categories relate to appearances (A137/B176):

> Pure concepts of understanding, on the other hand, are quite heterogeneous from empirical intuitions (indeed sensible intuitions generally) and can never be encountered in an intuition. How, then, can an intuition be *subsumed* under a category, and hence how can a category be *applied* to appearances—since surely no one will say that a category (e.g. causality) can also be intuited through senses and is contained in appearances?

Thus, as Pendlebury (1995) notes, there is already an ambiguity here in Kant's double use of *subsumption* and *application*, which further complicates the issue as to whether the imagination applies categories through schematization in synthesis to non-conceptually given things, or whether the object synthesized always already has a conceptual unity, which makes it possible to subsume such an object.[4]

The classical comparison in Allison (2004, 213–215) and Guyer (1987, 170–172) of Kant and Wittgenstein on rule-following, while certainly present in the text, does not help much here, since both arrive at the necessity of transcendental time-determinations with radically different emphases on what the schematism chapter does in modifying our understanding of the categories. For Allison, the transcendental time-determinations are in effect those same "formal intuitions" that Kant refers to in the B Deduction at B160n, which here then are supposed to emphasize the immediacy of schemata with their quasi-non-conceptual origin in the activity of the imagination, while still carrying with them essentially normative functions as rules for construction (cf. Allison 2004, 206–207). With Guyer, his characterization of transcendental time-determinations, while much more conflicted as to the possibility of determining these without reference to spatial determinations (to which I will return later), does point out that the transcendental time-determinations do seem to have successive states in time as not immediately perceptible, and thus requires determination through schematized categories for time-series to be interpretable;

it thus takes on what one might call the conceptualist horn of the dilemma (following the treatment of this distinction with regard to the activity of the imagination in Onof and Schulting 2015) of how to understand the activity of the imagination.

Determining the role of schematism is, in the end, important for understanding why Kant thinks that the logical use of the categories needs a restriction in order to provide the "true and sole conditions for . . . reference to objects and hence with *signification [Bedeutung]*" (A146/B185). In other words, the categories depend on schematism in order for them to have any "real" meaning at all, since otherwise, no objects could be synthesized according to "universal rules" and "fit for thoroughgoing connection in one's experience". This makes the "abstract" meaning of the categories lack proper objects, and so, the debate on conceptualism and non-conceptualism functions as a crucial background framing question for interpreting this chapter.

2. Schematism as Time-Determination

Although Kant does not define schema in a sentence of the form "By schema, I mean such–and–such", he does give a definition (at A138/B177) of what is supposed to account for the mediation between sensibility and the understanding as "a mediating representation [which must be] pure (i.e. without anything empirical), and yet must be both *intellectual*, on the one hand, and *sensible*, on the other hand." This is then called a "transcendental time determination" three sentences later. Kant further characterizes a schema as "always only a product of the imagination", which further aims at "the unity in the determination of sensibility" (A140/B179), and this leads him to distinguish schematizing proper from the production of images. This is important, then, for understanding that schemata, insofar as they relate to appearances, do not pick out what is particular about an image—i.e., its intuitive character—but rather their generality, such that the image can be grasped as an instance falling under a general concept. The first example he uses to illustrate this is the image of the number five in five successive dots (•••••) which he then also contrasts with the number one thousand, which cannot be intuitively represented in such a way as to grasp the image in its intuitiveness—i.e., in its direct character. The next example, that of the schema of triangle, is also illuminating, since Kant contrasts the variety of different kinds of triangles with that function of unity which is supposed to make it possible that we understand any triangle as a triangle. Thus, the schema picks out "a rule of synthesis of imagination" by which we can conceive of the unity of a given intuition.[5] For this reason, we can also see why Kant always insists on emphasizing the inadequacy of any image to its concept, regardless of whether the concept is of pure sensibility, empirical, or transcendental—even though the gap between the former two and the latter is infinitely wide. An image *simpliciter*, as something intuited, is still not adequately determined, unless there is some way one can recognize the rules by which one can determine a singular instance of some "this–here–now" as also being "such–and–such", which in turn requires us to use a concept by way of its schematized form. It is here again where Kant appeals to the notion of the *in concreto*, this time with regards to empirical concepts, in service of making this point about determination.

Kant does not think that one can, as such, bring the categories to the level of determination that we find in images, since schematizing concerns "the determination of inner sense as such, according to conditions of that sense's form" (A142/B181). This entire passage is fraught with obscurity, and very difficult to comprehend in any detail. However, I do think some clarity can be gathered from looking at Kant's treatment of the schema of magnitude (A142–143/B182):

> The schema of magnitude (*quantorum*) for outer sense is space, whereas the pure image of the magnitudes of all sense objects as such is time. But the *pure schema of magnitude* (*quantitatis*) taken as a [pure] concept of the understanding is *number*, which is a representation encompassing conjointly the successive addition of one time to another (homogeneous item). Therefore number is nothing other than the unity in the synthesis of the manifold of a homogeneous intuition as such, a unity that arises because I myself produce time in apprehending the intuition.

First, we must distinguish here between two senses of magnitude that Kant uses in developing the schema of magnitude, indicated by his use of the Latin "*quantorum*" and "*quantitatis*". Longuenesse (1998) already drew attention to the importance of "quantitative syntheses" for understanding Kant's theory of judgment and synthesis in the first *Critique*. Indeed, she places Kant in the trajectory that led to Frege's definition of number, without prefiguring him, by pointing to the fact that Kant "form[ed] the concept of number [as depending] on constituting *sets of objects thought under the same concept*" (257). While I certainly agree with her exposition of Kant's determination of number as the schematization of the category of magnitude, I think we must pay closer attention to the paradigm example that Kant refers to when discussing magnitude. While he does not give any examples in the Schematism chapter, there is one example that he returns to time and again in the Transcendental Analytic: drawing the line in inner intuition.

First is the following passage in the A edition Transcendental Deduction, which occurs in the section On the Synthesis of Reproduction in the Imagination (A102):

> Now, obviously, if I want to draw a line in thought, or to think the time from one noon to the next, or even just to represent a certain number, then I must, first of all, necessarily apprehend in thought

one of these manifold representations after the other. But if I always lost from my thoughts the preceding representations (the first part of the line, the preceding parts of the time, or the sequentially presented units) and did not reproduce them as I proceeded to the following ones, then there could never arise a whole representation; nor could there arise any of the mentioned thoughts—indeed, not even the purest and most basic representations of space and time.

The second occurs in §24 (On Applying the Categories to Objects of the Senses as such) of the B edition Transcendental Deduction (B154–155):[6]

> This [need for figurative synthesis], moreover, we always perceive in ourselves. We cannot think a line without *drawing* it in thought . . . And even time we cannot represent except inasmuch as, in *drawing* a straight line (meant to be externally figurative representation of time), we attend merely to the act of the manifold's synthesis whereby we successively determine inner sense, and thereby attend to the succession of this determination in inner sense. Indeed, what first produces the concept of succession is motion, taken as act of the subject (rather than as determination of the object)* and consequently as the synthesis of the manifold in space, if we abstract from this manifold and attend merely to the act whereby we determine *inner sense* according to its form. Hence by no means does the understanding already find in inner sense such a combination of the manifold; rather the understanding *produces it*, inasmuch as the understanding *affects* that sense.

Kant adds the following footnote where I put an asterisk (B155n):

> Motion of an *object* in space does not belong in a pure science, and consequently not in geometry. For the fact that something is movable cannot be cognized a priori, but can be cognized only through experience. But motion taken as the *describing* of a space is a pure act of successive synthesis, by productive imagination of the manifold in outer intuition as such, and belongs not only to geometry but even to transcendental philosophy.

Finally, Kant discusses the drawing of a line in the Axioms of Intuition (A162–163/B203):

> Extensive is what I call a magnitude wherein the representation of the parts makes possible (and hence necessarily precedes) the representation of the whole. I can present no line, no matter how small, without drawing it in thought, i.e. without producing from one point onward all the parts little by little and thereby tracing this intuition in the first place. And the situation is the same with every time, even the smallest. In any time I think only the successive progression from

one instant to the next, where through all the parts of time and their addition a determinate time magnitude is finally produced.[7]

These examples are repeated in many passages across the Kantian corpus, both Critical and pre-Critical (cf. Ferrarin 1995, 133), and while I do not want to diminish the dissimilarities of these passages or their respective function within the arguments from which they are lifted, I do want to highlight a number of features that these passages have in common: (a) time is understood as a succession of instances of moments— i.e., "nows";[8] (b) the successive apprehension of every moment is crucial for apprehending an object as temporal *and* spatial; and (c) the apprehension of a unified object, through the successive synthesis of moments, is a cognitive achievement of the subject.[9]

Of the features that I delineated above, I take (c) to be the most important for understanding the general tenor of how one should read the first two features, in that the cognitive achievement that lies at the basis of understanding temporal succession, as well as how temporal succession gives rise to manifolds that have both spatial and temporal properties, involves the "self-affection" of the subject, in the sense of highlighting the influence of the understanding on the imagination's productive synthesis. While this may prematurely emphasize a conceptualist understanding of the activity of imagination, I want to highlight that there is a sense in which we can understand the subject as "self-moving".[10] In the above-quoted passage at §24 of the B Deduction, where Kant defines imagination, he emphasizes that the imagination shares "blindness" with sensibility, as well as "spontaneity" (B151–152) with the understanding, such that the transcendental synthesis of the imagination is indeed the "first application" of the understanding on intuitions. As such, this synthesis is an "action", which I take to be indicative of the essential role of the subject's freedom as spontaneity, which makes space possible, not only as a form of intuition, but also as a form of intuition which is essential to the experience of given objects *simpliciter*. Thus, in the same way that synthesis, as an aspect of the spontaneity of the understanding, is spontaneous (in the sense in which I characterized the schematizing of the imagination as being free in its tracing of the shapes of given objects), so also is the transcendental synthesis of the imagination, as a determination of inner sense. As spontaneity, the subject must be active in order to affect in itself the determination of the given object, such that it can understand a given object as determined in some sense. Further, it is necessary that the subject can trace the object in such a way as to make the object amenable to further mathematical description, which then requires a further secondary schematism that only relates to space as a *quantorum* rather than *quantitatis*—although even here, the conceptualist would insist that the *quantum* is still only made possible through a schematized logical category.[11]

What is interesting here in this respect is that Heidegger also realized this distinction between different concepts of magnitude, and while his account of the Schematism chapter in *Kant and the Problem of Metaphysics* (1929) may only give a very truncated exposition of his reading of schematism, it is present in his seminar course from 1925 to 1926 (published in Heidegger 1976/2016), just prior to writing *Being and Time* (1927). Thus we find Heidegger saying this about schematism (1976/2010, 314–315):

> The process of constituting the true and proper provision of an image goes as follows:
>
> - Now–this, then another now–this—a manifold of this's, if you will.
> - But this manifold is already and antecedently present in the preview of quantity, i.e., of "how much."
> - Therefore, in the synthesis a "this" is already antecedently understood as a "one."
> - Moreover, "and" of the synthesis is already understood to be characterized by quantity: one and one and one, etc.

This understanding of time returns as a theme in Heidegger's treatment of schematism in *Kant and the Problem of Metaphysics* (1929/1997), when he singles out perception as a "taking–in–stride of . . ." (122, 126):

> In distinguishing time, our mind must already be saying constantly and in advance "now and now and now," in order to be able to encounter "now this" and "now that" and "now all this in particular." Only in such a differentiating of the now does it first become possible to "run through" and collectively take up the impressions.

We can thus see that the notion of time-determination in Kant anticipates phenomenological treatments of time, and so, turning to how phenomenologists understand time systematically, we may find new tools for interpreting Kant's work and understanding the contours of the debate.

3. Phenomenological Approaches to Time-Determination

Looking to what a phenomenological analysis of time-consciousness might contribute to interpretations of Kant, we have to be careful. Apart from Heidegger's reading of the Kantian texts themselves, we might look to how Husserl approaches this problem, given also how broadly Husserlian arguments are usually advanced in favor of non-conceptual theories of perception. However, we have to be careful about exactly what aspect of Husserl's theory we ought to look at in order to find helpful suggestions for understanding Kant's schematism.

While Husserl was not a scholar of Kant,[12] his phenomenological philosophy does intersect with Kant's transcendental idealism in various
ways with regards to the theory of schematism. First of all, Husserl, like
Kant, realizes that we need a "third" to mediate (by way of articulating
features at the level of universality) between the sensible particular and
our constitution of that particular in experience. For this, Husserl uses
the notion of a type, which gives the rule for how any possible instance
of a universal could be encountered in experience.[13] Now, turning to
time-consciousness, and with it the problem of transcendental time-
determination in the Schematism, many of course will know from *On
the Phenomenology of the Consciousness of Internal Time* (1966/1991)
that the experience of time for Husserl is always structured by inten-
tionality into a structure of the "now", protention, and retention—i.e.,
the currently experienced moment always carries with it a retention of
past moments with an expectation of some future moment (Husserl
1966/1991, 3–88). Further, consciousness of objects in time is always
structured according to some schema of "intention" and "fulfillment"—
i.e., some thought always includes certain expectations as to how their
intentional content may be fulfilled in an experience (Husserl 1901/2001,
210–211). One aspect that Husserl emphasizes about the experience of
temporality is that one has to distinguish first of all between "noetic and
noematic temporality" (Husserl 2001, 121–124, all translations mine)—
that is, between the temporality of an object considered as *noema* (i.e., as
the intentional object[14] of what exists outside of me in space and in "objective" time), and temporality considered merely noetically (i.e., as it is
experienced in its lived and sensuous quality). Thus (121–122), for

> an immanent object [*Gegenstand*], a hyletic Datum lasts [*dauert*],
> and the given duration is filled with hyletic point data [*Punktdaten*],
> which are given moment by moment as present. . . . The whole time-
> constituting consciousness, in which not only the perduring tone,
> but furthermore, not only the present tone, but also the past, and
> the expected tone, is constituted moment by moment . . . in short,
> moment by moment a continuum of temporal modalities and in
> the whole process the continuum of these continua [is constituted],
> in which a single line is constituted as the immanent tone built up
> through the integration of its duration.

Husserl here draws attention to how consciousness of time is not
merely a registering of processes external to oneself, but that it already
includes determinations of objects of consciousness, as well as of the acts
of consciousness in time as a whole. Paying attention to the modi-
fications that attend our experience of time contains then an element
that is non-reducible to spatial determinations. In some remarks devoted
specifically to the difference between how space and time are given in

experience, Husserl notes aptly (2001, 92): "The 'now' changes itself necessarily—the 'here' changes only with motion (of things or in the 'I move', free change of my orientation). I cannot change my temporal orientation freely."

A similar distinction could be drawn from Kant's discussion of causality in the Second Analogy—viz., between the sequence of temporal determinations that occur arbitrarily when circling a house and the temporal determinations attending a ship passing downstream. While with the Kantian examples, the previous worry about the necessity of spatial determinations to establish the necessity attending the particular causal determination remains, yet we might establish an analogy with the phenomenological focus on time-consciousness in discovering what aspects of time are essential to the structuring of experience. Investigating the protention in this way may give interesting new avenues to understand how Kant's transcendental time-determinations may be structured.[15]

4. Schematism and the Problem of Spatial Determinations

Now, I return to a problem mentioned earlier: Paul Guyer (1987) stated in his characterization of the theory of schematism as a determination of inner sense that this lack of referring spatial determinations essentially dooms the argument of the Schematism chapter to failure (and highlights that the theory of schematism was a late addition to the *Critique* as a whole). Guyer interprets the whole of the Analytic of Principles as an argument that ultimately shows the necessity of spatial objects for the objective reality of the categories of experience (167–168), as well as for the refutation of external world skepticism. Now, while this is not inconsistent with Kant's emphasis on time-determinations in the Schematism chapter, as Guyer himself notes, "spatial relations themselves are also not always directly perceived, and recognition of them in turn may depend upon knowledge of dynamic relations among objects in space" (168); there are passages in both editions of the first *Critique* that point to the relative de-emphasizing of time in favor of space in the Analogies.[16] Specifically, for Guyer, it seems that, by 1787, Kant clearly thinks that "in order to render the temporal relations which constitute the schemata of the categories actually *determinable* in inner sense, empirical judgments about the latter must in turn be grounded in intuitions of outer sense" (169).

Thus, the theory of schematism faces two substantial problems from Guyer's interpretation: on the one hand, cognition requires more than just rules in inner sense that order the manifold of intuition such that it can represent the world through objectively real categories, which are not even hinted at in the Schematism; on the other hand, the Schematism seems to fail at giving the conditions for applying the categories even with respect to time, since knowledge of succession (as well as any other temporal relation) has more epistemic conditions than what we can merely assume with time as the form of inner intuition. These are of course features that have since also been picked up by commentators like Förster (2012) and Westphal (2006), among others, on the issue of the transition from the first *Critique* to the *Metaphysical Foundations of Natural Science*, and in discussing the gap in Kant's philosophy between transcendental philosophy and the special metaphysics that undergirds the principles of causal judgments.

While these are indeed hard objections to counter, I think we can counterbalance them with some considerations on the character of time-determinations with respect to how these relate to the merely logical meaning of the forms of judgment.[17] More recently, in response to Eckart Förster's (2012) account of the shift from the first *Critique* to the *Metaphysical Foundations of Natural Science*, Eric Watkins (2013, 95) states that one might retreat from the strong reading that Guyer anticipates by stating that "temporal determination must occur by way of substances that are in fact spatial . . . [maintaining] that such an assertion is consistent with temporal determination occurring without any determination that is itself explicitly spatial."

The reading I am proposing here, in keeping with Watkins' suggestion of a more moderate reading of the Schematism, taken together with the Analogies and the Refutation of Idealism, is merely to suggest that temporal determinations have a certain logical priority over spatial determinations. This reading might even lead to the conclusion that the problem which the first *Critique* articulates in the Analytic of Principles is one that could only be prepared there, while the substantial answer, relating to a schematism that involves spatial determinations, needed to be carried out at the level of the *Metaphysical Foundations*. More work needs to be done than what is presented here to show how the schema of magnitude can be explicated merely through the use of temporal determinations, but the foregoing at least begins to clarify this.

5. Conclusion

I want to offer here, in conclusion, some comments on what my position may contribute to the debate around conceptualism and non-conceptualism. The heterogeneity problem only makes sense given Kant's "cognitive dualism" about the distinct, and thus irreducible, contributions that sensibility and the understanding make in the constitution of experience. Thus, Kant's focus in the Schematism chapter on providing schemata can only be understood against the backdrop of a non-conceptualist understanding of Kant's theory of cognition, one that hopefully takes it as uncontroversial that Kant's theory of cognition distinguishes between two sources, or "roots"—i.e., sensibility and the understanding. Thus, we ought to distinguish between: (a) debates over the necessary conceptuality of the content of cognition, which might be better understood as a continuation of the Hegelian critique of Kant regarding the "separability" of representations into "intuition" and "concept" (see Pippin 1976,[18] 1989, and 2013 for one example of such a strategy); and (b) debates over whether there is experience with non-conceptual content apart from the synthetic activity of the understanding. While both of these issues are interdependent, it is unclear what the grounds are for the disagreement between the conceptualist and non-conceptualist on whether cognition, for Kant, requires something from outside of the conceptual order for any cognition to have the determinacy and unity that it has.[19] While the main focus of the Schematism chapter is to give conditions of restriction to the use of concepts, limiting their application to spatio-temporal objects, the Schematism also shows that such a primitive notion as number already requires a schematizing activity on behalf of the imagination, guided by the understanding. Thus, while the original unity of space, which does not presuppose a synthesis of the understanding, provides a richly determined manifold prior to any activity of the understanding, it seems as if the capacity to build a foreground–background relationship already requires the capacity to form a notion of number, such that the object (or objects) in said manifold could be adequately discriminated from each other. If this is the case, then any richly determined manifold given in experience is still subject to some conceptual constraint by which any subject could interpret the data such that they would yield the sort of recognition of the object that is required for it to amount to a cognition of the object in that manifold, which would be true of both animal and human subjects.[20]

Finally, I hope that these considerations may move the debate on Kant's conceptualism or non-conceptualism, along with assessments of the viability of his position, further from considerations solely about the arguments of the Transcendental Deduction. As I have demonstrated, we must also scrutinize the Schematism chapter, along with the Analytic of Principles as a whole, in order to work out the details of his views.

Notes

1. I want to acknowledge contributions from the participants at the Kant in Asia II: Intuition, East and West conference for pushing me on the issues of conceptualism and non-conceptualism with regards to reading the Schematism chapter, as well as for suggestions on how this relates to Husserl's work on time-consciousness. I also want to acknowledge my debt to Dietmar Heidemann, under whom I wrote my MA thesis on this topic and whose comments and suggestions were very helpful in developing the material I presented at the conference. Finally, I want to acknowledge Kenneth Westphal for alerting me to the issues around spatial determination, which Kant left underdeveloped in the Schematism chapter.
2. All translations of Kant are from Pluhar (1996), with the exception that I retranslate every instance of "*Vorstellung*" as "representation".

3. Either that of Marburg Neo-Kantianism (see Onof and Schulting 2015 for examples) or of contemporaries like McDowell (1994/1996).
4. Pendlebury is more concerned in his paper on giving an explication of how the schematization would work for empirical concepts, and so the "transcendental problem" is only mentioned.
5. Where most commentators see Kant responding here to the problem of universals that the British Empiricists were dealing with—in particular Berkeley's objection to Locke's theory of general ideas—Kant also echoes Descartes (2006, 40) in the Sixth Meditation on our apparent incapacity to imagine a chiliagon. While Descartes there highlights the superiority of our conceptual capacities for understanding mathematical terms, even when these cannot be immediately recognized, Kant emphasizes that, if given an instance of such a figure, it is still necessary to refer back to the synthesizing activity of the imagination, which produces the schemata that underlie not only our pure intuitions, but also our pure sensible concepts.
6. Again, I leave aside here any discussion of the role of this passage within the structure of the B Deduction for reasons of space and relevance.
7. I do not intend the selection of these passages to be exhaustive, but merely to highlight certain features of the example, which I think relevant to the schema of magnitude.
8. See Heidegger (2016, 313–319) for an interpretation of the Schematism chapter that explains magnitude as the "combining" of successive moments into a determinate time, which for all intents and purposes could be understood as a "specious present".
9. Sacha Golob (2016) discusses some of these aspects with reference to the Axioms of Intuition, also with reference to the example of the line. Here he points out that the "simple argument" for the conceptual content in experience required for the perception of parts is too weak (since its appeal to the intuitiveness of "drawing the line" seems to be tenuous), and the complex argument (drawn from various sections of the first *Critique*, but focusing in particular on the results of the Axioms) might fail against standard objections to non-conceptualism. I am sympathetic to the treatment given here, although I think that the unity of space may be given too much emphasis over the unity conferred by the synthesis of the understanding. (See Onof and Schulting 2015 on the "unicity" of space in relation to the unity conferred by the action of the imagination.)
10. See Ferrarin (1995, 143) for a similar use of "motion".
11. This, then, would further provide a way of distinguishing between the different senses of unity that are attributed to space (and consequently also to time), which Onof and Schulting (2015) point out on the distinction of form of intuition and formal intuition at B160n.
12. See Kern (1964). It is clear from Husserl's notes and his lecture plans that he was most familiar with more popular texts, like the *Prolegomena*.
13. For a more detailed comparison between the Kantian schema and the Husserlian type, see Lohmar 2003.
14. To avoid a possible confusion: The *noema* is not merely the external/"transcendent" object that exists outside of one's experience, but rather the immanent object of experience that constitutes the meaning for a subject of what is experienced. See Husserl (1913/2014, 73–75).
15. It ought to be noted here that expectation and protention are distinct, while interlinked, aspects of experience. Expectation is always in some sense founded on previous experience and so resembles recollection. Protention is rather a structural moment of the experience of time in its pointing to the

future, with retention being the corresponding moment pointing toward the past. However, precautions ought to be taken before analogizing too quickly, as the analysis here functions at the level of the "primordial impression" (*Urimpression*) rather than fully constituted objects. See Rodemeyer 2003.

16. Guyer (1987) cites A183,192, B219, 225, 233, 257, and 291–293 as examples of this.
17. Heidegger (1997; see also 2016) provides good examples of the treatment of time from a phenomenological perspective; also, Nenon (1986) contains a fruitful discussion of Kant's focus on time as the aspect of sensibility required for the theory of schematism emphasizing the position of the finite cognizer.
18. Pippin (1976) also discusses the topic of the "mediating third" in the Schematism chapter, and compares it to the Platonic problem of the third man. While he does draw attention to the non-metaphysical character of the formulation of the problem in Kant, this problem is a general feature of relating particulars to the general kind terms in grouping or classifying them, and it ought to be addressed in the conceptualism/non-conceptualism debate. This fits with Pippin's insistence (171) that the imagination's transcendental function be understood as one " 'guided' not by an 'in–itself', but only by the concept as rule."
19. For example, McDowell (1996, 28) writes: "Now if we are to give due acknowledgement to the independence of reality, what we need is a constraint from outside *thinking* and *judging*, our exercise of spontaneity. The constraint need not be from outside *thinkable contents*." With regards to the notion of determination, we ought to consider Kant's treatment of the problem of incongruent counterparts in the *Prolegomena* and other texts (cf. Birrer 2016).
20. See Golob (2016) for an account that accommodates the conceptualist worries to a non-conceptualist reading of Kant. Given how Kant's theory of judgment and perception has this interpretative element, it seems to me that the argument from rogue objects in Hanna (2011) ought to be reexamined for what it actually can tell us about the overall debate. It seems clear that any interpretation of Kant has to respect that intuition delivers contents independently of our ability to conceptually determine them—e.g., as in the example of incongruent counterparts. However, it does not seem to justify the inference to accepting "rogue objects" (409)—i.e., "nomologically ill-behaved" objects or processes, particularly with reference to "spontaneous goal-directed behavior (life, consciousness, freedom)." Hanna singles out spontaneous goal-directed behavior (i.e., free acts). Engaging with these matters would require at least a paper-long treatment of this topic. However, I will note two things. First, the capacity to recognize events as freely caused requires an application of the idea of freedom. Thus it requires an interpretation of events as being possible through that idea. The event itself however, is just as thoroughly determined by natural causality as any other, so nothing given in the experience itself suggests its "rogueness". With respect to the consciousness of freedom, Kant points out in the second *Critique* (5:42–50) that we require reason even to be able to think and justify freedom, so our consciousness of that freedom is thoroughly conditioned by our grasp of a rational idea (and thus, in our sense, it is conceptual). Even "mere" self-consciousness is already a product of the understanding (B157). How we determine how this fits into the rest of the system is, however, a matter of ongoing debate, and I only want to highlight the difficulty in maintaining a consistent non-conceptualist reading in the way Hanna (2011) proposes.

References

Allison, Henry (2004). *Kant's Transcendental Idealism: An Interpretation and Defense*, 2nd ed. New Haven: Yale University Press.

Birrer, Matthias (2016). Kant on the Originality of Time (and Space) and Intellectual Synthesis. In: *Contemporary Studies in Kantian Philosophy* 1, 1–21.

Descartes, René (2006). Trans. and ed. R. Ariew and D. Cress, *Meditations, Objections, and Replies*. Bloomington: Hackett Publishing Company.

Ferrarin, Alfredo (1995). Construction and Mathematical Schematism: Kant on the Exhibition of a Concept in Intuition. In: *Kant Studien* 86(2), 131–174.

Förster, Eckart (2012). *The Twenty Five Years of Philosophy: A Systematic Reconstruction*. Cambridge: Harvard University Press.

Gardner, Sebastian (1999). *Routledge Philosophy Guidebook to Kant and the Critique of Pure Reason*. London: Routledge.

Golob, Sacha (2016). Kant as Both Conceptualist and Nonconceptualist. In: *Kantian Review* 21(3), 367–391.

Guyer, Paul (1987). *Kant and the Claims of Knowledge*. Cambridge: Cambridge University Press.

Hanna, Robert (2011). Kant's Non-Conceptualism, Rogue Objects, and the Gap in the B Deduction. In: *International Journal of Philosophical Studies*. 19(3), 399–415.

Heidegger, Martin (1927/1962). Trans. J. Macquarrie and E. Robinson. *Being and Time*. New York: Harper and Row.

——— (1929/1997). Trans. R. Taft, *Kant and the Problem of Metaphysics*. Bloomington: Indiana University Press.

——— (1976/2016). Trans. T. Sheehan, *Logic: The Question of Truth* Bloomington: Indiana University Press.

Husserl, Edmund (1901/2001). Trans. J. N. Findlay and D. Moran (ed.), *Logical Investigations*, Vol. 2. London: Routledge.

——— (1913/2014). Trans. D. Dahlstrom, *Ideas I*. Bloomington: Hackett Publishing Company.

——— (1966/1991). Trans. J. Brough, *On the Phenomenology of Internal Time-Consciousness (1983–1917)*. Dordrecht: Kluwer Academic Publishers.

——— (2001). R. Bernet and D. Lohmar (eds.), *Die 'Bernaur Manuskripte' über das Zeitbewußtseins 1917/18*. Dordrecht: Kluwer Academic Publishers.

Kant, Immanuel (1996). Trans. W. S. Pluhar, *Critique of Pure Reason*. Indianapolis: Hackett Publishing Company.

Kern, Iso (1964). *Husserl und Kant*. The Hague: Martinus Nijhoff.

Lohmar, Dietmar (2003). Husserl's Type and Kant's Schemata: Systematic Reasons for their Correlation or Identity. In: D. Welton (ed.), *The New Husserl*. Bloomington: Indiana University Press, 93–124.

Longuenesse, Béatrice (1998). *Kant and the Capacity to Judge*. Princeton, NJ: Princeton University Press.

McDowell, John (1996). *Mind and World*. Cambridge: Cambridge University Press.

Nenon, Thomas (1986). *Objektivität und endliche Erkenntnis: Kants transzendentalphilosophische Korrespondeztheorie der Wahrheit*. Freiburg: Verlag Alber.

Onof, Chris and Dennis Schulting (2015). Space as Form of Intuition and as Formal Intuition: On the Note to B160 in Kant's Critique of Pure Reason. In: *Philosophical Review* 124(1), 1–58.

O'Shea, James (2012). *Kant's Critique of Pure Reason: An Introduction*. London: Routledge.

Pendlebury, Michael (1995). Making Sense of Kant's Schematism. In: *Philosophy and Phenomenological Research* 55(4), 777–797.

Pippin, Robert (1976). The Schematism and Empirical Concepts. In: *Kant Studien* 67(2), 156–171.

——— (1989). *Hegel's Idealism: The Satisfactions of Self-Consciousness*. Cambridge: Cambridge University Press.

——— (2013). What is Conceptual Activity? In: J. K. Schear (ed.), *Mind, Reason, and Being–in–the–World: The McDowell–Dreyfus Debate*. London: Routledge, 91–109.

Rodemeyer, Lanei (2003). Developments in the Theory of Time-Consciousness: An Analysis of Protention. In: D. Welton (ed.), *The New Husserl*. Bloomington: Indiana University Press, 124–155.

Watkins, Eric (2013). Shifts and Incompleteness in Kant's *Critique of Pure Reason*? In: J. Haag and M. Wild (eds.), *Übergänge, diskursiv oder intuitiv?: Essays zu Eckart Försters Die 25 Jahre der Philosophie*. Frankfurt am Main: Klostermann, 81–95.

Westphal, Kenneth (2006). *Kant's Transcendental Proof of Realism*. Cambridge: Cambridge University Press.

10 Negative Certainties

Nāgārjuna's Challenge to Kant on the "Togetherness" of Intuition and Concepts

Ellen Y. Zhang

1. Introduction

In *Critique of Pure Reason*, we find an often-quoted statement by Kant: "Thoughts without content are empty, intuitions without concepts are blind. . . . Only from their unification can cognition arise" (A51/B76). This is sometimes known as the Kantian "togetherness principle" (e.g., Hanna 2013b, 91), which leads to two major ideas allegedly held by Kant: (1) intuitions without concepts do not exist; and (2) intuitions without concepts, if existing, are simply meaningless. Recently, however, some Kantian scholars such as Robert Hanna, Lucy Allais, and others have argued that Kant is a non-conceptualist about intuition, and that intuitions in Kant refer to the objectively representational that can be essentially independent of concepts. This interpretation is different from the traditional reading of the togetherness principle, whereby intuition and cognition cannot be realized in the absence of the application of concepts; this application, in turn, gives rise, through the connection of concepts to cognition, to judgment, in terms of which knowledge in Kant's philosophy is properly understood.

In this chapter I will discuss the togetherness principle and relate it to Madhyāmika Buddhism via Nāgārjuna's argument on the relationship between intuition and concept. I will explicate Nāgārjuna's skeptical view of the semantic dependence of intuition on concepts in light of his critique of "conceptual proliferation", with an intention to show that the togetherness principle does not fully address the nature of immediate representations that can be non-conceptual. In addition, I will appropriate the role of intuitions in conjunction with Kant's Critical position on mystical experience, and thus bring Kant into conversation with Nāgārjuna and post-Nāgārjuna Ch'an (Zen) Buddhism. I will conclude by contending that we need to draw a line between intuition as an experiential intake and any explanation or understanding of that experience which involves a post-experiential and discursive interpretation. Understanding in terms of conceptualization and rational analysis, as maintained by Nāgārjuna, belongs to a realm of "conventional truth", which is conceptually dependent and cognitively important, yet without exhausting all kinds of intuition and knowledge.

2. The Kantian Togetherness Principle

Kant's so-called *togetherness principle*, that "[t]houghts without content are empty, intuitions without concepts are blind" (A51/B76), is often taken as establishing the cognitive necessity of a semantic interdependence between intuitions and concepts. Understanding, in this view, is an act of combining an intuition and a concept which arises out of the cognitive dualism between the faculties of sensibility and understanding (A50–51/B74–76):

> Intuition and concepts . . . constitute the elements of all our cognition, so that neither concepts without intuition corresponding to them in some way nor intuition without concepts can yield a cognition. . . . Thoughts without content are empty, intuitions without concepts are blind. It is thus just as necessary to make the mind's concepts sensible (i.e., to add an object to them in intuition) as it is to make its intuitions understandable (i.e., to bring them under concepts). Further, these two faculties or capacities cannot exchange their functions. The understanding is not capable of intuiting anything, and the senses are not capable of thinking anything. Only from their unification can cognition arise.

According to Kant, intuitions represent objects and are immediate and particular, whereas concepts represent the form that those objects take and are general and derivative. Intuitions relate to objects perceived immediately, while concepts relate to objects perceived mediately. It follows that a concept as such, instead of relating to an object directly and singularly, it is always related to some other representation of it, whether it be an intuition or itself already a concept (A68/B93). The question then is whether a mental representation as "mere intuition" points to the actual existence of a "cognizer" who does not possess conceptual representation but is capable of generating objectively valid empirical intuitions rather than a subjective perception.

When discussing Kant's theory of mental representation, David Landy points out (2015, 99) that how one interprets "intuition" makes a significant difference on how one understands Kant's theory of representation. He then contends that Kant understands concepts as functioning as forms of "meta-representation" in which consciousness or the thought process is the condition for cognitive experience. In this regard, intuitions are dependent on the act of understanding, and concepts must be constructed by the faculty of cognition. Kant distinguishes between our experience of "mere intuition" and "intuition and concept", and the latter fits his togetherness principle. Thus, he insists (A656/B684): "The understanding can intuit nothing, the senses can think nothing. . . . The understanding cognizes everything only through concepts; consequently, however far it goes in its divisions [of lower concepts] it never cognizes through mere intuition but always yet again through lower concepts." Kant uses "empty" concepts and "blind" intuitions to refer to a cognition that is not objectively valid. In terms of his togetherness principle, Kant's notion of intuition indicates a cognition (i.e., a conscious objective representation) rather than a mere (subjective) experience or perception: the former is concept-oriented, whereas the latter may not be. The togetherness principle suggests the possible application of a concept—viz., the concept of an object in general (the categories) and the thought of the self, both of which play a necessary role in the unity of consciousness in Kant's theory. It also applies to Kant's transcendental idealism, where the unity of apperception is viewed as the unity through which all the manifold given in an intuition is united in a concept of the object. In other words, the act of arranging what is given in intuition is a synthesis of the manifold. Therefore, the togetherness requirement suggests that intuitions and concepts are cognitively complementary and semantically interdependent for achieving objectively valid judgments.

While committed to the togetherness principle, which encapsulates a classical form of conceptualism, Kant also speaks of the independence and autonomy of intuitions in his idea of pure intuitions. He also accepts the idea that objects can indeed appear to us without necessarily having to be related to functions of the understanding (A89/B122). For example, space and time are, according to Kant, pure intuitions—i.e., intuitions that are concept-free—since these are *a priori* conditions of our sensibility which determine exactly how we are "receptive" to affectations. Accordingly, pure intuitions in this case do not fit the togetherness principle, which claims that intuitions without concepts are blind.

But if Kant allows any intuitions that are essentially non-conceptual cognitions, the togetherness principle cannot be a universal formula to be used to deny the possibility of the existence of pure intuitions. Are there any other types of pure intuition that are meaningful, apart from the intuitions of time or space? Kant's explanation seems to be ambiguous on this. The ambiguity lies in either the polyvalent meaning of "intuitions" used by Kant or different interpretations of Kant's concept of "intuitions". Wilfrid Sellars (1963), for example, points out that in the togetherness principle Kant introduces the dichotomies of intuition–concept and sensibility–understanding as reflecting the opposition between the receptivity for impressions and the spontaneity of concepts. Receptivity involves the capacity (of the subject) to be affected by objects while spontaneity involves freedom and autonomy in understanding. So Kant's theory of intuition can be illustrated as follows:

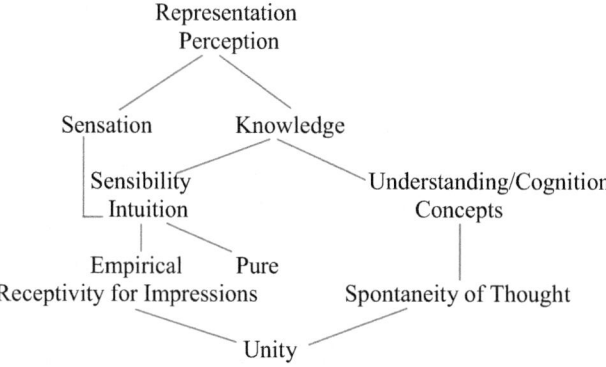

Figure 10.1 Kant's theory of intuition

But such characterization of receptivity and spontaneity, for Sellars, does not resolve the problem of ambiguity, since intuitions—or at least, those intuitions capable of giving us an object—cannot proceed entirely from mere receptivity.

John McDowell, who takes a stronger conceptualist position than Sellars, notes that Kant is firm that sensibility alone does not yield cognition, and that perceptual content, in order to be able to justify perceptual judgment, needs to be fully propositional (McDowell 2006, 312). Thomas Land also holds a similar position, arguing that "if intuition, in order to exhibit the requisite unity, does depend on the involvement of conceptual capacities, then the unity of sensory experience is the same as the unity of conceptual thought, in the sense that sensory experience is propositional in structure" (Land 2006, 190). Lucy Allais suggests that the togetherness principle shows that, for Kant, neither intuitions nor concepts alone can give us a direct perceptual presentation of a particular. "The fact that Kant thinks concepts alone cannot supply distinct perceptual particulars", says Allais, "does not mean that he thinks intuitions alone could do so either; the point about the mutual dependence of intuitions and concepts could be that both ingredients are necessary" (Allais 2009, 399).[1]

The ambiguity of Kant's togetherness principle leads to the contemporary debate in Kantian scholarship as to whether Kant endorses a conceptualist or non-conceptualist idea of intuition. Robert Hanna, a representative of a non-conceptualist approach to Kant's intuition, contends that the conceptualist and non-conceptualist interpretations of Kant's philosophy influence the way we interpret Kant's theory of cognition in general and his theory of judgment in particular. Hanna holds that sensible intuitions in Kant's formula possess wholly non-conceptual representational content (2005, 248): "Non-conceptualism holds that non-conceptual content exists and is representationally significant. . . . Non-conceptual cognitive content in the contemporary sense is, for all philosophical intents and purposes, identical to intuitional cognitive content in Kant's sense." Hanna thus elucidates the possibility of independence of intuitions from conceptualization and forms of thinking in Kant, pointing out that the reason for such a possibility is because Kant uses the term "cognition" both in a narrower and a broader sense. While "cognition" in the togetherness principle is used in a narrower sense, as referring to "objectively valid judgment", "cognition" in other contexts is used in a broader sense, as "conscious objective representation" that can be over and above conceptual content. In this way, Hanna (2013a) contends that "blind intuition" for Kant does not mean either "bogus intuition" or "wholly meaningless intuition"; rather, it means "autonomously and independently objectively valid intuition/essentially non-conceptual cognition."

The debate on Kant's togetherness principle is significant when we try to decipher the meaning of intuitions in Kant's theoretical framework concerning forms of thinking or categories at both phenomenal and noumenal levels. The question of conceptuality or non-conceptuality is particularly perplexing when Kant does not make it clear whether the noumenal object is meant to be identical with phenomenal objects or distinct from them, or whether the kind of intuitions that apply to the noumenal object is identical with intuitions that apply to phenomenal objects.[2] Since the textual evidence pulls in both directions, the issue remains controversial.

3. Nāgārjuna's Intuition or Intuitive Insight (*prajñā*)

Nāgārjuna (ca. 150–250 CE) was the founder of the Madhyāmika (Middle Way) School and the systematizer of the doctrines of Māhayāna Buddhism. He is well-known for his skeptical position on perception, cognition, and conceptual language. In contrast to Kant, Nāgārjuna takes a more negative position on sense perception, the faculty of receptivity, and the conceptual structure of understanding as major sources of knowledge. Although perceptive representation seems to be the key base for the further development of empirical judgment, yet in reality it cannot be intelligently established because of the illusion created by the "thinking I". Sensibility that includes the ability to imagine can also be the root of illusion.

In his writing *The Fundamental Wisdom of the Middle Way* (*Mūlamadhyamakakārikā*, hereafter *MMK*), which offers a systematic analysis of all important philosophical issues in the second century C.E., Nāgārjuna discusses sense faculties, sense organs, and the subject's sensory experience of the object in a critical manner:

Seeing, hearing, smelling.
Tasting, touching, and mind

Are the six sense faculties.
Their spheres are the visible objects, . . .
That very seeing does not see
Itself at all.
How can something that cannot see itself
See another.
From the non-existence of seeing and the seen it follows that
The other four faculties of knowledge do not exist.
And all the aggregates, etc.
Are the same way.[3]

The awareness (*saṃjña*) of the perceptive object that is associated with affectations and sensations is limited to one's experience, apperception, and judgment. The key point for Nāgārjuna is, however, not to deny perceptive knowledge *per se*, but to say that all faculties of knowledge through sensations are devoid of self-being (i.e., absolutely true in itself) and as such are "empty". This is reason Nāgārjuna claims that the very seeing organ does not see itself at all. In Buddhism a distinction between an act of awareness (i.e., the sensing of the object) and the object is often clearly made. A sense-datum as a relational property of perceptual experience that is sensed points to the item and to sensory consciousness simultaneously. Nāgārjuna's approach to perceptual experience, however, is from the haphazard doubt about an object all people experience in their everyday lives, not only due to the illusion of an object that is often given to us, but also due to the conditioned self that is unable to make a conceptual formulation of such perceptual experience.

For Nāgārjuna, this rejection of the self-being or self-existence of faculty knowledge does not lead to the conclusion that "emptiness" (*śūnyatā*) is the ultimate reality; otherwise there would be no need for him to make such an effort to explicate its conception and provide information on its epistemological basis. Then what is emptiness, according to Madhyāmika Buddhism? Nāgārjuna states that all things in the world are devoid of self-being or self-nature (*svabhāva*) in the sense of being dependently or causally (*pratītya*) originating (*samutpāda*). Emptiness (*śūnya*) as such should be understood not as nothing or non-being, nor as something that has exhausted all theories on knowing or understanding.

Now, let us turn to Nāgārjuna's idea of intuition or intuitive insight (*prajñā*). According to T.R.V. Murti, a well-known Buddhist scholar, the goal of Nāgārjuna's philosophy is to take us through the three stages of the dialectic: that is, from dogmatism (knowing) to criticism (negation of knowing) and, finally, to intuition (beyond knowing and not-knowing). Murti calls Nāgārjuna's intuition or intuitive insight "absolute knowledge" (1955, 140). Such an interpretation, however, has an essentialist orientation that is problematic for Nāgārjuna's critical theory. Nevertheless, Murti correctly points out that intuition for Nāgārjuna means a suspension of all conceptual constructions. The result is the disclosure of reality as it is, or truth free from dependence on rational judgments that respond to thought constructions.

To clarify this point, let us use Nāgārjuna's concept of twofold truth—namely, the "conventional truth" and the "ultimate truth". For Nāgārjuna, perceptive and conceptive cognitions belong to the realm of conventional truth, and all our knowledge that depends on the involvement of conceptual capacities is relative in the sense that are causally conditioned (i.e., limited by our perceptive and cognitive experiences and rational judgment). By contrast, there is another kind of knowledge, called "intuition" or "intuitive insight", that belongs to the realm of ultimate truth.[4] To illustrate this point, Madhyāmika Buddhism speaks of fourfold negation, based on Nāgārjuna's method of *tetralemma*, or "four points of argumentation" that consist of these propositional possibilities: (1) X, (2) -X, (3) both X and -X, and (4) neither X nor -X. Using this method, we can depict the four twofold levels as follows:

As shown above, each level from level one to level three involves twofold truth—that is, the conventional and the ultimate, as well as a conjunction and a disjunction. The fourth level indicates that the language of "two" (i.e., the twofold truth in terms of C and U) at the first three levels of discourse should be perceived as different levels of the conventional or conceptual truth. The ultimate truth at the fourth level, in contrast to the first three levels, is "beyond" any discursive discourse. The fourfold progression thus involves a gradual negation at each level, characterized by a double strategy of affirmation and negation. The ultimate truth, as

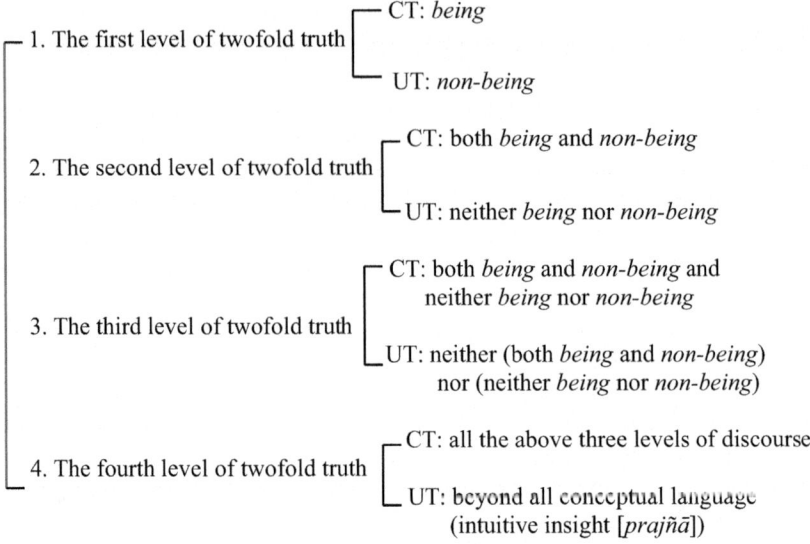

1. The first level of twofold truth
- CT: *being*
- UT: *non-being*

2. The second level of twofold truth
- CT: both *being* and *non-being*
- UT: neither *being* nor *non-being*

3. The third level of twofold truth
- CT: both *being* and *non-being* and neither *being* nor *non-being*
- UT: neither (both *being* and *non-being*) nor (neither *being* nor *non-being*)

4. The fourth level of twofold truth
- CT: all the above three levels of discourse
- UT: beyond all conceptual language (intuitive insight [*prajñā*])

Figure 10.2 Nāgārjuna's method of *tetralemma*

stated above, cannot be put into words and concepts; as such, it ends with the fourth level of negation. The ultimate level is also identified with the level of "speech-forgetting and thinking-terminating", as the Chinese commentator Jizang calls it (Ho 2012, 13), which points to Nāgārjuna's notion of pure intuition.

It follows that Nāgārjuna speaks of intuition as a mental faculty of immediate knowledge, a kind of super sense-perceptual experience, and he thus puts the term "intuition" beyond the mental process of conscious thinking, arguing that the conscious intellect cannot necessarily access subconscious information, or render such information into a conceptual form. According to Nāgārjuna, an intuitive knowing of reality leads to the path of enlightenment; thus he warns against "conceptual proliferation" (*prapañca*)—that is, the attempt to conceptualize reality through the use of ever-expanding language and concepts (*MMK* 18:5). Philosophical argument, in a sense, can be mental fabrication caused by the "thinking I", which reduces a direct experience of reality to concepts.[5] This is why Nāgārjuna sees conceptual argument in light of conventional truth. Conventional truth allows things to arise, to exist, as well as to fade away. In this vein, Nāgārjuna speaks of the peaceful cessation of being attached to concepts (*MMK* 25:24), maintaining a kind of "intellectual intuition" that is independent from concepts and all fixed views.

Murti (1955, 140) contends that the "ultimate truth" or the "absolute truth" transcends discursive thought, which means it is unreachable through the use of conceptual configuration and rational judgment. But at the same time, Murti insists that Madhyāmika's "no–doctrine–about–the–real" does not lead to a negation of reality and truth; instead, it intends to make the distinction between the phenomenal world of samsāra and the noumenal reality of nirvāna. Murti sees Nāgārjuna as an absolutist rather than a nihilist. Concerning this argument, Andrew P. Tuck notes that Murti, like Kant, "must be committed to the absolute reality of both the thing–in–itself and the notion of the constituting capacity of the mind" (Tuck 1990, 53). Perhaps Murti is too eager to defend Nāgārjuna against the charge of being nihilistic, insisting that the Madhyāmikan "no–doctrine–about–the–real" position should not be taken as a "no–reality" doctrine (Murti 1955, 52). However, such a defense ignores the fact that Nāgārjuna's critique of attachment to concepts and conceptualization at the level of conventional truth also applies to the level of ultimate truth. To put it otherwise, "no–doctrine–about–the–real" means no attachment to either the conventional or the ultimate, rather than indicating a distinction between the phenomenal world and noumenal reality. The question for us is whether Kantian noumenal perception also allows the same kind of silence. After all, Kant insists that human beings experience, in a sense, only appearances, not things in themselves, which suggests that the ultimate truth postulated by Buddhism would be inaccessible to human understanding for Kant.

4. Non-Conceptuality Via Negativity

No doubt, the Buddhist idea of "sacred silence" points to a gesture of negativity. This negativity, in terms of the "intuitive insight" maintained by Buddhism in general and Nāgārjuna in particular, has generated a heated debate in contemporary scholarship concerning the possibility of religious perception or experience of the nature of reality that can be concept free. What intrigues me is that scholars such as Steven T. Katz, W.T. Stace, and Robert Forman are strongly influenced by Kant, yet their different interpretations of Kant's theory of intuition lead to their different understandings of religious experience, especially what is labeled as "mystical experience".

Katz follows Kant's argument that no intuition without concepts can yield a cognition, arguing that any experience, including what is called "pure, intuitive, and mystical experience" is always context laden, and mediated through conceptual language. That is, without the application of a particular category in a particular context, mystical experience is impossible (Katz 1978, 26). Such an approach to mystical experience leads to Katz's critique of the Ch'an/Zen notion of "pure experience", a concept based on Nāgārjuna's understanding of "intuitive insight", and further articulated by Kitaro Nishida, a Japanese Zen scholar (Nishida 1993, 121–123). It seems that Katz's dismissal of the mystics' claim is also tied up with his rejection of the notion of what is "given", which is compatible with thinking that intuition presents us "something" independently of the application of concepts.

However, Katz's contextualist or conceptualist position is challenged by Robert Forman, who claims to be a "decontextualist" and supports the idea of "pure consciousness events" (Forman 1990, 30). Forman's position is close to that held by Stace, who attempts to find an underlying core experience common to all mystical traditions, or what he calls the "universal introvertive experience" (Stace 1961, 79). Both Forman and Stace accept an experiential representation which is "directly intuited" or "given" without any mediation through language and concepts.

I think it would be helpful to draw a line between "intuitive experiences" and understanding that involves discursive and "post-experiential interpretations". This differentiation is based on Kant's division between "experience" and its "interpretation", but at the same time, it preserves the idea that intuition involves a kind of knowing. For Buddhists, "pure experience" is perceived as a product of a certain mind-set, which is believed to be "beyond thinking and non-thinking". Is this perception an objectively valid judgment? It might be a wrong question for the Buddhist since the question itself still operates within a dualist scheme of subject and object, in the sense that "I, the subject, know this object."

If Kant admits that God cannot be an object of intuition, then Kant must suggest another form of knowledge which is different from knowledge of the phenomenal, with its togetherness principle. Although the notion of intellectual intuition in Kant is used in a negative sense, it does not rule out any intuitions that are independent of concepts. Steven DeLay, for example, observes that when Kant claims that the understanding can make no other use of concepts than to judge by means of them, "he is not saying that concepts are meaningful only in the context of objectively valid judgments, or meaningful only in the context of any kind of judgment, since noumenal concepts, quite apart from any kind of judgment, are obvious counterexamples" (DeLay 2014, 88). Therefore, despite it being true for Kant, according to the togetherness principle, that intuitions and concepts must be combined with one another in order to generate objectively valid judgments, nevertheless intuitions/ essentially non-conceptual cognitions can also occur both autonomously from and independently of concepts and still remain objectively valid.

Stephen R. Palmquist, on the other hand, has a different opinion on Kant's view on mysticism. In his reading of Kant's *Dreams of a Spirit-Seer* along with the *Critique of Pure Reason*, Palmquist argues that Kant's goal is "to reject the uncritical (speculative and fanatical) forms of mysticism, not in order to overthrow all mysticism, but to replace it with a refined, *Critical* version, directed towards *this* world and our reflection on it from various perspectives" (Firestone 2009, 115). It is interesting to note that Palmquist (1989, 84) uses the term "Critical mysticism" to describe Kant's critique of mysticism:

> Kant's treatment of the "unity of apperception" does indeed have a certain mystical flavor. For Kant is not referring simply to the ordinary man's empirical sense of "I", but to a deeper, *transcendental* limit of all human experience—a limit which comes into view only as we gradually *forget* about (i.e., hold in abeyance) the empirical diversity of our ordinary experiences. And this, like Kant's overall a priori approach, is remarkably similar to the mystic's claim that in order to experience God . . . we must first go through an experience of *unknowing*.

Here, Palmquist has noted elements of the *via negativa* in Kant. He further points out that "Kant's belief in God was based not on theoretical proof, but on an existential 'conviction that dawns most spontaneously in all minds', which is quite close (if not identical) to the sort of immediate certainty of the transcendent claimed by mystics" (79). It is significant that Palmquist has disclosed a dimension in Kant's schema of unity of apperception that has been ignored by most Kantian scholars. If Kant's notion of self presupposes the distinction between the phenomenal and the noumenal, then Kant's notion of experience must also entail the distinction between the perceptive cognition experienced by the phenomenal subject and cognition as experienced by the noumenal subject.

To a certain degree, Kant is critical about, if not totally hostile towards, "mystical claims" because of an implied moral privilege in the idea of *unio mystica*. On this note, Nāgārjuna would agree with Kant when the claim about the oneness of ultimate reality (such as emptiness) is absolutized. But at the same time, I will argue that Kant's epistemological scheme allows non-conceptual intuitions and even a qualified version of mysticism. But it still remains a question if Kant (or Christian mystics) and Buddhists talk about the same kind of experience. After all, the cloud of unknowing maintained by Christian mystics is not the same as the cloud of nothingness/emptiness argued by Nāgārjuna and Buddhism. For Nāgārjuna, nothingness or emptiness is more methodological than metaphysical, since the ultimate truth is not totally "the other". It is in this sense that most modern interpreters of Nāgārjuna reject seeing him through the lens of Kant's absolutism. On the other hand, although we allow ourselves to make a distinction between "experience itself" and "post-experiential accounts or interpretations of that experience", we have to admit that our knowledge of mystical experience tends to be "textual" (or "conceptual" as Kant has suggested) and textual experience cannot be exactly the same as lived experience.

When Kant introduces his concept of the transcendental unity of apperception, he tries to explain the uniting and building of coherent consciousness out of different elementary inner experiences. But who is the "I" here in the self-consciousness that makes synthetic and transcendental unity possible? Stace argues that, if a person empties his mind of all empirical contents, he would get into a state of "pure consciousness" with no content except itself, which Stace identifies with the Kantian transcendental unity of apperception (1961, 86).[6] In addition, Stace assimilates mystical experiences to his universal introvertive experience by distinguishing between experience and interpretation, stating that the introvertive experience is the same across cultures and only interpretations differ. This is Stace's non-conceptual appropriation of Kant.[7]

It needs to be noted that Nāgārjuna's view on intuitive insight into ultimate reality is pragmatic and soteriological instead of descriptive and explanatory.[8] Nāgārjuna extends the teaching of the Buddha, and he thinks it is pointless to engage in philosophical debate, since what really matters is how to release oneself from all kinds of suffering in life. To follow this line of thinking, it would be questionable to call Nāgārjuna's intuitive insight "mystical". In other words, Nāgārjuna's anti-conceptualism seems to be more pragmatic than mystical.

5. Negative Certainties: A Concluding Remark

Nowadays, to answer questions left by Kant, phenomenologists speak of the representational or "intentional" content of a mental state. Mental states are intentional—that is, have intentional content—when they are directed towards some actual or possible object, property, or state of affairs. In his argument on a phenomenological approach to theology, Jean-Luc Marion contends that the transcendental as an object is irreducible to consciousness since what he calls the "saturated phenomenon" is so "overwhelming" and "bedazzling" that it defies all attempts to comprehend, categorize, and conceptualize it (Marion 2002, 159). According to Marion, some phenomena give more intuition than is needed to fill a subject's intention. Such phenomena are "saturated" with intention and exceed any concepts or limiting horizons that a constituting subject could impose upon them. As such, Marion's concept of being given articulates what one has perceived as a phenomenon that gives itself without any conditions being imposed upon it. Such a phenomenon, says Marion, is "saturated with intuition" to the point that intention cannot grasp it, and no easy signification can be given because such givenness is required before phenomena can show themselves in consciousness.

Marion's notion of "givenness" intentionally transgresses the Kantian categories of understanding, in terms of the ordinary conditions of quantity, quality, relation, and modality. For Kant, our mind formats our understanding of representation as experience via these forms of thinking, or categories. Kant, of course, regards these categories of quantity, quality, relation, and modality as conditions for the possibility of experience. Marion, however, insists on the intentional horizon as a conditioning manifestation. Hence, he claims (2008, 34): "The saturated phenomenon exceeds the categories and the principles of understanding—it will therefore be invisible according to quantity, unbearable according to quality, absolute according to relation, and incapable of being looked at according to modality".[9] Marion holds that what is shown in a phenomenon should be regarded as the thing itself rather than as a representation of something else. Marion's "saturated phenomenon" is similar to the Buddhist idea of a "direct experience", in which reality appears as itself and of itself. That is, reality appears without being reduced to the "I", as Marion puts it, and the phenomenon in question is not something constituted by the I; instead, the I experiences itself as constituted by it (40). Here we see Marion's "alteration" of Kantian subjectivity—namely, the subjectivity between the self's self-constitution and its being constituted from the outside (Alvis 2014, 25).

The phrase "negative certainties" (*certitudes négatives*) is employed by Marion (2015) to suggest that our knowledge of certainty is the starting point rather than the conclusion. To use Nāgārjuna's twofold truth formula: certainty in terms of discursive knowledge can be made only at the conventional level, but not at the ultimate level, since we tend to attain knowledge by reducing the thing in itself to an object or concept. Meanwhile, similar to a theology *via negativa* or the negative formula, *neither . . . nor*, in Nāgārjuna's negative philosophy, Marion maintains that in the self-giving phenomena intuition exceeds any concepts, exemplified by his conception of God as "impossible" (Marion 2007, 24). Although Kant would like to maintain thinkability and intelligibility as a general principle, he might agree with negative certainties to an extent in his philosophy, since he also suggests that one cannot say what the noumenal world is, yet one can say what it is not.

In sum, for Buddhists in general and Nāgārjuna in particular, an intuitive insight into reality is the means to limit the state of the consciousness of the self. It is the same case with Ch'an/Zen meditation, where thought is said to be freed from the presence of the "I" for the cognitive act. The object is no longer known via the series of past representations or current contextualization; rather it is given directly. While Buddhism in general is more skeptical about the (seemingly Kantian) togetherness of empirical intuitions and cognition, some post-Nāgārjuna Buddhist schools are more positive on a form of intuitive wisdom that transcends ordinary experience and understanding.

Notes

1. Some scholars speak of a distinction between strong Kantian conceptualism and weak Kantian conceptualism: whereas the weak variety at least minimally preserves Kant's cognitive dualism of faculties, and also some sort of semi-independent cognitive role for intuitions, the strong variety does not countenance any of these concessions to non-conceptualism, and thereby, in effect, strong Kantian conceptualism explanatorily reduces the faculty of sensibility to the faculty of understanding. See Hanna 2013a.
2. Kant maintains that, unlike the empirical world or the world of appearances, we can say nothing about the noumenal world—that is, things in themselves.
3. *MMK* 3:1, 2, and 8. For the text of *MMK*, I use Garfield's 1995 translation. The words "all the aggregates" here refer to the five types of aggregates (*skandhas*) that serve as the bases for designating persons or personhood.
4. Early Buddhism speaks of the ultimate in terms of space (*akāśa*) and nirvāṇa, and neither of them is causally conditioned. Nāgārjuna, however, tends to employ them in a negative way to indicate the ultimate in order to avoid the trap of conceptual analysis.
5. It should be noted that there is also soteriological concern for Nāgārjuna's negative argument. After all, for Buddhism freedom from suffering rather than philosophical arguments is the final goal. Hence, Nāgārjuna simply follows the teachings of the Buddha to relieve suffering. Through fourfold negation, he attempts to do away with all forms of clinging, including clinging to his own views.
6. When speaking of mysticism, Stace identifies a universal, "monistic", introvertive experience that "looks inward into the mind" to achieve "pure consciousness"—that is, an experience phenomenologically not of anything (Stace 1961, 86). Stace calls this kind of mystical experience a "unitary consciousness".
7. It is interesting to note that both Katz as a contextualist and Stace as a perennialist use Kant to argue for a conceptualist and non-conceptualist position, respectively.
8. For discussion on pragmatic and soteriological dimension of Nāgārjuna's argument, see Garfield 1994.

9. Marion (2002, 23) argues that there is a range of phenomena that exceed any intentional horizon (whether perceptual, anticipatory, re-collective, imaginative, or so on), and, with a backwards look at Kant's table of categories, he offers a typology of this excess by way of the event (saturation of quantity), the idol (saturation of quality), the flesh (saturation of relation), and the icon (saturation of modality).

References

Allais, Lucy (2009). Kant, Non-Conceptual Content and the Representation of Space. In: *Journal of the History of Philosophy* 47(3), 383–413.

Alvis, Jason (2014). Subject and Time: Jean-Luc see Marion's Alteration of Kantian Subjectivity. In: *Journal for Cultural and Religious Theory* 14(1), 25–37.

DeLay, Steven (2014). God and Givenness: Towards a Phenomenology of Mysticism. In: *Continental Philosophy Review* 47, 87–106.

Firestone, Chris L. (2009). *Kant and Theology at the Boundaries of Reason.* London and New York: Routledge.

Forman, Robert K. (1997). *The Problem of Pure Consciousness.* Oxford: Oxford University Press.

Garfield, Jay L. (1994). Dependent Origination and the Emptiness of Emptiness: Why Did Nāgārjuna Start With Causation? In: *Philosophy East and West* 44, 219–250.

Hanna, Robert (2005). Kant and Nonconceptual Content. In: *European Journal of Philosophy* 13(2), 247–290.

——— (2013a). Kant's Conceptualism, Kant's Non-conceptualism, and The Togetherness Principle. In: *Stanford Encyclopedia of Philosophy*. Online: https://plato.stanford.edu. Accessed June 27, 2018.

——— (2013b). Kant's Non-Conceptualism, Rogue Objects, and The Gap in the B Deduction. In: D. H. Heidemann (ed.), *Kant and Non-Conceptual Content.* London and New York: Routledge, 87–103.

Ho, Chien-hsing (2012). The Non-duality of Speech and Silence: A Comparative Analysis of Jizang's Thought on Language and Beyond. In: *Dao: A Journal Comparative Philosophy* 11(1), 1–19.

Katz, Steven T. (1978). Language, Epistemology, and Mysticism. In: S. T. Katz (ed.), *Mysticism and Philosophical Analysis.* Oxford: Oxford University Press.

Land, Thomas (2006). Kant's Spontaneity Thesis. In: *Philosophical Topics* 34, 189–220.

Landy, David (2015). *Kant's Inferentialism: The Case Against Hume.* London and New York: Routledge.

Marion, Jean-Luc (2002). Trans. J. L. Kosky, *Being Given: Toward a Phenomenology of Givenness.* Stanford: Stanford University Press.

——— (2007). The Impossible for Man–God. In: John Caputo and Michael Scanlon (eds.), *Transcendence and Beyond: A Postmodern Inquiry.* Bloomington: Indiana University Press.

——— (2008). Trans. C.M. Gschwandtner, et al., *The Visible and the Revealed.* New York: Fordham University Press.

——— (2015). Trans. S.E. Lewis, *Negative Certainties.* Chicago: The University of Chicago Press.

McDowell, John (2006). Sensory Consciousness in Kant and Sellars. In: *Philosophical Topics* 34(1–2), 311–326.

McLear, Colin (2011). *Kant on Animal Consciousness*. Ithaca: Cornell University Press.

—— (2014). The Kantian (non)-Conceptualism Debate. In: *Philosophy Compass* (7 November), 1–34.

Murti, T. R. V. (1955). *The Central Philosophy of Buddhism*. London: Allen and Unwin.

Nāgārjuna (1995). Trans. J. L. Garfield, *The Fundamental Wisdom of the Middle Way: Nāgārjuna's Mūlamadhyamakakārikā*. Oxford: Oxford University Press.

Nishida, Kitaro (1993). An Inquiry into the Good. In: *International Journal for Philosophy of Religion* 34(2), 121–123.

Palmquist, Stephen R. (1989). Kant's Critique of Mysticism: (2) The Critical Mysticism. In: *Philosophy and Theology* 4(1), 67–94.

Rao, K. Ramakrishna (2005). *Consciousness Studies: Cross-Cultural Perspectives*. Jefferson, NC: McFarland and Company.

Sellars, Wilfrid (1963). Empiricism and the Philosophy of Mind. In: W. Sellars (ed.), *Science, Perception, and Reality*. New York: Humanities Press, 127–196.

—— (1968). *Science and Metaphysics: Variations on Kantian Themes*. London: Routledge and Kegan Paul.

Stace, W. T. (1961). *Mysticism and Philosophy*. London: Macmillan.

Tuck, Andrew P. (1990). *Comparative Philosophy and the Philosophy of Scholarship*. New York and Oxford: Oxford University Press.

Part III

The Sublime and the Challenge of the East on Intuiting the Supersensible

11 The "Sublime", the "Supersensible Substrate", and "Spirit"—Intuitions of the Ultimate in Kant's Third *Critique*

John H. Zammito

An immense gulf is fixed between the domain of the concept of nature, the sensible, and the domain of the concept of freedom, the supersensible, so that no transition from the sensible to the supersensible (and hence by means of the theoretical use of reason) is possible, just as if they were different worlds, the first of which cannot have any influence on the second; and yet the second *is* to have an influence on the first, i.e., the concept of freedom is to actualize in the world of sense the purpose enjoined by its laws. Hence it must be possible to think of nature as being such that the lawfulness in its form will harmonize with at least the possibility of [achieving] the purposes that we are to achieve in nature according to the laws of freedom. So there must after all be a basis *uniting* the supersensible that underlies nature and the supersensible that the concept of freedom contains practically . . .

(*CPJ* Intro. §ii, 5:176)[1]

1. Introduction

When one takes up the question of "intuition" in an East/West context, the prospect arises that what is for one tradition ultimate can seem to another infantile. I am thinking here of a famous instance of this failure to connect that arose in the 1920s, when the great French poet, Romain Rolland, having steeped himself for some time in Asian thought, raised with Sigmund Freud the question of what he described as an "oceanic feeling"—a sense, a *feeling*, of participation in a vaster unity of nature or being.[2] Freud took up the question in two of his most famous works, *The Future of an Illusion* and *Civilization and its Discontents*, only to assert that while Rolland might have had such a feeling, he himself had not. He therefore inferred it must be an illusion, if not a delusion: a sign of improper development into adult autonomy, the persistence of infantile lack of boundaries (Freud 1989, 11–13). Freud was, to borrow a phrase from Max Weber, religiously unmusical. The question motivating my paper is whether in this matter he was being spiritually obtuse.

And my recourse is to a philosopher hardly known for any infantile self-indulgence, namely Immanuel Kant.[3]

The place to start, I think, is with Kant's conceptualization of intuition, and there are many ways to construe it. I set out from some contrasts that situate the notion for at least initial approximation and engagement. Intuition is not reason. It is attentiveness. It is, moreover, *embodied* attentiveness; that is, it is *felt*. So the question at issue in intuition, whether for East or for West, is *what we can feel*, and even more, what we can *grasp* through such feeling. In Western thought, intuition has either been confined with all philosophical rigor to *aisthesis*, the processes of sense perception, or left to wander beyond the pale as the stuff of fancy and imagination, of subjective inclinations and sheer guesswork. Often intuition is also quite condescendingly gendered, as a female predilection. When poets have written of the "ineffable", of the *je ne sais quoi*, philosophers from Plato onward have shaken their heads and invoked rigor and reason. I profess deep ambivalence regarding this "ancient quarrel of the philosophers and the poets" (Plato, *Republic*, 607b5–6). It seems to me that Shakespeare was not altogether beyond the mark in the rejoinder his Hamlet uttered to Horatio ("There are more things in heaven and earth, Horatio,/ Than are dreamt of in your philosophy"). That renders me far more attentive to the intuitions of Eastern thought. But, again, I want to harvest a rejoinder from a highly unlikely source: the rationalist philosophy of Immanuel Kant.[4]

The "sage of Königsberg" had definite ontological and theological preferences, which became increasingly explicit over the 1780s and took on exceptional prominence in the *Critique of the Power of Judgment* (1790). That tendency drew Kant close to the kinds of speculations in metaphysics which his Transcendental Dialectic of the *Critique of Pure Reason* (1781/1787) had proscribed. There are strong grounds for the view that Kant's thinking evolved beyond the posture of the first *Critique*, and that a historical appreciation of his philosophizing must take into account a tendency in his later thought to try to resolve certain dilemmas which haunted that first great effort.[5] The architectonic of his Critical philosophy came more and more to rest on its tangency with a "supersensible substrate" until, in the third *Critique*, that notion of a transcendent ground featured decisively in rounding his system to a close. The degree of determinacy to which his thinking edged in the discussion of the "supersensible"—both within human beings and as a ground without which the coherence of the sensible world would be impossible—suggests that his Critical shield had to it an element of transparency, beneath which a profoundly metaphysical Kantianism lay clear for any who wished to see it.[6]

To be sure, Kant rescued all this from "dialectical" dogmatism by repeated admonitions that such speculations, taken in a strict, cognitive-epistemological light, represented "mere thinking". Yet there can be no real doubt about the seriousness of his convictions on the score of the-ism or on the related issue of human moral freedom. A large part of his Critical philosophy can be interpreted as an effort to balance his recognition of the limitations of speculative rationalism or "dogmatic metaphysics" with his affirmation of the essential human interest in met-aphysics. In the *Prolegomena to any Future Metaphysics* he wrote that the demand for metaphysics would never disappear "since the interests of human reason in general are intimately interwoven with it" (*PFM* 4:257). In his Introduction to the first *Critique* he went even further (A3/B7): "Indeed, we prefer to run every risk of error rather than desist from such urgent inquiries, on the ground of their dubious character, or from disdain and indifference. These unavoidable problems set by pure reason itself are *God, freedom* and *immortality.*" These decisive *ideas of reason* had their ground in its *immanent interests*, what Kant termed the "*requirements (Bedürfnisse)* of reason" in the essay "*Was heisst: sich im Denken orientieren?*" (*WOT* 8:136). In the third *Critique* (*CPJ* §72, 5:390), Kant made explicit what he had intimated in that essay of 1786: "There is, then, indeed a certain presentiment of our reason or a hint, as it were, given us by nature, that, by means of this concept of final cause, we go beyond nature and could unite it to the highest point in a series of causes."[7] And again: ". . . the natural things that we find possible only as purposes supply the best proof of the contingency of the world-whole . . . " Indeed, Kant's personal metaphysical preferences come to clear expression immediately after this statement, when he writes (*CPJ* §75, 5:398–399):

> . . . to the common understanding and to the philosopher alike they are the only valid ground of proof for its dependence on and origin from a Being existing outside the world—a Being who must also be intelligent on account of its purposive form. Teleology, then, finds the consummation of its investigations only in theology.

2. The Transcendental Relevance of Feeling

For Kant there is a very important transcendental relation between feeling and reason. In addition to the pure rational self-appraisal entitled "apper-ception", there is another dimension of self-awareness upon which we can count for evidence of mental states and mental functions: the sphere of feeling and the reflective judgment about them. While transcendental self-consciousness ("apperception") attends principles of pure reason *a priori* in "transcendental reflection", reflective self-consciousness (*Lebensgefühl*) attends feelings as keys to its state (*Gemütszustand*), and thus undertakes aesthetic reflection (Makkreel 1990, 88–107, a reworking of Makkreel 1985). Feelings turn out to have great value in the subjective reckoning of consciousness regarding its states and its purposes (Schrader 1976).

Feeling can be the mark of the existence of a relation of reason. As a mark of existence, it is empirical. But it refers, subjectively to be sure, to an *a priori* rational principle. Reflection arrives at the same result that pure rational apperception achieves. This transcendental potential of feeling is most striking in the later *Critiques*. The relation of imagination and understanding is marked by the distinctive feeling of beauty. The relation of imagination and reason is marked by the distinctive feeling of the sublime. And the relation of will to reason is marked by the distinctive feeling of respect. Feeling is possible because man is sensible, but not all feelings are caused by sense. The peculiar feeling of respect is the crucial instance of this. As Kant writes in the second *Critique* (*CPrR* 5:76): "Sensuous feeling . . . is the condition of the particular feeling we call respect, but the cause that determines this feeling lies in the pure practical reason."

In the aesthetic experience, i.e., via feeling, reflection is pointed towards the ultimate meaning of subjectivity which no exertion of the understanding in determinant judgments could ever attain, an insight into the unity not only of reason, but of being, in the supersensible ground. Kant wrote (*CPJ* §59, 5:353):

> Hence, both on account of this inner possibility in the subject and of the external possibility of a nature that agrees with it, it finds itself to be referred to something within the subject as well as without him, something which is neither nature nor freedom, but which is yet connected with the supersensible ground of the latter. In this supersensible ground, therefore, the theoretical faculty is bound together in unity with the practical in a way which, though common, is yet unknown.[8]

The unity of reason in the supersensible substrate: this was the point to which all the antinomies "forced" us, in Kant's view.

In his *Critique of the Power of Judgment* Kant moved from a negative to a positive notion of the antinomy: from "discipline" (critique) to speculation (metaphysics).[9] The positive sense urges us to "think" the unity of reason as the ground of our own subjectivity (*CPJ* §57 Remark I, 5:341). In Remark II to §57 (344), Kant argued that the point of all the antinomies was to "force" us to recognize "an intelligible substrate (something supersensible of which the concept is only an idea and supplies no proper knowledge)." This he articulated with even more eloquence and importance in §57 itself (341):

> And thus here, as also in the *Critique of Practical Reason*, the antinomies force us against our will to look beyond the sensible and to seek in the supersensible the point of union for all our a priori faculties, because no other expedient is left to make our reason harmonious with itself.

That Kant used the word "force" in both contexts is striking. He suggested with it that the mind resisted the notion that there is a supersensible realm over and above the sensible one. Such resistance derived from two quarters: the natural impetus to regard the sensible world as the only world (common sense), and the sophisticated philosophical suspicion of warrant for such a transcendent world (skepticism). Kant claimed that the first resistance could be overcome once it was demonstrated that nothing fundamental to the actual needs of ordinary men was lost by such a distinction, but rather a great deal gained for their ultimate meaning.[10] Against the second resistance, Kant argued that reason, upon which skeptics rely for critical efficacy, could not itself remain coherent without resort to such a distinction.

Kant went on to argue that the judgment of taste ultimately entailed the assertion of the reality not only of "the subjective purposiveness of nature for the judgment", but also of a "determining ground", the "supersensible substrate of humanity". In a reflective judgment, "the mere rational concept of the supersensible, which underlies the object (and also the subject judging it), [is] regarded as an object of sense and thus phenomenal" (*CPJ* §57 Remark II, 5:340). That is clearly "dialectical" subreption in terms of the first *Critique*. As determining, rather than determined, the supersensible "which lies at the basis of all sensible intuition" (339) could never be a true object of cognition.[11] Kant now stressed, however, that it could be *thought*, and—more importantly for my current concern—it could also be *attended via reflection* (i.e., *felt* aesthetically). What understanding could not prove, reason could *think*, reflection could *feel*. What they both pointed to was the *supersensible*, conceived not only as the "substrate of phenomena" but also as a "subjective principle"—i.e., "the indefinite idea of the supersensible in us."

Kant articulated three aspects of this idea in his Remark II to §57. There was the idea of the supersensible in general, as the substrate of nature, which corresponded to the idea of the thing–in–itself or transcendental object in the "Transcendental Analytic", and also, perhaps, to the idea of nature as a whole in the "Transcendental Dialectic" of the first *Critique*. There was the principle of freedom and its conformity to moral law, or the idea of transcendental or noumenal freedom as developed in the second *Critique*. And finally there was the principle of subjective purposiveness of nature for our cognition, or the imputed "technic of nature" involved in the transcendental principle of logical reflective judgment, the theme of the third *Critique*. Hence each of the three *Critiques* explored an idea of the supersensible. The question implied by this articulation was whether there was some *unity* to the idea of the supersensible which was more than nominal, and which could then stand as a universal ground for both nature and freedom. Kant asserted in the first *Critique* that such unity was methodologically indispensable for the function of reason, but remained merely a formal or heuristic principle, hence objectively nominal. The new conception of antinomy seemed to raise again the question whether there were grounds for considering the supersensible ultimately real.

In his important essay, *What Does Orientation in Thinking Mean?*, Kant explored the rational problem of orientation in the utterly obscure realm of the supersensible, in which concepts had no experience to rely upon to establish objective validity. The quandary could only be resolved by a subjective recourse, the "feeling of reason's own requirement [*das Gefühl des der Vernunft eigenen Bedürfnisses*]" (*WOT* 8:136). He characterized this as "a subjective ground of discrimination of its own faculty of judgment [*einem subjektiven Unterscheidungsgrunde in der Bestimmung ihres eigenen Urtheilsvermögens*]". These two passages are of decisive importance in discerning the distance Kant had come in his stance on transcendental faculties and transcendental deductions since the first *Critique*. Kant now wrote of "judgment" and a "faculty of judgment", anticipating the vantage adopted in the third *Critique*. The anticipatory relation looms even more strongly when we examine the two crucial terms "feeling" (*Gefühl*) and "requirement" (*Bedürfnis*) which Kant introduced in the article.

Kant clarified his formulation in a footnote somewhat later in the essay in the following terms (*WOT* 8:139n): "Reason does not feel; it recognizes its shortcoming [*Mangel*] and incites [*wirkt*] via the *drive for knowledge* [*Erkenntnistrieb*] the feeling of a need [*Bedürfnis*—better rendered as *requirement*]." Kant went on in the footnote to compare this to his notion of the "moral feeling" in the crucial sense that the feeling is the consequence, not the instigator of reason. Reason engenders a feeling, but it does so for reasons of its own: that is why *Bedürfnis* must not be read too literally as itself a feeling or need. Reason has an immanent, transcendentally prior propensity to systematicity, to totality, to logical closure. This immanent principle regulates the entire function of the mind—feeling, understanding and reason itself. It is this which makes knowledge a "drive". It is this which spurs imagination to visions of coherence in the world and in the self. We find ourselves in the innermost reaches of Kantian phenomenology of subjective consciousness: the relation among the faculties. The connection of this relentless law of reason with the proceedings of the other faculties, I submit, forms the systemic foundation for Kant's third *Critique*.

In the absence of any objective reference, reason tries to find the next closest approximation. If it cannot form a determinate insight into its supersensible object, it tries to reason about the *relation* of this object to the objects of experience, and to bring this relation under logical rules. Hence *analogy* is the rational form of orientation in the realm of the supersensible. Analogy cannot establish existence; only sense intuition can provide this. On the other hand, there are representations in the mind to which no sense intuition corresponds. One such representation without correspondence in sense intuition must draw our attention (*WOT* 8:137): "the concept of an original being, as the highest intelligence and at the same time the highest good." This notion of an *ens realissimum* or *ens perfectissimum*, Kant argues, is a necessary idea for our rational process. We can only grasp particulars in their concreteness within the conspectus of something all-encompassing. But what Kant insists is that this idea is "regulative"—i.e., heuristic, not ontological. What sort of status does such an idea then have? It is cognitively indispensable and objectively indeterminate. For such a notion, Kant offered the apt term *Vernunftglaube*, rational belief.[12]

3. From *Lebensgefühl* to *Geistesgefühl*

How is self-consciousness, immediately via the feelings of internal state, possible? In §1 of the third *Critique* (*CPJ* §1, 5:204), Kant wrote of

> a quite separate faculty of distinction and judgment . . . comparing the given representation in the subject with the whole faculty of representations, of which the mind is conscious in the feeling of its state [*das ganze Vermögen der Vorstellungen . . . , dessen sich das Gemüt im Gefühl seines Zustandes bewußt wird*] . . . Here the representation is altogether referred to the subject and its feeling of life [*Lebensgefühl*], under the name of the feeling of pleasure or pain.

Kant argues that by reflection we can infer from a feeling to the rational structure which determines it. When the mind attends its "feeling" it attends its subjective processes. Pleasure and pain are not the final terms of that consciousness, but only the data, the matter for interpretation, for judgment. *Lebensgefühl* is grounded in Kant's theory of subjective self-consciousness under the rubric of reflection. Kant is loath to call this cognition, yet it is self-consciousness of the subject not as merely passive but as active. The mind has the power to respond to its appraisals of its states, and to alter them. And it has at least one criterion by which this data—pleasure or pain—is to be evaluated: the feeling of life.

What does *Lebensgefühl* point to, what does it mark by its data of pleasure? Life, for Kant, is the property of an intelligent will, the capacity to choose, to act (*MFNS* 4:544). More concretely, it is freedom of will in its actuality: *Willkür*, in Kant's precise sense. The *feeling* of life, therefore, is the awareness of our empirical freedom, our status as practically purposive in the world of sense. Pleasure, in that context, is either what fosters our consciousness of this freedom, or what accompanies and underscores its efficaciousness. In either case, pleasure is bound up with the *materiality* of man, his capacity to sense, his bodily existence. Kant referred to Epicurus in this connection (*CPJ* §29GR, 5:277–278):

> [A]s Epicurus maintained, all *gratification* or *grief* may ultimately be corporeal . . . because life without a feeling of bodily organs would be merely a consciousness of existence, without any feeling

of well-being or the reverse . . . For the mind is by itself alone life (the principle of life), and hindrances or furtherances must be sought outside it and yet in the man, consequently in union with his body.

Similarly, in §54 (§54, 331), Kant connects gratification with a "feeling of the furtherance of the whole life of the man, and consequently also of his bodily well-being, i.e., his health." Thus *Lebensgefühl*, like *Willkür*, is involved in that complex dualism of human experience as between pure reason and embodiment. It can be read simply physiologically, and then assuredly we are in the realm of empirical psychology, not only with *Lebensgefühl*, but also with *Willkür*. But it can also be read transcendentally, in accordance with the technical sense of Kant's term life. In the latter sense, both *Lebensgefühl* and *Willkür* point to a pure rational determination.

Kant believed that there is (or ought to be) a difference between "sensuous" and "intellectual" pleasure, not so much in terms of psychophysical response as in terms of rational significance (*APP* 7:230; see also *CPrR* 5:118). Sensuous pleasure is occasioned by the senses or the imagination; intellectual pleasure by concepts or ideas. For Kant not all feelings were homogeneous quantities (such that, opposed, they would cancel one another), for both in the *Anthropology* and in the third *Critique* he identified circumstances in which it makes sense to find pain justified and joy bitter. As Kant put it in the *Anthropology* (*APP* §64, 7:237), "a *higher* satisfaction or dissatisfaction with ourselves (namely, a moral one) [serves to] judge enjoyment and pain." In the third *Critique* Kant explained (*CPJ* §54, 5:331): "The satisfaction or dissatisfaction here depends on reason and is the same as *approbation* or *disapprobation*; but gratification and grief can only rest on the feeling or prospect of a possible . . . *well-being* or its opposite."

If all that mattered were quantitative gratification, Kant argued in §3 of the third *Critique* (*CPJ* §3, 5:206), "the impressions of sense which determine the inclination, fundamental propositions of reason which determine the will, mere reflective forms of intuition which determine the judgment, [would be] quite the same as regards the effect upon the feeling of pleasure." If our goal were simply happiness, we would not scruple over the source of pleasure, but simply maximize it; indeed, there would be no moral issue at all, only a question of efficiency. But obviously for Kant a moral issue profoundly colored his view of mere gratification. Thus Kant introduced a crucial complication: there were conflicting criteria for the evaluation of states of mind and for actions taken to alter them. He discriminated between the feeling of life (*Lebensgefühl*) and a feeling of autonomous spirituality (*Geistesgefühl*).[13]

In §54 Kant connected gratification with a "feeling of the furtherance of the whole life of the man, and consequently also of his bodily well-being, i.e. his health". But he then made what was for him the key distinction:

between gratification which was merely "animal [*animalische*], i.e., bodily sensation" (*CPJ* §54, 5:331), and that which was a "*spiritual* feeling [*geistigen Gefühl*] of respect for moral ideas" (§54, 335). While *Lebensgefühl* operated on the natural assumption that health and well-being were good, *Geistesgefühl* introduced the question of worth, of value in an ultimate sense, which threw just this natural assumption into suspicion. Humans must evaluate all in terms of their spiritual estate, their moral purpose. Consequently life itself, empirical freedom, and the capacity to enjoy it, must come under a sterner criterion. In that light (*APP* §66, 7:293), "life as such . . . has no intrinsic value at all . . . it has value only as regards the use to which we put it, the ends to which we direct it." "The value of life for us, if it is estimated by that *which we enjoy* . . . sinks to zero . . . There remains then nothing but the value which we ourselves give our life . . . " (*CPJ* §83, 5:434n).

The full significance of the tension between *Lebensgefühl* and *Geistesgefühl* lies in the recognition of our supersensible destiny. In the sphere of feeling, that recognition is called "respect". Kant writes of it as (*CPrR* 5:74) "a positive feeling not of empirical origin . . . which can be known a priori . . . a feeling produced by an intellectual cause." Since respect is for law, for the necessitation of duty (78), it is "a tribute we cannot refuse to pay to merit whether we will or not" "Respect is properly the representation of a worth that thwarts my self-love" (*GMM* 4:401n). The subject experiences a pain, but reflection upon this pain, i.e., judgment about the state of mind via *Lebensgefühl*, leads to the recognition of a relation to its own immanent rationality, and of the authority of that rationality in the subject, and this produces a feeling of "intellectual pleasure" or, more precisely, approbation. It is a feeling which refers to the supersensible. It is not *Lebensgefühl* but *Geistesgefühl*.

Kant argues that in the experience of respect for the law (*CPrR* 5:77), "the soul believes itself to be elevated in proportion as it sees the holy law as elevated over it and its frail nature [*die Seele sich in dem Maße zu erheben glaubt, als sie das heilige Gesetz über sich und ihre gebrechliche Natur erhaben sieht*]." The verb Kant used is in its nominal form the term for the sublime. Again, in describing duty, Kant writes (86) it is "something which elevates man above himself as part of the world of sense, something which connects him with an order of things which only the understanding can think [*was den Menschen über sich selbst (als einen Theil der Sinnenwelt) erhebt, was ihn an eine Ordnung der Dinge knüpft, die nur der Verstand denken kann*]". And Kant uses the nominal form of sublimity as well: "the sublimity of our own supersensuous existence . . . subjectively effects respect for their higher vocation in men" (89).

The parallellisms between the feeling of respect and the feeling of the sublime are obvious. The first parallel is in the psychology of the experience. Both respect and sublimity are "mixed feelings" or complex states of mind involving change. Thus the subjective experience of both respect and sublimity is a movement in mental states, a *Rührung*, a stirring of emotions.[14] Both start out with a feeling of displeasure or pain. But this feeling in the sensible subject is discerned to be caused by the subject's own rational determination, and this induces a new feeling of approbation, which is pleasant but in a different manner. The sublime and respect are not merely similar in subjective process, however. In both cases, the experience is no longer merely a feeling of life [*Lebensgefühl*]—i.e., the actual efficacy of the will. It is a feeling of spirit [*Geistesgefühl*]—i.e., the rational authority in the will.

Thus the connection is extremely close between the feeling of respect and the feeling of the sublime. Yet they can and should be distinguished.[15] Precisely what distinguishes the moral feeling from the sublime is that the moral feeling attends the subjective supersensible directly. The sublime, on the other hand, involves a "subreption", whereby it seeks the supersensible in an object of nature.[16] Sublime subreption at the same time reveals the *limitations* of the merely phenomenal presence of nature. Thus Kant defined the feeling of the sublime as "an object (of nature) *the representation of which determines the mind to think the unattainability of nature regarded as a presentation of ideas.*" The experience of seeking such an "objective correlative", such a "sensible illustration", in nature demonstrates the process of reason itself, "as the faculty expressing the independence of absolute totality [*als Vermögen der Independenz der absoluten Totalität*]." That is, what really gets presented is "the subjective purposiveness of our mind in the employment of the imagination for its supersensible destination" (*CPJ* §29GR, 5:268). Yet this subreption was fruitful precisely for the metaphysical openness it occasioned, namely to the harmony of nature with *Geist*, and hence the possible ontological unity of the supersensible ground of nature with the supersensible ground of man.[17] *Geistesgefühl* points to two key elements: first, to the tension between natural inclination and "supersensible destination" (i.e., *moral* self-consciousness); and, second, to the metaphysical potential in the idea of *Geist*, especially as Kant articulated it in §49.

4. The Sublime

Evidence for the supersensible destination of the subject, it must be reemphasized, can take the form of a *feeling*. Reflection can attain to the sense of the supersensible destination of the subject through the experience of the sublime. Not only did Kant limit reason to make room for faith, he also elevated aesthetics to the medium of the expression of reason's interests and insights in the supersensible realm. Through *metaphor*, Kant could permit the articulation of the metaphysical concerns which he prohibited within the sphere of cognition proper. There would be no recourse to metaphor unless there was an ineluctable incapacity of discursive reasoning to secure *metaphysics*. Aesthetic feelings therewith assume a central place in culture. They are the vehicle through which the supersensible gives token of its real presence; aesthetic feeling offers symbolic access to the ultimate. Imagination functions not only according to the (mechanically) natural laws of association but also "in accordance with principles which occupy a higher place in reason (laws, too, which are just as natural to us as those by which understanding comprehends empirical nature)." This connection with reason gives art, via genius (*CPJ* §49, 5:314), the power to work up "the material supplied to us by nature . . . into something different which surpasses nature." Its primary purpose is to *express* the supersensible.

Both aesthetic feelings, the beautiful and the sublime, in so far as they have their origins not in mere sense, but in reflection, are "purposive in reference to the moral feeling." That is, they contribute to the awareness and acceptance of the moral principle in complex human beings (animal as well as spiritual). As a result, Kant wrote (*CPJ* §29GR, 5:267), "the moral feeling . . . is . . . so far cognate to the aesthetical judgment and its formal conditions that it can serve to represent the conformity to law of action from duty as aesthetical, i.e., as sublime or even as beautiful, without losing purity." That is to say, one can *symbolize* moral considerations via the aesthetic feelings, because the feeling evoked by moral law in the subject is "cognate" with these feelings. The sublime shows a much closer fit than the beautiful; hence Kant's qualifier "even". Kant made the point about the closer proximity of the sublime to the moral feeling a bit later in the General Remark (271):

> The object of a pure and unconditioned intellectual satisfaction is the moral law in that might which it exercises in us over all mental motives *that precede it*. This might makes itself aesthetically known to us through sacrifices (which causing a feeling of deprivation, though on behalf of internal freedom, in return discloses in us an unfathomable depth of this supersensible faculty, with consequences extending beyond our ken) . . . Hence it follows that the intellectual, in itself purposive, (moral) good, aesthetically judged, must be presented as sublime rather than beautiful, so that it rather awakens the feeling of respect (which disdains charm) than that of love and familiar inclination . . .

As embodied rational agents, humans experience this supersensible not as play but as obligation. While this supersensible ground is essentially transcendental freedom, the nature of that freedom as experienced concretely is duty. Consequently, once again, there is a closer approximation between the experience of the sublime and the moral than between the experience of the beautiful and the moral (268–269):

> [In the] immediate pleasure in the beautiful of nature . . . freedom is . . . represented as in *play* rather than in law-directed *occupation* which is the genuine characteristic of human morality, in which

reason must exercise dominion over sensibility. But in aesthetical judgments upon the sublime this dominion is represented as exercised by the imagination, regarded as an instrument of reason.

Kant's whole theory of the sublime revolved around "subreption"—viewing an object of nature as though it were the origin of a feeling which in fact had its source in the self. As Kant put it (*CPJ* §23, 5:246), "We must seek a ground external to ourselves for the beautiful of nature, but seek it for the sublime merely in ourselves and in our attitude of thought, which introduces sublimity into the representation of nature." More concretely, Kant wrote (§27, 257): "the feeling of the sublime in nature is respect for our own destination, which, by a certain subreption, we attribute to an object of nature." Representations of the "formless", the "boundless", the infinite, arouse "a feeling of purposiveness lying *a priori* in the subject (perhaps the supersensible determination of the subject's mental powers)" (*CPJ*, FI §12, 20:250).[18]

The feeling of the sublime inadvertently reveals transcendental freedom and, hence, the supersensible ground of subjectivity. In short, what the sublime illuminates is *metaphysics* (*CPJ* §29GR, 5:274–275).[19] Kant confirmed this point by terming his consideration of the sublime a *Kritik des Geistesgefühls*, a critique of spiritual feeling (*CPJ*, FI §12, 20:250–251). It might appear that such "critique" should entail only a subjective reference, and consequently at most, a subjective metaphysics. But that the sublime *projects* this experience onto an object of intuition in fact demonstrates our capacity to *symbolize*—i.e., to take an actual object, however inadequate, as an illustration, a metaphor, for a supersensible idea. Kant formulated it as follows (*CPJ* §25, 5:250):

> But because there is in our imagination a striving toward infinite progress and in our reason a claim for absolute totality, regarded as a real idea, therefore this very inadequateness for that idea in our faculty for estimating the magnitude of things of sense excites in us the feeling of a supersensible faculty.[20]

That reason can think such absolute greatness as a whole, that it "renders it unavoidable to think the infinite (in the judgment of common reason) as *entirely given* (according to its totality)" establishes that this faculty is itself beyond sensibility—i.e., it "surpasses every standard of sensibility"—or is, itself, noumenal. As Kant puts it (§26, 254–255): "*The bare capability of thinking* this infinite without contradiction requires in the human mind a faculty itself supersensible."

The feeling which attends this discovery is "a different feeling, namely, that of the inner purposiveness in the constitution of the powers of the mind" (*CPJ*, FI §12, 20:250). Kant defines it precisely as "the feeling of our incapacity to attain to an idea *which is a law for us*" (*CPJ* §27,

5:257). The moral resonance of that definition is unmistakable. But reason imposes laws, "regulates" the faculties of the mind, and imposes "requirements" not simply in its practical form, but also in its theoretical form.[21] The experience of the sublime "arouses in us the feeling of this supersensible destination" inherent in our rationality, because reason sets down a law for imagination which it cannot fulfill (§27, 259): "Thus that very violence which is done to the subject through the imagination is judged as purposive *in reference to the whole determination* of the mind." Kant here presses a metaphysical interpretation of genius (§49, 314):

> By this means we get a sense of our freedom from the law of association (which attaches to the empirical employment of the imagination), with the result that the material can be borrowed by us from nature in accordance with that law, but be worked up by us into something else—namely, what surpasses nature.

Genius presents "aesthetic ideas"—i.e., imaginative representations through which ideas of reason find symbolic expression and therewith cultural articulation ("universal communicability") (§57 Remark I, 344).

The *First Introduction* to the *Critique of Judgment* stressed the parallel between "reflection" as a cognitive enterprise and "art". Kant wrote (*CPJ*, FI §5, 20:213–214): "The reflective judgment thus works . . . not schematically, but *technically*, not just mechanically, like a tool controlled by the understanding and the senses, but *artistically*, according to the universal but at the same time undefined principle of a purposive, systematic ordering of nature." Judgment "posits a priori the *technic of nature* as the principle of its reflection", but its grounding is not merely methodological; it is transcendent ("supersensible"). And just because this transcendent grounding is beyond the extent of understanding, i.e., beyond determinant judgment and its schematism, the only recourse available to it is *symbolical* expression.

In §49 of the *Critique of the Power of Judgment*, Kant gave a new definition of aesthetical ideas (*CPJ* §49, 5:313–314):

> by an aesthetical idea I understand that representation of the imagination which occasions much thought, without however any definite thought, i.e. any *concept*, being capable of being adequate to it; it consequently cannot be completely compassed and made intelligible by language. We easily see that it is the counterpart (pendant) of a *rational idea*, which conversely is a concept to which no *intuition* (or representation of the imagination) can be adequate.[22]

The aesthetic idea initiates a movement of the mind; it "occasions in itself more thought than can ever be comprehended in a definite concept and which consequently aesthetically enlarges the concept itself in an unbounded fashion." By exhausting understanding's capacity to determine the concept, the imagination presents a reflective judgment which cannot be converted into a determinant one, which cannot be explained definitively, i.e., cognitively, but only reflected upon at a higher level, and hence reason, the faculty of intellectual ideas, intervenes. Such an aesthetic idea "brings the faculty of intellectual ideas (the reason) into movement" (§49, 313–315); spirit [*Geist*], as the "animating principle of the mind . . . is no other than the faculty of presenting *aesthetical ideas*."

Kant called the aesthetic idea "the counterpart (pendant) of a *rational idea*" (*CPJ* §49, 5:314). "Counterpart", taken as "pendant", suggests that Kant does not wish to develop simply the formal symmetry of converse propositions but rather a substantive relation between the two. Counterpart as pendant signifies precisely an *expressive* potential—i.e., a symbolical relation between aesthetic ideas and rational ideas. Not only is the faculty of reason mobilized by the inadequacy of the understanding, it was in fact the origin of the very enterprise, and the aesthetic idea is its own symbolic project. If we wish to view this proceeding merely from the vantage of aesthetic *reception*, however, the point only turns out to be the same, for what we will be describing is simply the experience of the sublime (§57 Remark I, 344):

> It can only be that in the subject which is nature and cannot be brought under rules of concepts, i.e. the supersensible substrate of all his faculties (to which no concept of the understanding extends), and consequently that with respect to which it is the final purpose given by the intelligible [part] of our nature to harmonize all our cognitive faculties.

The dynamic requirement of reason as the supersensible unity of the subject now emerges as the real ground of genius, as the source of its quest for metaphorical expressions of its own immediate but indeterminate essence: *Geist*.

5. Kant's Speculations About *Geist*

All of Kant's metaphysical intimations culminated in the idea of *Geist*. His discussion of *Geist* in §49 opens up astonishing depths of Kantian metaphysics: " 'Spirit [*Geist*]' in an aesthetical sense, signifies the animating principle [*das belebende Princip*] in the mind" (*CPJ* §49, 5:313)[23] "Animating", "enlivening", "life"—a whole series of words which previously arose in connection with Kant's characterization of the "harmony of the faculties"—here achieve renewed prominence. Kant elaborates in the following terms (§49, 313): "But that whereby this principle animates the soul—the material which it employs for that purpose—is that which sets the mental powers into a swing that is purposive, i.e., into a play which is self-maintaining and which strengthens those powers for such activity." In his criticism of rational psychology in the first *Critique*, Kant had intimated (negatively) the potential in the notion. He observed (A379–380): "Neither the transcendental object which underlies outer appearances nor that which underlies inner intuition, is in itself either matter or a thinking being, but a ground (to us unknown) of the appearances which supply to us the empirical concept of the former as well as of the latter mode of existence." The inaccessibility of the transcendental subject and the universality of its impositions upon the empirical ego's experience of inner sense are such that it can in no way be established whether it is something different in each individual or something which in fact encompasses all such empirical individuals—indeed, all reality, i.e., not merely the transcendental subject but the transcendental object as well—within the totality of its own noumenal nature. Earlier, he stated (A360): "If . . . we compare the thinking 'I' not with matter but with the intelligible that lies at the basis of the outer appearance which we call matter, we have no knowledge whatsoever of the intelligible, and therefore are in no position to say that the soul is in any inward respect different from it." Thus the entertainment of such speculations as the ground for a subjective idealism could not preclude their extension to an even vaster objective idealism.[24]

By the time of the third *Critique*, Kant had come to be "forced" to make explicit the notion of *Geist* as the noumenal ground or substrate of human freedom. The whole thrust of his reformulation of the antinomy in the Dialectic of Aesthetic Judgment was to "force" us to consider the "supersensible substrate" of human nature and reason as a "unity" (*CPJ* §57, 5:341). But this line of speculation carried beyond a subjective to an objective idealism. In §ii of the Introduction, Kant wrote (§ii, 176): "there must be a ground of the *unity* of the supersensible, which lies at the basis of nature, with that which the concept of freedom practically contains. . . . " In Remark II to §57, Kant made the same metaphysical argument, and he took it up again in the culminating section of that whole Dialectic, §59, in the following terms (353):

> Hence, both on account of this inner possibility in the subject and of the external possibility of a nature that agrees with it, it finds itself to be referred to something within the subject as well as without him, something which is neither nature nor freedom, but which yet is connected with the supersensible ground of the latter. In this supersensible ground, therefore, the theoretical faculty is bound together in unity with the practical in a way which, though common, is yet unknown.

Despite his epistemological scruples, Kant insisted on the legitimacy of rational belief in this unity of the supersensible (§91, 474):

> We have therefore in us a principle capable of determining the idea of the supersensible within us, and thus also of the supersensible without us, for knowledge, although only in a practical point of view . . . Consequently the concept of freedom (as fundamental concept of all unconditioned practical laws) can extend reason beyond those bounds within which every natural (theoretical) concept must remain hopelessly limited.

In this context it would appear that Kant's notion of practical reason did entail a "knowledge" which extended reason beyond the theoretical parameters of "understanding". This was a kind of knowledge which had a higher validity than mere "belief", and which also had clearly *metaphysical* implications.

The richest insight into the metaphysical potential in Kant's concept of *Geist* is to be found in his *Reflections* of the late 1770s.[25] These private speculations, which proved more daring than his published writings, set out from the definition of *Geist* which Kant would enunciate in §49 of the third *Critique*—namely, the "animating principle of the mind" (5:313). He formulated this definition already in 1771 (perhaps earlier) in R740 (15:326). Yet in the *Reflections* Kant was more candid about the latent metaphysical potential of the notion. In R782 (1772–1775), Kant wrote of the *geistige Gefühl* as a sense of "participation in an ideal whole", and he identified this ideal whole with the "fundamental idea of reason" (15:342). In R824 (1776–1778), he wrote: "the feeling of spiritual life [*das Gefühl des geistigen Lebens*] has to do with understanding and freedom, for man has within himself the bases of knowledge and well-being" (15:367). For Kant, *Geist* was this "secret spring of life". It was not subject to volition, but welled up spontaneously, "from nature". That was what it meant to say that what arises from spirit is "original" [*ursprünglich*].[26] *Geist*, Kant wrote in R844 (1776–1778), was the "inner principle of activity". It occasioned the "sustained exertion of the mind" (15:375).

In some linked reflections from the late 1770s, Kant developed the idea in its most remarkable form. Again in R844 (1776–1778), Kant writes (15:375):

> In us there are delightful and compelling, but also enlivening causes of mental power; this last principle has its own quite unique nature and laws. Nothing is enlivened but a certain universality which the mind fastens upon prior to all particulars, and from which it fashions its viewpoint and its products. That is why genius resides in this capacity to create the universal and the ideal.

Geist is the "generative ground [*Erzeugungsgrund*] of ideas." The "expression of the idea through manifold and unified sensibility is proof of spirit." It is the source of "system" as contrasted with mere aggregation. It is no particular talent, but the "animating principle of all talents" (R933 [1776–1778], 15:414). *Geist* is the active principle; "soul" is what gets animated. *Geist* is the source of all animation, and can be derived from nothing prior (R934 [1776–1778], 15:415). This line of thought brought Kant to his ultimate consideration regarding the concept (R938 [1776–1778], 15:416):

> Because spirit involves the universal, it is so to speak *divinae particula aurae* [a particular emanation of the divine] and it is created out of the universal spirit. That is why spirit has no specific properties; rather, according to the different talents and sensibilities it affects, it animates in varying ways, and, because these are so manifold, every spirit has something unique. One ought to say not that it belongs to the genius. It is the unity of the world soul.

If *Geist* means "world soul", Kant's trajectory of thought has carried him very far towards his idealist successors. With the third *Critique*, Kant signaled to the succeeding generation of German idealism and Romanticism the vision they were to try to realize. Kantianism itself made idealism inevitable. The metaphysical potential of the idealist concept of *Geist* was already fully latent in the repressed speculations of Immanuel Kant, and it filtered through, above all in the third *Critique*, to stimulate his successors to its outright articulation. Reading the third *Critique* created an urgent and specific philosophical problem for Kant's successors. What Kant believed, and the vivid formulation of those beliefs in his works, seemed to his followers to cry out for a more wholehearted articulation and defense. What Kant could intimate as rational belief, they sought to articulate as metaphysical truth. What Kant had locked away in an inaccessible transcendence, they retrieved as a transfiguring immanence. His successors wished to reestablish *Geist* at the center of philosophy as reason's own reality. They came to believe that the involuntary spontaneity Kant associated with the active, transcendental subject as well as the essential, ontological ground of human nature, should be understood as *Geist*. That is, they identified generative ("spontaneous") and systemic reason with the metaphysical ground of being.

That is a very complicated story, and one worth setting in an East/West context. But I return to my original thesis. I conclude: Immanuel Kant, via his notions of the sublime, the supersensible substrate, and spirit (*Geist*), offered a Western affirmation of that "oceanic feeling" Rolland would later derive from Eastern thought. Kant reproved Freud long before the latter even mustered his condescension.

Notes

1. Quotations from *CPJ* are from the translation by J.H. Bernard (Kant 1790b).
2. Rolland wrote of a "religious sensation which is . . . the simple and direct fact of this feeling of the eternal (which may well not be eternal, but simply without perceptible boundaries, as if oceanic)." (Letter to Sigmund Freud, December 5, 1927, in Rolland and Freud 1993, 303–304).
3. ([This note and subsequent ones in parentheses represent responses to the generous and perceptive comments of Robert Clewis; I have left the original text largely unchanged in order for his comments to have their full weight.] I am clearly *using* Kant, not necessarily arguing that just this was his primary concern.)
4. (Kant's primary concern was to entrench human moral freedom and responsibility, but he situated that in epistemological and metaphysical frames.)
5. (I part company firmly with those who see *no* fundamental changes in Kant's postures after 1781.)
6. (In this, I deliberately open the possibility that "an idealist, metaphysical story of *Geist* as intimating the supersensibly real" [Clewis] *can* be construed in Kant's works. The German idealists may have been *wrong*, but they were not completely prevaricating.)
7. (If we "go beyond nature" to the "highest point in a series of causes", I submit, we are in metaphysical, not simply practical terrain. Clewis is correct that Kant's prime concern was with the latter, but just for that sake, he *needed* the former. That is the upshot of Kant's *Orientation* essay, for example. That is why he *needed* to "limit reason to make room for faith".)
8. (I wish to retrieve the repeated Kantian gestures to a *more than* subjective-practical character in the supersensible. That may not have been *his* most important concern, but it is there, and it serves *my* purpose, here. I certainly acknowledge that I neglect, accordingly, just that practical concern that Clewis rightly insists was one of the keys to Kant's "dynamic" sublime and that has led him, in his fine monograph (Clewis 2009), to conceive, on Kant's behalf, the idea of a "moral sublime".)
9. On the idea of "discipline" as the defense against dogmatists (atheistic and otherwise) see A738–794/B706–822. On the positive aspect of the antinomy, see *CPJ* §57 Remark II (5:345).
10. This argument for transcendental idealism was made especially in the Preface to the B version of the first *Critique*, then reiterated in the third.
11. This is parallel to the argument regarding transcendental apperception in the Paralogisms of the first *Critique*.
12. The term *Vernunftglaube* was articulated in the *Kanon* of the first *Critique*, A820–830/B848–858.
13. (Clewis has chided me [gently] to stick to Kant's own express words and meanings. But *Geistesgefühl* is Kant's term, and I am simply taking seriously *his* discrimination.)
14. (Clewis terms this a "clog–and–release" process. The notion of a stirring feeling, a "mixed pleasure", was central to the whole tradition of discourse of the sublime, starting with Longinus. See Doran 2015.)
15. Kant writes in *CPrR* (5:77) that respect "applies to persons only, never to things." A bit later (82n) he clarifies himself still further: "respect can never have other than a moral ground." This accords with the argument he made in the *Groundwork* (GMM 4:401n, 400): "All respect for a person is properly only respect for the law . . . of which the person provides an example." Thus Kant comes back to his basic assertion: "only the law itself can be an object of respect." In others and in oneself, what causes respect is the law.

Subjectively it is duty. Objectively it is the moral law and, behind it, the autonomy of the will in rational freedom.

16. What Kant is referring to by admiration and astonishment for such things as "lofty mountains, the magnitude, number, and distance of the heavenly bodies, the strength and swiftness of many animals, etc." (*CPrR* 5:77) is what is called the "natural sublime". Kant also discusses admiration, astonishment, awe and their distinctions in *Anthropologie*. In the third *Critique* these distinctions are revived in connection with the sublime. That awe Kant evoked in the magnificent apostrophe which ended the second *Critique*: "Two things fill the mind with ever new and increasing admiration and awe . . . the starry heavens above me and the moral law within me . . ." (162).

17. (This is the essential point I am trying to harvest: a prospect raised by Kant of relevance to the contest of East and West over intuition and the "oceanic feeling".)

18. The tentativeness of the term "perhaps" and the parenthetical formulation of the whole idea suggest the diffidence with which, at the point of composing the *First Introduction* to CPJ, Kant still regarded discussion of the supersensible. That tentativeness vanished in the full "ethical turn" of late 1789 and early 1790.

19. (That is, it invites or incites considerations about the ultimate interior of the subject and the ultimate exterior of its context, and even the prospect that these may be indisseverably united.)

20. The phrase "striving toward infinite progress" is redolent with the metaphysics of Fichte and the sensibility of Romanticism.

21. (Therefore I agree with Professor Clewis and see this legislation as ubiquitous for Kant.)

22. (Here, my reading, while constructive, seeks a coherence in Kant's arguments across the corpus of the Critique of Aesthetic Judgment. I do not think that anything that comes *after* the discussion of the sublime can be construed to ignore it. Nor does it seem to me that we need insist that all that came after that discussion should already have been explicitly articulated in the discussion of the sublime. Instead, we need to seek a more comprehensive sense of the development of the argument, and the earlier articulation of the sublime dramatically inflects the idea of the aesthetic, especially regarding genius and art.)

23. (Here Clewis raises what is for me the most important of his reservations: namely, that I am misconstruing what Kant meant by *Geist*. There are anticipations of his concern in a translator's note in Pluhar's rendition of the *Critique of Judgment* (Kant 1790a, 205n): "The *Geist* here [§54] is obviously not the 'spirit in an aesthetic sense,' the 'animating principle in the mind,' our 'ability to exhibit *aesthetic ideas*' (§49, Ak. 313). Since the qualification, 'in an aesthetic sense,' is not repeated anywhere as Kant goes on to discuss *that* kind of *Geist*, it would be misleading if 'spirit' were used again to render '*Geist*' in a *non* aesthetic sense . . . 'Intellect' seems closest to what Kant has in mind here, in the broad sense in which Kant has been using the term '*intellektuell*' all along in this work." My response to both reservations is the same. We must read the discussion of *Geist* against the entire backdrop of Kant's—and his time's—usage. And we must be sensitive to the notion that in this text Kant is trying to use "an aesthetic sense" precisely to access the ultimate nature of human subjectivity and of metaphysical grounding.)

24. (Again, it is the *possibility* for such a rational conception that I wish to harvest from Kant.)

25. (Here, Clewis challenges me to provide some methodological justification for drawing upon unpublished notes composed decades earlier to illuminate

158 John H. Zammito

what Kant wrote in 1790. First, one of the crucial methodological principles that informs Kant studies of our times is that *all* of Kant's writings should play a part in our historical–philosophical reconstructions. Second, another emergent principle is that many of the ideas articulated in the *Critique of Judgment* had been developed long before, even in the early, "pre-Critical" period. Third, and for me decisive, the formulations in the third *Critique* take up and use precisely formulations in those earlier reflections and the latter illuminate in ways that are striking the metaphysical possibilities that Kant is contemplating in 1790, even if he is not prepared to go so dogmatically far in asserting the cognitive certainty we may attain regarding them, which is precisely why I believe he inserted the qualifying phrase "in an aesthetic sense".)

26. The insistent wordplay with "spring" is certainly not inadvertent. See Kant's *Reflexion* #831 from 1776–1778 (15:371).

References

Clewis, Robert (2009). *The Kantian Sublime and the Revelation of Freedom.* Cambridge: Cambridge University Press.

Doran, Robert (2015). *The Theory of the Sublime from Longinus to Kant.* Cambridge: Cambridge University Press.

Freud, Sigmund (1989). *Civilization and Its Discontents.* New York: W.W. Norton and Company, Inc.

Kant, Immanuel (1790a). Trans. W. Pluhar, *Critique of Judgment.* Indianapolis and Cambridge: Hackett Publishing Company, 1987.

——— (1790b). Trans. J. H. Bernard, *Critique of Judgment.* New York and London: Haffner Publishing, 1968.

Makkreel, Rudolf (1985). The Feeling of Life: Some Kantian Sources of Life-Philosophy. In: *Dilthey–Jahrbuch für Philosophie und Geschichte der Geisteswissenschaften* 3, 83–104.

——— (1990). *Imagination and Interpretation in Kant.* Chicago and London: University of Chicago Press.

Rolland, Romain and Sigmund Freud (1993). *Sigmund Freud et Romain Rolland: Correspondance 1923–1936.* Paris: University Presses of France (PUF).

Schrader, G. (1976). The Status of Feeling in Kant's Philosophy. In: *Proceedings of the Ottawa Congress on Kant, 1974.* Ottawa: University of Ottawa Press, 143–164.

Appendix to Chapter 11
Spirit and Sublimity, Pleasure and Freedom

Robert R. Clewis

1. "Latent" German Idealism?

I begin my comments on Professor Zammito's intriguing chapter where he began and ended—that is to say, with Sigmund Freud. There is a certain irony, intended or not, in Zammito's using Freudian language (latency, repression) to defend Kant against Freud's implicit criticism of an intuition of the supersensible—that is, a feeling of oneness with the whole. At the end of *The Future of an Illusion* and in *Civilization and Its Discontents*, Freud had touched on the sublime (though without using that word). He was critical of, or at least confessed an inability to experience, what Rolland had called a feeling of the eternal that is "as it were oceanic" (e.g., Freud 1989, 723), a sensation of oneness with the universe or the unbounded. Freud rejects Rolland's claim that this feeling could explain the origin of religion and instead offers his own psychological explanation of the feeling: the oceanic feeling, if present, is a remnant of an early stage in the ego's development. Zammito writes: "The metaphysical potential of the idealist concept of *Geist* was already fully latent in the repressed speculations of Immanuel Kant, and it filtered through . . . to stimulate his successors to its outright articulation" (p. 155, above; cf. Zammito, 305).[1] I doubt Zammito intended this characterization to be ironic, but I nevertheless find irony in the claim that the potential of the concept of *Geist* would be "latent", and that Kant would have "repressed" speculations.

Professor Zammito wishes to read this oceanic feeling as a kind of the sublime, which seems just fine; indeed, there seems precedent for that in the wider aesthetic tradition. But the "oceanic feeling" does not strike me as resonating with Kant's theory. To me it sounds much more Nietzschean or (even better) Schopenhauerian—not necessarily *anti*-Kantian, but at least post-Kantian or non-Kantian. Intuitions of the ultimate, of oneness with the universe, and of the unity of all beings: this kind of sublime is reminiscent of Nietzsche (*The Birth of Tragedy*) and Schopenhauer (*World as Will and Representation*), who in turn was heavily influenced by classical Indian philosophy. But, in all of this metaphysics, reflected in the title of Zammito's chapter, where did the practical go?

2. Transition From Nature to Freedom

In other words, what happened to the transition from the way of thinking about nature, to that of freedom, as expressed in the following key passage from *CPJ* (Introduction §ii 5:175f), quoted (in a different translation) by Zammito (p. 139, above; cf. Zammito 1992, 265f)?

> Now although there is an incalculable gulf fixed between the domain of the concept of nature, as the sensible, and the domain of the concept of freedom, as the supersensible, so that from the former to the latter (thus by means of the theoretical use of reason) no transition is possible, just as if there were so many different worlds, the first of which can have no influence on the second: yet the latter should have an influence on the former, namely the concept of freedom should make the end that is imposed by its laws real in the sensible world.

I agree that this passage is crucial: explaining the "transition" is an excellent way to understand the place of the sublime in Kant's project. However, I would focus on the practical implications of this passage more than on the metaphysical. The place of the sublime in Kant's philosophical project is somewhere in the middle, functioning as a kind of bridge between the origin (i.e., nature) and goal (i.e., morality) (Clewis 2015b, 168).

If Kant denies that we can have immediate epistemic access to (a direct intuition of) freedom or our supersensible selves, how can the experience of the sublime make the will palpable (*fühlbar*)? How are we best to understand Kant's claims that: (1) the sublime is not technically an intuition or cognition of freedom, yet (2) the sublime makes palpable the will, in that one feels "raised" or "elevated" above nature? Kant holds that one cannot explain how it is possible that we are free, nor understand how freedom can be a causal power. The sublime does not give rise to or offer a theoretical cognition or proof that human beings are free. If it is a "recognition" of the powers of reason, it is only a sensible intimation, a feeling (i.e., a feeling of *spirit*) rather than a cognition or intuition. Even if it can be used in the service of morality, the feeling remains only a sensory indication or hint.

At the same time, Kant claims that the concept of the sublime in nature can "make palpable in ourselves a purposiveness that is entirely independent of nature" (*CPJ* 5:246)—that is, it shows us the will, determined by a moral vocation or destiny (*Bestimmung*). In the experience of the (dynamical) sublime, the imagination presents those cases in which "the mind can make palpable to itself the sublimity of its own vocation even over nature" (262). It is as if by failing to provide an *intuition* of freedom, the imagination initiates and is part of a stirring experience that provides a sensible hint or feeling of freedom (but still only a hint).

3. Spirit and Sublimity

When it comes to the connection between aesthetic and rational ideas, genius, *Geist* (spirit), and the sublime (Zammito 1992, 283–289), I wonder whether Kant's texts actually say what Zammito implies they do. I thus raise some hermeneutic–methodological questions. The quote from Kant's Remark I to §57 (*CPJ* 5:344), which Zammito quotes in the context of discussing the sublime, in fact concerns the *beautiful*: "it is not a rule or precept but only that which is merely nature in the subject, i.e., the supersensible substratum of all our faculties (to which no concept of the understanding attains)". (The translation that Zammito uses in his chapter [p. 152] begins, "It can only be . . .".) In §57, which appears well beyond the Analytic of the Sublime (§§23–29), Kant is commenting on his resolution of the antinomy of *taste*.

Now, some interpreters, including Zammito, attempt to connect genius, as the capacity for the expression of inexponible, unbounded, even formless, *aesthetic* ideas, and the sublime, as involving the intuitive response to rational ideas. This connection is grounded on the fact that in the sublime, the rational idea exceeds any attempt by perception or imagination to represent, present, or imagine it in intuition. However, such readings gloss over a crucial difference between the two kinds of ideas. With aesthetic ideas, there is *too much* imaginative–sensory–perceptive material—too much intuition. But with ideas of reason, there is not enough intuition—i.e., reason gives a command that the imagination in principle cannot fulfill. In the Analytic of the Sublime, Kant simply does not explain the sublime in terms of aesthetic ideas or genius. More textual support and commentary would be helpful in order to validate such connections between *Geist* and sublimity. In addition, I worry that, on Zammito's reading, the emotional–imaginative experience and *aesthetic* feeling of the sublime will be overlooked or overcome in an idealist, metaphysical story of *Geist* as intimating the supersensibly real.

This brings me to another methodological point. Zammito cites (among others from the 1770s) *R938*, which dates from circa 1776 (see also Zammito 1992, 303f). The marginal note's unpublished status and date are significant. The text was an unpublished note and was written about fourteen years before the publication of the third *Critique* in 1790, so I invite Zammito to comment on his methodology in using this marginal note. While I do not object to the use of literary remains, correspondence, and student lecture notes (see Clewis 2015a), it would be useful to hear Zammitto's take on this methodological issue.

4. Sources of Pleasure in the Sublime

What is the source of the pleasure in the sublime? The answer usually emphasized in the scholarly literature is that the pleasure derives from a person's recognition of their powers of reason. (Zammito, for instance, mentions the subject's "recognition of a relation to its own immanent rationality" [p. 147].) To supplement this, however, I would like to underline two other sources mentioned by Kant: the expansion of imagination (as it tries in vain to provide an intuition of the unconditioned), and the release of the vital forces.

On the first point, Kant is not alone. Many other modern authors, such as Joseph Priestley, David Hume, Henry Home, Anna Aikin, Helen Maria Williams, and William Wordsworth, offer a version of the claim that a stretching of the mind or of imagination is one of the sources of pleasure in the sublime.[2] According to John Baillie, when an object is vast yet uniform, "there is to the imagination no limits of its vastness, and the mind runs out into infinity, continually creating as it were from the pattern" (quoted in Kirwan 2005, 9). William Duff claims that a poet who contemplates "these awful and magnificent scenes in his musing mind" thereby "labours to express in his compositions the ideas which dilate and swell his Imagination" (Ashfield and de Bolla 1996, 174–175). And Thomas Reid holds that "it requires a stretch of imagination to grasp them ['vast objects'] in our minds" (Ashfield and de Bolla 1996, 178–179). Like Kant, these authors propose that the stretching of the imagination induces a feeling of pleasure.

This theory has not gone unnoticed by twentieth-century Kant commentators such as Rudolf Makkreel (1990) and Jean-François Lyotard (1994). Lyotard, for instance, observes that, according to Kant's account, the striving of the imagination leads to a pleasant exhilaration. Reason commands the imagination to seek the unconditioned (like the principle of reason that Grier 2001 calls P_1), and the imagination responds by trying to keep up, to take it all in and comprehend it in a single moment or glance (*Augenblick*). The imagination is expanded in the process.[3]

A second source of pleasure is the release of the vital sources. Here Kant says that the sublime contains a "negative pleasure". The feeling of the sublime (*CPJ* 5:245, emphasis added)

is a pleasure that arises only indirectly, being generated, namely, *by the feeling of a momentary inhibition of the vital powers and the immediately following and all the more powerful outpouring of them*; hence as an emotion it seems to be not play but something serious in the activity of the imagination. Hence . . . since the mind is not merely attracted by the object, but is also always reciprocally repelled by it, the satisfaction in the sublime does not so much contain positive pleasure as it does admiration or respect, i.e., it deserves to be called negative pleasure.

The italicized phrase in this quote reveals what I call Kant's "clog–and–release" view. That view is expressed in §14, in which Kant claims that the sublime could be combined with a "sensation in which agreeableness is produced only by means of a momentary inhibition followed by a stronger outpouring of the vital force" (226).[4] I like to interpret this as a feeling of the promotion of life, even if Kant does not put it that way.[5]

As Zammito notes, the sublime is a *Geistesgefühl*. The sublime is negative pleasure in part because it is a kind of respect, which, generically, is a "feeling of the inadequacy" of our capacity for the attainment of a rational "idea" that is a "law" for us (257). (Here I have perhaps a small quibble with Zammito's reading: the "law" in question that generates respect need not be read as the *moral* law, but can be law in general.)

On page 147 (cf. Zammito 1992, 299), Zammito seems to read the life-feeling as *leading to* the intellectual or spiritual feeling (*Geistesgefühl*):

> The subject experiences a pain, but reflection upon this pain, i.e., judgment about the state of mind via *Lebensgefühl*, leads to the recognition of a relation to its own immanent rationality, and of the authority of that rationality in the subject, and this produces a feeling of "intellectual pleasure" or, more precisely, approbation. It is a feeling which refers to the supersensible. It is not *Lebensgefühl* but *Geistesgefühl*.

If forced to find a relation between the spiritual/intellectual feeling and the life feeling, I would prefer to say that the spiritual feeling *enables* (or makes possible) the clog–and–release of the vital forces. I would prefer to say not so much that the *Lebensgefühl* leads to the *Geistesgefühl*, as that the two kinds of reflection operate on different, yet compatible, levels—the physiological–psychological and the rational–intellectual—in explaining the pleasures in the sublime.[6]

5. Freedom(s) and the Sublime

Finally, Zammito writes: "As embodied rational agents, humans experience this supersensible not as play but as obligation. While this supersensible ground is essentially transcendental freedom, the nature of that freedom as experienced concretely is duty" (p. 149, above; cf. Zammito 1992, 293). He adds: "The feeling of the sublime inadvertently reveals transcendental freedom, and hence the supersensible ground of subjectivity. In short, what the sublime illuminates is *metaphysics*" (p. 150, above; cf. Zammito 1992, 280, citing *CPJ* §29GR). I would have handled this slightly differently. In my view, *three* distinct senses of freedom (transcendental, negative practical freedom, and positive practical freedom) are reflected in three distinct types of the sublime (mathematical, dynamical, and moral). I take this to be a claim about the *conceptual* relations found in Kant's writings, that is, in his corpus broadly construed. How they map onto the real world is another matter.

A brief explanation of the "moral sublime" is called for, since I have created or constructed this aesthetic type on Kant's behalf—and I fully recognize that it does not appear in the third *Critique* as a kind of the sublime. First, one should not be misled by the word "moral" in the phrase. What is being designated is the *aesthetic* appreciator's response to the moral law: the disinterested person does not engage the will or attempt to obey the moral law, but takes an aesthetic stance toward the moral law, as fittingly demonstrated in the second *Critique*'s renowned encomium to duty ("Duty! Sublime and might name" [*CPrR* 5:86]) and in the book's Conclusion (where "the moral law within me" evokes admiration and reverence [161]). The observer or spectator, not the agent, views the moral law or duty with aesthetic pleasure and disinterest. Of course, according to Kant, moral agents are "disinterested" too, but in another sense: they are impartial and do not make exceptions of themselves. Indeed, it is precisely for such reasons that we should identify at least five distinct senses of disinterestedness and interest (Clewis 2009, 146–168).

How then, briefly, do I characterize Kant's view of the relation between sublimity and freedom? First, the mathematical sublime can be said to disclose transcendental freedom, as the idea of infinity stops the time series or freezes the "time-condition" in the progression of the imagination (Clewis 2009, 17). The faculty of reason commands the imagination to attempt to comprehend infinity, and such violence results in the (merely subjective) blocking of the progression through time required by a causal series. Second, the dynamical sublime reveals practical freedom in the *negative* sense (negative practical freedom)—that is, freedom from impulses, desires, and inclinations. The sublimity of my practical freedom becomes palpable; I am in a position to see (if I so reflect) the merely relative value of such goods as health and wealth and to acknowledge the absolute value of (negative practical) freedom, which, as we know, for Kant is then determined by the moral law. The moral law (or some representation having moral content) more evidently emerges in the third and final type. Here, the moral sublime, when or if there is such a partly intellectual but still aesthetic experience in response to the moral law, duty, or a representation having moral content, discloses *positive* practical freedom—that is, moral autonomy. This sensory disclosure is analogous to how the moral law functions as the *ratio cognoscendi* of freedom (*CPrR* 5:5n)—that is, it is yet another way we can become aware of our freedom, even if there is no claim to knowledge or cognition of it via intuition.[7]

Notes

1. In the following, I will cite any relevant or parallel discussions found in Zammito 1992.
2. For an anthology of representative texts, see Clewis 2018.

3. Kant employs faculty language that is sometimes interpreted as giving empirical–psychological descriptions, but he might instead be more fruitfully read as giving a transcendental or regressive analysis of the experience.
4. Kant also offers an "oscillation" account, according to which the feeling wavers between repulsion and attraction.
5. Pleasure is the feeling that expresses a life-promoting condition, while displeasure corresponds to life's hindrance. In my view, Kant should have acknowledged that the release of vital forces is experienced as a "promotion of life".
6. In the original version of my comments (hence the basis for Zammito's response in his note 13), I had asked: "What is the basis or ground of the [Zammito's] appeal to the concept of a *Geistesgefühl*? . . . What reasons can be given for following Kant here?" But I now see (in response to the first question) that not only was Zammito taking up and employing Kant's terminology, but also (in response to the second) that a philosophical defense of conceiving of the sublime as an intellectual feeling (*Geistesgefühl*) would have been beyond the scope of his chapter.
7. I am grateful to have been granted the opportunity to comment on Professor Zammito's chapter.

References

Ashfield, Andrew and Peter de Bolla (1996). *The Sublime: A Reader in British Eighteenth-Century Aesthetic Theory.* Cambridge: Cambridge University Press.

Clewis, Robert R. (2009). *The Kantian Sublime and the Revelation of Freedom.* Cambridge: Cambridge University Press.

—— (2015a). *Reading Kant's Lectures.* Berlin: Walter de Gruyter.

—— (2015b). The Place of the Sublime in Kant's Project. In: *Studi kantiani* 28, 149–168.

—— (2018). *The Sublime Reader.* London: Bloomsbury.

Freud, Sigmund (1989). Civilization and Its Discontents. In: P. Gay (ed.), *The Freud Reader.* New York: W.W. Norton and Company, Inc., 722–727.

Grier, Michelle (2001). *Kant's Doctrine of Transcendental Illusion.* Cambridge: Cambridge University Press.

Kirwan, James (2005). *Sublimity.* New York and London: Routledge.

Lyotard, Jean-François (1994). Trans. E. Rottenberg, *Lessons on the Analytic of the Sublime: (Kant's "Critique of Judgment," sections 23–29).* Stanford: Stanford University Press.

Makkreel, Rudolf (1990). *Imagination and Interpretation in Kant.* Chicago: Chicago University Press.

Zammito, John H. (1992). *The Genesis of Kant's Critique of Judgment.* Chicago: University of Chicago Press.

12 Kant's Impure Sublime
Intuition, Comprehension, and *Darstellung*

Bart Vandenabeele

1. Introduction

Kant unwarrantedly downgrades the aesthetic credentials of the mathematical and dynamical sublime, by unduly emphasizing not merely its
moral significance but also, and especially, the moral ground of the pleasure we take in it and of the communicability of the aesthetic judgment
based upon it. I argue that Kant is wrong both in grounding the sublime
in morality and our susceptibility to moral ideas, and in grounding sublime *pleasure* in the awareness of our moral superiority over nature. On
Kant's account, I contend, despite his averments to the contrary, the judgment of the sublime is not *purely* aesthetic.[1]

2. The Mathematical Sublime

Kant distinguishes two varieties within the classification of the sublime:
the mathematical and the dynamical sublime. In keeping with the traditional eighteenth-century distinction between a sense of sublimity connected to size and one connected to power, Kant's mathematical sublime
is connected to what is excessively or absolutely large and cannot be
grasped fully by our senses and imagination. The dynamical sublime is,
on the other hand, connected to an overwhelming power (of, for instance,
a hurricane or a volcano) which surpasses the power of imagination.
Despite their differences, both varieties of the sublime are, according to
Kant, united in putting us in touch with our moral powers and sensibilities
and, as we shall see, the pleasure they yield is ultimately grounded in our
moral superiority over nature. In the mathematical sublime, our senses
are pushed to the limits of their powers through the overwhelming size of
natural objects or phenomena. Although Kant clearly holds that "nature
is sublime in those of its appearances whose intuition carries with it the
idea of their infinity", he meaningfully adds that "the only way for this
to occur is through the inadequacy [*nicht anders geschehen, als durch die
Unangemessenheit*] of even the greatest effort of our imagination to estimate an object's magnitude."[2] In Kant's view, the sublime is certainly not

a transcendent experience of the absolute, nor does it involve a (sense of) timelessness. Time does not stand still when faced with the sublime. We do, however, experience the limitations or the "maximum" of the power of our senses—i.e., our imagination. Kant specifies this in a complex passage that is worth quoting in full (§26, 251; italics added):

> Now even though there is no maximum [*Grösstes*] for the mathematical estimation of magnitude (inasmuch as the power of numbers progresses to infinity), yet for the aesthetic estimation of magnitude there is indeed a maximum. And regarding this latter maximum I say that when it is judged as absolute measure beyond which no larger is subjectively possible (i.e., possible for the judging subject), then it carries with it the idea of the sublime and gives rise to that emotion which no mathematical estimation of magnitude by means of numbers can produce (except to the extent that the basic aesthetic measure is at the same time kept alive in the imagination). For a mathematical estimation of magnitude never exhibits more than relative magnitude, by a comparison with others of the same kind, *whereas an aesthetic one exhibits [darstellt] absolute magnitude to the extent that the mind can take it in one intuition.*

Kant argues that judging the sublime involves not a mathematical method of measuring, but an attempt to grasp the whole through "aesthetic comprehension". Since there is never a first or original measure to estimate the magnitude of objects, however, he claims (§26, 5:251) that

> our estimation of the magnitude of the basic measure must consist merely in our being able to take it in directly in one intuition and to use it, by means of the imagination, for exhibiting numerical concepts. In other words, all estimation of the magnitude of objects of nature is ultimately aesthetic (i.e., determined subjectively rather than objectively).

The sublime is thus indeed a limit experience, but not in the sense that it involves a transcendent, timeless experience of the absolute (or of the absolutely large, or of "that which is large beyond any comparison"), but is rather a double-edged experience of the limits of sensory perception. It is a feeling of the "basic measure" upon which all reflective judgments are based—the "horizon", as it were, which accompanies any estimation of magnitudes—as well as of the limitations of imagination to *comprehend* the absolutely large (i.e., the maximum of simultaneously presentable magnitude in a single image). The sublime is, hence, an experience not of an absolute existing beyond the power of imagination (e.g., God), but of the absolute nature of the unsurpassable limits of our senses to comprehend large wholes in a single image. Our appreciation of the mathematical sublime in nature begins with aesthetically comparing the size of the vast object, but we are soon lost in the comparison. For through the failure of imagination to comprehend incomparably vast magnitudes, that is to say, to present them in a single image, we become aware of "the feeling of a supersensible power in us", namely reason's striving for totality and its urging imagination to come up with a measure that is suited to take in incomparably great wholes (§25, 250). Thus Kant argues that imagination's failed effort reveals reason's ability to *think* the absolutely large as a rational idea of infinity (§26, 255). This *felt* inadequacy of imagination is, so Kant argues, precisely what manifests the immense power of reason at the level of human sensibility and makes us aware of the "higher ends" of our rational being—i.e., our ultimate vocation, which is moral. Kant insists that the inadequacy of imagination to intuit infinite magnitudes is still pleasurable, as the judgment of the sublime is ultimately purposive for the power of reason and is in harmony with rational ideas.

Surprisingly, to say the least, the Kantian sublime almost loses sight altogether of the aesthetic *object*, since our admiration and astonishment for its vastness is ultimately due to a so-called "subreption" (§27, 5:257). Nature is actually mistakenly called sublime, for it is *the mind that makes the sublimity of its own moral vocation palpable to itself.* Sublime objects seem to be reduced to merely offering "occasions" to enjoy our own superiority as moral subjects. No matter how deeply concerned Kant really is with pointing out the aesthetic nature of judgments of the sublime, and no matter how sophisticated his analysis, the core significance of the Kantian sublime is undeniably moral, since it offers "an expansion of the mind that feels able to cross the barriers of sensibility with a different (a practical) aim" (§26, 255), and "thus nature is here called sublime *merely* because it raises our imagination to the point of exhibiting those cases where the mind can come to feel the sublimity of its own [moral] vocation, which *elevates it even above nature*" (262, italics added).

I maintain that we do not have to presuppose that the mathematical sublime is necessarily grounded in the awareness of the superiority of our moral vocation. To experience the mathematical sublime, it suffices that *theoretical* reason challenges the imagination to surpass its own limits and present to the senses what is "absolutely large" in a single image, which it obviously fails to do and through which we experience displeasure. For the pleasure in the sublime results from the peculiar awareness—which makes itself felt *only* through the displeasure of imagination's inadequacy, and hence, *at the level of sensibility*—that we, as rational beings, have the power to think ideas which we cannot comprehend in a single intuition.[3] The conflict between reason and imagination would then be inextricably linked up with our awareness of the tremendous power of reason in its *theoretical* capacity, which keeps striving for absolute totality even if this implies perturbing or distorting sensory perception. The question now arises as to whether Kant is able to offer a more plausible account of the other variety of the experience of the sublime—namely, the dynamical sublime.

3. The Dynamical Sublime

In the dynamical sublime, it is power and not just size that is overwhelming to the senses and imagination. Although we feel ourselves to be in safety, we are still overwhelmed by the might of nature. Kant writes (§28, 5:261):

> Bold, overhanging and, as it were, threatening rocks, thunderclouds piling up in the sky and moving about accompanied by lightning and thunderclaps, volcanoes with all their destructive power, hurricanes with all the devastation they leave behind, the boundless ocean heaved up, the high waterfall of a mighty river, and so on. Compared to the might of these, our ability to resist becomes an insignificant trifle. Yet the sight of them becomes all the more attractive the more fearful it is, provided we are in a safe place. And we like to call these objects sublime because they . . . allow us to discover in ourselves an ability to resist which is of a quite different kind, and which gives us the courage to believe that we could be a match for nature's seeming omnipotence.

Kant concurs with Edmund Burke that the feeling of the dynamically sublime arises only "provided we are in a safe place", but (*contra* Burke) Kant argues that the concomitant pleasure does not result from realizing our personal safety but from realizing that we have in us "an ability to resist [nature's might] which is of a quite different kind". By this Kant clearly means our ability as moral persons, who are oriented towards suppressing sensible inclinations in order to behave morally. Being in a safe place enables us to judge the might of hurricanes, volcanoes, and so on, as sublime without undergoing real fear.

Moreover, this type of aesthetic judgment is not merely "similar to the moral disposition" (General Comment, 5:268); it also prepares us not merely for loving nature, as beauty does, but "for esteeming it even against our interest (of sense)" (267). And, even more crucial to Kant's analysis of the dynamical sublime, the pleasurable aspect of the sublime "vibration" (*Erschütterung*), as Kant calls it, is essentially based on our susceptibility to morality, for it is a "feeling of this supersensible vocation" that we, as rational beings, all have. "The violence that the imagination inflicts on the subject" is experienced as pleasurable merely because it is "judged purposive *for the whole vocation of the mind*", which is (in Kant's view) purely moral. It even "reveals in us at the same time an ability to judge ourselves independent of nature, and reveals in us a superiority over nature" (§28, 261). Although the sublime does not necessarily involve any conscious intellectual recognition of our moral vocation, the pleasure that we may experience, provided we believe our-selves to be safe, is based upon "discovering" in our mind "a superiority over nature itself in its immensity", since "it reveals in us an ability to judge ourselves independent of nature" (§28, 261), which "keeps the humanity in our person from being degraded, even though a human being would have to succumb to that dominance of nature" (262). Although Kant sometimes seems to suggest otherwise, the dynamical sublime arises through an activity of the imagination, is based on feeling and does not necessarily require any cognitive recognition of our power of reason.

It is hard to see, though, how the revelation of our moral independ-ence and superiority over nature can come about without any conceptual basis for our judgment.[4] Thus, not only the purported moral basis of the pleasure threatens the Kantian sublime's purely aesthetic nature, but also Kant's emphasis that the sublime allows us to *recognize* ourselves as moral beings.

What is perhaps more perplexing than this quasi-moralization of the sublime, and even more damaging to his aesthetic doctrine, is that Kant, when discussing the modality of the judgment of the sublime in §29 (5:265, italics added), argues that it "*has its foundation . . . in* something that, along with common sense, we may require and demand of every-one, namely *the predisposition to the feeling for (practical) ideas, i.e., to moral feeling.*" Kant emphatically claims that *the sublime is founded on our predisposition to moral feeling,* and despite his attempt to safeguard the sublime's aesthetic credentials, this definitely affects the purely aes-thetic nature of the judgment of the sublime.[5] It is obviously right that the sublime may have a propaedeutic function with regard to morality, and that this does not necessarily turn the sublime into moral feeling.[6] The Kantian sublime is indeed merely akin to moral respect, since it does not suppress our sensible inclinations (*Neigungen*) but rather violates as well as expands our imagination, offering us a mixed feeling of pleasure and displeasure which is analogous (and hence, not identical) to the struggle with sensible inclinations involved in behaving morally.[7]

However, what many commentators seem to have overlooked but actu-ally proves far more damaging to the purely aesthetic nature of the judg-ment of the sublime, is that one of the vital *a priori* requirements of pure aesthetic judgment—namely, its necessary universal communicability (some-times inappropriately called, its intersubjective nature)—cannot be met by the judgment concerning the sublime, unless it is grounded in morality.[8]

4. The Impurity of the Sublime

What has often been downplayed in the literature, but seems to me to be one of the determining aspects of the Kantian sublime, is that, compared to judgments of natural *beauty*, "we cannot with the same readiness count on others to accept our judgment about the sublime in nature" (§29, 5:264). Kant has a number of reasons for claiming this, three of which are especially worth emphasizing.

First, unlike beauty, the sublime does not provide an "attunement [*Stimmung*] of the cognitive powers that is required for cognition in general" and "without which cognition . . . could not arise" (§21, 5:238; see also §39, 293). This "attunement" purportedly grounds the judgment of beauty's universal validity, and since it fails to occur in the sublime, which does not offer a harmonious play between imagination and understanding but a turbulent struggle between imagination and reason, the sublime cannot "with the same readiness" demand to be universally shared. (We shall shortly see exactly why this is the case and also why this severely damages the sublime's purely aesthetic status.)

Second, to be able to judge vast or mighty natural objects as sublime one needs *culture*—or, at least, more culture is required compared to what is needed to appreciate natural beauty (see §29, 5:265). One must be receptive to rational ideas, in order to become properly *attuned*, as Kant puts it, to the feeling of the sublime. Thus, instead of urging that the sublime merely *prepares* us for morality, Kant in fact argues that people who have not been sufficiently prepared by culture to appreciate the sublimity of overwhelming nature will simply be frightened and repelled by such overwhelming natural phenomena: they will not be able to take pleasure in what is violent, overwhelming, and potentially destructive to them. Only if one is sufficiently susceptible to rational ideas can one judge mighty objects as sublime—that is to say, as not merely chaotic, harmful, dangerous, and frightening, but also as ultimately purposive. It should be clear from the above passage that it is, again, reason (and not understanding, as in the beautiful) that grounds the feeling of the sublime. Reason actually uses—or rather, abuses—imagination so as to confront nature's destructive powers in order to reveal its own superior might. The sublime is indeed "a pleasure involved in reasoning contemplation [*Lust der vernünftelnden Kontemplation*]" (§39, 292).

Thirdly, the *modality* of the judgment of sublimity is, as Kant says, "one principal moment for a critique of judgment" (§29, 5:266), but it has received surprisingly little attention from most commentators.[9] Its importance can hardly be overlooked, however, for it is supposed to convince us of the thought that, as Brady (2013, 74) contends, despite "important differences between the sublime and the beautiful, these differences do not undermine a case for the sublime as aesthetic." I concur with Brady that questioning the aesthetic status of the Kantian sublime simply by referring to its intimate links to our moral disposition and the moral feeling of respect, may not be altogether convincing. For whilst it is true that the sublime may somehow prepare us for treating nature with admiration and persons with respect, that in itself is no reason to question the sublime's aesthetic nature. For pure beauty, too, prepares us to love nature and even symbolizes morality, yet this does not therefore turn the feeling of the beautiful into a moral feeling. On the contrary, this might actually work in the opposite direction. It is only because beauty exclusively belongs to the aesthetic domain that it may enhance moral capacities and teleological understanding, and be a sign of a genuinely moral disposition. Moreover, that Kant attends to the formless character of sublime objects might further support its aesthetic character as, for instance, Brady (74–79) and Gibbons (1994, 136, 148f, 150–151) contend. Judging the sublime is clearly connected to peculiar features of "raw nature [rohe Natur]" (§26, 5:253), which engage imagination and "expand it commensurately" with reason's power (§25, 5:249), through which it "acquires an expansion and a power that surpasses the one it sacrifices" (General Comment, 274, 269; see also §28, 262).

Even though, as I attempt to show in Vandenabeele (2015b), Kant's doctrine of the sublime can be upgraded to a genuinely aesthetic exploration of the sublime (in art) and as such can offer a more positive evaluation of imagination's productive activity and presentational powers, at least one striking and, to my mind, insurmountable difficulty still remains. For, whilst on Kant's official view, judgments of beauty and sublimity share the general characteristics of aesthetic judgments—they please without necessary reference to concepts, they claim universal validity, they are subjectively purposive, and they are subjectively necessary—yet, unlike judgments of beauty, judgments about the sublime cannot immediately demand universal assent, unless quite a "detour" is made (namely, via practical reason). What Kant does not sufficiently emphasize is that, despite all that beauty and sublimity have in common, the modality of the two judgments is far from similar, and this severely tarnishes the sublime's aesthetic credentials.

What, then, are the most striking differences between judgments of beauty and judgments of the sublime, with regard to their modality? First, Kant argues that the sublime requires more culture—i.e., Kultur, in the sense of the development of moral ideas—than the beautiful (§29, 5:265). This is of utmost importance. For, according to Kant, the beautiful testifies to a felt harmony, not only between imagination and understanding but also between the mind (Gemüt) and the purposive forms of nature, which tightly connects beauty to natural teleology. The feeling of the sublime, on the other hand, by no means presupposes nor engenders such a harmonious continuity between our mind and nature. In the sublime, Kant contends, reason is felt to be triumphant over nature, for "we judge the sensible in the presentation of nature to be suitable for a possible supersensible use" (§27, 258). Furthermore, the sublime can "present . . . imagination and reason as harmonious by virtue of their contrast" and give rise to a purposiveness by the very conflict of imagination and reason (258). The overwhelming object is excessive for the imagination, "against our interest of sense" and even "repulsive to mere sensibility", and pleasure can arise solely because *reason uses nature* to force imagination to surpass its limits in order to make palpable the moral vocation of the mind, which is infinitely superior over nature (see General Comment, 267).

Second, whilst the exemplary necessity of the judgment of beauty is based on the free yet harmonious play of our cognitive powers, which is purportedly conducive to any type of cognitive operation, the pleasure accompanying the judgment of the sublime cannot be immediately shared by all, as the sublime is not a matter of taste, says Kant, but of *feeling*. Importantly, the pleasure in the sublime is "a pleasure involved in *reasoning* contemplation" (§39, 5:292, italics added). Its demand that everyone approve refers to "subjective bases as they are purposive", not for "the benefit of the contemplative understanding", as with the beautiful, but merely "in relation to moral feeling" (General Comment, 267). Kant even insists that "what is sublime, in the proper meaning of the term, cannot be contained in any sensible form but concerns only ideas of reason . . . Thus the vast ocean, heaved up by storms, cannot be sublime. The sight of it is horrible" (§23, 245). I concur with commentators such as Malcolm Budd and Katie McShane, who correctly interpret Kant's theory as overly directed at the sublimity of the (moral) subject and with Ronald Hepburn, who justly argues that Kant's doctrine downgrades "nature's contribution in favor of the one-sided exalting of the rational subject".[10]

Also, someone lacks feeling, not taste, Kant contends (§29, 5:265), "if he remains unmoved in the presence of something we judge sublime." Therefore—and this is an extremely important point—contrary to judgments of beauty, the sublime cannot demand immediate communication (*unmittelbare Teilnehmung*). The principal reason for this is that, whereas assenting to judgments of taste can be "demanded unhesitatingly from everyone" (266, italics added):

> In the case of feeling, on the other hand, judgment refers the imagination to reason, our power of ideas, and so *we demand feeling only under a subjective presupposition* (though we believe we are justified and permitted to require fulfilment of this presupposition in everyone): *we presuppose moral feeling in man.* And so we attribute necessity to this kind of aesthetic judgment as well.

From this follows that, despite all similarities between judgments of beauty and sublimity, which Kant is keen to point out, there is an immense difference between the ways they are able to meet the modal requirement of pure aesthetic judgments—i.e., the crucial *a priori* requirement to be universally communicated or shared. *Pace* Brady and numerous other commentators, I do not think this is a minor point which leaves the sublime squarely in purely aesthetic territory. On the contrary, it deeply affects the purely aesthetic character of the Kantian sublime. For the requirement of universal assent is one of the transcendental conditions that is supposed to logically distinguish aesthetic from non-aesthetic judgments. It forms the very heart of Kant's *critique* of aesthetic judgment.

Furthermore, whereas the beautiful lays claim to *immediate* participation (*Teilnehmung*) and universal assent, the sublime demands universal participation, merely because it "presupposes . . . a feeling of our supersensible vocation, a feeling which, however obscure it may be, has a moral foundation" (§39, 5:292). And as the sublime reveals the *presence* of moral freedom and thus endows us with a value infinitely superior to nature, its demand to be universally shared can be based solely on the transcendental idea of moral freedom. Kant expressly specifies this in §39, which has been usually downplayed by commentators, possibly because it does not feature in the Analytic of the Sublime as such. Yet, what Kant writes is crucial and unambiguous (292): "I may require that liking too from everyone, but only by means of the moral law, which is in turn based on concepts of reason." What demands and legitimates the necessity of the sublime's universal shareability is neither cognitive nor aesthetic, but moral.

Does this, then, turn the feeling of the sublime into moral feeling? By no means, for the feeling of respect is not aesthetically pleasurable. (It is definitely not *Wohlgefallen*.) Furthermore, as already indicated, in the sublime "the imagination thereby acquires an expansion and a power that surpasses the one it sacrifices" (General Comment, 5:269; see also §25, 249), which is (although clearly grounded in practical reason's impossible demand to present what cannot be presented) obviously a matter of *aesthetic* presentation (*Darstellung*); and the latter cannot be confused with moral action and the feeling of respect.

As already noted, however, the story of the Kantian sublime does not end here. The Kantian sublime is not merely analogous to moral struggle. For Kant is adamant that what *grounds* not only the universal communicability of the sublime but also the pleasure we take in it—hence, what supposedly resolves the paradox of the sublime—is really the "nonpathological" feeling of moral respect. Thus, the feeling of the sublime is not itself a moral feeling, but both its requirement to be universally shared, which is supposed to guarantee its purely aesthetic credentials, and its pleasurable aspect do presuppose the ability to take pure interest in the moral law. Hence, contrary to pure judgments of beauty, judgments about the sublime cannot be *immediately* shared, as their demand to be assented to by all others purportedly needs to be mediated by morality.

This obviously tarnishes the sublime's *purely* aesthetic character. For, as Kant writes (General Comment, 5:271), "from the aesthetic side . . ., the pleasure is negative, i.e. opposed to this interest, but considered from the intellectual side it is positive and connected with an interest." No matter how hard Kant and several of his sympathetic commentators attempt to safeguard the sublime's purely aesthetic nature, one ought to concede that the demand of the sublime for universal assent stems solely from "the intellectual side" of the feeling—i.e., the universal validity of the moral law, which is intimately tied up with the palpable *presence* of the idea of moral freedom in the mind.[11] There can thus be neither a *completely* disinterested judgment of the sublime nor a sublime *sensus communis*. It is necessarily an impure or "dependent" judgment.[12] This might also ultimately explain the healthy *"madness"* which is typical of sublime affects, such as enthusiasm (275).[13]

Sublime "vibration" (*Erschütterung*), as Kant calls it in §27, cannot be purely aesthetic, as it really belongs to two separate realms or territories, the moral and the aesthetic—or, rather, to neither of them as such. The sublime, indeed, simultaneously involves "repulsion and attraction" (§27, 5:258). The Kantian sublime is, like a monster in a horror film, interstitial.[14] It is a radically split feeling dwelling in two distinct domains, and is torn between their opposite requirements.[15]

Notes

1. Arthur Schopenhauer offers a more plausible theory of the sublime in *The World as Will and Representation*, which safeguards the sublime's aesthetic credentials and moves beyond Kant's in numerous meaningful ways, as I argue extensively in my book, *The Sublime in Schopenhauer's Philosophy* (Vandenabeele 2015a). There I offer a profound critique of Kant's and Schopenhauer's doctrines. Drawing on recent insights in philosophy of mind and psychology, I also offer a critical alternative to their theories of the sublime.
2. §26, 5:255. All Kant quotations are from his *Kritik der Urteilskraft*. As is customary, I indicate the section number, followed by the *Akademie Ausgabe* volume and pagination. The English translations are my own, but are based largely upon Kant (1790) and the Cambridge Edition translation.
3. "Intuition" is often used to mean "ineffable insight", and the sublime has frequently been associated with this kind of (quasi-)mystical understanding. I here use "intuition" in the strictly Kantian sense of an imaginative synthesis of the manifold's appearance.
4. Here I take issue with Emily Brady's all-too-charitable "aesthetic" reading of the Kantian sublime. See Brady, 189 and *passim*.
5. See Brady, 61: "My reading of Kant's sublime places it firmly within the aesthetic domain. While there are key links made to practical reason, the foundation of Kantian morality, it is important to emphasize that this type of judgment, like the beautiful, only *prepares* us for morality". This is misguided, since for Kant the modality of the sublime—i.e., its *demand* to be universally shared—"has its foundation in human nature: in something that . . . we may require and demand of everyone, namely, the predisposition to the feeling for (practical) ideas, i.e., to moral feeling" (§29, 5:265). Therefore, someone who cannot appreciate the sublime in nature is "someone who has no *feeling*" (265). Hence the sublime does not merely prepare us for morality, but is actually *based upon* our predisposition to moral feeling. Moreover, its claim to universal communicability is construed as grounded in the (unwarranted) assumption of a susceptibility to moral ideas in all human

beings. It might be no coincidence that Kant usually puts "practical" between brackets in §29, as he often does in the context of the sublime. Perhaps he sensed the threat that such a close link to morality would pose to the purely aesthetic nature of the sublime. But unfortunately, Kant could not resist what Malcolm Budd aptly calls "his inveterate tendency to evaluate everything by reference to moral value" (Budd 2002, 68 and 84). My view is that Budd is right and that Brady's reading is overly charitable.

6. Here I disagree with Melissa McBay Merritt (2012, 46–47), who holds that "moral feeling is a mode of the Kantian sublime: it is an elevated state of mind, registering as the subject's attraction to an ideal conceived through the moral law." Merritt overlooks the fact that, in Kant's view, unlike the sublime, respect is a "non-pathological" feeling (§12, 5:222). Kant does say at one point (§23, 245) that "the liking for the sublime contains not so much positive pleasure as rather admiration and respect, and so should be called a negative pleasure." From this it does not follow, however, that Kant implies that the moral feeling of respect is identical to the feeling of the sublime, and it would be rather odd if he did. He even explicitly acknowledges that "the moral law in its might" is "the object of a pure and unconditioned intellectual liking" and, hence, not aesthetically sublime itself. It is only "if we judge aesthetically . . . the moral good, [that] we must *present* it not so much as beautiful but rather as sublime, so that it will arouse a feeling of respect" (General Comment, 271, italics added). Kant thus holds that moral feeling is analogous to the sublime, not that it is identical with it, and that the sublime *may* give rise to a feeling of respect.

7. Katerina Deligiorgi even argues that sublime pleasure "comes from the mere thought that we have the capacity for agency" (2014, 32).

8. Already in the pre-Critical *Observations* Kant draws a connection between the sublime and morality. See Clewis 2009, 13. Still, the connection between sublimity and morality is much tighter in his Critical work.

9. One notable exception is Lyotard (1994, 224–239).

10. See Brady, 70–71. Here I side with McShane (2013) and Hepburn (1996, 201).

11. As Robert Clewis justly points out: "for Kant the sublime discloses that the subject belongs to a realm of freedom" (22).

12. Whether intentionally or not, Kant actually seems to leave room for dependent or partly intellectual judgments of the sublime, by insisting (§26, 5:252–253): "if the aesthetic judgment [of the sublime] is to be *pure* (*unmixed with any teleological* and hence rational judgment), . . . then we must point to the sublime not in products of art (e.g. buildings, columns, etc.), where both the form and the magnitude are determined by a human purpose, nor in natural things *whose very concept carries with it a determinate purpose* (e.g. animals with a known determination in nature) but rather in raw nature [*an der rohen Natur*] (and even in it only insofar as it carries with it no charm, nor any emotion aroused by actual danger), that is, merely insofar as raw nature contains magnitude." Kant does not really make clear what "raw nature", which allegedly occasions pure sublimity, exactly is, but he does seem to allow the occurrence of impure or dependent sublimity.

13. Like Lord Kames (Home 2005), John Dennis (2003), and others, Kant connects enthusiasm (*Enthusiasmus*) and the sublime. He does so in a rather confusing passage in the General Comment, in which he first claims that enthusiasm merely "seems to be sublime" (5:272), then also asserts that enthusiasm is as blind as any other affect and can by no means "deserve to be liked by reason". Yet, he adds in the following sentence that "enthusiasm is sublime aesthetically because it is a straining of our forces by ideas that

impart to the mind a momentum whose effects are mightier and more permanent than are those of an impulse produced by sensory representations". Further in the same section, he distinguishes between fanaticism (*Schwärmerei*),
madness (*Wahnsinn*), mania (*Wahnwitz*), and enthusiasm proper (*Enthusiasmus*). Kant now suggests that fanaticism and mania are closely related
and not compatible with the sublime, whereas enthusiasm is (see General
Comment, 257). See also Lyotard (2009). For a critical rebuttal of Lyotard's
interpretation, see Clewis, 21–23.
14. For the complicated relation between the sublime and the monstrous (*unge-
heuer*), see §26, 5:253. For a controversial reading of Kant's account of the
relation between the monstrous and the sublime, see Rogozinski, 159–168.
For an inspiring account of monsters in art-horror, see Carroll, especially
31–33, 42–49, 176, and 185.
15. I wish to thank all who have asked questions about the conference talk upon
which this paper is based. I am especially grateful to Robert Clewis, Jonathan Johnson, Clinton Tolley, John Zammito, and Zhengmi Zhouhuang for
their very helpful comments.

References

Brady, Emily (2013). *The Sublime in Modern Philosophy: Aesthetics, Ethics, and Nature*. Cambridge: Cambridge University Press.

Budd, Malcolm (2002). *The Aesthetic Appreciation of Nature*. Oxford: Oxford University Press.

Carroll, Noël (1990). *The Philosophy of Horror or Paradoxes of the Heart*. New York: Routledge.

Clewis, Robert (2009). *The Kantian Sublime and the Revelation of Freedom*. Cambridge: Cambridge University Press.

Deligiorgi, Katerina (2014). The Pleasures of Contra-Purposiveness: Kant, the Sublime, and Being Human. In: *The Journal of Aesthetics and Art Criticism* 72(1), 25–35.

Dennis, John (2003). *The Advancement and Reformation of Modern Poetry: A Critical Discourse*. Farmington Hills: Thomson Gale.

Gibbons, Sarah (1994). *Kant's Theory of Imagination: Bridging Gaps in Judgement and Experience*. Oxford: Clarendon Press.

Hepburn, Ronald (1996). Landscape and the Metaphysical Imagination. In: *Environmental Values* 5(3), 191–204.

Home, Henry (Lord Kames) (2005). *Elements of Criticism*. Indianapolis: Liberty Fund.

Kant, Immanuel (1790). Trans. W. S. Pluhar, *Critique of Judgment*. Indianapolis: Hackett Publishing Company, 1987.

Lyotard, Jean-François (1994). *Lessons on the Analytic of the Sublime*. Stanford: Stanford University Press.

——— (2009). *Enthusiasm: The Kantian Critique of History*. Stanford: Stanford University Press.

McShane, Katie (2013). Neosentimentalism and the Valence of Attitudes. In: *Philosophical Studies* 164(3), 747–765.

Merritt, Melissa McBay (2012). The Moral Source of the Kantian Sublime. In: T. M. Costelloe (ed.), *The Sublime: From Antiquity to the Present*. Cambridge: Cambridge University Press, 37–49.

Rogozinski, Jacob (2011). The Sublime Monster. In: D. Loose (ed.), *The Sublime and Its Teleology: Kant, German Idealism, Phenomenology.* Leiden: Brill, 159–168.

Vandenabeele, Bart (2015a). *The Sublime in Schopenhauer's Philosophy.* Basingstoke: Palgrave MacMillan.

——— (2015b). Kant, the Mannerist and the Matterist Sublime. In: *Journal of Aesthetic Education* 49(3), 32–49.

13 Turn from Sensibility to Reason

Kant's Concept of the Sublime[1]

Zhengmi Zhouhuang

1. Introduction

There are various dichotomies in Kant's philosophy: sensibility vs. reason, nature vs. freedom, cognition vs. morality, noumenon vs. phenomenon, among others. There are also different ways of mediating these dichotomies, which is the systematic undertaking of Kant's *Critique of the Power of Judgment*. One of the most important concepts in this work is the sublime, which exemplifies the connections between the different dichotomies; this fact means the concept's construction is full of tension. On the one hand, as a pure reflection of aesthetic judgment, the sublime must be without interest or purpose, but on the other hand it has its foundation in moral feeling (*CPJ* 5: 265, 292). On the one hand, the sublime "represents merely the subjective play of the powers of the mind (imagination and reason) as harmonious" (258), but on the other hand, reason "exercises dominion over sensibility" and the imagination is "purposively determined in accordance with a law" of reason (268f). Taking into account these problems concerning the essential definition the sublime, this chapter will first illustrate how the sublime embodies the *a priori* principle of aesthetic judgment through contrasting the judgment of the sublime with the judgment of taste in order to establish a basic logical frame for the judgment of the sublime. Second, this chapter redefines the boundary between the mathematically and dynamically sublime in order to reveal both the coexistence of contemplation and movement within the sublime and the unrevealed function of reason and imagination. Finally, contrasting the sublime with moral feeling, this chapter elaborates the turning-structure (from sensibility to reason and from object-intuition to idea-exhibition) of the sublime.

2. Beauty and the Sublime

During the pre-Critical period Kant had already made a distinction between beauty and the sublime. Because he was influenced by British empirical aesthetics (especially Edmund Burke), his philosophy concentrated on the empirical and psychological distinctions between the two concepts. This changed in *CPJ*, when he developed an *a priori* principle to define beauty and art, which distinguished aesthetics from cognition and morality. Thus, aesthetics became an independent discipline with *a priori* universality and objective necessity.

Kant's three disciplines of philosophy—theoretical, practical, and aesthetic—are built on the use of three different faculties of the mind, their application based on three higher cognitive faculties, and their *a priori* principles. In theoretical philosophy, understanding provides the faculty of cognition with *a priori* categories; in practical philosophy, reason provides the faculty of desire with moral law; and in aesthetic philosophy, judgment provides the faculty of the feeling of pleasure and displeasure with the *a priori* principle of subjective purposiveness. Though judgment plays an important role in both theoretical and practical philosophy, it serves only understanding and reason and does not have its own operating mechanism (reflection) or its own *a priori* principle. The judgment of taste is defined by Kant as such an activity: we compare given representations not with others, but with our faculty of cognition, and in the consciousness of the harmonious relationship between imagination and understanding we feel pleasure. On the one side, Kant criticized German rationalist aesthetics, which defined beauty as the perfection of an object, by grounding beauty in subjective feeling (as a judging criterion); on the other side, he differentiated himself from empirical aesthetics, which offered only a psychological description of aesthetic phenomena by endowing empirical feelings with an *a priori* principle.

The judgment of the sublime as a kind of aesthetic judgment is also an application of the reflecting power of judgment and follows subjective and formal purposiveness. The judgment of the sublime and the judgment of taste are regarded as the "two principal parts" of Kant's critique of the aesthetic power of judgment (*CPJ* 5:192). The connection and differentiation between these two parts, therefore, will then be the main line to comprehend and classify the sublime. I start this chapter by looking at the judgment of taste.

Guided by the table of logical functions in the first *Critique* (A70/B95), Kant examined the judgment of taste using four moments. First of all, in the moment of quality the judgment of taste is without any interest, regarding not only material and sensible interest (being different from what is agreeable), but also moral and intellectual interest (being different from what is good). Concerning the moment of quantity, the judgment of taste claims to have universal validity. In the moment of relation, the judgment of taste is based on the form of the purposiveness of an object, but without representation of an end. Concerning the moment of modality, judgment of taste involves universal assent and should have objective necessity. These accounts about the judgment of taste come from a perspective of reflection on the inner state of the mind: it begins with a rejection of interest (negation), asked for by the purity of reflection, and the reflected state of mind has a universality (totality), a subjective purposiveness (reverse causality),[2] and necessity of the accordant state of mind.

There is also another way to look at the judgment of taste, from which Kant analyzed taste in a more empirical way that is more in accordance with our daily life. The judgment of taste can be expressed like this: "X is beautiful because it brings us satisfaction". In this judgment, the moment of quality is about the way a predicate states the feeling of satisfaction (i.e., the reality of a "feeling of life"). The quantity of the judgment is not aesthetic, but logical. This suggests that judgments of taste are singular. Concerning relation, beauty can be seen as the attribute of an object (substance and accident) and a concrete judgment which, made in the experience, embodies a kind of actuality. In this way we can differentiate two lines in the analysis of a judgment of taste: one is reflective, aesthetic, and *a priori*, while the other is empirical, logical, and grammatical.

The analysis of the sublime is also guided by the logical functions of judging and develops from those previously described four moments. Kant pointed out several basic similarities between taste and judgment of the sublime: both involve satisfaction and the pure use of reflecting judgment (quality), both involve singular judgments with universal validity (quantity), and both are purposive and necessary (relation and modality). However, there are also differences. First, the analysis of the sublime begins with a moment of quantity rather than quality. The sublime relates not only to the amount of the object to be judged but also to the amount the object possesses. The reflecting judgment involves not only judging subjects (universality) but also the subjective capacity for comprehending infinity and totality, no matter what endeavor of imagination is need to comprehend infinity or the demand of reason for totality.

In the judgment of the sublime, the estimation of the magnitude of objects is not logical and mathematical, but sensible and aesthetic. In the former, we estimate an object by means of a given objective measure, which is united with numbers. In this type of estimation, there is no "greatest", because a numerical series can progress to infinity. But in aesthetic estimation we compare an object not with any objective measure, but only with our own subjective measure, as expressed through the faculties of apprehension and comprehension of imagination in the inner sense. When we try to comprehend partial representations of an oversized object into a whole, our imagination reaches its maximum and cannot complete the image. To try to comprehend the whole of an object can thus provoke feelings of imaginative inadequacy; our imagination does not continue trying to perceive the object, but "sinks back into itself" (*CPJ* 5:252). Through reflection of our mind a supersensible faculty (reason) is found and evoked. Reason claims an absolute totality, whether an object is given or infinite. Upon reason's request our imagination strives to comprehend all representations into an intuition, but this request goes beyond the faculty of imagination. Despite the incapability of imagination, the act of striving embodies the vocation of reason and is purposive for the reason.

Regarding the moment of quality, the sublime is not a pure and direct pleasure but one that is complex (mixed with displeasure) and indirect (evoked through striving). In the aesthetic estimation of magnitude, the limitation of imagination is contrapurposive for reason, but its striving for rational ideas is purposive, so displeasure and pleasure are felt at the same time. Different from the direct affirmation and stimulation of the feeling of life present in the judgment of taste, in the sublime there is a stronger and inner feeling of life, or "feeling of spirit" (*CPJ* 5:192), that is aroused from inhibiting the sensible feeling of life.

Regarding the moment of relation, we can still regard beauty as a property of an object.[3] Though for Kant a feeling of pleasure is aroused through reflecting on one's state of mind, a state of mind is still related to an object—in other words, stimulated by intuition of the form of an object. So from pleasure we can see the harmonious relationship not only between the faculties of mind, but also between ourselves and the object, which cannot actually expand "our cognition of natural objects, but our concept of nature, namely as a mere mechanism, into the concept of nature as art: which invites profound investigations into the possibility of such a form" (*CPJ* 5:246). The sublime, on the other hand, cannot be seen as a property of an object. The absolutely great is not the object, but the supersensible idea aroused by the object. The feeling of the sublime in nature is actually respect for our own vocation, "which we show to an object in nature through a certain subreption (substitution of a respect for the object instead of for the idea of humanity in our subject)" (257). In this sense, we could say that the sublime describes the properties and nature of a subject.

In the reflected perspective of the moment of relation, we can distinguish the purposiveness in the sublime from the purposiveness in beauty in the following two ways. First, unlike the direct purposiveness in beauty, the purposiveness in the sublime is indirect, achieved through a lack of purposiveness or even contrapurposiveness. Kant regarded this as "[t]he most important and intrinsic difference between the sublime and the beautiful" (*CPJ* 5:245). Second, the purposiveness in the beautiful corresponds with sensible purpose. The free play between imagination and understanding is in harmonious and undetermined relationship, in which understanding serves the imagination. Without the constraint of understanding, the imagination creates "voluntary forms of possible intuitions" (241). But the purposiveness in the sublime corresponds to the purpose of reason. Imagination and reason exist in a serious and intense relationship. No matter how imagination tries to expand itself to reach the infinite (in the mathematical sublime) or to overcome power and promote itself to the supersensible world (in the dynamically sublime), it merely serves reason as a tool to accomplish the business of reason, despite the fact that imagination is also expanded and strengthened.

Concerning the moment of modality, common sense (*Gemeinsinn, sensus communis*) as an ideal norm demands universal assent to the judgment of taste and ensures the necessity that it be universally communicable (*CPJ* 5:237f). Kant defined common sense as a disposition of the cognitive powers (imagination and understanding) for cognition in general, and it is assumed to be a necessary condition for the universal communicability of cognition (238f). However, in the case of the sublime the disposition is not about imagination and understanding, but imagination and reason, so it has nothing to do with the subjective condition of cognition. This kind of disposition can only be based in our "predisposition to the feeling for (practical) ideas" (265), because a determined correspondence between reason and sensibility lays the foundation for the undetermined correspondence between reason and imagination.

3. The Mathematically Sublime and the Dynamically Sublime

In addition to the concrete differences between the beautiful and the sublime in the four moments described above, Kant also added to his composition of the sublime something that did not exist in the concept of beauty: a distinction between the mathematically sublime and the dynamically sublime. Through this differentiation Kant underlined the different states of mind when conceiving of the beautiful and the sublime. A judgment of taste is contemplative, and "[e]motion, a sensation in which agreeableness is produced only by means of a momentary inhibition followed by a stronger outpouring of the vital force, does not belong to beauty at all" (*CPJ* 5:226). But a judgment of the sublime always accompanies movement, which can be compared to a "vibration, i.e., to a rapidly alternating repulsion from and attraction to one and the same object" (258). The contemplation of the beautiful can only be regarded mathematically, which is similar to the contemplation that occurs in theoretical cognition; and the emotion present while discerning the sublime is more dynamic, similar to the indispensable incentive (*Triebfeder*; i.e., driving force) in moral praxis.

Kant concretely defines the mathematically and dynamically sublime using two kinds of functions (modes) of imagination in emotions. Imagination is related either to the faculty of cognition or to the faculty of desire, and then has one of two dispositions: mathematical or dynamical. The purposiveness of the given representation is judged only in the respective disposition of imagination. According to this distinction, Kant correlated the moments of quality and quantity to the mathematical sublime and the moments of relation and modality to the dynamical sublime. But how should we understand this distinction? It is conceivable that imagination relates to the faculty of cognition, but how does it relate to the faculty of desire? In this arrangement, the two kinds of sublime have only two moments in which to be elucidated. Does this mean there is a kind of incompleteness and asymmetry between the mathematically and dynamically sublime? I shall use these questions to examine Kant's definitions and applications of the mathematically and dynamically sublime.

In the *Critique of Pure Reason* Kant splits the understanding of the sublime into different classes. The first class is concerned with intuitive objects and the second with existence (see B110). Considering how pure concepts could be applied to possible experience, Kant also divided synthesis of the pure concepts of understanding into two types: mathematical and dynamical. Both are combinations of a manifold of representations, but the former is composed of a homogeneous manifold wherein the parts do not necessarily belong to each other, whereas the latter is composed of a heterogeneous manifold wherein the parts do necessarily belong to one another (see B199f). In the Transcendental Dialectic, Kant also distinguished the two perspectives to define the cosmological ideas behind these two categories. The mathematical whole (world) is an aggregation of all appearances in reference to their quantity (both in the great and the small, or their progress through composition and division). The expression of the dynamical whole (nature) emphasizes the necessary unity in the existence of appearances (A418f/B446f). In this way, we can summarize the distinction between the mathematical and dynamical sublime in three points: (1) intuition vs. existence, (2) homogeneous vs. heterogeneous, and (3) unnecessity vs. necessity. Returning to Kant's analysis of the sublime in the *Critique of the Power of Judgment*, we can verify that these distinctions are present there as well.

In respect to the first distinction within the judgment of the sublime—between intuition and existence—intuition is present not in the theoretical sense, but in an aesthetic one. Intuition involves the use of judgment's reflecting power, not only as it is related to the intuition of objects but also as it is associated with the relationship between a given object and cognitive faculties—i.e., with the reflection of a specific state of mind. Therefore, the distinction between the mathematically and dynamically sublime lies not only in the distinction between intuition and existence, but also in the distinction between intuition and reflection, or between the intuition of an object and the reflected state of existence of the subjective mind.

It is also worthwhile to mention that the existence of a subject here is not real, but only an imaginary existence that occurs when we confront an object with irresistible power. Though one might imagine that this object could destroy everything and endanger one's own existence, one actually remain safe, so that one can stay in "a mood of calm contemplation" and make "an entirely free judgment" (*CPJ* 5:263). As Kant pointed out, in the dynamically sublime the imagination is related to the faculty of desire (247). The constraint of nature on the sensible faculty of desire (e.g., self-protection) as well as one's powerlessness to resist is only represented in the imagination, and the purposiveness of reason aroused by the contrapurposiveness of sensibility only concerns the power of representation. Therefore, reason is not the determining ground of the faculty of desire and is little related to one's capacity of action to bring about an object; reason is only sensibly aware in the reflection. The horror and astonishment that are felt when we view the sublime in nature are not an actual fear for our safety, "but only an attempt to involve ourselves in it by means of the imagination, in order to feel the power of that very faculty, to combine the movement of the mind thereby aroused with its calmness, and so to be superior to nature within us, and thus also that outside us" (269). In this sense, the dynamically sublime also has a contemplative character and a mathematical dimension.

The second distinction, between homogeneous and heterogeneous within the sublime, is not as explicit as it is in Kant's theoretical philosophy. In the mathematically sublime, the partial representations of an object that are to be comprehended are homogeneous; the increasing degrees of the power that is to be resisted can be regarded as successive and homogeneous. But there are also heterogeneous elements in both the mathematically and the dynamically sublime. In the former, we discover a supersensible capability providing the idea of totality from the limits of our imagination (*CPJ* 5:250). In the latter, we find a power both alien and superior to nature (i.e., the personality of rational beings and the moral idea), arising from our physical disability in the face of the power of nature, so that we can remove ourselves from sensible frustration. In this way, heterogeneity not only lies in the difference between objects being judged—intuited objects—and the reflected subjective state of mind, but also in the transformation of functional authority from the sensible being to the moral being.

Further support for this can be found in Kant's description of the mixed feelings in both types of the sublime. In both circumstances, there is a repulsion from and attraction to an oversized and overpowerful nature, as well as a complex feeling: the inhibition of sensible vital powers and the more powerful outpouring of rational vital powers. In Kant's 1786 *Metaphysical Foundations of Natural Science*, he defines the dynamical connection as a combination of "the original forces of repulsion and attraction" (*MFNS* 4:532). Thus, the boundary between the mathematically sublime and the dynamically sublime is not as settled as it seems.

The last differentiation between the two types of sublime is the necessary connection between partial representations. The crucial problem is whether the transformation of the heterogeneous, from imagination's contrapurposiveness when intuiting objects to the purposiveness of reason, is necessary. Though Kant said that contrapurposiveness, together with displeasure, "at the same time" (*CPJ* 5:258) is represented as purposive for reason, this transformation does not constantly occur. For example, when experiencing ugliness displeasure is also caused by the

contrapurposiveness of the relationship between imagination and understanding, but from this contrapurposiveness no purposiveness for anything is revealed. Kant also admits that "not every object that arouses
fear is found sublime in our aesthetic judgment" (260). Another example
is contributed by Kant himself: a man without a moral conscience feels
only a fear of danger when viewing icy mountains, but the sight arouses
no moral feeling (265).

Comparing these counterexamples, we can find some unexplored elements in the transformation from contrapurposiveness to purposiveness.
The first pertains to features of an object. We feel something is ugly or
awful for various reasons: weirdness, loathing, etc. But only those objects
in nature, which have something in common (e.g., infinity, power) with
the sublime in ourselves (e.g., the starry heavens and the sea) can be
in accordance with the purpose of reason and can thus be described as
sublime. The similarity is more obvious when sensible representations
serve as attributes of supersensible ideas: for example, correlating the
rational idea of a cosmopolitan disposition to the movement of the sun,
or describing a rise in virtue as a sunrise (see *CPJ* 5:316). This is not only
grounded in the conventional usage of language, but also necessary for
Kant's construction of the judgment of sublime. Ideas can elevate the subject only when the supplement provided by the ideas has a similar aspect
to what is lacking from sensibility. It is only through this similarity that a
connection between the largeness and power of the outer object and the
infinity and transcendence of the inner rational capacity is possible. This,
in turn, makes possible the transformation from contrapurposiveness to
purposiveness. This connection can only be accomplished through the
function of the association of imagination.

The second example is related to the inner capabilities of the subject.
We will only see danger and distress when faced with the power of nature
if our reason is not sufficient to propel us from powerlessness and make
us aware of the supersensible idea; this rids us of our fright and turns to
satisfaction with our own personality. Thus, in the turn from contrapurposiveness to purposiveness, reason as supersensible power is not only
found, but also initiates the turn. Despite the fact that this is not a practical incentive that can affect will and action, but an imaginative one that
affects only the mind, reason pushes us to go deeper in our reflection:
Not only is the relation between cognitive faculties reflected in this state
of mind, but also the ultimate ground for this relationship. Thus, reason
is not only awoken, but also lets itself be exhibited.

Though Kant portrays the mathematically and dynamically sublime as
a neat distinction, this division is actually not so neat. The dynamically
sublime also contains a mathematical element that limits the sensibliza-
tion of rational ideas only to contemplation. Likewise, in the mathematically sublime there is also a dynamical element that allows rational ideas
to be revealed. To make this interplay possible, a spontaneous capacity

is necessary—i.e., reason. To connect the intuited object in nature to the reflected idea of reason, a capacity of association (i.e., imagination) is needed; it prevents judgment from falling apart as a result of the interplay.

4. The Sublime and Moral Feeling

In the *Critique of Practical Reason*, Kant created a new definition of moral feeling that is differentiated from the traditional understanding of the concept in English empiricism. The moral feeling of respect, according to Kant, is an *a priori* feeling based in practical reason. It serves as an incentive for pure reason (i.e., the subjective determining ground of one's will) and drives a person to obey the moral law in actions. As a feature of feelings, the feeling of respect is divided into two types: negative and positive. The first refers to the pain and displeasure felt when denying a sensible inclination, while the latter refers to the pleasure and satisfaction that comes when one's intellectual personality is realized and affirmed.

There are many similarities between moral feeling and the sublime: concerning the subjective formal condition, both are pure, having no connection with natural need (neither an empirical nor sensible interest). Therefore, both are universal, though the universality of the former is imperative, while for the latter it is a claim for others' assent to our own judgment. In reference to the complexity of feelings, both are combined with complex feelings of displeasure and pleasure; in both cases, displeasure comes from the suppression and frustration of sensibility and pleasure from the consciousness and affirmation of reason.

The essential affinity between the sublime and moral feeling lies in the fact that the disposition of the sublime is based on the disposition of moral feeling, since the undetermined correspondence between imagination (as the sensible capacity of representation) and reason in the sublime has its foundation in the determined correspondence between the sensible capacity of desire and reason in moral feeling (cf. *CPJ* 5:265, 256). Kant wrote that "a feeling for the sublime in nature cannot even be conceived without connecting it to a disposition of the mind that is similar to the moral disposition" (268), and that "the intellectual, intrinsically purposive (moral) good, judged aesthetically, must . . . be represented . . . as sublime, so that it arouses more the feeling of respect" (271).

On one hand, an affinity with moral feeling provides a foundation for the universality and necessity for the judgment of sublime. On the other hand, it challenges the purity of this judgment. If the sublime is based on an idea of practical reason, how can we say that judgment is without any interest or end, even though its interest/end is practical and intellectual? Concerning one's inner state of mind, Kant thought that "reason must exercise dominion over sensibility" in both the sublime and moral feeling (*CPJ* 5:268f). He argues that the latter serves the business of former as its instrument, which is quite different from the free play in the judgment of taste. However, Kant also explicitly states that the sublime does not have a determinate concept as its ground: "[I]t represents merely the subjective play of the powers of the mind (imagination and reason) as harmonious even in their contrast" (258). Is the judgment of the sublime then determined and dominated or free and without purpose?

A possible solution is to divide the judgment of the sublime into two stages: the first is a free play of the cognitive faculties when intuiting objects and the second stage is the determination and dominion of reason over the imagination when exhibiting the idea of reason. The two stages are connected and exist together in turn (*Umschlag*).[4] When we start to intuit an object, we do not presuppose the end of reason,[5] yet the idea of reason is subsequently revealed and evoked. This revelation and evocation lie in both our sensibility and our reason. Without the empirical condition—the frustration of sensibility in intuition of an object as stimulation—it would be impossible. It would also be impossible without the *a priori* condition, the idea of reason and the moral disposition, as foundation. Therefore, unlike the purposiveness of reason in moral feeling, which always has an end in view, the purposiveness of reason in the sublime is without an end, and the correspondence between imagination and reason is brought out through the contrast and conflict that they freely generate. Negative freedom turns into positive freedom, and the free play in aesthetic reflection turns into free will with a moral task.

Except for the turn from contrapurposiveness to purposiveness, the mode and effect of the purposiveness of reason in the sublime is different from that of moral feeling, though in both cases sensibility is determined by reason purposively. First, reason in the sublime is not determinate—it could be practical reason or theoretical reason—yet theoretical reason is directed at, and ultimately based on, practical reason. Second, the dominion of reason over sensibility lies in the exhibition of supersensible ideas with imagination. Through this exhibition, "hidden" (*CPJ* 5:269) ideas can be sensibly exhibited, and imagination can also be enlarged and strengthened, so that it can exceeds the limitations of nature and "look[s] out upon the infinite, which for sensibility is an abyss" (265). In moral feeling, determined sensibility is imagination not as faculty of representation, but as faculty of desire. Moral feeling, as an incentive of practical reason, serves as a subjective ground for desire. It relates not to a feeling as much as to the capacity of desire. Though there is also affect and enthusiasm in the sublime, these are merely feelings that relate to the present state of mind but not to a future action (*APP* 7:251). The following table provides an overview of the differences between beauty, the sublime, and moral feeling.

	beauty	the sublime	moral feeling
the object	the reflected state of mind concerning the given object	the reflected idea of reason (the object as stimulation)	moral vocation (personality)
relation and state of the mind	free play between imagination and understanding	from free play to determined correspondence between imagination and reason	determined correspondence between reason and the sensible capacity
mode of purposiveness	subjective purposiveness without purpose	subjective purposiveness without purpose (from contrapurposiveness to purposiveness)	purposiveness with purpose
features of purposiveness	purposiveness of nature	purposiveness of freedom found in nature	purposiveness of freedom
the purpose in purposiveness	sensible power of life	purposive of reason (theoretical and practical)	purposive of practical reason
state of mind	contemplation	combination of contemplation and movement	incentive to moral action
effect in the inner mind	animation of the imagination	exhibition of ideas of reason, enlargement and strengthening the imagination	subjective determination of reason over the will
similarities between two of the three	application of aesthetic reflecting power of judgment, subjective purposiveness without purpose, beginning with the object in nature, contemplation		
		realization of end of reason; dominion of reason over sensibility; conflicting feelings	
similarities between all three	negative freedom—i.e., without sensible interests and inclinations; universal validity		

Figure 13.1 Differences between beauty, the sublime, and moral feeling

5. Turn and Unity

With the turn, we can explain the conflict between the aesthetic purity and the rational foundation of the sublime; but it is also worth noticing that the turn does not split judgment of the sublime into two things, but only two stages. In order to emphasize the unity of these two stages,

Kant claimed that sensibility's subjective contrapurposiveness is "at the same time" represented as reason's objective purposiveness (*CPJ* 5:257, 259, 261). By using the phrase "at the same time", Kant pointed out that our consciousness of sensibility's limitation and the revelation of reason's superiority come from the same act of reflection, in which the imagination strives under the regulation of reason to expand itself, mathematically or dynamically, with or without being conscious of the regulation. This insight does not conflict with the notion of a turn, which contains a logical as well as a temporal sequence.

There is also a tension between the object of nature and the ideas of reason. Kant continually emphasized that the object of the sublime is not an object in nature but our own supersensible capacity and that the former is merely a subreption for the latter (*CPJ* 5:257). Nature is a schema for the ideas of reason, albeit a failed one, because exactly through the failure is the "unattainability" (268) of the ideas revealed. Kant's emphasis on the distance and difference leads to the similarities and connections mostly being ignored, even though Kant admits that sensible representation can serve as an attribute of the ideas of reason and also animate it. The tension between the break and connection can be seen as Kant's protection of his dichotomous system (nature and freedom) on the one hand, and on the other hand his endeavor to find connections.

Despite the isolation between nature and freedom from an external perspective (nature outside us and freedom inside us),[6] Kant is more optimistic about the connection between them (nature within us and freedom inside us) in the subject. The human being can be cultivated to be more sensitive to morality by narrowing the distance between sensibility and reason and finding various ways of correspondence between them (e.g., sensible or intelligible, determined or undetermined). On the one hand, compared to the ideas of reason, imagination is insignificant; its limitations have to be overcome so that we can prepare for supersensible ideas. On the other hand, we do not abandon sensibility but force it to expand toward the supersensible, so that it can exhibit the latter in its own way. Unlike the determination of understanding over imagination in cognition, which involves the content of concepts and is constitutive, the determination of reason over imagination is only regulative for its expansion. Despite deprivation because of the dominion of reason, imagination obtains through this dominion "an enlargement and power which is greater than that which it sacrifices" (*CPJ* 5:269).

In this way, on the one hand, we can see conflict and a break between sensibility and reason in the sublime; on the other hand, we can also find the possibility of a transition between nature and freedom through the movement of self-promotion (*sich selbst erheben*)[7] from it. We can regard the sublime as a preparation for the realization of a moral end through overcoming the obstacle of nature both outside and inside of us, but also as a mutual promotion whereby reason rescues sensibility and the latter honors the former by animating it. In this tension, we can see the maximal embodiment of Kant's dichotomy, as well as his endeavor to coordinate it with the spontaneity of reason, as he always did.

Notes

1. A previous version of this chapter was published in Chinese, in the Chinese journal, *World Philosophy* 2 (2017) 2, 67–76.
2. Kant defined an end as an "object of a concept insofar as the latter is regarded as the cause of the former (the real ground of its possibility)" (*CPJ* 5:220). So there is a relationship between the concept as cause and the object as effect, based on causality. By contrast, purposiveness is "the causality of a *concept* with regard to its *object*" (220).
3. He "speaks of beauty as if it were a property of things" (*CPJ* 5:212). "When we call something beautiful, the pleasure that we feel is expected of everyone else in the judgment of taste as necessary, just as if it were to be regarded as a property of the object that is determined in it in accordance with concepts" (218).
4. This does not mean that there is always a turn in the feeling of the sublime. The turn exists only when the feeling of the sublime comes from intuiting an object in nature. We can also have a direct feeling of the sublime regarding our moral vocation, but this feeling is not brought about through aesthetic reflection, but intellectual consciousness.
5. Just as when we observe an object, but do not automatically presume it to be beautiful.
6. The connection between nature and freedom from an external perspective is not yet possible here, but possible in the second part of the third *Critique*, on teleology.
7. The German Word "*das Erhabene*" (the sublime) comes from the verb "*erheben*" (to promote, raise).

References

Allison, Henry E. (2004). *Kant's Theory of Taste: A Reading of the Critique of Aesthetic Judgment*. Cambridge: Cambridge University Press.

Busche, Hubertus (1991). Die spielerische Entgegnung der Idee auf die ernste Natur. Versuch über Kants Analytik des Erhabenen. In: *Zeitschrift für philosophischeZeitschrift für philosophische Forschung* 45(4), 511–529.

Foessel, Michaël (2008). Analytik des Erhabenen. In: Otfried Höffe (ed.), *Immanuel Kant: Kritik der Urteilskraft*. Berlin: Akademie Verlag, 99–119.

Guyer, Paul (1982). Kant's Distinction between the Beautiful and the Sublime. In: *Review of Metaphysics* 35(4), 753–783.

Loose, Donald (2011). *The Sublime and Its Teleology*. Leiden: Brill Press.

Nahm, Milton C. and Bryn Mawr (1956). "Sublimity" and the "Moral law" in Kant's Philosophy. In: *Kant-Studien* 48(4), 502–524.

14 The Ubiquity of Transcendental Apperception

Werner Moskopp

To give us a common past, I shall start this chapter with a short preview of the main topics of the following text. It is the movement of thoughts that makes this preview a review, for the text is already written and, in fact, its hypotheses can now, *ex post facto*, be listed like this: (1) In direct relation to Chong-fuk Lau's interpretation of Kant, the following thoughts are based on the assumption that in Kant's philosophy, transcendental idealism coincides with empirical realism. We just have to be aware of the perspective of our cognitive operation in each case: Is it an epistemic claim or is it an ontological thesis, and so on? (2) Hence, the main problem of defining intuition lies in considering the affection of inner or outer impressions (*Empfindung*) on the one hand and mere thinking on the other hand. In this chapter, transcendental apperception is placed in the center of any possible epistemological question, especially in the center of the metaphysical and the transcendental discussion of intuition, plus the dark power of the *Einbildungskraft* (imagination) in connecting *Sinnlichkeit* (sensibility) and *Verstand* (understanding). (3) If the arguments for these two standpoints are correct, I conclude (to say it in accordance with Hegel) that every philosophy East or West, *a fortiori*, has to be an idealism. Thus, philosophy searches for universal and necessary cognitions that constitute every possible claim of knowledge. So, as I understand transcendental philosophy, it is a pure methodology and, in so far as it concedes universal methodological structures for any reasonable being, it is at any concrete time at any place a real access of reason to the *philosophia perennis* (see Kaulbach 1982, 6).

At the end of these opening remarks, it seems quite clear that the following arguments stand in the context of transcendental idealism. Therefore, I take philosophy as a critical and pragmatistic project that searches for the universal way (method) towards self-reliance, say, that searches for self-improvement or *ren* or *yoga* or *ethos*. I will discuss this project in two steps: The first one points out my interpretation of Kant's Critical philosophy and asks what that interpretation means for "intuition West"; the second step asks what it means for "intuition East".

Comparing different epistemologies from different cultures all over the world, no doubt, works by investigating relations in words, in texts, in abstracted cultural backgrounds, in associations of logical structures. What seems to be a relativistic position, at first glance, takes its objectivity from a phenomenological point of view: The universality of human cognition lies in the congruity of the many faculties of the mind. Of course, all things that we think about are given by the affection of our inner and outer senses; and the senses in turn are embedded in particular environmental/natural and social contexts. Now, the claim to contextualize all experiences is in itself a generalization of our understanding (*Verstand*) and so a principle regulates all possible experiences of a steady world in the community of things as they appear to a (single) observer (cf. the principles of pure understanding in *Critique of Pure Reason*, A148f/ B187f). In that principle of a transcendental analogy of the first *Critique*, all experiences affirm the presupposition that categories and intuitions are constituted by the synthesis of factual apperception (A106):

> Every necessity has a transcendental condition as its ground. A transcendental ground must therefore be found for the unity of the consciousness in the synthesis of the manifold of all our intuitions, hence also of the concepts of objects in general, consequently also of all objects of experience, without which it would be impossible to think of any object for our intuitions; for the latter is nothing more than the something for which the concept expresses such a necessity of synthesis.

Any true claim of transcendental Criticism demands universality and necessity in its synthetic validity—and this validity reaches beyond the generality of inductions and therefore beyond the binding of intuitions. When thinking refers to pure intuition it finds one of its own capabilities. In a second step, if it refers to itself in order to describe its own capabilities, there are pure forms of consciousness reflecting themselves as a special kind of universal knowledge, that is: These forms have to be acknowledged by every reasonable being that is reflecting its thinking, because they are independent of (not: unconditioned by) the knower's concrete location and historical placement. But the independence of the material context does not mean that the forms of thinking already count as a cognition—every cognition is bound to the necessary conditions of pure intuitions (space and time) as they can be described by pure reason.

What does that mean for the "intuition West"? "Intuition" has several meanings in German philosophy: "*Anschauung*" is the Kantian word that is translated here into the English "intuition" and that in the long run gives access to the so called "intellectual intuition" in Schelling's work.[1] Even Spinoza's third type of cognition in his *Ethica*, "*sub specie aeternitatis*" (1977, 670; Pars V, Propositio XXIX) can be seen as a "direct

jump" from reason to divine evidence, as a kind of revelation, or as a connection of the highest parts of human intellect to the world logos (*nous,
Vernunft, Geistseele*)—i.e., as an inspiration, a second sight or a mantic
or ecstatic act. As we can see, the common semantic frame concerning all
these aspects of intuition is built by metaphors of the extended body and
the bodylike solids (*geometrische Körper*) that surround it, like buildings, rooms, etc. This dimension, therefore, describes a spatio-temporal
process that, say, penetrates the skin/the senses/the borders of the living
organism. In the way we typically think about human experiences, this
process is imagined as a movement from the outside–in, or as an "*Empfindung*"/sensation of the inner sense.

But Kant takes the problem of a wrong assignment of these structures
seriously, as we can see in the Amphiboly chapter, where he warns not
to mix up the material of outer or inner intuition with concepts of the
intellect. Therefore, the difference between mere thinking and synthetic
cognition is crucial. And that means for us that we must not confuse the
inner sense with the unity of apperception. The inner sense works in its
sensation of moods and its temporal tendencies of the *Empfindung* as a
kind of underlying feeling, a basic tactual sense, maybe as "*das Erleben*"
(*qualia*) or "*das Dasein*" (being).

Therefore, our "*Dasein*" bears only acts of transcendental cognition
as far as it bears a synthesis of intuition and concepts to "my" continuous consciousness. Especially the synthetic judgments *a priori* claim
universality and necessity because their function is independent of any
empirical material, but reason has to describe it in a pure succession
(*Nacheinander*). These functions, however, are only possible if the content of thoughts itself is constituted by the form of a deeper synthesis.
You can analyze this form in all judgments I make, because they all consist of a combination of "3 to the power of 4" (i.e., 81) possibly judging
forms that depend on the categories and succession.

In contrast, the separation of an isolated esthetical feeling, which is
reflected as my first-person experience of being ("*Erleben des Daseins*")
at a moment in the past, (for the understanding) is only a remembrance
of the fact of the *Dasein*. Analytic judgments concerning the continuum
of the *Dasein* remain mere tautological explanations. Hence, they own
no knowledge of the self, the *Dasein*, or any of these metaphysical topics,
because, as Ernst Bloch puts it (1985, Ch.20), every "*Erleben*" (*qualia*,
or actual first-person experience or intuition, in the way Bergson uses it)
is just "*Gelebtes*" (a description of what was formerly *qualia* that is too
late to catch the *qualia* itself).

At first glance, we can envision an algorithm or an assembly belt
for the production of cognition, wherein the pure intuition works and
stamps its forms into an amorphic/manifold material, just as if cognition
fabricated its parts of the production process. But because of the "reflex
arc" of thinking, maybe we would better think of a system of inclusions

that can be illustrated by concentric circles: in the center lies the synthetic power of relations and in the widest circle you find the relation of the observer-apperception to the things as they appear and, by the conditions of being related as phenomena, to the relations of the things as they appear in a community (reciprocity).[2] In this illustration, all kinds of empirical scientific thoughts, based on external or internal intuitions of sensibility (such as psychology, anthropology, etc.) are composed of synthetic judgments *a posteriori*. But both the constitutive and the regulative principles of scientific laws, including the axioms of intuition, are themselves connected by the effects of synthesis. As I mentioned before, that is the central point where I expect the source of universality to be (i.e., "transcendental apperception"). But, as far as we know, there is no possibility to catch this power in itself, neither as a thing in itself nor as the content of any intuition.

So, what on earth am I writing about? We have to handle a hard and tragic limitation, because we prefer to name this power of living consciousness "Ego", "I", or "my inner self". At least, we know something about the concept of the synthesis in knowing that there is no possible knowledge we could formulate about it. And we know by reflection that every act of cognition in itself is synthetic, and therefore has an idealistic relation to the ego. Thus, we end up with a Critical result: we can know what is not to be known by limitation and we can show what kind of theories altogether transcend the safe ground of synthetic cognition. The Hungarian philosopher, Zeno Vendler, brings the effort of this combination of transcendental idealism and empirical realism to the point (Vendler 1984, 117):

> Of course, the transcendental self does not operate by itself, *in vacuo*, but as anchored in you or me. For this reason the idea of a possible world not containing rational creatures is mere speculation. I exist, by Descartes's argument, since I perceive and think and act in *some* subject in the world, which *happens to be* this mind and this body. To use Kant's terminology: the transcendental unity of apperception does not determinate *my* perspective; it is the rule for all possible perceptions.

From my methodological point of view, the human self is nothing when we think of it in concepts of categories (for example "substance") or when we imagine it in bodily or temporal metaphors, because the transcendental synthesis is, as far as we can follow its trace, the "*Bedingung der Möglichkeit*" (conditions of the possibility) of the cognition of all these principles, concepts, and intuitions. In this respect, it is not a thing in itself and not a thing as it appears; it is the *conditio sine qua non* under which any consciousness can be anchored ("*je und je*") as its own "now and here" and consequently as an inertial system of every single ego.

I want to emphasize the universality of "every single ego", in contrast to the generalization, "all egos", since the extension of the concept, "self" or "ego", contains no object in the world of facts.

As Wittgenstein tried to show: The ego is not an atomic fact/state of affairs of the world, but it is the one transcendent power that all other activities of the mind are related to. Therefore, I select the term "ubiquity" to denote the universal claim that can be made by every consciousness in the same way. The German language has an equivalent expression that can convey my purpose: "*Selbigkeit*" refers not only to the same but also to a pure selfhood, *atman* and *advaita*. David Velleman (2013, 67) uses the term "ubiquity" to express the coincidence of every single concrete thinking and the realization of formal structures in moral psychology. The advantages are clear: Velleman can argue on the structural level of moral grounds, while at the same time he is mapping the field of actual moral beliefs worldwide by empirical studies.

In Kant's *Lectures on Logic* (JL 9:102–133), we can see that inductive generality and comparative judgments have the same tendency to describe the "insufficient" material issues of the world. Only the pure synthetic judgments *a priori* are considered to be universal, and in fact that does not mean that they exist in a world of ideas, but that every reasonable being has no other possibility to build its cognitions. Hence, ubiquity emphasizes a kind of cognition that—if we think in structures of things—is nothing in itself (has no substance) and is everything in its transcendental moment of pure synthesis.

What does that mean for "intuition East"? We should remember that there was an inclination toward "Chinoiserie" in Kant's time that was slowly transforming into an "Indomania" in the time of the Romantic philosophers and of German idealism (Friedrich Schlegel, Schopenhauer, and Hegel in some regard). From the "weird" standpoint of Western philosophers, Paul Deussen (to select one of many) writes in "*Vedanta, Platon und Kant*" (1917, 8; my translation):

> We have proved that Kant's main theorems serve as indispensable presuppositions to all religions. This is not to say that it was only through Kant that religion became possible in the world, but rather that Kant's main thought existed long before Kant, and that all religious minds always presupposed unconsciously or half consciously the great truth, which indeed by Kant's proof was initially exalted to scientific evidence.

No doubt, Kant's *Critiques* show the limits of human faculties in questions of the ontological state of the self and the unity of "*Seyn*". By this means, the ubiquity of the transcendental ego can be read with a negative connotation as an equivalent standpoint to *Anatta* or nothingness and with a positive connotation as the "*tat twam asi*" (that you are) of the

Chandogya Upanishad. In both ways, the illusion of a constant "personal core" of a soul is excluded from possible cognitions, because its concepts occur without formal or material (here: inner or outer) intuition. Hence, there is no knowledge of the self in itself, and within a Critical philosophy there can be no knowledge of birth or rebirth because there can be no epistemic claim about the substance of a soul that could be born at all. The common ground for thinking about *Anatta* or nothingness and for *Atman* or allness lies in the formal apperception (B157):

> In the transcendental synthesis of the manifold of representations in general, on the contrary, hence in the synthetic original unity of apperception, I am conscious of myself not as I appear to myself, nor *as* I am in myself, but only *that* I am. This *representation* is a *thinking*, not an *intuiting*. Now since for the *cognition* of ourselves, in addition to the action of thinking that brings the manifold of every possible intuition to the unity of apperception, a determinate sort of intuition, through which this manifold is given, is also required, my own existence is not indeed appearance (let alone mere illusion), but the determination of my existence can only occur in correspondence with the form of inner sense . . .

At this point, we outline the (affirmative) speculative speech of "ineffability" in metaphysics,[3] while the directions of thoughts are staying the same East and West: inner and outer mystic (see Underhill 2013), top–down or bottom–up processes of redemption (Neoplatonism), holism (Spinoza), or mere reduction. This is where the ubiquity of transcendental methodologies all around the world shows its advantages: ubiquitous "thinking" emphasizes a primacy of practical reason and a normative dimension of the relation between means and ends; therefore, *ren* and self-realization (cf. Naess 2013) do not only call for an improvement of one's own ego, but they postulate the perfection of a nameless apperception that is "mine" in each case (*eigentlich*)—however, the pronoun "mine" intends to retrospectively reflect on a separated object "I", where there is no object at all but a state or a process that cannot be expressed by any object-related language. So to say, we deal with living nothingness, as Nishitani puts it in *Religion and Nothingness* (1982).

It is a pity that I cannot do better here than to refer to Bergson's method of "intuition" in the way of a "pure" empirism (see Bergson 1999)—or "radical empiricism" as William James (2003) calls it. Even if Bergson criticizes Kant for his transcendental method that is built, in Bergson's opinion, on a dualism of analyzing and synthesizing features of scientific thinking. Although Bergson criticizes Kant for his transcendental method, which in his opinion is based on a dualism of scientific analysis and synthesis, it allows us to see some subtleties by differenciating between reflective and pre-reflective concepts of consciousness (cf.

Frank 2015). However, I would like to emphasize that Kant's "transcendental synthesis" is not a mere methodological feature, but an ongoing process that should be read as an actual condition of the possibility of knowledge and action as a whole. It is up to Kant's supreme wisdom to declare any description of this state (in itself and even as a phenomenon) as inadequate, for it shows the limits of human knowledge, or the limits of any Critical philosophy that will ever appear as a science.

One could compare Kant's claims about these limits with a lot of passages in the *Tao Te Ching* (Lao Tzu 2012, 5 [Ch. 1]):

> The Tao that can be told is not the eternal Tao. The name that can be named is not the eternal name. The nameless is the beginning of heaven and Earth. . . . These two spring from the same source but differ in name; this appears as darkness. Darkness within darkness. The gate to all mystery.

And I think that even Kant could tolerate a "metaphysical oneness" like the *tao*, when it is formulated as a practical "*Besinnungsmoment*" or transcendental apperception: in a short appendix of *Conflict of the Faculties*, called On A Pure Mysticism in Religion (*CF* 7:69f), we find a description of the mystical way of life in Karl Arnold Wilmans' letter to Kant (73): "In a word, if these people [i.e., the mystics/separatists] were philosophers they would be (pardon the term!) true Kantians." This—here I am in absolute agreement with Palmquist (2000, 306)—is carefully endorsed by Kant's footnote (69n): "However, I do not mean to guarantee that my views coincide entirely with his."

Notes

1. See e.g., the fourth lecture of his *Philosophy of Revelation* (Schelling 1985, 664), where he refers to "the immediate content of reason" (my translation of "der allein unmittelbare Inhalt der Vernunft").
2. Compare the distinction of Chong-fuk Lau (2016, 5; quoting A373) between two levels of status of the "*außer uns*": "Bei der Frage nach der ontologischen Position Kants kommt es also darauf an, ob und inwiefern sich der transzendentale Idealismus auf die Existenz äußerer Dinge festlegt, d. h., ob und inwiefern es material-körperliche Gegenstände gibt, die nicht in unserem Bewußtsein, sondern außer uns existieren. Diese Frage muß allerdings auf zwei verschiedenen Ebenen getrennt beantwortet werden. . . . Dieser [sc. der Ausdruck 'außer uns'] kann einmal in seinem gewöhnlichen Sinne empirisch verstanden werden, indem er sich auf Dinge bezieh[t], die nicht innerlich im Bewußtsein, sondern äußerlich im Raum existieren. Er kann aber auch "im transzendentalen Sinne" als etwas verstanden werden, das unabhängig von allen Bedingungen des erkennenden Subjekts als Ding an sich selbst existiert. Als erste Annäherung könnte Kants komplexe Theorie des empirischen Realismus und transzendentalen Idealismus als eine zweifache These aufgefaßt werden, die die Existenz 'äußerer Dinge' im empirischen Sinne anerkennt, aber dieselbe im transzendentalen Sinne leugnet. Auf der empirischen Ebene

legt sich Kant auf die Existenz äußerer Dinge fest. Was im empirischen Sinne außer uns existiert, sind im Raume anzutreffende Dinge. Dabei wendet sich Kant entschieden gegen den empirischen oder materialen Idealismus."
3. Both have their primacy in practical reason, so that our thinking might lead us to a pragmatic field, where we find what Charles Sanders Peirce might have called the "synechism" (i.e., continuity) of intuition East and West. I quote just one single thought from Peirce's *oeuvre* (Peirce 1992, 2): "Nor must any synechist say, 'I am altogether myself, and not at all you.' If you embrace synechism, you must abjure this metaphysics of wickedness. In the first place, your neighbors are, in a measure, yourself, and in far greater measure than, without deep studies in psychology, you would believe. Really, the selfhood you like to attribute to yourself is, for the most part, the vulgarest delusion of vanity. In the second place, all men who resemble you and are in analogous circumstances are, in a measure, yourself, though not quite in the same way in which your neighbors are you."

References

Bergson, Henri (1999). *An Introduction to Metaphysics*. Indianapolis: Hackett Publishing Company.

Bloch, Ernst (1985). *Das Prinzip Hoffnung*. Frankfurt am Main: Suhrkamp.

Deussen, Paul (1917). *Vedanta, Platon und Kant*. Wien: Urania Bücherei.

Frank, Manfred (2015). *Präreflexives Selbstbewusstsein: vier Vorlesungen*. Stuttgart: Reclam.

James, William (2003). *Essays in Radical Empiricism*. Mineola and New York: Dover Publications.

Kaulbach, Friedrich (1982). *Immanuel Kant*. Berlin: De Gruyter.

Lao Tzu (2012). Trans. J. Legge, *Tao Te Ching*. New York: Simon and Brown.

Lau, Chong-fuk (2016). Ist Kant ein Idealist? Lecture at the Rheinisch–Westfälische Technische Hochschule Aachen (May 3, 2016).

Naess, Arne (2013). *Die Zukunft in unseren Händen*. Wuppertal: Peter Hammer Verlag.

Nishitani, Keiji (1982). Trans. J. V. Bragt, *Religion and Nothingness*. Berkeley: University of California Press.

Palmquist, Stephen R. (2000). *Kant's Critical Religion: Volume Two of Kant's System of Perspectives*. Aldershot: Ashgate.

Peirce, C. S. (1992). *The Essential Peirce: Selected Philosophical Writings*. Bloomington: Indiana University Press.

Schelling, F. W. J. (1985). *Ausgewählte Werke*. Bd. 5.1. Frankfurt am Main: Suhrkamp.

Spinoza, Benedictus de (1977). Trans. J. Stern, *Ethica/Ethik*. Stuttgart: Reclam.

Underhill, Evelyn (2013). *Practical Mysticism*. Hamburg: Tredition Classics.

Velleman, David (2013). *Foundations for Moral Relativism*. Cambridge: Open Book Publishers.

Vendler, Zeno (1984). *The Matter of Minds*. Oxford: Clarendon Press.

15 Intuition as a Blend of Cognition and Consciousness

An Examination of the Philosophies of Kant and Krishnamurti[1]

Krishna Mani Pathak

1. Introduction

Intuition (*Anschauung*)[2] is one of the central components of Kant's theory of knowledge in the sense of its role in the process of mental representation and production of knowledge.[3] Human knowledge is generated distinctively in three ways: (a) by *experience*, (b) by *reason*, and (c) by the *union* of the two, and can be expressed as *analytic* or *synthetic* judgments.[4] It is well known that empiricists advocate for human experience as the only source of knowledge whereas rationalists believe in human reason as the ultimate originating faculty of knowledge. Kant doesn't find either experience or reason to be independently capable of yielding adequate knowledge of objects, truth, and reality, and therefore he does not subscribe to these theories. He rather believes in the unity of the two with primacy given to reason.

Kant criticizes the propounders of empiricism and rationalism for two reasons: (1) both empiricists and rationalists have failed to identify the two essentially inclusive components of human knowledge regarded as *a priori* and *a posteriori*, or so to say, *innate* and *experienced*, and (2) they also fail to observe the unified functional role of both the mind and the senses in representing objects to them together in order to convert the representation as knowledge. Having established the points for his criticism of both of these theories of knowledge, Kant comes up with the idea of a compromise or synthesis between the two and offers a new theory of knowledge that we can call *Kantianism* or Kant's *syntheticism*. This seems to be clear from Kant's assertion of two roots of knowledge, sensibility (*Sinnlichkeit*) and understanding (*Verstand*): "there are two stems of human cognition, which may perhaps arise from a common but to us unknown root, namely sensibility and understanding, through the first of which objects are given to us, but through the second of which they are thought" (B29). Sensibility and understanding are respectively regarded as two distinct faculties of knowledge. The former is the faculty that yields sensuous knowledge whereas the latter is the faculty that yields knowledge of concepts or ideas.

The two components of *a priori* and *a posteriori* can be understood respectively as knowledge whose validity can be established *independent of* all experiences and knowledge whose validity is *dependent on* experiences. The former, according to Kant, is universal and necessary whereas the latter is particular and contingent or dispensable. As generally believed, *a priori* knowledge can be in the form of either analytic or synthetic judgments but *a posteriori* knowledge is mostly in the form of synthetic judgments, although some scholars like Aldrich (1968) and Palmquist (1987 and 2012), contrastingly with different epistemological approaches to Kant's theories, attempt to prove that *a posteriori* analytic judgments are possible. I propose to deliberately skip the debate on the distinction between analytic and synthetic, due to the specific concern of this chapter, despite the fact that Kant's epistemology is woven in such a manner that nothing can be less meaningful.

Kant's epistemological quest is to deal with the question pertaining to the origin of *a priori* synthetic judgment, since he seems to have believed that the existence of *a priori* analytic and *a posteriori* synthetic judgments have no difficulty at all because they rest, as the case may be, upon the concept constructed by the mind or the perception or experience of objects (Prichard 1909, 2). But, why does Kant want to explore the possibility of having synthetic *a priori* judgments? Kant's answer can be found in his first *Critique*, where he admits that metaphysical claims pertaining to God, freedom, and immortality are made most often in synthetic *a priori* judgments without any appeal to human experience. So to validate those claims of metaphysics we must first ascertain whether such synthetic *a priori* judgments do really exist. This is what has encouraged Kant to demarcate the range within which both sensibility and understanding play their distinct roles in generating (*a priori*) human knowledge.

Intuition is said to be a conscious cognitive activity of mental representation that is related to sensibility and sometimes to intellect, known as sensible intuition and intellectual intuition. But by and large human intuition, Kant believes, is not intellectual; rather it is sensible only. It is solely sensible simply because it is dependent on the existence of sensible objects and thus it fails to have spontaneous immediate reflection in its representation. Intellectual intuition or immediate knowledge, on the other hand, can only be possessed by primordial beings like God, although Kant is skeptical about this as well since the activity of intuition can never take place without sensibility. I will discuss this aspect of the Kantian notion of intuition in detail in subsequent sections.

Unlike Kant, Jiddu Krishnamurti (see note 1, above) does not give any systematic notion of intuition, but his thought on human knowledge does indeed reflect significant philosophical insights, if we examine how he uses the word "knowledge", be it right or wrong, in the psychological

202 *Krishna Mani Pathak*

sense of knowledge that arises as a result of the gathering of experiences (Krishnamurti 1996). Knowledge of this kind is limited because it is born out of experiences, and thoughts dependent of such knowledge would eventually be limited, leaving many more to be known by other means. Krishnamurti seems to have criticized the empiricist account of knowledge for the purpose of differentiating it from both non-empirical and immediate knowledge. This is what makes him concerned about whether the human mind can, by any means, transcend its thoughts based on empirical knowledge. I will explain this point and his definition of intuition as intelligence with the help of Krishnamurti's idea of self-knowledge in subsequent sections.

Although both Kant and Krishnamurti do not seem to be keeping intuition and intellect (intelligence) entirely separate, there are some notional contrasts between their definitions and understandings of human intuition as a means to mental representation. One such contrast is that Kant is more pessimistic towards humans' intellectual intuition when he says that one's cognition cannot intuit anything without sensibility, whereas Krishnamurti is more optimistic when he says that intuition is the whisper of the human soul and can express itself without any mediation.

2. Two Patterns of Mental Representation[5]

Mental representation is usually understood as a cognitive process or state of the mind that involves under some conditions a string of activities, such as receiving images and data, thinking about and analyzing events, classification of received data into different categories, cognizing objects, and making judgments. All these are taken together as mental contents. What is contextually relevant to know is how the mind (re)presents the internal or external reality to itself before it yields cognition of one kind or another. More precisely, it is to know the process of how the mind reaches the object to cognize it as anything A or B or C since philosophers working in the area of epistemology and cognitive science believe that the mind "is able to represent the world" and "the basic problem of mental representation is that of better understanding this relationship between mind and world" (Clapin 2002, 2).

Among many key notions present in Kant's epistemology, one is the notion of *Vorstellung* (a representation), which Kant discusses in reference to objectively produced cognitive judgments, be they *a priori* or *a posteriori* (Dickerson 2004, Ch. 1). According to Kant, the mind involves its two radically different but cognitively powerful faculties of sensibility and understanding to reach to an object of experience. These two faculties exhibit two different sides of the mind: sensibility exhibits the *receptive* aspect, how the mind is related to the object, whereas understanding exhibits the *spontaneous* aspect, how it presents to itself its own construction of concepts or thoughts without regard to any relation to the object. These two faculties represent two different kinds of contents to the mind: sensibility produces intuition and understanding produces concepts, and for any form of cognition to be complete both intuition and concepts (via sensibility and understanding) must participate in the cognitive process. For Kant, all human knowledge requires the object of knowledge to be presented both by receptivity and spontaneity together. This is the idea Kant has advanced while discussing the roles of these two faculties in the process of mental representation (A50–51/B74–76):

> Our cognition arises from two fundamental sources in the mind, the first of which is the reception of representations (the receptivity of impressions), the second the faculty for cognizing an object by means of these representations (spontaneity of concepts); through the former an object is given to us, through the latter it is thought in relation to that representation (as a mere determination of the mind). Intuition and concepts therefore constitute the elements of all our cognition, so that neither concepts without intuition corresponding to them in some way nor intuition without concepts can yield a cognition. Both are either pure or empirical. . . . Without sensibility no object would be given to us, and without understanding none would be thought. Thoughts without content are empty, intuitions without concepts are blind.

Kant believes that although our knowledge begins with our experience through the receptive representation made by our senses, it is not the case that all our knowledge arises from experience (B1). The complete process of knowledge through mental representation involves the unity of both receptivity and spontaneity.[6] In other words, what Kant says is that our knowledge arises out of the compound made between our sensuous impressions and understanding of concepts, which the mind spontaneously receives from itself. We can explain this with an example. A person who has the knowledge of different colors can better explain the rainbow seen in the sky on the basis of what she perceives as a bow-like colored object and what she possesses as concepts of red, green, blue, and so forth. A two-year-old child, on the other hand, can identify the rainbow only as *something* if she has no knowledge of any color and any object like a bow, because what she perceives is merely sense impressions without any appeal to concepts of different colors.

These two mental faculties of sensibility and understanding show two different patterns of representation through receptivity and spontaneity. Receptivity is the pattern of presenting the object of knowledge to the mind in the form of sensations or sense impressions generated through contact with the sense-object. The receptive mind in this kind of representation is merely a receiver of those sense impressions and is therefore said to be involved passively since it does not do anything with those impressions at this stage. Knowledge does not arise at this level. The mind actively acts in the next moment when its faculty of understanding brings the mind to the spontaneity mode, where the mind conforms those sense impressions to its concepts to produce knowledge. In other words, receptivity is merely sensuous perceptions and spontaneity is mental conceptions, and no knowledge arises, Kant claims, without the realization of the two together.[7] Further, these two faculties have two distinct kinds of contents: sensibility has a direct reach to objects and understanding has a direct reach to concepts; but indirectly, both faculties supplement each other. Now if we exclude immediate intuition and revelation as direct means of knowledge from our discussion on Kant, we have sufficient reasons to support Kant and his syntheticism.

Krishnamurti discusses the nature of mental contents from a different perspective of mental paradigms, which he classifies into knowledge and wisdom. Unlike Kant, who distinguishes between perception and conception, Krishnamurti asserts that wisdom is above all kinds of knowledge. He says (1992, 122):

> What is knowledge, and why does the mind give such extraordinary importance to knowledge? . . . A mind must be free to be wise. The essence of wisdom is the denial of experience, and the denial of experience is the denial of knowledge, because experience has become our authority. . . . Everything is an experience, and we question that experience. I say a mind that merely experiences and accumulates is an immature mind, and the mind that is beyond and above experience is the free mind, is the new mind, is the young mind.

Krishnamurti seems to have believed that all kinds of (mental and perceptive) knowledge, dependent on human experience, are inferior to wisdom because "wisdom cannot be brought; it is natural, spontaneous, free. . . . Wisdom, I say, has nothing to do with knowledge" (Weeraperuma 1986, 222). A question arises here: Does Krishnamurti mean that *a priori* concepts are natural, spontaneous, and free, and therefore become the content of wisdom which is ultimately possessed by the mature mind? We cannot answer this with certainty because Krishnamurti, as it has been said before, is not a systematic philosopher. His metaphysical and epistemological thoughts are scattered and sometimes amalgamated everywhere in his writings, interviews, and discussions. So, it is quite difficult to extract and present them to the readers in the manner Kant has profoundly presented his philosophy. However, one thing is clear, that Krishnamurti, like Kant, gives priority to (*a priori*) spontaneous knowledge over (*a posteriori*) experienced knowledge (Mehta 1973, 161–162):

> For all acts of perception there are three agencies that have to be considered—the sensorial apparatus, the brain and the mind. The

sensorial apparatus is concerned with sensations, the brain is concerned with the formulation of perceptions and the mind with the creation of concepts. Perceptions deal with forms or structures of things and events, it is the conceptual activity which is concerned with the naming process. In fact the name and the concept are not two different things. To put anything into a framework of concept is to assign a name to it. It is quite obvious that if the perception is incomplete or inadequate then the concept or the name assigned to that perception cannot be correct.

Thus, the faculty of sensibility that gives rise to perception and the faculty of understanding that gives rise to conception are taken to be two such agencies without which no knowledge is possible since the object, as it is rightly believed by Kant and to some extent by Krishnamurti, cannot be given to us without sensibility and be thought of without understanding. The epistemic symmetry between Kant and Krishnamurti is become clearer to us since both the philosophers classify the content of knowledge into experienced and non-experienced and subjective and objective. Objectively the object is presented to the mind through intuition as it appears to our senses; subjectively the object is brought under conceptions of the mind as it fits into them. When both these subjective and objective processes of representation take place, knowledge eventually arises. This is why "all representation", Kant writes, "is either sensation or cognition" (*VL*, 24:805).

3. Intuition and Its Epistemic Content[8]

As indicated before, intuition works under the faculty of sensibility and plays a crucial epistemological role in constructing mental contents to be used as material for generating knowledge. In the beginning of *CPR* (A19/B34), Kant has made it clear that intuition is the only means through which the mind has a direct reach to the object before it assembles the sense data with the help of its concepts in order to convert them into knowledge. In this context, I would like to cite two of the most quoted passages from Kant's writings to substantiate my observation (A19/B34 and *JL* 9:91):

I. In whatever way and through whatever means a cognition may relate to objects, that through which it relates immediately to them, and at which all thought as a means is directed as an end, is intuition. This, however, takes place only insofar as the object is given to us; but this in turn, is possible only if it affects the mind in a certain way. The capacity (receptivity) to acquire representations through the way in which we are affected by objects is called sensibility. Objects are therefore given to us by means of sensibility, and it alone affords us intuitions; but they are thought through the understanding, and from it arise concepts. But all thought, whether straightaway (directe) or through a detour (indirecte), must ultimately be related to intuitions, thus, in our case, to sensibility, since there is no other way in which objects can be given to us.

II. All cognitions, that is, all representations related with consciousness to an object, are either intuitions or concepts. An intuition is a singular representation (repraesentatio singularis), a concept a universal (repraesentatio per notas communes) or reflected representation (repraesentatio discursiva). Cognition through concepts is called thought (cognitio discursive).[9]

These two passages clearly indicate that intuition is receptive in nature and always presents particular objects to the mind, which cognizes the objects with the help of its universally valid concepts. The objective representation is done by the intuition without which the object cannot be given to the mind and the subjective representation is done by the concept without which the object cannot be cognized or thought of. Kant's *Tractatio Logices* in the Vienna Logic discusses in detail the process of representation and both kinds of cognitive components, which create knowledge (*VL*, 24:805):

All our cognitions can be considered in two relations.

1. In relation to the object. This is representation.
2. In relation to the subject. This is consciousness of the representation.

. . . All representation is either sensation or cognition. It is something that has a relation to something in us. Sensations do affect, but they quickly vanish, too, because they are not cognition. For when I sense, I cognize nothing. Cognition is of two kinds, either intuition or concept. The former is singular, the latter is universal. For a concept belongs to all.

Although there are some genuine problems pertaining to the English translation of *Anschauung* as *intuition*, I think one can easily come to Kant's basic idea of intuition and the kind of role it plays to directly represent the object to the knower to let him have the cognition about it. Precisely, one can draw the following key points to be discussed in more detail:

(a) Intuition and concept are two basic components of human cognition or thought and none of them alone can constitute knowledge.
(b) Intuition, which always works through sensibility, refers to be the direct relation between the cognition of the knower and the object

known. And sensibility in this process of cognizing things through intuition refers to the receptive capacity of the knower through which she acquires representations about the objects.

(c) Conception, unlike intuition, always works through understanding and refers to be the cognitive framework through which the knower participates in thinking.

The epistemic content of intuition is undoubtedly the object of sensuous perception. Intuition in this sense is the channel through which sense data are transferred to the mind before it applies its various conceptual categories or frameworks upon them. Kant has talked about two kinds of intuition: sensible and intellectual. Sensible intuition is the most common form of intuition; it is common because any normal human agent with sound sensuous receptivity can experience this. We can also call it *mediate intuition* where sensibility is the mediator between the mind and the object. All common knowledge or knowledge of all common people comes under this category. Kant even makes a more general statement that human intuition is in all respects sensible (B72): "Our mode of intuition is dependent upon the existence of the object and is therefore possible only if the subject's faculty of representation is affected by that object . . . it is derivative (intuitus derivatives), not original (intuitus origainarius), and therefore not an intellectual intuition."

Intellectual intuition, on the other hand, is likely to be immediate and non-sensuous; we can call it *immediate intuition*. It does not depend on sensibility or any other means to give objects to the mind; rather it represents the objects directly to the mind as they are without any mediation. There is no sensuous receptivity involved in this form of intuition; rather it is based on direct spontaneity. If that is so, can we call it spontaneous intellectual intuition? Do humans have intuition of this kind? If not, can some of them have it? We must think. As far as Kant's own response is concerned, he has clearly indicated that humans do not and even cannot have intellectual intuition. There are some minds that can have intellectual intuitions, but these minds, according to Kant (B71; cf. B138), do not belong to humans; rather, they belong to superior minds, like that of God. But here Kant is skeptical about how this form of intuition takes place in God's mind without sensibility.[10]

Kant's classification of intuition into sensible and intellectual seems to be based on his approach to the objective existence (physical reality) of the object and the subjective existence (non-physical reality) of God. He argued in the Dialectic of the first *Critique* that the existence of God cannot be objectively proved as real, and a God who is not physically real would certainly not have sensation. So, God, if we follow Kant, can be said to have neither sensuous intuition nor intellectual.[11] I don't think those who believe in the existence of an omniscient God would subscribe Kant's interpretation. Spinoza, for example, believes that "intuitive knowledge is that kind of knowing which proceeds from an adequate idea of the formal essence of certain attributes of God to the adequate knowledge of the essence of things" (Spinoza 1985, E IP40/S$_2$).[12] Similarly in eastern philosophical traditions of Advaita Vedanta and Buddhism, intuition is taken to be the only direct means to higher knowledge, which is neither subjective nor objective and is therefore beyond the knower, the known, and the act of knowing. This direct intuition is known as *prajna*, which is beyond the reach of language, logic, and the senses.[13]

Krishnamurti claims that no knowledge, be it mental or intellectual, can take the knower to the reality simply because there is a dualistic gap between the knower or the subject and the known or the object. But unlike Kant, he argues that since the mental or intellectual knowledge is conditional and conceptualized, it keeps us away from the truth and reality. The mind cannot keep itself free from those conditions and concepts as the mind itself is conditioned by them. It can give us sensuous knowledge or knowledge based on understanding and reason but such knowledge, according to Krishnamurti, is not true knowledge. What is true knowledge then, and how does it originate in the human mind?

According to Krishnamurti, it is intuitive knowledge that brings truth directly to the mind without any mediation in the process. Intuitive knowledge—or say, intuition—happens when the mind is unconditioned or free from all concepts and sensuous representations. It is spontaneous apperception about the object. Intuition, for him, is intelligence. This is what he said in an interview with Stokowski: "you cannot divide intuition from intelligence in the higher sense. . . . Intuition is the highest point of intelligence . . . It is the apotheosis, the culmination, the accumulation of intelligence" (Krishnamurti 1970, 76).[14] In another place Krishnamurti says (2007, 67): "To me intuition is intelligence, and intelligence is not past experience, it is the understanding of past experience . . . If there is spontaneous action in the ever-moving present, in that action is intelligence and that intelligence is intuition. Intelligence is not to be separated from intuition."

Krishnamurti distinguishes intuition by ordinary people and intuition by people of higher intelligence. He claims to have not denied intuition but he is a little skeptical to consider intuition of ordinary people since he believes that what "the usual people calls intuition . . . is something without reason, validity, without understanding behind it" (2007, 23). Krishnamurti also made a distinction between intellect and intelligence. Intellect, according to him, is "thought functioning independently of emotions, whereas intelligence is the capacity to feel as well as to reason" (Lee 1995, 130 and 157). Or as Krishnamurti himself puts it (1981, 51):

> Intelligence is much greater than intellect, for it is the integration of reason and love; but there can be intelligence only when there is self-knowledge, the deep understanding of the mind process of

oneself . . . Intelligence is the spontaneous perception which makes a man strong and free. Intelligence is not the accumulation of experience and knowledge; but intelligence is the highest form of sensitivity.

Krishnamurti, unlike Kant, has not given a clear systematic theory of knowledge.[15] This is one reason why he defines intuition sometimes in reference to intelligence, sometimes in reference to intellect, and some other times in reference to insight. That a clear systematic theory of intuition and its epistemic content is missing in Krishnamurti's philosophy may be due to his intellectual growth being shaped by the components of spirituality and mysticism found in the Indian philosophical tradition, both classical and modern. Despite this fact, one can easily extract a number of philosophical statements from his interviews and works to conclude that Krishnamurti, like Kant, does believe in intellectual intuition. What is distinct in their views is that Kant's notion of intellectual intuition seems to be speculative, abstract, and unreal whereas Krishnamurti's notion bears a deep sense of direct acquaintance with the object of knowledge, be it material or nonmaterial. However, both of them appear to have advanced the idea that intuition is an integral part of conscious cognition that further becomes a pathway of representation and knowledge.

4. Cognition, Consciousness, and Intuition

Two things or ideas can be said to be blended if they are inseparably mixed together to form a new thing. Intuition, in Kant's writing, is like that. It is a blend of cognition and consciousness. Cognition (*Erkenntnis/cognitio*), according to him, is an objective perception that is either intuition or concept. This means that intuition is a form of cognition or knowledge that gives an object to the mind. In *CPR* (A320/B377) Kant writes that intuition is a mode of cognition which "relates immediately to the object and is single." Conception helps intuition to complete the process of generating knowledge. The question arises whether the mind knows that it is intuiting when it actually intuits. And if it does, then the question is how?

One can have an answer to this question only when one thinks over Kant's concept of consciousness, which plays a significant role in the entire cognitive process of knowing. Although Kant doesn't seem to have given any systematic definition of consciousness but there are enough literary materials to help us know about what Kant has in mind about consciousness. Some scholars like Serck-Hanssen (2009) has rightly pointed out that consciousness is apperception or comprehending the object of knowledge; it can be understood as one's capacity to be aware of one's spontaneity or spontaneous activities. Does it follow that the mind knows what it intuits with the help of its spontaneous awareness of the concepts without which cognition cannot arise?

It is better to say that intuition, being mainly *intellectual*, is a blended form of both cognition and consciousness rather than to say that intuition is a mode of cognition as such. The point is that if intuition does not carry the elements of cognition or if intuition is simply a sensuous representation, it can never give rise to cognition. In fact, it does carry the elements of cognition through the united thread of sensibility and understanding which the mind is continuously aware of—or so to say, that the mind is aware of each and every activity that takes place in the process. This definition, broadly speaking, will better help us defend Kant's idea of intellectual intuition.

If we closely analyze the pattern of mental representation framed by Kant, we come to have Figure 15.1:

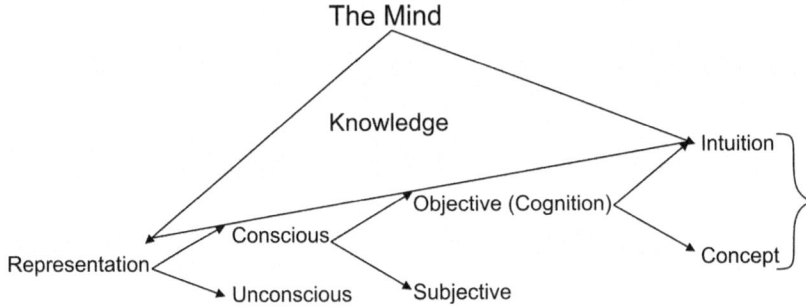

Figure 15.1 Kant's Model of Mental Representation

The triangular shape in the figure indicates how the mind receives representation starting from intuition and concept through cognition and consciousness. The subjective cognition and unconscious representation are excluded from the cognitive conscious process of knowing. Intuition is thus taken to have two different forms: (1) It is regarded as an objective conscious mental representation that is an intrinsic part of the process of knowing, and (2) it is referred to as a state of mind connected with the sensation of the object. Many scholars, like Allais (2015), have emphasized the distinct frameworks of these two forms—i.e., *intuition–as–conscious–objective–representation* and *intuition–as–sensation*.[16] I have taken the first form of intuition to substantiate my claim that intuition is not empty; rather it a unitary means of knowledge where one's consciousness and cognitive capacity make intuition happen in one's mind. Compared to this, intuition–as–sensation lacks these features and therefore cannot be said to be competent to generate knowledge.

Sensible intuition being mediate in nature does not have any such blend of cognition and consciousness; rather it is, some may argue, simply sensuous raw impressions which are the results of merely sense object contact. The mind may or may not be aware of these impressions. Intellectual intuition, on the other hand, is immediate, direct, or, so to say, spontaneous. This cognitive quality of spontaneity is explicit in intellectual intuition. It is this quality which helps the mind cognize the object. Krishnamurti also takes this quality as efficient in making novel cognition possible in unconditioned human minds, as he writes (1991, 129):

> Thought is always bound to this collected experience, and the question is: Can thinking be free? Because it is only in freedom that one can observe, it is only in freedom that one can discover. It is only in a state of spontaneity, where there is no compulsion, no immediate demand, no pressure of social influence that real discovery is possible. Surely, to observe what you are thinking, why you think, and the source and motive of your thought, there must be a certain sense of spontaneity, of freedom, because any influence whatsoever gives a twist to observation.

Krishnamurti advocates for a free, mature, and unconditioned mind which can perceive the truth and reality directly. He is certainly not talking about different versions of intuition advanced by psychologists and scientists like Bruner (1966), among others, because these versions of intuition, according to him, are often deceptive. He is talking about the process of *knowing intuitively*. To be more specific, we can discover three kinds of intuition found in the writings of Kant and Krishnamurti: *sensory*, *imaginary*, and *cognitive*. It is the cognitive intuition which is taken to be such a blend because both sensory and imaginary intuitions are limited and hence incapable to convert their contents into knowledge. What is particular in cognitive intuition, on the other hand, is the coexistence of consciousness, cognition, and spontaneity. Or, so to say that "the simple objects of intuitions are identical with the objects of consciousness" (Jardine 1874, 201).

5. A Concluding Note

I conclude this chapter with an assertive note that intuition has been understood from the perspectives of both the common mind and the cognitively superior mind. Although there are many symmetries and asymmetries in the philosophical deliberations of Kant and Krishnamurti, the comparative reading of their works definitely helps us locate the parallels of their intellectual exercises, particularly to understand the source, nature and domain of human intuition, from the perspective of the east and the west. It also helps us understand the limitations and restrictions of the human mind. Kant's idea of sensible intuition is distinct from Krishnamurti's idea of intuition linked to one's desire but both philosophers seem to have some close notional resemblances on intellectual intuition with some difference of views on who are qualified to have this higher level of intuitive knowledge.

Notes

1. The life stories of Jiddu Krishnamurti compiled by C. V. Williams (2004) may be of great help to understand his philosophical journey and intellectual growth.
2. For better apprehension of the term, the readers may be interested in Carus (1892).
3. Intuition is also used as a philosophical method to have immediate knowledge about reality and truth by looking into oneself and is believed to be free from logical reasoning. See P.T. Raju (1952).
4. An *analytic* judgment is believed to have conceptually contained its predicate in its subject and therefore does not extend our knowledge. For instance, the judgment "my bachelor friend is unmarried" is analytic in nature since the concept of "unmarried" is contained in the concept of "bachelor". In contrast to this, a *synthetic* judgment that is believed to have its predicate conceptually out of its subject but belongs to the subject in some kind of relationship with it. A synthetic judgment in this sense is potentially able to extend our knowledge. For instance, the judgment "the wall of my office is yellow" is synthetic since the concept of "yellow" is not a part of the concept of "the wall" but it is related to it, saying something new about the wall. Some may even add other means of knowledge, such as revelation.
5. There are two groups of scholars who give different interpretations to Kant's idea of mental representation, especially on the very basic question of whether sensory representation made through intuition can be done without concepts. One group argues that such sensory representations of the object can be done only with concepts whereas the other group argues just the opposite to it. The two groups are respectively known as conceptualist and non-conceptualist. I deliberately skip the details of this conceptualist–nonconceptualist debate to restrict my focus on the topic.
6. Kem and Smyth (2006) have given a detailed account of receptivity and spontaneity discussed in Kant's epistemology. There is some other suggestively relevant literature on this topic of understanding Kant's idea of mental representation. See for example Perconti (1999, Ch. 2).
7. Indian philosophical schools of both orthodox and heterodox traditions define these two faculties as two different stages of cognition: indeterminate (*nirvikalpa*) and determinate (*savikalpa*). It is generally believed that the former (indeterminate) stage is merely the awareness of existence of the object as "something" whereas the latter (determinate) stage is a kind of cognition categorized as "something A or B". That is, the former is merely sense impressions and the latter is knowledge with cognitive judgments. For better comparative apprehension of the epistemological symmetry between Kant's idea of mental representation discussed above and that of Indian logic, see Grimes (1989, 274); Vidyabhusana (1920, reprint 2006, 390); and Sharma (2000, 194).
8. Wilson (1975) has given a lucid interpretation of Kant's idea of intuition to help us understand its epistemological framework.
9. Also see Natterer (1998/2010, 22). For scholarly discussion on these two aspects of singular and general representations, which Kant discusses in his *Lectures on Logic*, see Thompson (1972).
10. Fitz (2001) has done a scholarly evaluation of intuition, defining it as "integral insight" and referring to it as one of many direct means to knowledge.
11. Hardly any Kant scholar would agree with this point since Kant clearly and repeatedly says that the concept of God is the concept of a being who possesses intellectual intuition. However, if one applies Kant's own logic

derived from his classification of sensuous and intellectual intuition, one can have sufficient reasons to theoretically believe that Kant's God does not have intellectual intuition; and God, being transcendent, obviously does not have sensuous intuition either. Scholars like Ando (1974) have rightly observed: "Intuition is usually understood as direct perception of an object; to limit it to the sensuous is a thought peculiar to Kant" (128); and "Kant never showed why our intuition should be confined to the sensuous; instead he only defined the sense as the faculty of receiving representation through being affected by an object. From this definition, it is a matter of course that every intuition is of sensuous character. That sense is passive and intellect is active was Kant's dogmatic assumption, which automatically ruled out intellectual intuition of any kind" (130).

12. The citation is taken from Edwin Curley's 1985 translation of Spinoza's works.
13. See Puligandla (1975). Burtt (1953) reflects some significant philosophical points of the eastern and western traditions.
14. Krishnamurti's conversation with Stokowski can also be accessed on www. jiddu-krishnamurti.net/en/1927-1928-1929-early-writings/krishnamurti-early-writings-12-a-conversation-with-stokowski
15. Sardesai (1996) has given a brief account of Krishnamurti's theory of knowledge that can be of some help.
16. Hanna (2015) has also examined aspects of the epistemic relationship between various components of consciousness, cognition, and intuition, and therefore may be of great help to have a comprehensive understanding of Kant's philosophy of intuition.

References

Aldrich, Virgil C. (1968). Analytic a Posteriori Propositions. In: *Analysis* 28(6), 200–202.

Allais, Lucy (2015). *Manifest Reality: Kant's Idealism and his Realism*. Oxford: Oxford University Press.

Ando, Takatura (1974). *Metaphysics: A Critical Survey of its Meaning*. The Hague: Martinus Nijhoff.

Bruner Jerome Seymour (1966). *On Knowing: Essays for the Left Hand*. New York: Atheneum.

Burtt, E.A. (1953). Intuition in Eastern and Western Philosophy. In: *Philosophy East and West* 2(4), 283–291.

Carus, Paul (1892). What Does *Anschauung* Mean? In: *The Monist* 2(4), 527–32.

Clapin, Hugh (2002). *Philosophy of Mental Representation*. Oxford: Oxford University Press.

Dickerson, A. B. (2004). *Kant on Representation and Objectivity*. Oxford: Oxford University Press.

Fitz, Hope K. (2001). *Intuition: Its Nature and Uses in Human Experience*. Delhi: Motilal Banarsidass Publisher.

Grimes, John (1989). *A Concise Dictionary of Indian Philosophy: Sanskrit Terms Defined in English*. New York: State University of New York Press.

Hanna, Robert (2015). *Cognition, Content, and the A Priori: A Study in the Philosophy of Mind and Knowledge*. Oxford: Oxford University Press.

Jardine, Robert (1874). *The Elements of the Psychology of Cognition*. London: Macmillan.

Kem, Andrea and Daniel Smyth (2006). Spontaneity and Receptivity in Kant's Theory of Knowledge. In: *Philosophy Topics* 34(1/2), 145–162.

Krishnamurti, Jiddu (1970). *Early Writings*, Vol. II. Bombay: Chetana.

—— (1981). *Education and the Significance of Life.* New York: Harper San Francisco.

—— (1991). *The Collected Works of J. Krishnamurti: Crisis in Consciousness*, Vol. XI. Dubuque, Iowa: Kendall Hunt Publishing Co. (Krishnamurti Foundation of America).

—— (1992). *The Collected Works of J. Krishnamurti: A Psychological Revolution*, Vol. 13. Dubuque, Iowa: Kendall Hunt Publishing Co. (Krishnamurti Foundation of America).

—— (1996). *Questioning Krishnamurti: J. Krishnamurti in Dialogue.* Michigan: Thomson/The University of Michigan Press.

—— (2007). *The Collected Works of J. Krishnamurti*, Vol. II. Delhi: Motilal Banarsidass Publisher.

Lee, R. E. M. (1995). *The Book of Life: Daily Meditations with Krishnamurti.* New York: Harper San Francisco.

Mehta, Rohit (1973). *J. Krishnamurti and the Nameless Experience: A Comprehensive Discussion of J. Krishnamurti's Approach to Life.* Delhi: Motilal Banarsidass Publisher.

Natterer, Paul (1998/2010). *Immanuel Kant's Logik. Ein Handbuch zu Vorlesungen.* URL: www.paul-natterer.de/images/Downloads/Kant_Jaesche_Logik.pdf. Accessed June 30, 2017.

Palmquist, Stephen R. (1987). A Priori Knowledge in Perspective: Naming, Necessity and the Analytic A Posteriori. *Review of Metaphysics* 41(2), 255–282.

—— (2012). Analytic Aposteriority and Its Relevance to Twentieth-Century Philosophy. *Studia Humana* 1(3/4), 3–16.

Perconti, Pierto (1999). *Kantian Linguistics: Theories of Mental Representation and the Linguistic Transformation in Kantism.* Muenster: Nodus Publication.

Prichard, H. A. (1909). *Kant's Theory of Knowledge.* Oxford: Clarendon Press.

Puligandla, Ramkrishna (1975). *Fundamentals of Indian Philosophy.* New York: Abingdon Press.

Raju, P. T. (1952). Intuition as a Philosophical Method in India. In: *Philosophy East and West* 2(3), 187–207.

Sardesai, Arundhati (1996). Epistemology of J. Krishnamurti. In: *Indian Philosophical Quarterly* 23(3–4), 455–466.

Serck-Hanssen, Camilla (2009). Kant on Consciousness. In: S. Heinamaa and M. Reuter (eds.), *Psychology and Philosophy*, Vol. 8. Netherlands: Springer, 139–157.

Sharma, Chandradhar (2000). *A Critical Survey of Indian Philosophy.* Delhi: Motilal Banarsidass Publisher.

Spinoza, Baruch (1985). Trans. and ed. Edwin Curley, *The Collected Works of Spinoza.* Princeton, NJ: Princeton University Press.

Thompson, Manley (1972). Singular Terms and Intuitions in Kant's Epistemology. In: *Review of Metaphysics* 26(2), 314–343.

Vidyabhusana, S. C. (1920). *A History of Indian Logic: Ancient, Medieval and Modern Schools.* Delhi: Motilal Banarsidass Publisher.

Weeraperuma, Susunaga (1986). *Sayings of J. Krishnamurti*. Delhi: Motilal Banarsidass Publisher.

Williams, C. V. (2004). *Jiddu Krishnamurti: World Philosopher (1895–1986): His Life and Thoughts*. Delhi: Motilal Banarsidass Publisher.

Wilson, Kirk Dallas (1975). Kant on Intuition. In: *The Philosophical Quarterly* 25(100), 247–265.

Part IV

East–West Perspectives on the Role of Intuition in Philosophy

16 *Philosophia in Sensu Cosmico*

Kant's Notion of Philosophy with Resonance from Chinese Antiquity

Tze-wan Kwan

1. Introduction

Notwithstanding Kant's contribution to so many areas of philosophy, his reflections on the very nature of philosophy itself should also be given due credit, for it is through such reflections that a new rule of thumb for doing philosophy has been pronounced, namely, that philosophy should always bear the mark of "situatedness" and that, rather than being just an intellectual game, doing philosophy should be made answerable to the world that confronts humanity.

2. Kant's Distinction Between Mathematics and Philosophy

Kant never wrote anything that treats exclusively of philosophy in general, but he did embark on this issue in crucial passages of his work. Besides the first *Critique*, we find relevant discussions in his *Logic* handbook and in his lectures on logic and on metaphysics. In all instances when Kant sets off to talk about the nature of philosophy, he without exception starts his discussion by comparing philosophy to mathematics. For Kant, philosophy and mathematics are both disciplines based on reason rather than on the collection of data, and it is upon this common ground that they diverge sharply in the ways they are performed. In Kant's own formulation, the difference between mathematics and philosophy is a very subtle one: whereas the former derives its knowledge "from the construction of concepts", the latter does so "from concepts" (A837/B865).[1] Despite the apparently enigmatic nature of this distinction, Kant's intention was very clear. Mathematics and philosophy have utterly different objects of study. Mathematicians can create their own objects, which Kant calls *mathema* (A736/B764), based on rational principles independent of whether such objects are empirically given or not. To explain this point, Kant gives simple geometric entities like "triangle" as examples (A713/B741), but he also accepts more complex entities as algebraic expressions and equations (A717/B745; A734/B762) as rationally constructable mathematical objects. Other examples we might readily give include conic sections such as "circle", "ellipse", "parabola" and "hyperbola", etc. If we want still more examples, we might include such abstruse mathematical objects in topology as the "Möbius strip" or the "Klein bottle", for these are precisely mathematical objects which are literally fictions "originally framed by the [human] mind itself" (A730/B758), as Kant would have so described.

Philosophy, on the contrary, cannot enjoy the same freedom as does mathematics—i.e., it cannot intuitively "construct" its own objects of study, but has to derive its objects "from concepts" (*aus Begriffen*). This requirement is, for those unfamiliar with Kant's language, not easily understandable. For Kant, human experience is the result of the combined effort of sensible intuitions and pure concepts of the understanding, or categories, which are 12 in number, with "substantiality" and "causality" being the most representative ones. Philosophy's need to derive its objects "from concepts" refers exactly to the employment of these pure concepts, which are nothing but the keys to man's capacity to comprehend worldly experiences in an orderly manner. This said, however, we must bear in mind that pure concepts of the understanding can never yield real experience by themselves, but always need to operate in conjunction with sensible intuition in order to have real application. Consequently, Kant's differentiation between philosophy and mathematics should be interpreted as an attempt to bring out, by means of comparison, the following characteristics about philosophy: (1) Whereas mathematics can define its own objects and operate freely and intuitively by relying on pure intuition, philosophy, in the last analysis, is always "discursive"— i.e., philosophical knowledge is basically mediated through our experience of the sensible world (A68/B92; A719–720/B747–748), provided for us through sensible intuition. (2) Mediation in this sense means that philosophers cannot use their reason to deal with objects so offhandedly without reverting to sensible experience. (3) While mathematics alone can truly "define" its concepts, philosophy typically can only "explain" what it is going to deal with (A730/B758). (4) Philosophers must not presumptuously attempt to "imitate mathematics" (A730/B758) to the point of "divert[ing] philosophy from its true purpose" (A735/B763). And (5) Philosophy cannot detach from worldly givenness, which is the final reference of its contemplative vocation.

This understanding of philosophy is in line with many aspects of Kant's doctrine. Even the very central notion of "transcendental philosophy" is described by Kant as being rooted in "the fertile *bathos* of experience" (*PFM* 4:380), which in fact is what the whole enterprise of transcendental philosophy is destined to "explain" or to account for. It is no wonder that Kant followed the European tradition by depicting philosophy as "*Weltweisheit*", an expression he used without any pejorative meaning both before and after his Critical period.[2]

If we now argue that Kant's notion of philosophy entails the demand for situatedness in a world of experience, then we must clarify that a world like this should not be understood from a solipsistic point of view as a realm of private experience, but as a communally shared world. As early as in his "*Geisterseher*" book of 1766, Kant already made the following remarks:

> Aristotle says somewhere: "When we are awake, we have a common world, but when we dream, each has his own." It seems to me that one should perhaps reverse the last proposition and could say: When different people each have their own world, then it is to be supposed that they are dreaming.[3]

In this connection I very much appreciate Friedrich Kaulbach's description (1969, 129) of human experience or appearance as "things for us" (*Dinge für uns*), as opposed to the supposedly independent existence of "things for themselves" (*Dinge an sich*), which for Kant is only a "limiting concept" (*Grenzbegriff*).

3. Kant's Distinction Between Philosophy in a Scholastic Sense and Philosophy in a Cosmic Sense

Of even greater importance is Kant's further distinction between two ways or two levels of doing philosophy, namely between philosophy in a scholastic sense and philosophy in a cosmic sense. Unlike what the term itself suggests, philosophy's scholastic sense has very little to do with scholastic philosophy in the middle ages, but refers to philosophy as institutional learning, or to what we in modern universities call academic philosophy. This type of philosophy "has . . . in view only the systematic unity appropriate to science and consequently no more than the logical perfection of knowledge" (A838/B866). Being bound by a scholarly tradition, this level of philosophy puts its emphasis on the systematic acquisition of philosophical concepts and theories, as well as on related argumentations and discussions, which Kant considers important and necessary as far as disciplinary learning is concerned, for such training brings the promise of sharpening the mind and equips the learner with intellectual skillfulness (*Geschicklichkeit*).

However, Kant opines that doing philosophy on this "scholastic" level alone is inadequate if the full meaning of philosophy is to be brought out. Kant astutely points out (*JL* 9:24) that, in doing philosophy the "scholastic" way, no matter how refined and skillful one might become, "[y]et in the end people always ask what purpose is served by this philosophizing and by its final end." Therefore, beyond philosophy in a scholastic sense Kant advocates philosophy in a cosmic sense, which he understands as "the [philosophical] science of the relation of all knowledge to the essential ends of human reason" (A839/B867). For Kant, it is this other concept of philosophy that "has always formed the real basis of the term 'philosophy'" (A838/B866). Indeed it is "[t]his high concept [that] gives philosophy *dignity*, i.e., an absolute worth, and which first gives a worth to all other cognitions" (*JL* 9:23–24). Whereas philosophy's scholastic sense has to do only with "skill", it is philosophy in a cosmic sense which renders philosophy "a doctrine of wisdom", in the sense that it makes philosophy truly "useful" (*JL* 9:24; cf. *Metaphysik L2* 28:534). Unlike logical skill, such "usefulness and utility [*Nützlichkeit und Brauchbarkeit*]" (*JL* 9:60) is not a matter of theory, but one of practice, for which the question "Useful for whom?" always applies! While Heidegger subsequently coined the term "*Worumwillen*" (literally "for the sake of whom") to deal with this issue, Kant simply considers the "usefulness" of the cosmic conception of philosophy to be "that in which everyone necessarily has an interest" (A840/B868). In other words, philosophy in a cosmic sense feeds back upon man himself. Being literally "mundane" or "worldly", it pertains to the ultimate concerns of humanity at large. To underscore this worth of philosophy as answerable to humanity's essential ends and to the world in which we dwell, Kant once described this philosophy with the alternative expression philosophy "*in sensu cosmopolitico*" or even philosophy "*in sensu eminenti*" (*Logik Pölitz*, 24:533–534).

All in all, Kant's distinction between mathematics and philosophy and his further distinction between the two levels of philosophy have in fact the same message to convey: namely, that in doing philosophy our situatedness in a world has always to be borne in mind. In other words, true philosophy is never a sheer "scholarly" mastery of philosophical doctrines and theories, but the free and active use of reason in solving "worldly" issues that haunt humanity.

4. The Notion of "*zhe*" as the Translation of the Western Notion of Philosophy

Kant himself very seldom uses the word "situation", and if at all, never in a philosophically significant way. But in contemporary philosophy, "situation" has become a keyword with "existential" connotations. In addition to this, many new but apparently unrelated philosophical terminologies are in fact in line with this plea for situatedness, Husserl's concept of lifeworld (*Lebenswelt*) being the best example. In Heidegger's *Sein und Zeit*, the term "situation" appears some 50 times. Besides, Heidegger's analytic of *Dasein* as "Being-in-the-world", as well as his concepts of "throwness" (*Geworfenheit*) and of "state of mind" (*Befindlichkeit*), are all related to the human condition of being always a situated existence.[4] Karl Jaspers (1969, 43f), on his part, dedicated a whole chapter of his massive work *Philosophie* to discuss the very notion of "situation". Then we have Merleau-Ponty, who reiterates the Heideggerian program on the completely new platform of bodily *Dasein*, which he once formulated as "my body–in–the–world" (Merleau-Ponty 2012, 142). For Merleau-Ponty, prior to the Cartesian "geometrical space" (100, 254, 302), we first encounter "situational spatiality" (102), which is "enveloped in the unique hold (*prise*) that our body has upon the world" (288). All of this I consider a Kantian legacy.

This Kantian legacy, besides being recapitulated and underscored in contemporary Western philosophy, finds quite unexpectedly a strong reverberation and a robust endorsement from the East, namely in the archaic Chinese character "哲, *zhe*".

In the early phase of the introduction of Western philosophy into China during the Ming Dynasty, the very term philosophy was first translated by an Italian missionary, Giulio Aleni (艾儒略, 1582–1649), through phonetic means, but the subsequently Romanized terms, having no appeal for the Chinese at all, did not survive. When later on the Japanese took turn to assimilate Western philosophy, a Leiden-trained scholar, Nishi Amane (西周, 1829–1897), when translating the Dutch word "*wijdbegeerte*", which is etymologically related to the German word "*Wißbegierde*" and refers to *Philosophie*, adopted a different principle of translation by borrowing from the Chinese script, and the result he got was *tetsugaku* (哲學, *zhexue* in Chinese), which means literally "the learning of wisdom" (Schmitz 2001, 267–276, esp. 272). This term became popular not only in Japan, but subsequently also in China through its promotion by Chinese scholars and students with Japanese connections. When later on, in 1912, the School of Philosophy (*zhexuemen*, 哲學門) was set up at the Peking University, the term *zhexue* became institutionalized.

Understandably enough, accepting the Chinese character "*zhe*" as pertaining to philosophy merely on the ground of its being derived from a Japanese translation is not an emotionally easy task for Chinese academia. For this reason, besides taking note of this being a fact, what I proposed earlier (in many contexts over the past few decades) is to see if we can exhaust Chinese sources that might help explain how in the graph, *zhe*, the notion of wisdom actually came about, so as to give us a philosophically good justification for such a choice of word.

Generally speaking, the use of *zhe* to translate the Western notion of philosophy is justified, insofar as the traditionally accepted lexical meaning of "*zhe*" is indeed "wisdom", which in the first place is in line with the etymology of "philosophy" in the West as "the love of wisdom".

In the *Thirteen Classics*, the character *zhe* occurs 38 times, notably in word compounds such as *mingzhe* (明哲), *junzhe* (濬哲), *shengzhe* (聖哲), *zheren* (哲人), *zheming* (哲命), etc., which all pertain to positive aptitudes of wisdom. In the *Book of Documents* 《尚書. 皋陶謨》, we read the definitive quote: "Knowing people is wisdom" (知人則哲). In *Erya* (爾雅), the oldest Chinese lexicon, we find the standard definition of the character: "*zhe*, it means wise/wisdom" (哲, 智也).

Besides this lexical evidence, it dawns on me that a paleographical approach might promise a deeper understanding of the issue. Whereas the contemporary form of the character *zhe* (哲) is made up of *zhe* (折) and *kou* (口 = mouth), we need to know that an earlier form of the character *zhe* (悊) was written with *zhe* (折) and *xin* (心) or "heart–mind" instead of with *kou*. In fact, it is with this earlier form of *zhe* (悊) that I shall start my exposition.

Regarding the component *zhe* (折), which has the same sound as the resultant character *zhe* (悊), one common opinion is that it functions basically as a phonetic tag. However, I consider that besides this phonetic function, the visual component of 折 is at the same time a semantically mean-ingful component, which means literally "to cut" or "to chop", as vividly demonstrated by the archaic script tokens (see Fig-ures 16.1 and 16.2), representing the scenario of a tree branch being cut or chopped into two pieces by an axe (斤).[5] And it is this compo-nent of 折 that teams up with the other visual component 心 (*xin* or

Figure 16.1 Oracle bone script token of *zhe* as cutting

Figure 16.2 Bronze script token of *zhe* as cutting

"heart–mind"), to make up the resultant meaning of 悊 (*zhe*), which later on was rewritten as 哲, which in turn was subsequently used as a transla-tion of the Western term, "philosophy".

This brings us back to our earlier question: How did the notion of wis-dom actually come about, with the meanings of the components of *zhe* (悊) now exposed? My reckoning is that the component *zhe* (折), should not be understood literally as the physical action of cutting, but rather as a deliberative action of differentiation or discernment, as the other com-ponent *xin* (心) clearly suggests.[6] But under what circumstances would there be such a need of "deliberative differentiation"? My answer is: there is such a need when one is intellectually perplexed by ambiguities or ambivalences, which in turn might involve two scenarios, either "theo-retically" when we need to tell the difference between two things or two states of affairs not easily discernible, or "practically" when we need to make up our mind to do a thing this way or otherwise. These needs for deliberative differentiation can best be explained by the Platonic concept of "division" or "distinction" (διαίρεσις, *diairesis*) on the one hand and the Aristotelian concept of "decision" or "choice" (προαίρεσις, *proaire-sis*) on the other. In Plato, *diairesis* can be understood as the method of conceptual distinction through dichotomy, which is the key to human theoretical understanding (see *Phaedrus*, 265d). *Proairesis*, a term basically coined by Aristotle (see *Nic. Eth.*, 1113a, 1139a), refers to the exercise of this deliberative capacity in practical life contexts, in the sense of making the decision whether to do this or that, or committing oneself as to which way to go in one's life situations by balancing our desires and our ends with our reason. To the last analysis, both *diairesis* and *proairesis* have to do with "judgment making", or as the Germans will put it, in "*Ur-teilen*" or "primal dividing", which is so much in line with the basic componential structure of the Chinese character *zhe* (悊).

We can therefore argue that it is precisely in this capacity of deliberative differentiation, whether in a theoretical or in a practical context, that in the character *zhe* (悊) the meaning of "wisdom" is brought about.

5. Further Explanation of *zhe* (哲/悊) by Considering Two Remarkable Bronze Script Tokens

Instead of stopping here with our account of the character *zhe* (哲/悊), let me take our paleographical analysis one step further.

In an attempt to further clarify how the connotation of "wisdom" came about for the character "*zhe*", I discovered some years ago two archaic script tokens of the character from two bronze utensils, *Dakeding* (大克鼎) and *Shiqiangpan* (史牆盤), which were excavated in 1890 and in 1976, respectively.[7] The reason for considering these two script tokens is that we find in them additional script components besides the "cutting" (axe on tree branch) and the "heart–mind" as hitherto known. In the *Dakeding* token, we find the additional component for *mu* (目) or "eye", which signifies very clearly that the act of "deliberative distinction" central to the wisdom of *zhe* has to be exercised on the condition of careful observation, or in Kantian terms, to rely on sensible intuition. Then in the *Shiqiangpan*

Figure 16.3 Token of *zhe* found in *Dakeding*

Figure 16.4 Token of *zhe* found in *Shiqiangpan*

token, we find besides the component "eye" still further the component *chi* (彳), a component I consider of great importance for bringing out the most subtle meaning of *zhe* (哲) as bound to situatedness. Let me explain.

This additional component, *chi* (彳), is in fact the left half of the character 行, which in contemporary Chinese carries a whole range of meanings including "to walk", "array", "deeds", "behavior", "conduct", etc., with different pronunciations. From an etymological point of view, among these meanings, there must be one meaning which is more primary, upon which other meanings are derived. Now with many tokens of this character identified for comparison, we might agree with Luo Zhenyu (羅振玉, 1866–1940), one of the most prominent scholars in oracle bone scripts, that 行 originally refers to "a crossroad leading to everywhere" (四達之衢) (quoted in Ding 1970, 808b). The renowned Swedish sinologist, Bernhard Karlgren (1889–1978), similarly defined 行 as "a drawing of meeting streets" (Karlgren 1957, 748a–d). I agree with both Luo and Karlgren, but consider 行 to imply a deeper and more philosophical meaning. "Street" and "crossroad" are social concepts. They signify the place, or the milieu, where one can expectantly get in touch with people, and deal with them for various reasons. This explains why for this one character 行, which originally means "crossroad", such other abstract meanings as "conduct" or "behavior", etc. have developed, which are only socially comprehensible and derivable. One very similar notion we can find in the Greek tradition is ἦθος (*ēthos*), which, among various meanings, can also refer to "an accustomed place" or ". . . the abodes of men" (Liddell and Scott 1996, 766).[8] Just as it is quite certain that ἦθος is etymologically related to the modern Western stem "ethic-", it is equally arguable that the original meaning of 行 as "crossroad" or meeting place is also related to its other more abstract meanings such as "conduct" or "behavior", or even to the Chinese character for morality (Figure 16.5).[9]

With the meaning of 行 as "crossroad" or as "milieu" clarified, we can get back to our newly unveiled component *chi* (彳), which is only the left half of 行. As is well known in Chinese paleography, *chi* (彳) and *chu* (亍), being the two halves of the character 行, can be used separately (or in conjunction) as script component(s) bearing the same meaning as 行 in forming more complex graphs. With this in mind, we can say that, in the token *zhe* in *Shiqiangpan* unearthed in 1976, the additional use of *chi* (彳) can be regarded as a clear indication that the entire talk of deliberative distinction, which makes up what we may call wisdom, can only make good sense within a "worldly" situation or horizon, in which not only physical environments, but also social circumstances have to be taken into account. If the component "eye" already implies

「行」字的甲骨文及金文字形

Figure 16.5 Tokens for 行 as "crossroad" or "meeting streets"

a world that awaits our observation, then this final and crucial component, "crossroad" or "milieu", makes this "situatedness" of the deliberating person in the world even more explicit.

To summarize, the meaning of the character *zhe*, as represented in the 1976 *Shiqiangpan* token, is informed by the compounding of 4 visual-semantic script components: namely, (a) "cutting" (with an "axe" on a tree branch), which signifies in conjunction with (b) the "heart–mind" an act of deliberative distinction, which requires the deliberating person to use her (c) "eye(s)" to observe what is going on in the surrounding world represented by (d) the "crossroad", which symbolizes the place or the milieu where the need of "deliberative differentiation" arises. We argue that these components that made up the archaic script token "*zhe*" and its connotation as "wisdom" are in fact universal traits that pertain precisely to what Kant aspired as "philosophy in a cosmic sense".

6. Philosophy in a Cosmic Sense: Its Implications for Kantian philosophy, With Further Echoes From Chinese Antiquity

After relating the Chinese character *zhe* to Kant's notion of philosophy in a cosmic sense, we find ourselves in a better position to see how this vision of Kant has influenced the way he treats other specific philosophical topics. I will limit myself to three such issues: (1) the primacy of the practical; (2) the concept of choice; and (3) the motto of enlightenment.

6.1. The Primacy of the Practical

It is well known that Kant advocated the primacy of practical reason in his second *Critique*. His justification was that despite the apparent discrepancy between speculative reason and practical reason in terms of their interest, they are after all "one and the same reason", involving different employments. And as long as the acting person is not "pathological" but is holding the moral law in respect, then reason should not assume its practical employment to be contradicting its theoretical employment just because of the latter's own "restriction of speculative folly" (*CPrR* 5:121), but should endorse the interest of the practical. In other words, within our "only one and the same reason" (121), the theoretical should not be considered as merely *co*-ordinated side by side with the practical, but as *sub*-ordinated to the latter by virtue of the latter's pure practical interest (as far as this subordination does not alter the stringency of theoretical cognition), hence the thesis of the Primacy of Pure Practical Reason" (see 119–121).

Independent of this explication in the second *Critique*, we find this thesis already entailed in Kant's notion of philosophy in a cosmic sense. On the one hand, Kant makes allowance for "scholarly" philosophy being able to guarantee a "sufficient supply of cognitions of reason, and . . . a systematic connection of these cognitions" (*JL* 9:23), but on the other hand he ascribes to philosophy in a cosmic sense the task of establishing the "relation of all knowledge to the essential ends of human reason (*teleologia rationis humanae*)" (A839/B867). In an attempt to clarify the relation between these two ways of doing *philosophy*, Kant proposes that under essential ends we need to differentiate between the "ultimate end" and "subordinate ends", and while subordinate ends, being "optionally chosen", are "connected with the former as means", the final end of philosophy is nothing less than "the whole vocation of man", so that "the philosophy which deals with it is entitled moral philosophy [*Moral*]" (A840/B868). For Kant, it is through this vocation to deal with the ultimate end of human reason that philosophy in a cosmic sense can acquire its "dignity" (*Würde*), or its "absolute value" (*Metaphysik L2* 28:532, my translation) and thus shows the "superiority which moral philosophy has over all other occupations of reason" (A840/B868). This explained, we see very clearly that the primacy of practical reason over speculative reason advocated by Kant in the second *Critique* is only a more precise formulation of the primacy of philosophy in a cosmic sense over philosophy in a scholastic sense. To underscore this primacy of the practical, Kant concludes his discussion thus: ". . . every interest is ultimately practical, even that of speculative reason being only conditional and reaching perfection only in the practical use" (CPrR 5:121).

Returning to the two archaic script tokens of *zhe* we found in *Dakeding* (1890) and in *Shiqiangpan* (1976), we see that with the additional components of "eye" and "crossroad" now in place, something very delicate might turn out as far as script-formation is concerned. First of all, we

「直」字的甲骨文及金文字形

Figure 16.6 Token for *zhi* as "straight"

may argue that the "eye", when conjoined to the vertical line above (borrowed from the tree branch)[10] results in the character *zhi* (直), which literally means "straight", but metaphorically interpreted by Xu Shen (許慎, 58–147) in *Shuowen* as 正見 or "the right(eous) view". And this graph *zhi* (直), if conjoined with the *xin* (心) or "heart–mind" below, will result in the graph *de* (悳), which is an old written form of the modern graph *de* (德). And if still further the component *chi* (彳) or "crossroad" is included, as in the case of the 1976 *Shiqiangpan* token, we yield straightaway the graph *de* (德) itself, which is the modern script for virtue or morality. Therefore, both archaic tokens for *zhe* (哲) can in fact be "stylized" as 㯱,[11] a fictitious but ideally conceived graph made up of "cutting" and   "morality", pertaining arguably to "moral judgment". Understanding the graph *zhe* in this way clearly brings out the "ultimate concern" of *zhe* or philosophy to be a matter of morality. Here we find another support for Kant's thesis of the primacy of the practical.

6.2. The Concept of Willkür or Choice

In my earlier discussion of the basic components of the character *zhe*, or philosophy in Chinese, I emphasized the importance of the notion of "to cut" as pertinent to the overall meaning of *zhe* as "deliberative differentiation", both in theoretical contexts and in practical ones, the latter being further confirmed by the component *chi* (彳), which suggests a social milieu. To convince myself of this notion of deliberative differentiation being central to the wisdom of philosophy, I have introduced the Platonic–Aristotelian discussion of *diairesis/proairesis* for comparison. Although an explicit etymological account of these two concepts cannot be found in Kant's *opus*, we can assume that such conceptual legacies should not be foreign to Kant. One marginal evidence we can find in his lectures is his mention of the notion of "distinction" (*Unterscheidung* [*distinctio*]) as the "knowledge of the differences of things" (*Metaphysik von Schön*, 28:495). Here Kant was using the Platonic concept of διαίρεσις (*diairesis*) to explicate his own ontological scheme, which is totally non-Platonic.

Regarding the Aristotelian concept of προαίρεσις (*proairesis*), there is clear evidence that this concept, which has been rendered as "*arbitrium*" since Saint Augustine, is indeed the predecessor concept of "*Willkür*", a key issue of paramount importance for the Kantian system, especially for his moral doctrines.[12] This concept of *Willkür* has been translated into English very disparately, namely, as will, volition, choice, choice^w, or power of choice. The translation of *Willkür* as "will" aims at showing the former to be a power of discretion, but this translation tends to mix up *Willkür* with *Wille*, which should be avoided. Volition is lexically a good translation, but might collide with Kant's Latin term "*voluntas*" which in fact refers to *Wille*. The translation of *Willkür* as "choice" is much more accurate, as it goes back to the original Aristotelian issue of *proairesis*, which is mostly translated as choice. In ancient Greek, the word αἵρεσις is derived from the verb αἱρέω, which means to take, or arguably also from αἱρέομαι, which means to choose, so that αἵρεσις or αἵρεσιν (in the accusative) is literally that which is being taken or chosen—i.e., choice (Liddell and Scott 1996, 41). In other words, αἵρεσις, being a common element shared by *diairesis* and *proairesis*, carries by itself already the meaning of choice in the sense of that which is taken. With the prefix προ- in place, *proairesis*, when also translated as choice, refers not to "the choice" (*Wahl*) itself, but rather to the "capacity" of making a choice, as the prefix pro- serves to underline the intention or commitment for so choosing. In other words, *proairesis* is not the choice (*Wahl*) itself, but the very capacity or power, or arguably even the principle of choice-making in practical situations that might be ambivalent and perplexing. In Aristotle's *Nicomachean Ethics* (1113a), we read: "Choice will be a deliberate desire of a thing in our power; for we first deliberate, then select and finally fix our desire according to the results of our deliberation."

With all this explained, we see how tightly the Kantian concept of *Willkür* is related to the Aristotelian tradition of *proairesis* as well as to the Chinese notion of *zhe*, which we defined precisely as "deliberative differentiation" and argued to be in total agreement with Kant's notion of philosophy in a cosmic sense. Let us also reiterate how Kant relates this in his *Logic* handbook (*JL* 9:24): "As for what concerns philosophy according to the worldly concept (*in sensu cosmico*), we can also call it *a science of the highest maxim for the use of our reason*, insofar as we understand by a maxim the internal principle of choice among various ends [*das innere Princip der Wahl unter verschiedenen Zwecken*]."

In Kant's moral doctrine, *Willkür* is understood as the original susceptibility of the human will to the influence of sensual desires on the one hand and to the dictates of the moral law on the other, as if before the acting person there are two paths to be chosen. In order to prevent this ambivalent situation for man to become totally "arbitrary", Kant further differentiates between animal *Willkür* (*arbitrium brutum*) and human free *Willkür* (*arbitrium liberum*) (A534/B562; 28:254; 27:267) but deprives the latter of the claim for complete ignorance of the moral law, so that when one "chooses" to indulge in sensual desires, one is making this choice with the awareness of one deviating from the other more worthy option.[13]

All in all, in Kant's practical philosophy, *Willkür qua* free *Willkür* is, though ambivalent, not totally arbitrary. We can imagine that in the various stages of one's life, one will be facing endless challenges to choose typically from two main options: to follow sensuous desire or to follow the moral law. For Kant, the option for wrongdoing must be "given" as this guarantees moral freedom. But wrongdoing or indulgence on the one hand and being moral on the other should not be considered as two arbitrarily "equal" (*gleichgültig*) options. This is because, as I just said, human *Willkür qua* free *Willkür* can never leave the moral law completely out of sight so that wrongdoings have always to deal with the call of conscience on the one hand and the self-indignation of being "worthless and contemptible" (*geringschätzig und verwerflich*) on the other (*CPrR* 5:161).

In Kantian philosophy, whether in theoretical or in practical contexts, judgment making is a matter of utmost importance. As explained earlier, judgment is an act of primal "dividing" or "*ur-teilen*".[14] In Chinese antiquity, besides the character *zhe* (哲), as discussed, we find in the classics equally rich evidences for the extensive use of the notions of "cutting", "differentiating", and "choosing" in moral practices.

In the Chinese language, the typical word for differentiation or distinction is *bian* (辨), which Xu Shen defines as follows: "*Bian* (辨), it means *pan* (判), and is pronounced as *bian* 莽." Structurally speaking, *bian* (辨) is composed of a knife (*dao*, 刀) which divides or intersects the graph 莽, which refers to two contesting testimonies before the court, into two halves.[15] Here the definiens *pan* (判) literally means "to judge". What is interesting is that both *bian* (辨) and *pan* (判) include a knife as a component, which is comparable to *zhe* (哲) comprising an axe! The etymological meaning of 辨 is still controversial, but one possible interpretation along Xu Shen's line is that it refers to the judgment made in favor of one or the other party of a litigation.[16]

Philosophically, we find in the *Book of Changes* much discussion on the importance of judgment making. Under the hexagram *Dayou* (大有) we find the explanatory phrase 《明辨哲也》, which can be rendered as "being able to discriminate clearly is wisdom."[17] Since the character *zhe* (哲) is considered equivalent to *zhe* (悊) or *zhe* (哲) in antiquity,[18] the semantic affinity between *bian* (辨) and *zhe* (哲) can be considered to have been definitively established. Then under the hexagram *Weiji* (未濟) we find in the *Xiang-Zhuan* commentaries the dictum 《君子以慎辨物居方》[19] which can be rendered as "The superior man arouses his own caution (慎) to discriminate (辨) between things, and to tell the positions they should occupy."[20] But most importantly, in the Commentaries, *Xici Xiazhuan* (繫辭下), in the comments on the hexagram *Kun* (困, Perplex), we read one of the most illuminating remarks of the *Book of Changes*: "困，德之辨也",[21] which I freely render as: "It is in the time of perplexity or difficulty that one can tell whether one is really virtuous or not." In other words, it is in real life situations, most probably in the times of need, poverty, exhaustion, or adversity that man as a moral agent is critically put to test. It is under such marginal circumstances that the decisions one makes would really make a difference. Following this same line of thought, we find in the *Analects* that Confucius repeatedly discusses two topics side by side, namely "respect for the Moral [Law]" (崇德) and

"Differentiation in Perplexities" (辨惑).[22] Here Confucius is admonishing us that when one is perplexed by bad intentions one should carefully sort out where the problems lie so that one can possibly deal with them and remove them, and in so doing, respect for the moral law should always be kept in view.

Besides the notions *bian* (辨), or *pan* (判), we also have the notion *duan* (斷), which also comprises "axe" as a component and means also "to cut", or metaphorically, "to decide", "to judge". In the *Book of Documents*, we read: "惟克果斷, 乃罔後艱", which Legge translates as "it is by means of bold decision that future difficulties are avoided."[23] Even in the *Shiji* 《史記》 we see the importance of judgment making duly emphasized: "臨事而屢斷, 勇也", which can be rendered as: "To manifest decision in the conduct of affairs is bravery."[24]

With the above paraphrases from the Chinese classics, we should be convinced that the need to make the correct choices in real-life circumstances is equally emphasized in the West as it is in the East. We should also be convinced how closely related Kant's concept of *Willkür* is to the notion of *zhe* (哲) as deliberative distinction in real life contexts.

6.3. *The Motto of Enlightenment*

In Kant's most influential article "Answer to the Question: What is Enlightenment?" we read from the first paragraph the famous motto of enlightenment (*AQE* 8:35): "Sapere aude! Have courage to use your own reason!" For Kant, enlightenment is a matter of self-education and public education at once. It is a matter of self-education because the average man in the "great unthinking mass" has the tendency to stick to his self-incurred tutelage or his reluctance to exercise his own reason. However, as Kant points out, there are always independent thinkers who can break off from such constraints and become self-enlightened to various degrees (as in the case of philosophers who manage to leave Plato's cave), and then the problem of enlightenment in the sense of public education will be on the shoulders of these people. For this to happen, and to supplement the general motto of enlightenment, Kant proposed an additional requirement: "public use of reason". Public use of reason is for Kant the opposite of "private use of reason", which he defines, though not totally convincingly, as the use of reason in the context of one's daily restricted workplace where one is expected to perform the professional duties one is trained for (37). On the contrary, "public use of reason" is for Kant the use of reason "as a member of the whole community or of a society of world citizens [cosmopolitical], and thus in the role of a scholar who addresses the public" (37). To illustrate his point, Kant uses the example of a clergyman who, while performing his duties following standard guidelines, might voice out his criticism of the church in his capacity as a free and responsible citizen (cf. Martin Luther). This example, naturally, might well apply to other roles in a civil society. In fact when talking about the so-called public use of reason, Kant's exact wording (36) was "public use of one's reason *in all matters*" (*von seiner Vernunft in allen Stücken öffentlichen Gebrauch zu machen*). If this extended Kantian motto of enlightenment can be followed through consistently enough, we might then be able to spot out "inappropriateness or even injustice" (37–38) in different walks of life more easily and have them rectified more readily. It is in this way that society as a whole will most benefit, very much in the sense of "piecemeal social engineering" as advocated by Karl Popper (1957, 64).

This lofty ideal of the "public use of reason" as a world citizen is in fact also entailed by Kant's notion of philosophy in a cosmic sense (or in a "cosmopolitical" sense), for in both cases, it is again the "situatedness" of the thinking agent as a social critic in the public sphere that really matters. In his polemical treatise, *The Conflict of the Faculties*, Kant assigns this social critical role to the philosophers, who, in their role as public intellectuals, will have to uphold the power of reason against all odds. I still remember vividly how I jumped out of my chair in awe and admiration when I first read the following sentence from this book (*CF* 7:27): "So the philosophy faculty, because it must answer for the truth of the teachings it is to adopt or even allow, must be conceived as free and subject only to laws given by reason, not by the government."

In *Mengzi*, Mencius gave me the same intellectual gratification with a lapidary statement: "說大人, 則藐之, 勿視其巍巍然。... 在彼者, 皆我所不為也; 在我者, 皆古之制也, 吾何畏彼哉?", a statement which James Legge rendered as follows: "Those who give counsel to the great should despise them, and not look at their pomp and display ... What they esteem are what I would have nothing to do with; what I esteem are the rules of the ancients. Why should I stand in awe of them?"[25] Here Mencius gave us another good example of what attitude one should take before political powers. Yet Mencius did not teach us to be critical indiscriminately against everything. Self-esteem and pride are valuable qualities, but they too have to obey our judgments based on reason. In another passage of *Mengzi*, Mencius interrupted, when two discussants were debating what "great valor" meant, by citing the following dictum of the Confucian sage Master Zeng (曾子): "自反而不縮, 雖褐寬博, 吾不惴焉; 自反而縮, 雖千萬人, 吾往矣", which Legge translates as follows: "If, on self-examination, I find that I am not upright, shall I not be in fear even of a poor man in his loose garments of hair-cloth? If, on self-examination, I find that I am upright, I will go forward against thousands and tens of thousands [of opponents]."[26] What we can learn from this whole discussion is that, before making our judgment on what we should agree or disagree with, we should first make room for self-enlightenment and self-criticism, and when actually making our judgment on what to agree or disagree with, righteousness should be our only criterion.

7. Conclusion

The above comparative study aims at rethinking the nature and purpose of doing philosophy, which in the layman's understanding is often regarded as a conceptual game, or as a scholarly discipline that treats merely of abstract objects. By comparing philosophy to mathematics, and further distinguishing between the two levels of doing philosophy, in *sensu scholastico* and in *sensu cosmico*, Kant tells us that true philosophy is not like that. This is because, as an intellectual endeavor of reflection and judgment making, philosophy has to "situate" itself in the world of reality with all sorts of problems, where it finds its real references beyond being just an intellectual game.

By bringing in the archaic Chinese script tokens of the character *zhe*, and by looking into its deep structures, we find in this very character, which subsequently was used as a translation for the Western notion of philosophy, indeed a lot of intellectual resources that are so close to what Kant aspires as philosophy in a cosmic sense, and to such issues as *diairesis* and *proairesis*, which are what in Western philosophy have been known and treasured since Plato and Aristotle.

With the above comparative study, we see that both Kant and his predecessors on the one hand and our Chinese ancestors on the other might have taken different paths to touch upon some basic and common traits of mental exercises which we might call "philosophy" in the broadest sense. Against such a comparative backdrop, we might claim in the first place that the emphasis of *philosophia in sensu cosmico* alone would suffice to qualify Kant as a world-philosopher. On the other hand, we might also say that, with such commonalities clarified, it would no longer make any good sense for us to keep on querying and debating whether the Chinese really have "philosophy" or not, just because of the apparently different paths of thinking they have taken!

Notes

1. In this chapter, references to Kant will be made flexibly. All quotations from *Critique of Pure Reason* are taken from the Kemp-Smith translation and will be cited with the original A/B pagination. All other citations, unless otherwise noted, will refer in the standard way to the *Akademie Ausgabe* (*Kants Gesammelte Schriften*). Translations from these other Kant texts are listed in the References.
2. See Kant's *Versuch den Begriff der negativen Grössen in der Weltweisheit einzuführen* (1763) and *Untersuchung über die Deutlichkeit der Grundsätze der natürlichen Theologie und der Moral* (1764), 2:167f. See also A15/B29, A325/B382, and A464/B492.
3. Kant 1766, *DSS* 2:342. Kant seemed to be unaware of the fact that this sentence was first proposed by Heraclitus.
4. Otto Pöggeler (1990, 61), when trying to explain the meaning of "Dasein as thrown projection" in Heidegger, once interpreted it as "being in the situation" (*In-der-Situation-sein*).

5. Archaic script tokens used by courtesy of the CHANT database developed at the D.C. Lau Research Centre for Chinese Texts, Chinese University of Hong Kong. The tokens can also be viewed under the respective head characters in the "Multifunction Chinese Character Database" now being implemented by the present author. URL: http://humanum.arts.cuhk.edu.hk/Lexis/lexi-mf/

6. Of course one needs to bear in mind that in Chinese antiquity the heart is considered as having an intellectual or deliberative function. In *Mengzi* we read "the heart is an organ for thinking" (心之官則思). See《孟子．告子上》.

7. I am referring to the bronze tripod *Dakeding* (大克鼎) from the late Western Zhou Dynasty, unearthed in 1890 (CHANT 2836), as well as to the bronze plate *Shiqiangpan* (史牆盤) from the middle Western Zhou Dynasty, excavated in 1976 (CHANT 10175).

8. Karl Schenkl (1897, 349) defined ἦθος as "der gewohnte Aufenthaltsort" and "Wohnungen der Menschen".

9. It should be noted that the characters for *dao* (道) and *de* (德), in their archaic script forms, are made up of two and only two types of components: (1) 彳 and often also 亍, which signify "crossroad" or a situation in general; and (2) 首, 止, 心, and/or 直 (目 + 丨), which are all body parts signifying human existence in general. Given that *dao* and *de* are conjoined in modern Chinese to mean "morality", we see clearly how important a role the components 彳 and 亍 have played in the constitution of the meaning of "morality" in archaic Chinese.

漢字―字例 \部件 \性質 Graphs-Examples\Components\Meaning	處境 Situation (crossroad)	象徵人的存在 Human existence (bodily parts)
dao 道：	彳、亍	首、止、人
de 德：	彳、亍	直（目、⊥）、心、止

10. This is what among paleographers is known as "*hewen*" (合文) or "combined script form".

11. See Li Xueqin (李學勤) (1978, 150) and Xu Zhongshu (徐中舒) (1978, 141). In Zhang Shichao (張世超) we read the incisive remark that "[the graph in] *Dakeding* adding an 'eye' 目 and [that in] *Shiqiangpan* adding 'crossroad' were probably the result of moral deliberation" ("克鼎增『目』，牆盤復增『彳』，殆受『德』類化而致。"). (Zhang 1996, entry 0149).

12. In fact Kant himself uses the word *arbitrium* in his Latin works to refer to *Willkür*.

13. Hence Kant's following statement about the free *Willkür* is rendered readily understandable (A802/B830): "A will [*Willkür*] which can be determined independently of sensuous impulses, and therefore through motives which are represented only by reason, is entitled freewill [*freier Willkür, arbitrium liberum*], and everything which is bound up with this will [*Willkür*], whether as ground or as consequence, is entitled practical."

14. In Kant, we find expressions such as "*moralische Unterscheidung*", "*moralische Beurteilung*" (*Praktische Philosophie Powalski*, 27:106u, 1432; 19:115), and "*Sittliches Urtheil*" (A808/B835; 19:133, 152), etc.

15. See the entry on 辨 in Xu Shen, *Shuowen*, p. 86.

16. See the related entry on 𢆉 in Xu Shen, *Shuowen*, p. 311.

17. *Book of Changes*, 《周易. 大有. 九四》.
18. See 楊慎〔明〕：《古音叢目. 古音附錄》, entry for「哲」.
19. *Book of Changes*, 《周易. 未濟. 象傳》.
20. *Book of Changes*, 《周易·未濟·象傳》. Translation from the Chinese by the present author.
21. *Book of Changes*, 《周易. 繫辭下》. Trans. James Legge, modified by the present author. All translations by Legge are made available in *Chinese Text Project*, URL: https://ctext.org/.
22. *Analects,* 《論語·顏淵. 10》.
23. *Book of Documents*, 《尚書·周官·4》.
24. Shima Qian (司馬遷), *Shiji*, 《史記·樂書》.
25. Mengzi, 《盡心下 - Jin Xin II, 80》, trans. J. Legge, URL: https://ctext.org/mengzi/jin-xin-ii (last accessed: Sept. 06, 2018).
26. Mengzi, 《公孫丑上 - Gong Sun Chou I, 2》, trans. J. Legge, URL: https://ctext.org/mengzi/gong-sun-chou-i (last accessed: Sept. 06, 2018).

References

Aristotle 1976. *Nicomachean Ethics*, (trans.) J.A.K. Thomson. New York: Penguin Books. References cite the standard, Bekker pagination.
Book of Changes. Trans. J. Legge in *Chinese Text Project*. URL: https://ctext.org/. Accessed June 21, 2018.
Book of Documents. 《尚書·周官》. Trans. J. Legge, made available in *Chinese Text Project*. URL: https://ctext.org/pre-qin-and-han?searchu8=惟克果斷. Accessed June 21, 2018.
Ding, Fubao (丁福保), ed. (1970). 說文解字詁林 (*A Forest of Glosses on the Shuowen Jiezi*). Taipei: 臺灣商務印書館 (Taiwan Commercial Press).
Jaspers, Karl (1969). *Philosophy*, Vol. I. Chicago: University of Chicago Press.
Kant, Immanuel (1766). Trans. G. R. Johnson and G. A. Magee, *Dreams of a Spirit–Seer Elucidated by Dreams of Metaphysic*. In: *Kant on Swedenborg: Dreams of a Spirit–Seer and Other Writings*. West Chester: Swedenborg Foundation, 2002, 1–63.
——— (1783). Trans Paul Carus, *Kant's Prolegomena to Any Future Metaphysics*. Chicago: Open Court, 1902.
——— (1784). Trans. L. W. Beck, *An Answer to the Question: What Is Enlightenment?* In: L. W. Beck (ed.), *Critique of Practical Reason and Other Writings in Moral Philosophy*. Chicago: The University of Chicago Press, 1976, 286–292.
——— (1781/1787). Trans. N. Kemp Smith, *Critique of Pure Reason*. London: Macmillan, 1929.
——— (1788). Trans. L. W. Beck, *Critique of Practical Reason*. Indianapolis and New York: The Liberal Arts Press, 1956.
——— (1798). Trans. M. J. Gregor, *The Conflict of the Faculties*. New York: Abaris Books, 1979.
Karlgren, Bernhard (1957). *Grammata Serica Recensa*. Stockholm: The Museum of Far Eastern Antiquities.
Kaulbach, Friedrich (1969). *Immanuel Kant*. Berlin: de Gruyter.
Kung Zi (Confucius). 論語 (*Analects*).
Li, Xueqin (李學勤) (1978). 論史牆盤及其意義 (On *Shiqiangpan* and its Meaning). In:考古學報 (*Journal of Archaeology*) 2.

Liddell, Henry George and Robert Scott (1996). *A Greek–English Lexicon.* Oxford: Clarendon.

Mengzi (Mencius). 《孟子·盡心下》. Trans. J. Legge, *Mencius.*

Merleau-Ponty, Maurice (2012). Trans. D. A. Landes, *Phenomenology of Perception.* London: Routledge.

Plato 1973, *Phaedrus*, and the Seventh and Eight Letters (trans.) Walter Hamilton. Harmonsworth: Penguin Books. References cite the standard, Stephanus pagination.

Pöggeler, Otto (1990). *Der Denkweg Martin Heideggers*, 3. Auflage. Pfullingen: Neske.

Popper, Karl (1957). *The Poverty of Historicism.* Boston: Beacon Press.

Schenkl, Karl (1897). *Griechish–deutsches Schulwörterbuch.* Wien: Carl Gerold's Sohn.

Schmitz, Christoph (2001). Nishi Amanes Verständnis der Philosophiegeschichte. In: *11. Deutschsprachiger Japanologentag in Trier*, Bd. 1, LIT-Verlag.

Shima, Qian (司馬遷). 史記 (*Shiji*). Trans. J. Legge, in *Chinese Text Project.* URL: https://ctext.org/pre-qin-and-han?searchu=臨事而屢斷. Accessed June 21, 2018.

Xu, Shen (許慎) (2013). 說文 (*Shuowen*), new edition. Beijing: 中華書局.

Xu, Zhongshu (徐中舒) (1978). 西周牆盤銘文箋釋 (Annotation and Interpretation of the Inscriptions on *Shiqiangpan* of the Western Zhou Dynasty). In: 考古學報 (*Journal of Archaeology*) 2.

Zhang, Shichao (張世超等), et al. (1996). 金文形義通解 (*A Compendium for Gestalt and Meaning of the Bronze Script*). Kyoto: Chinese Press.

17 The Problem of the Two-World Interpretation and Postmetaphysical Thinking

Mou Zongsan's and Lao Sze-kwang's Interpretation of Kant's Philosophy

Chun-yip Lowe

1. Introduction

The discussion between the two-world interpretation and the two-aspect interpretation is a major topic in contemporary Kant studies, since these models of interpretation largely influence how the main thrust of Kant's transcendental philosophy is construed. Briefly, the argument in the two-world interpretation is that the appearance and the thing in itself (*Erscheinung und Ding an sich*) are two distinct objects, and that the relationship between them is an ontological one. By contrast, in the two-aspect interpretation the two are two aspects of the same object, which are dependent on the spatiotemporally cognitive conditions of a rational agent, with the focus being on the conceptual relationship between a cognitive agent and objects.[1] In comparison with studies on Kant that have been conducted in the West, it seems that such a discussion has been given insufficient attention in Chinese-speaking regions of the world. However, in scrutinizing some important Chinese works on Kant's philosophy, such as those of Mou Zongsan (牟宗三, 1909–1995)[2] and Lao Sze-kwang (勞思光, 1927–2012), one can hardly deny that, despite the lack of thematization, they have already significantly participated in the debate about both interpretations.[3]

While Mou and Lao, as key figures in modern Chinese philosophy, are very much influenced by Kant, they take different approaches to Kant's philosophy. In his *Intellectual Intuition and Chinese Philosophy* and *Appearance and Thing in Itself*, Mou on the one hand criticizes weaknesses in Kant's philosophy, which Chinese philosophy is able to overcome, while on the other hand he uses many notions of Kant's philosophy to build up a metaphysics of *jingjie* (state, 境界), focusing on the reality of subjectivity in the practical sphere. Given his account of two levels of ontology,[4] which can be considered from a practical perspective, he can be associated with the camp of the "two-world" interpretation.

Although in his early interpretative work Lao does not point out which models of interpretation he would apply to Kant's philosophy, in reading his account it is evident that his argument primarily focuses on the conceptual relationship between objects and a cognitive agent (Lao 2001, 47–48, 209). With the help of Kant's theory of subjectivity, in the work of his middle phase, the *History of Chinese Philosophy* (Lao 1983), Lao attempts to establish a *non-metaphysical* model to elucidate and evaluate different schools in Chinese philosophy. Moreover, according to the recording of his lecture on Kant's philosophy and his account of Carnap's linguistic framework,[5] we are told that Lao's interpretation of Kant's philosophy is closely related to the two-aspect interpretation. Accordingly, comparing the accounts of Mou and Lao can help us to understand the development of the two-world and two-aspect interpretation in Chinese-speaking academic regions. At the same time, I shall argue that because of the development of modern philosophy, it is more reasonable for us to accept the two-aspect interpretation.

This chapter is divided into four parts. Since there is a considerable difference between Mou and Lao in their understanding of Kant's account of the empirical world and freedom, the next part of this chapter contains a brief sketch of that account in Kant's philosophy. In the third part, Mou's argument for the two-world interpretation, especially his account of intellectual intuition, is examined. The fourth is devoted to Lao's argument for a two-aspect interpretation and his application of Carnap's linguistic framework. In the fifth, I shall explain that against the background of postmetaphysical thinking (*nachmetaphysisches Denken*) (Habermas 1992 and 2012), the two-world metaphysical interpretation would lead to a closed system, in which some open elements of Kant's philosophy would be unable to function.

2. The Compatibility Between Hard Determinism and Freedom

According to Kant, all possible objects of experience must comply with the cognitive conditions of a rational agent, namely, a spatiotemporal intuition and categories. Within this spatiotemporal framework we are told that Kant's notion of the empirical world is a mechanistic worldview. For example, in discussing the second analogy, the "principle of temporal sequence according to the law of causality", Kant points out that "all alterations occur in accordance with the law of the connection of cause and effect" (B232). In other words, the causal explanation of all possible objects of experience must lie in the laws of nature.

Under this mechanistic worldview, as a physical object a rational agent is also strictly governed by the laws of nature. For example, according to modern science, our actions, including those stemming from our so-called free choice, can also be explained by either the operation of neurons or

DNA. In other words, in a phenomenal world all of the activities of a rational agent are determined by another empirical cause. As Kant points out, "one can therefore grant that if it were possible for us to have such deep insight into a human being's cast of mind, as shown by inner as well as outer actions, that we would know every incentive to action, even the smallest, as well as all external occasions affecting them, we could calculate a human being's conduct for the future with as much certainty as a lunar or solar eclipse" (*CPrR* 5:99). For this reason, such causal relations within a spatiotemporal framework can be called hard determinism, which belongs to the anti-thesis of the Third Antinomy. While the thesis fully complies with empirical science, it does not make sense in relation to our actions, since we still attribute the notion of *obligation* to a rational agent for its action. When all actions are determined by the laws of nature, it is impossible to make "my choice" or "your choice". For Kant, in order to make sense of the notion of the obligation of a rational agent, another causality is required, namely, the causality of freedom, where we act in accordance with our self-imposed rules, referring to the categorical or hypothetical imperative. Thus, regardless of which imperative a rational agent imposes, it is necessary to assume the idea of transcendental freedom, referring to "an *absolute* causal *spontaneity* beginning from itself" (A446/B474), as a cause of a rational agent, which is the incompatibilism of the thesis of the third antinomy.

In order to further elucidate the causal relation between a rational agent and its action, Kant introduces a distinction between the intelligible character and the empirical character of *Willkür*. The former refers to an incompatibilist conception of freedom and the latter to a compatibilist one (A539/B567). Although the latter provides a rich and attractive version of compatibilism and can serve as an explanatory model for action (A539–541/B567–569; A546–557/B574–585), it still cannot make sense of the notion of obligation, since the compatibilist conception of freedom can be reduced to physical conditions governed by the laws of nature. For this reason, Kant still insists on the incompatibilist conception of freedom, or the idea of transcendental freedom, which "in the practical sense is the independence of the power of choice from necessitation by impulses of sensibility" (A533–534/B561–562). Furthermore, since both characters refer respectively to incompatibilist and compatibilist freedom, Kant attempts to show the "compatibility between compatibilism and incompatibilism" (Wood 1984, 74).

Obviously, Kant's treatment of the notion of freedom is based on his mechanistic worldview. Given that a human being is a finite being who possesses merely sensible and not intellectual intuition, as an object of noumena the reality of freedom cannot be captured in a spatiotemporal framework. That is why, while elucidating the possibility of morals in the second *Critique*, Kant argues that the notion of freedom should be merely regarded as a postulate of moral law (*CPrR* 5:46).[6]

3. Intellectual Intuition and the Ultimacy of the state (*jingjie*, 境界) of the Moral Subject

With respect to sensible intuition and categories, Mou agrees with Kant's justification that they serve as necessary conditions for empirical knowledge. Mou's substantial disagreement lies in the denial of the reality of freedom in Kant's mechanistic worldview, since Mou thinks that considering freedom as a postulate would result in the complete failure of moral philosophy, and even of the whole of Chinese philosophy, in which the notion of morality is the main thrust. According to Mou, the only way to save morality is to establish the ontological status of freedom, rather than a merely conceptual understanding of it, since only the former can provide a solid basis for grounding morality and the latter would lead to skepticism. Because of his concern about Chinese philosophy, Mou's basic assumption in interpreting Kant's philosophy is to affirm the ultimacy of freedom. Consequently, if a scientific theory conflicts with freedom, he would have firmly denied it, e.g., the theory of evolution (Mou 31:10). Since Mou's argument often involves the interpretation of Chinese philosophy, in the following I shall point out some significant concepts that can show Mou's two-world interpretation.

As previously noted, one major assumption in Kant's philosophy is the finitude of a rational agent that possesses a sensible rather than an intellectual intuition, because of which we can only consider the notion of freedom as a postulate. Hence, in order to show the ultimacy of freedom, Mou attempts to provide a justification for the argument that a finite rational being has an intellectual intuition. His justification can be divided into two steps. The first is to reconsider the relationship between the thing in itself and a cognitive agent. In this regard, despite Mou's strong disagreement with Heideggger's interpretation in *Kant and The Problem of Metaphysics*, Mou implicitly adopts one of Heidegger's treatments, the main thrust of which lies in the word "object" in German, *Gegenstand*. According to the rules of German grammar, *Gegenstand* can be rewritten as the verb *entgegenstehen*, which means to "stand opposed to". Following from this, Heidegger (1990, 59) uses "das reine Gegenstehen-lassen von . . ." ("the pure letting–something–stand–against . . .") to characterize the cognitive relationship between subject and object. So construed, in investigating the antecedent condition between object and subject, we can say that to cognize an object is to let something stand in opposition to me, which entails the notion that object and subject were originally united in the ontological sense (Mou 20:42–43). In other words, the object is nothing other than the product of the splitting of the subject, or the object is derived from the subject. Accordingly, we can further subordinate all sensible data to the subject considered as the origin of the empirical world and the irreducible substance (20:259).

According to Mou, the claim that subjectivity serves the origin of the empirical world entails attributing intellectual intuition to the subject, which means that it is something that is not in the cognitive but the moral sphere. Moreover, Kant has mentioned that pure practical reason is more fundamental than speculative reason (*CPrR* 5:50–57, 119–121). Thus, Mou sees these two spheres as having a hierarchical relationship and the moral subject as negating itself and splitting into the cognitive subject and the thing in itself (Mou 21:127–133), a process that he calls moral conscience self-negation (*liang zhi zi wo xian kan*, 良知自我陷坎). For this reason, the function of the intellectual intuition of the moral subject is not only to create a thing in itself that grounds the phenomenal world, but also to show the presence of a moral conscience in the ontological sense. What makes that presence real is the act of morally reflecting on oneself, which is called retrospective verification (*ni jue ti zheng*, 逆覺體證) (20:252). Furthermore, in order to show that the state of the subject genuinely reaches an autonomous level, Mou argues that this reflection also contains an astonishingly moral feeling (*ben xin zhen dong*, 本心震動) (21:82, 105–109). Moreover, Mou often uses the word *ti* (體, body, the essentials of, the substance of) to characterize the ontological status of the moral subject: e.g., *zhi ti* (知體), *xin ti* (心體), and *xing ti* (性體). For these reasons, to claim the presence of the *jingjie* of an autonomous subject is equivalent to claiming that the intellectual intuition in that subject initiates the thing in itself, or morality, which is Mou's main assertion that men are finite but could be infinite (21:24–31).

By and large, according to Mou, if we have no intellectual intuition, this will inevitably lead not only to the collapse of morality, but also to the impossibility of a phenomenal world. Mou also indicates that because of Kant's denial that finite beings have such intuition (*CPrR* 5:99), he could only establish the *metaphysics of morals*, although his real intention is to build up a *moral metaphysics* (Mou 21:38–41). Hence, for Mou, moral metaphysics plays an essential role in establishing the ontology of adherence and without adherence—namely, the ontology of phenomena and noumena.[7]

From Mou's argument, we can see that his insistence on the presence of moral conscience focuses on the ontological role of a moral entity as grounding the phenomenal world. Thus, we are right to regard his argument as a two-world interpretation. Moreover, from his two-world interpretation it is also evident that Mou attempts to use moral language to solve the problem of being, which is quite different from the approach taken by other Kantian scholars, since they conceive of two worlds from the epistemic perspective. However, whether this moral metaphysics possesses better explanatory power is still in question; needless to say, the reality of moral conscience in a mechanistic world poses considerable difficulties, since the notion can be traced back to an antecedent cause within a spatiotemporal framework. With respect to this, we should in turn consider Lao's two-aspect interpretation.

4. Linguistic Frameworks and the Independence of Moral Language

In comparison with Mou's understanding of Kant's mechanistic world-view, Lao accepts the view, reflected in his discussion of Carnap's unity of science, that all empirical objects, including the actions of rational agents, can be reduced to physical language (Lao 2007a; see also 2014, 54–64). Obviously, hard determinism is assumed here. Nevertheless, this does not mean that Lao denies the notion of freedom; on the contrary, that notion plays a significant role in his philosophy of culture. How does he solve the problem of freedom based on that deterministic world-view? If we scrutinize his early interpretation of Kant's philosophy, it is evident that Lao's understanding is closer to the two-aspect interpretation. For example, he repeatedly argues that the notion of thing in itself should be regarded as a principle of the thinking of a rational agent, not derived from a supersensible being (Lao 2001, 47, 160–161). In other words, for Lao the notion of the thing in itself is merely an expedient way of elucidating the possibility of cognitive activity on the part of a rational agent. In his late period, Lao's interpretation takes a sharp turn in a non-metaphysical direction. Since the main thrust of his interpretation concerns the different functions of language, we shall consider Lao's discussion of Carnap's linguistic framework.

In defending the theory of linguistic frameworks, Carnap (1956) indicates that using a language poses an internal and an external problem. The former refers to entities within the language framework: when choosing a language framework we have to justify some objects that exist in that sphere and at the same time rule out other objects that do not exist in that sphere. We should understand that an object could have a meaning either with or without real reference. With respect to the external problem, we should justify choosing that language framework, which involves explanatory power. We should also bear in mind that while the internal and external problems require justification, the meanings of the justifications differ greatly.

Applying this theory of linguistic frameworks to Kant's philosophy, we can see that Lao construes Kant's use of language as follows. In the first *Critique* Kant assumes that in a given world a rational agent has already used cognitive language to describe empirical objects. However, the validity of this language still needs to be proven. For this reason, the concepts of Kant's epistemology are put forward to justify that validity—namely, to deal with the external problem in a linguistic framework, rather than to describe the operation of our cognitive system or to describe metaphysical entities. Lao points out that, so construed, Kant merely analyzes the cognitive conditions of a rational agent that empirical objects should comply with and never discusses the origins of those manifolds.

Lao denies that he is developing a metaphysical approach against a mechanistic worldview. On the contrary, with the help of the theory of linguistic frameworks, he attempts to establish a plausible conception of freedom under that worldview. As mentioned above, in choosing a linguistic framework we have already determined what objects can be presented. If all actions are reduced to cognitive language, it is impossible for us to form any kind of moral judgment. This is because corresponding to the mechanistic worldview, cognitive language cannot acknowledge any absolutely spontaneous objects. However, we have already used axiological language to construe the action of a rational agent (e.g., whether a person should or not should do something, self-determination, and taking responsibility); in doing so, we have assumed that the conception of freedom is a necessary condition. In other words, without assuming the notion of freedom we cannot make sense of our axiological language, and using axiological language imposes a *necessary supervenient structure* on the mechanistic world. So construed, the notion of freedom, as well as subjectivity, should carry out the explanatory function rather than the descriptive one that is used to speak about any metaphysical entity.

Given this linguistic framework, we need not ask the traditional metaphysical question about where the freedom comes from; we only need to explain the reasoning behind the adoption of such axiological language (Lao 2007a, 158). Against this background, Lao further points out that axiological language can be valid and independent of any metaphysical language, and that introducing metaphysical language to justify moral language would be to impose an *unnecessary supervenient structure* (Lao 2007a, 159; see also 2007b). Needless to say, mechanistic metaphysics and free will are incompatible, since metaphysical language would deny the existence of any spontaneous entity in a rational agent.

It seems that the two-aspect interpretation is better than the two-world one, since the former not only avoids the problem of the justification of substance, but is also closer to Kant's intention of denying metaphysics. "The proud name of an ontology, which presumes to offer synthetic *a priori* cognitions of things in general in a systematic doctrine . . ., must give way to the modest one of a mere analytic of the pure understanding" (A247/B303). In an open letter to Fichte, Kant (*C* 12:370) also stressed that,

> If the transcendental philosophy is correct, such a task requires a passing over into metaphysics. But I am so opposed to metaphysics, as defined according to *Fichtean* principles, that I have advised him, in a letter, to turn his fine literary gifts to the problem of applying the *Critique of Pure Reason* rather than squander them in cultivating fruitless sophistries.

Nonetheless, it can hardly be denied that in the first *Critique* and in the second *Critique* Kant provides ammunition for both interpretations, which has generated continuing debate over Kant's transcendental idealism. Which interpretation should we adopt? In considering both interpretations, we should think about the characteristics of modern philosophy. Lao suggests that, given that the whole determines the function of its parts, we are already in the modern world and cannot isolate a philosophical theory from the worldly background, since there are complex interactions between different philosophical theories and that background (Lao 1993, 189–190). As Habermas points out, the main characteristic of modern philosophy is postmetaphysical thinking. Thus, in the following I shall explain the role played by postmetaphysical thinking in the development of modern philosophy, and the problem of metaphysics, which creates a closed system.

5. Postmetaphysical Thinking and the Problem of a Closed System

Postmetaphysical thinking in modern philosophy refers to a way of thinking that departs from the tradition of classical metaphysics.[8] By arguing for this way of thinking Habermas attempts to show that the communicative reason of intersubjectivity can be used to tackle philosophical problems. While we may not fully agree on his theory of communicative reason, it does not influence his important observation on the history of philosophy (Lao 2014, 92–106). When using the word "modern", different phases of historical development are involved, namely, premodern, modern, and postmodern. In order to understand postmetaphysical thinking on modern philosophy, it is helpful to consider the characteristics of premodern philosophy, which refers to the era before the Enlightenment, especially the history of philosophy before Kant.

In examining the history of philosophy, we find that one of the distinctive characteristics of premodern philosophy is that many philosophers endeavor to establish all-inclusive metaphysical systems explaining the operation of the empirical world.[9] Accordingly, premodern philosophy can be characterized as metaphysical thinking. For Lao, metaphysics includes three crucial features: ultimacy, substantiality, and incorrigibility. Whether theoretical or practical metaphysics, it is evident that in all metaphysical systems of thought the aim is to search for the ultimate reality that serves as the origin of all being rather than for any rules or principles of activities, which would imply an ultimate substance independent of any sensible objects. Following from this, we must also assume that this ultimate reality can provide us with incorrigible knowledge by virtue of its perfection (Lao 2007a, 130–132). Since these three characteristics mean that we can actually obtain absolute knowledge, metaphysical thinking can be called absolutism or a closed system. For these reasons, absolutism is a key feature of premodern philosophy as well as of premodern world history.

However, because of scientific developments, a scientific explanation rather than a metaphysical model has come to occupy a dominant position in understanding how the world operates. For this reason, as Weber points out, saying that the world has entered the modern period refers to a process of disenchantment (*Entzauberung*), which began from the Enlightenment (Weber 1994, 9 and 2004, 13). At the same time, this process of disenchantment has also affected the sphere of philosophy, into which postmetaphysical thinking has been introduced because of the rise of Kant's philosophy. Following from this, it is clear that there is a distinct difference between premodern and modern thinking.

In spite of the strong trend towards postmetaphysical thinking in the modern period, Lao does not mean to say that we should entirely eliminate metaphysics. As mentioned above, Lao merely argues that we should not use metaphysics to tackle the problem of knowledge and morals, since the validity of epistemic and moral language does not depend on any metaphysical language (Lao 2007a; see also 2014, 101–102). Instead, Lao suggests that metaphysics should be repositioned, such that ultimacy, substantiality, and incorrigibility have an *orienting function* that serves as the final purpose for establishing sound knowledge (Lao 2014, 109–113). Lao's account of the repositioning of metaphysics is beyond our current concern. However, it is sufficient to say that postmetaphysical thinking requires us to avoid using metaphysical language to explain the empirical world, since this language cannot explain that world. Moreover, since absolutism will inevitably lead to a closed system that refuses to communicate with other philosophical traditions, some universal elements in that system cannot perform their functions. As Lao points out, such elements can be called open elements that are beyond different philosophical traditions and are universally valid for every rational agent. For example, Kant's treatment of categories and causality of freedom provide a plausible basis for us to explain different activities of rational agents. By contrast, metaphysics inevitably involves many closed elements that merely function in a particular historical period; as such, it has lost its objective reference in the contemporary world. For example, in the Chinese philosophical tradition, Zhu Xi (朱熹) established an influential metaphysics that largely consists in the cosmology of *yin* and *yang*, and the five elements (陰陽五行), such as the mention of five sounds (*wuyin*, 五音), five colors (*wuse*, 五色), five tastes (*wuwei*, 五味), and five cardinal relationships (*wulun*, 五倫) (Lao 1993, 185).

Accordingly, it seems that Lao's two-aspect interpretation is a better interpretative model for Kant's philosophy than Mou's two-world interpretation. It not only possesses better explanatory power but also, in this modern period of postmetaphysical thinking, it enables us to avoid applying a metaphysical interpretation to Kant's philosophy.

Notes

1. For a detailed discussion about the two different interpretations, see Allison 2004.
2. References to Mou's works are given in parentheses; the volume and page numbers that are indicated refer to his complete works (2003).

3. Both Mou and Lao are also regarded as leading figures in modern Chinese philosophy in that they have largely applied the Kantian notion of subjectivity to interpret traditional Chinese philosophy. Since as an important member of New Confucianism (*xiandai xinruxue*, 現代新儒學), Mou's aim is to revive traditional Chinese philosophy, Kant's philosophy is a plausible basis upon which to reconstruct the moral metaphysics that is considered the leitmotif of that philosophy. Given that in his early works Lao has also agreed that Kant's philosophy indicates the right direction to reconstruct Chinese philosophy, many commentators have associated Lao with New Confucianism. However, in scrutinizing their works, some irreconcilable differences between Mou and Lao become apparent, one of which is reflected in their interpretations of Sung–Ming Confucianism when applying the Kantian notion of subjectivity. Simply put, Mou champions the three threads theory (*san xi shuo*, 三系說), which holds that a moral subject and the way of heaven (*tiandao*, 天道) are two sides of one coin metaphysically grounded in morality (Mou 2003, volumes 5–7; Billioud 2011, 34–43). By contrast, Lao champions the one thread theory (*yi si shuo*, 一系說), which holds that the notion of subjectivity itself is sufficient to explain the main thrust of the Confucian emphasis on self- and social transformation; thus, we do not need to appeal to moral metaphysics to justify the ground of morality (Lao 1983).

4. Mou characterizes these two levels of ontology as ontology of adherence (*you zhi cun you lun*, 有執存有論) and ontology without adherence (*wu zhi cun you lun*, 無執存有論). Here the notion of 執 means to grasp, hold, and capture, which refer to Kant's categories. Accordingly, ontology of adherence means "phenomena" and ontology without adherence, "noumena".

5. I thank the Research Center of Prof. Lao Sze-kwang at Huafan University for lending me the recording of Lao's lecture on Kant's philosophy (Lao 2003).

6. As Allison's reciprocity thesis (1990, 201–213) suggests, in the moral sphere the notion of freedom and moral law imply each other.

7. Although Mou uses the terms "moral metaphysics" and "the ontology without adherence" interchangeably to discuss the reality of morality, they are fundamentally different. The former refers to the ground of morality, the latter to the unity of two heterogeneous beings, phenomenon and noumenon. Before publishing Phenomenon and Thing in Itself in 1975, Mou often used the term "moral metaphysics" to express his intention to deal with the reality of morality. However, after publishing that work, he attempted to use the notion of the ontology of adherence and without adherence to tackle problems in Chinese and Western philosophy. Admittedly, Heidegger's Kant Book certainly led to a change in Mou's philosophy (Lau 2013, 346–347). For detailed discussion of Mou's moral metaphysics, please see Billioud (2011, 93–122).

8. Habermas argument on postmetaphysical thinking can be misleading, since he would deny all metaphysics. However, as Baynes has pointed out, the notion of postmetaphysical thinking does not involve a rejection of the sort of inquiry pursued in the more recent revival of analytic metaphysics. By metaphysical thinking Habermas means "the tradition of classical metaphysics from Plato, on through the medieval period, and up to the modern 'philosophy of the subject' that arose in response to the emergence of science as a competing form of knowledge" (Baynes 2016, 205–206). Moreover, while Habermas associates Kant with the metaphysics of subjectivity, in this chapter I will not regard Kant's philosophy as a metaphysical doctrine because of the two-aspect interpretation.

9. One may argue that some post-Kantian philosophers—e.g., the German idealists Fichte, Schelling, and Hegel—are regarded as modern philosophers who attempt to establish metaphysical theories. It seems that metaphysical theory

is still developed in modern philosophy. While the rise of modernity dissolves the validity of premodern metaphysical theories, it does not mean that premodern thinking will immediately disappear. Thus, for Lao, because of their insistence on metaphysical thinking, the mentality of many post-Kantian philosophers is similar to that of premodern philosophers, although they live in the modern era and apply some notions of modern philosophy, especially subjectivity, to establish their theories (Lao 2007a, 167–171).

References

Allison, Henry E. (1990). *Kant's Theory of Freedom*. Cambridge: Cambridge University Press.

—— (2004). *Kant's Transcendental Idealism: An Interpretation and Defense*, 2nd ed. New Haven: Yale University Press.

Baynes, Kenneth (2016). *Habermas*. London: Routledge.

Billioud, Sebastien (2011). *Thinking Through Confucian Modernity: A Study of Mou Zongsan's Moral Metaphysics*. Leiden: Brill.

Carnap, Rudolf (1956). Empiricism, Semantics, and Ontology. In: *Meaning and Necessity: A Study in Semantics and Modal Logic*, enlarged ed. Chicago: University of Chicago Press, 205–221.

Habermas, Jürgen (1992). *Nachmetaphysisches Denken: Philosophische Aufsätze*. Frankfurt am Main: Suhrkamp Verlag.

—— (2012). *Nachmetaphysisches Denken II: Aufsätze und Repliken*. Berlin: Suhrkamp Verlag.

Heidegger, Martin (1990). Trans. R. Taft, *Kant and the Problem of Metaphysics*. Indiana: Indiana University Press.

Lao, Sze-kwang (1983). *History of Chinese Philosophy*. Taipei: Sanmin.

—— (1993). 中國文化路向問題的新檢討 (*Problem of the Direction of Chinese Culture: Reinvestigation*). Taipei: Dongda.

—— (2001). Kwan Tze-wan (ed.), 康德知識論要義新編 (*Essentials of Kant's Theory of Knowledge*). Hong Kong: Chinese University Press.

—— (2003). *Lecture on Kant's Philosophy (sound recording)*. Taipei: Research Centre of Prof. Lao Sze-kwang at Huafan University.

—— (2007a). 論非絕對主義的新基礎主義 (On New Foundationalism of Non-Absolutism). In: Lau Kwok-ying (ed.), 危機世界與新希望世紀—再論當代哲學與文化 (*A World of Crisis and the New Century of Hope: On Contemporary Philosophy and Culture [II]*). Hong Kong: Chinese University Press, 129–181.

—— (2007b). 儒佛心性論的異同 (*Difference and Sameness between Confucianism and Buddhism*). Taipei: Research Centre of Prof. Lao Sze-kwang at Huafan University.

—— (2014). Wang Qi (ed.), 當代西方思想困局 (*Predicaments of Contemporary Western Thought*). Taipei: Commercial Press.

Lau, Po-hei (2013). Book Review of Sebastien Billioud's *Thinking through Confucian Modernity: A Study of Mou Zongsan's Moral Metaphysics* (in Chinese). In: *Chinese Studies* 31(1), 341–347.

Mou, Zongsan (2003), 牟宗三先生全集 (*Mou Zongsan's Complete Works*). Taipei: Linking Publishing.

Weber, Max (1994). *Wissenschaft als Beruf 1917/1919 Politik als Beruf 1919. Studienausgabe der Max Weber-Gesamtausgabe Band I/17.* Tübingen: Mohr Siebeck.

———— (2004). Trans. Rodney Livingstone, *The Vocation Lectures: "Science as a Vocation" and "Politics as a Vocation".* Indiana: Hackett Publishing Company.

Wood, Allen (1984). Kant's Compatibilism. In: A. W. Wood (ed.), *Self and Nature in Kant's Philosophy.* Cornell: Cornell University Press, 73–101.

18 A Confucian Account of Intelligible Intuition in the Teachings of Liu Zongzhou

Simon Sai-ming Wong

1. Introduction

In his *Phenomena and Noumena* (Mou 1996, 3), Mou Zongsan famously claims that "if it is true that human beings cannot have [intelligible] intuition", as Kant argues, "then the whole of Chinese philosophy must collapse completely, and the thousands years of effort must be in vain".[1] Alerted by such an important claim, many commentators have tried to resolve the apparently conflicting views between Kant and Mou, not only in Chinese but also in English academia. The literature, however, might have failed to appreciate accurately the philosophical implications of Mou's critique against Kant, for they fail to acknowledge a few important complications behind the debate.

First, Mou's concept of *zhi de zhi jue* (Mou's intelligible intuition, 智的直覺)[2] is a concept of practical philosophy rather than theoretical philosophy. In *Phenomena and Noumena*, not long after the previous citation, Mou alleges that an account of intelligible intuition can be offered by an elucidation of "the free infinite mind, which manifests itself in our moral consciousness" (1996, 6). Commentators are usually aware of this claim, but if their interpretations of "the free infinite mind" and "our moral consciousness" are not accurate, they cannot possibly interpret Mou's account of intelligible intuition correctly. For instance, Mou would not agree that his critique is partly prompted by an urge to defend "a strong cognitive component" in moral development, in which "the sage, at least, [sees] what ordinary people and gentlemen do not see or do not see clearly" (Bunnin 2013, 53). To the contrary, Mou unequivocally maintains that intelligible intuition cannot be found in the cognizing human subject, no matter how rational and logical he or she is (see Mou 1996, 15–16).

Second, Mou's critique is largely provoked by the customary English translation of Kant's *intellektuelle Anschauung*, i.e., *intellectual intuition*. While the word "intuition" is itself an imperfect translation of Kant's *Anschauung*, its meaning is further distorted when it is translated into Chinese as *zhi jue* (intuition or direct awareness, 直覺). In Chinese, *zhi* (直)

literally means "direct" and *jue* (awareness, 覺) may convey a wide array of different meanings that can be philosophically significant.[3] The case is further complicated by the fact that when combined with the Chinese translation of the word *intellectual* into *zhi de* (智的), the final term *zhi de zhi jue* (智的直覺) happens to allude to one of the most important concepts in Neo-Confucianism, *ming jue* (perspicacious awareness, 明覺). As a result of the misleading translation, in the eyes of Mou, Kant's denial of *zhi de zhi jue* (Kant's *intellektuelle Anschauung*, 智的直覺) does seriously jeopardize the keystone of Confucian philosophy and a forceful defense is required. The debate goes on until Lo, a student of Mou for decades, finally clarifies that Kant's denial of *intellektuelle Anschauung* coincides perfectly with Mou's own philosophical insights and the Confucian notion of *ming jue* is by no means threatened by Kant's denial of *intellektuelle Anschauung* (see Lo 2010). Due to limit of space, I am not going to cite Lo's arguments here, but it should be noted that Lo's finding is still largely unknown to English scholarship.

Third, Mou's critique against Kant is written in Chinese, and when English-speaking readers interpret and cite his writings, the term *zhi de zhi jue* (Mou's intelligible intuition, 智的直覺) is mechanically translated back into *intellectual intuition* without investigating carefully, as Lo did, what Mou means by the term. The apparent "conflict" between Mou and Kant is thus established, while in fact Kant's *intellektuelle Anschauung* is significantly different from Mou's intelligible intuition.

As Lo (2010) has already given a very good account of the distinction between Kant's *intellektuelle Anschauung* and Mou's intelligible intuition, this paper will focus on another issue that is closely related to the debate—i.e., the primary meanings of *jue* (awareness, 覺) in Confucianism. A detailed explanation in English of the Confucian term *jue* (覺) is indispensable for the ultimate resolution of the prolonged debate. In this paper, I choose to introduce the concept of *Jue* (覺) in the teachings of Liu Zongzhou (劉宗周, 1587–1645), for reasons stated in the following section.

2. Meanings of *jue* (覺)

Broadly speaking, the character *jue* (覺) can be used, along with other Chinese characters, to name various activities of the mind (*xin*, 心) when the activities convey a sense of subjectivity or spontaneity. For instance, in its everyday and non-philosophical usage, *jue* (覺) can be seen in such expressions as *zhi jue* (intuition, 直覺), *zhi jue* (perception, 知覺), *jue cha* (awareness, 覺察), *jue wu, jue xing* (awakening or enlightening, 覺悟, 覺醒), and is usually associated with the attainment of intuitive and spontaneous wisdom. It is thus not surprising to note that *jue* (覺) is a crucial concept in Buddhism, for many of its primary connotations are deeply in tune with the core spirit of the teachings of Buddha, whose name literally means *the awakened* in Sanskrit and could have been translated as *jue zhe* (覺者) in Chinese.

While the teachings of Buddha revolve around the theme of awakening from the *three poisons*—passion (*raga*), aversion (*dvesha*) and ignorance (*moha* or *avidya*)—and thereby embarking on the path towards *nirvana*, *jue* (覺) does not play as important a role in the classical teachings of Confucius and Mencius. In the *Analects*, for instance, *jue* (覺) appears only once (see *Analects*, 14:31),[4] where it is meant to describe a desirable and adequate awareness in our dealings with others, a meaning that could not be interpreted as a critical constituent of the central theme of *ren* (benevolence, 仁) in the text. In Mencius, on the other hand, although *jue* (覺) is used in a more significant passage, in which Mencius asserts that it is the duty of the awakened to enlighten those who are not awakened yet (see Mencius 5A:7 and 5B:1), the notion of *jue* (覺) is not given any more emphasis than that in the whole volume. *Jue* (覺), which means *to be awakened* and *to enlighten* in the passage, is thus a subordinate concept that could be understood only under the principal ideas of *ren* (仁) and *yi* (righteousness, 義) in Mencius—i.e., in the context of his moral philosophy.

The implication of the concept of *jue* (覺) in Confucianism was elaborated at a more philosophical level in the Song and Ming dynasties (1368–1644) by Neo-Confucian thinkers, arguably in response to the widespread influence of Buddhism in China. This was not achieved without any complications though, not least because most of these Neo-Confucian thinkers were very familiar with Buddhism and might have been consciously or unconsciously influenced by the Buddhist way of thinking in their interpretations. Due to limits of space, it is impossible to discuss the various uses of the concept of *jue* (覺) in all Neo-Confucian thinkers. Instead, this paper will focus on the philosophical implications of *jue* (覺) in the teachings of Liu Zongzhou, the last prominent Neo-Confucian thinker in the Ming dynasty. Unlike many of his predecessors, Liu rightly and decisively interprets *jue* (覺) not merely as awakening or enlightening, but as a concept denoting the overall subjectivity and spontaneity of the mind (心) in connection to its moral capability and other cognitive powers. Without a robust account of the subjectivity and spontaneity of the mind as such, which should be the most fundamental meaning of *jue* (覺), the viability of any attempts to explain the awakening or enlightening of the mind is questionable, for the latter should be seen as the necessary manifestation of the former.

In the following discussion, I will interpret Liu's philosophical doctrine as an elaboration and development of the teachings of Confucius and Mencius. I will show that the philosophical implications of the concept of *jue* (覺) in Liu amounts to a forceful response on behalf of the two classical Confucian thinkers against the philosophical assertions by the Buddhists. Liu's doctrine will also be compared with Kant's, following the finding of Mou Zongsan that classical Confucianism and Kant's philosophy share the same fundamental philosophical insights and could be explained with the aid of each other. I will adopt this interpretive strategy in this chapter not because either Liu or Kant requires the support of the other, but because English-speaking scholars are generally more familiar with Kant's philosophy, and it would require a much longer paper to properly translate the work by Liu without the theoretical resources available in English with regard to Kant's philosophy.

3. *Jue* (覺) and the Activities of the Mind (心)

Liu's philosophical doctrine is not developed around the concept of *jue* (覺), but around the more fundamental concepts in Confucianism including mind (*xin*, 心), nature (*xing*, 性), heaven (*tian*, 天), the way (*dao*, 道), will (*yi*, 意), knowing (*zhi*, 知), and thing (*wu*, 物). Yet, as a concept denoting the subjectivity and spontaneity of the mind (心), *jue* (覺) could be rightly associated with any of these terms in Confucian philosophy. For the purpose of illustration, I shall start with the most primitive meaning of *jue* (覺) in Liu and progress step by step to the most refined and unique meaning in his teachings. The most primitive meaning of *jue* (覺) can be identified in the following passage (Liu 2:312): "From *zhi jue* [(literally perceptions)], we have the idea of the mind. [由知覺，有心之名。]"[5]

Jue (覺) is here identified as the perceptions (*zhi jue*, 知覺) from which we have the very first idea of the mind (心). *Zhi jue* (知覺) in Liu is a general term to describe our perceptions, which could be read as a phenomenal account of the general activities of the mind (心). This is evident when Liu associates the words *zhi jue* (知覺) with *yun dong* (運動) (Liu, 2:550), which literally means the activity of perception, and attributes such activities in the phenomenal sense also to animals (see 550). This phenomenal activity is necessarily perceived externally, or else it cannot be attributed to animals. This attribution should also be seen as a result of inference by analogy, according to Kant, "from the comparison of the similar mode of operation in the animals (the ground for which we cannot immediately perceive) to that of humans (of which we are immediately aware)" (*CPJ* 5:464), an inference that could allow us to assign the phenomenal concept of the activity of perception to animals.

Zhi jue yun dong (知覺運動), therefore, is a phenomenal observation that leads us to have a primitive idea of the mind (心), which does not yet offer any further determination about its characteristics or capabilities. If we stop at the phenomenal account of the mind (心), and try to interpret the mind (心) merely from such an account, Liu warns that we would end up with an illusionary idea of it that is either too imprudent to be useful, or too ambiguous to be meaningful (see Liu 2:312). In order to elucidate the more fundamental and refined concept of the mind (心)

in Confucianism that could shed light on the genuine subjectivity and spontaneity of humans, Liu hints that we must further examine the governing power behind the phenomenal *zhi jue* (知覺) (see 281). According to Liu, the self-governing power in the mind (心), and hence in *jue* (覺), is called the *will* (意) (see 481). It is therefore necessary to examine the meaning of the will (意), before we could further interpret *jue* (覺) in Liu's philosophy.

4. The Mind (心) and the Will (意)

In his *Original Mind*, Liu introduces the first and foremost meaning of the mind (*xin*, 心) as follows (Liu 2:327, my translation):

> Among all the things in nature, humans are the only one born as an intelligence. Their causality is independent of any empirical condition, and thus belongs to an intelligence. The highest self-governing power of human is called the *Mind*, and the *Mind* is considered the highest causality of all. [(盈天地間，皆物也。人其生而最靈者也。生氣宅於虛，故靈，而心其統也，生生之主也。]

Here I have translated 生氣 (literally "a power to create") as "causality" and 虛 (literally "void" or "empty") as "independent of any empirical condition". The word 靈, which is often translated as the adjective "intelligent" in English (see, e.g., Chan 1963), is translated here as the noun "intelligence", as an attempt to correlate it with Kant's *Intelligenz* (*CPrR* 5:125): "Now, a being capable of actions in accordance with the representation of laws is an intelligence [*Intelligenz*] (a rational being), and the causality of such a being in accordance with this representation of laws is his will."

The similarity between the two citations is strikingly conspicuous, though in Liu's passage, the mind (心) is being considered, while in Kant's it is the will. Instead of reducing the mind (心) to a synonym for the will too hastily, we might actually regard the word mind (心) in Confucianism as the collective name for all the powers of the mind, with the will being one of them. Before referring to Liu's own explanation on the connection between the mind (心) and the will (意), we can refer to Kant's idea of the primacy of pure practical reason—i.e., the will, in its connection to all the powers of the mind, as explained in a section of *CPrR* titled On the Primacy of Pure Practical Reason in Its Connection with Speculative Reason (5:120): "To every faculty of the mind one can attribute an interest, that is, a principle that contains the condition under which alone its exercise is promoted. Reason, as the faculty of principles, determines the interest of all the powers of the mind but itself determines its own."

According to Kant, the will, or pure practical reason, determines the exercise of all the powers of the mind, including its own exercise. It is, therefore, also appropriate to assert that all the power of the mind, when considered as a synthetic whole, are capable of determining their own exercise, which is essentially the meaning conveyed by Liu's assertion that "the mind is the highest self-governing power of humans" (心其統也). If we take one step further, considering Liu's insight that humans are the only being born as an intelligence, the mind (心) can then be rightly regarded as "the highest causality of all" (生生之主).

In Liu, the mind (心) is the highest self-governing human power (see Liu 2:327) and yet the will (意) is considered the governing power in *jue* (覺) and hence in the mind (心) (481). This could be explained very well by the passage about the primacy of pure practical reason from Kant, quoted above, which is also echoed by Liu himself in his elucidation on the relation between the mind (心) and the will (意):

> Though it cannot be observed, the will is capable of self-determination and hence it is where the primary and essential capability of the mind resides. [動之微而有主者，意也，心官之真宅也。]
>
> (327)

> The will is the primary essence of the mind. [意則心之所以為心也。]
>
> (457)

> The *ti* of the mind is nothing but the will. [心無體，以意為體。]
>
> (531)

Ti (體) is a concept in Confucianism that does not have any convenient equivalence in English. In essence, *ti* (體) is used to denote the necessary ground over which alone the performance, or *yong* (用), of the corresponding capability could be understood. The primary function of the mind (心) is being the highest self-governing human power, and the will (意) is considered the ground over which this governing capability is possible. As the *ti* (體) of the mind (心), Liu also designates the will (意) as what is preserved in the mind, rather than something manifested by the mind (心) (see Liu 2:457 and 459), though he also reminds us that the preserved and the manifested correspond to the same faculty (489). To be the governing power that resides within the mind (心) (459):

> The will is what is preserved in the mind, and is thus the most unchanging of all . . . The will itself is neither good nor evil, but is itself the liking of the good and disliking of the evil. Liking and disliking is the origin of the capability of the mind, the *ti* that cannot be observed. [意為心之所存，則至靜者莫如意 . . . 意無所謂善惡，但好善惡惡而已。好惡者，此心最初之機，惟微之體也。]

It is worth noting that liking and disliking is constituent of a faculty of desire called the will (意) that is not yet directly connected to the actual experience of any specific affectivity. Liking and disliking should be compared with Kant's notion of the faculty of desire and aversion (*CPrR* 5:58): "The only objects of a practical reason are therefore those of the good and the evil. For by the first is understood a necessary object of the faculty of desire, by the second, of the faculty of aversion, both, however, in accordance with a principle of reason." The faculty of desire and the faculty of aversion are not two different faculties but one and the same faculty of desire considered in association with the two possible objects, the good and the evil. Evil, however, as the object of aversion, cannot be seen as originating from the faculty of desire. The will (意) in Liu, or practical reason in Kant, is thus considered essentially good in both Kant and Liu (see *GMM* 4:393 and Liu 2:459).

The liking and disliking of the will (意) is the ground over which the mind (心) can be the highest self-governing human power and the highest causality of all. The liking and disliking of the will (意) is unchanging and self-determining, the preservation of which is the preservation of the primary and essential capability of the mind (心). In Confucianism, and hence in Liu's philosophy, there is yet another concept that serves to account for the liking and disliking of the will (意), and that is *zhi* (知).

5. The Mind (心), the Will (意), and *zhi* (知)

Notably following the teaching of the classical Confucian text *The Great Learning*, Liu explains the relationship between the mind (心), the will (意) and *zhi* (知) in the following sequence:

> The will is the primary essence of the mind, *zhi* is the primary essence of the will. [意則心之所以為心也，知則意之所以為意也。]
>
> (Liu 2:457).

> The *ti* of the mind is nothing but the will, the *ti* of the will is nothing but *zhi*. [心無體，以意為體；意無體，以知為體。]
>
> (531).

The will (意) is the necessary ground—i.e., the *ti* (體)—to explain the primary and essential capability of the mind (心), and now *zhi* (知) is considered the necessary ground to explain the capability of the faculty of desire—i.e., the will (意). Liu explains why *zhi* (知) is the necessary ground of the will (意) as follows (Liu 2:457–458):

> The initial function that is necessary for the will is nothing but the capability to determine liking and disliking. This is why the will cannot be deceived. Hence we know *zhi* is contained in the will, but not initialized by the will. [又就意中指出最初之機，則僅有知好知惡之知而已，此意之不可欺者也。故知藏於意，非意之所起也。]

The Chinese word *zhi* (知) literally means "know" or "knowledge" and is thus often translated as such. However, judging from this passage where Liu explains the initial function of *zhi* (知) that lies at the ground of the will (意), which is to "know" liking and disliking, *zhi* (知) is arguably more appropriately translated as a capability to determine, for there is nothing external to *zhi* (知) and the will (意) that *zhi* (知) could literally "know" in order to ground the liking and disliking of the will (意). In other words, *zhi* (知) indicates the self-determination of the will (意) and hence the mind (心), and this is exactly why Mencius asserts that *zhi* (知) is essentially *liang* (良)—i.e., intrinsic (see Mencius 7A:15). In his refutation against Wang Shouren's interpretation of *liang zhi* (良知), Liu specifically denies that *zhi* could be defined as a capability to know what is good and what is evil (Liu 2:372):

> If one compares *zhi* of good and evil and *zhi* of love and respect, they might sound similar but are in fact very different. In the *zhi* of love and respect, *zhi* is inherent in the love and respect; while in *zhi* of good and evil, *zhi* is external to the good and evil. When *zhi* is a constituent of love and respect, there is no impurity to the contrary, and thus the corresponding *zhi* should be rightly regarded as the intrinsic *zhi*. When *zhi* is external to good and evil, and all *zhi* could do is to distinguish between the two, it should be regarded as a manifestation of the intrinsic *zhi*, but it is not the most fundamental but only a derived function of the intrinsic *zhi*. [知愛知敬, 知在愛敬之中。知善知惡, 知在善惡之外。知在愛敬中, 更無不愛不敬者以參之, 是以謂之良知。知在善惡外, 第取分別見, 謂之良知所發則可, 而已落第二義矣。]

Zhi (知) denotes the capability of the will (意), as a faculty of desire and hence a faculty of causality, to determine itself, and Liu cites the famous example of love and respect by Mencius to indicate that the determining ground of the good lies within the human himself and should be considered as intrinsic (Mencius 7A:15). In this regard, as asserted by Liu, the *causality* (生氣) of humans is *independent of any empirical condition* (宅於虛) and *thus belongs to an intelligence* (故靈) (see Liu 2:327). Such a concept of causality, as Kant notes, also always "brings with it that of laws in accordance with which, by something that we call a cause, something else, namely an effect, must be posited" (*GMM* 4:446). This causality of the will (意), therefore, cannot be seen as lawless. Rather, it "must instead be a causality in accordance with immutable laws but of a special kind", "for otherwise a free will would be an absurdity" (446). This causality, according to an intelligible order, is thus nothing but a causality "in accordance with the representation of laws".

Zhi (知), therefore, is nothing but the self-legislating capability of the will. In Confucianism and in the teachings of Liu, *zhi* (知), or *liang zhi* (良知), is thus equivalent to *tian li* (the unchanging principle, 天理). *zhi*

(知) is not a knowledge of something external to the mind but the self-determination of the will, and hence the mind, according to the unchanging principle. *Tian li* (天理) is not a principle that is external to the mind and ready to be known or learned by *zhi* (知), but it is the same self-determination (by the necessary means of self-legislation) of the will (意) and hence the mind (心). *Zhi* (知) and *tian li* (天理) should therefore be seen as strictly interchangeable in Liu's philosophy and Confucianism.

6. The Mind (心) and *jue* (覺)

At the beginning of this chapter, I asserted that *jue* (覺) can be used to name any activity of the mind (心) that conveys a sense of subjectivity and spontaneity. The second section identified the phenomenal activity of perception as the most primitive meaning of *jue* (覺) in the teachings of Liu, from which we have the very first idea of the mind. The third and fourth sections introduced the concepts of the will (意) and *zhi* (知) in order to illustrate the most essential capability of the mind (心) (Liu 2:398): "In the *Five Classics* and the *Four Books*, the mind is always considered as the will and *zhi* combined. [凡五經、四書之言心也，皆合意知而言者也。]"

When considered as the will (意) and *zhi* (知) combined, the mind (心) is considered in its primary and essential capability—i.e., to determine itself according to its own unchanging principle. The manifestation of this capability demonstrates the genuine subjectivity and spontaneity of the mind (心). The meaning of *jue* (覺) is thus elevated to a new level. According to Liu (2:313): "It is not sensible to demand an account of *jue* without paying regard to reality. Whenever we speak of *jue*, therefore, we are speaking of *jue* of li. [世未有懸空求覺之學，凡言覺者，皆是覺斯理。]" An account of *jue* (覺) without paying regard to reality is one that does not consider the mind (心) as the will (意) and *zhi* (知) combined—i.e., one that does not consider the capability of the mind (心) to determine itself according to its own unchangeable principle. This is an accusation Liu makes against Buddhism (see, e.g., 331–332, 405), an accusation that cannot be discussed in this short paper. In essence, Liu is warning that any merely phenomenal account of *jue* (覺) is groundless and illusionary (312), as the subjectivity and spontaneity of the mind (心) could be explicated only by investigating the necessary grounds over which the apparent activities of *jue* (覺) are possible. Once the grounds are clearly explained, Liu argues that we can coherently speak of a single account of the mind (心) that should definitely include *jue* (覺) as a necessary concept (457):

> The mind is one. When its fundamental nature is considered, the mind is called *ren*. When its fundamental nature is not considered,

it is called *jue*. *Jue* is nothing but the affectivities felt in *ren*, but we should not consider *jue* as *Ren*, just like we cannot consider the mind merely as *xing*. [心一也，合性而言，則曰仁，離性而言，則曰覺。覺即仁之親切痛癢處，然不可以覺為仁，正謂不可以心為性也。]

In Confucianism, *ren* (仁) means humanity (see Liu 2:305) and is the *ti* (體) of the mind (心) (see 2:330). It is therefore incorrect to explain *ren* (仁) through an account of *jue* (覺), for the former is the ground of the latter. *Ren* (仁) and *jue* (覺), however, are both an account of the same mind (心), the only difference being that when *jue* (覺) is in question, it is the felt affectivities of the mind (心) that are being considered. *Ren* (仁), on the other hand, is humanity as explained by the refined account of the mind (心) as the will (意) and *zhi* (知) combined. These two perspectives presuppose each other. *Ren* (仁) as humanity presupposes its manifestation in the affectivities in the mind (心). *Jue* (覺) presupposes *ren* (仁) as the ground over which it is possible. These mutual presuppositions lead to Liu's claim, in the above passage, that "*jue* (覺) is nothing but the affectivities felt in *ren* (仁)". Following this interpretation, Liu hence declares that the mind (心) is *jue* (覺) (2:311–312) if we consider at the same time that the mind is *ren* (仁) (2:312):

The mind is the truest and the sincerest of all, of which we have no other clues but those manifested in its *jue*. In *jue*, we see the governing power in the mind. When the mind is governing itself properly, it is solid and sound. When the mind fails to govern itself, it is void. When the mind is solid and sound, there is no place for evils. When the mind fails to govern itself, evils prevail. When the mind is governing itself, it is like having a leader in a group where the group is directed by the leader. When the *jue* is self-governing, it is like having a clear mirror where the beautiful and the ugly immediately manifest themselves. In the past, people call the mind the "master" and ask, "Is the master always awake and aware?" I answer, if the mind is not always awake and aware, where is the master to be seen? [此心一真無妄之體，不可端倪，乃從覺地指之。覺者，心之主也。心有主則實，無主則虛。實則百邪不能入，無主焉反是。有主之心，如家督在堂，群奴為之奔走。有主之覺，如明鏡當空，妍媸於焉立獻。昔人呼心為「主人翁」以此。又曰：「主人翁常惺惺否？」若不是常惺惺，又安見所謂主人翁者？]

Jue (覺) is thus nothing but the awakening and awareness of the master in the mind (心). *Jue* (覺) therefore represents the genuine and refined idea of subjectivity and spontaneity in the activities of the mind (心) in Confucianism, for this is where we are conscious of the self-determinability of the mind (心).

As Lo (2010) argues, Mou's theory of intelligible intuition is in fact a direct inheritance of the concept of *jue* (覺) or *ming jue* (明覺), proposed by various Neo-Confucians, including Liu. This chapter therefore serves to support Lo's claim, for the meanings of Mou's term, *zhi de zhi jue* (intelligible intuition, 智的直覺) can now be properly explained with reference to the above discussion. The use of the Chinese character *zhi* (直) before *jue* (覺) is meant to convey a sense of directness in the consciousness of the freedom of the will (意) and the self-determinability of the mind (心). The use of *zhi de* (智的), on the other hand, highlights the independence of the mind (心) from sensibility. Both of these implications can be found in the teachings of Liu, as discussed above. The notion of *zhi de zhi jue* (智的直覺), or intelligible intuition, is thus meant to be an elaboration of the concept of *jue* (覺) in Confucianism. It is a strictly practical concept and has nothing to do with Kant's use of "*intellektuelle Anschauung*". Instead, as is evident from the unmistakable practical, rather than theoretical, nature of the concept, Mou's "intelligible intuition" should be compared with Kant's consciousness of oneself as an intelligence (*GMM* 4:458), the self-consciousness of a pure practical reason (*CPrR* 5:29), our consciousness of the moral law (see, e.g., 31, 46, 75), and the consciousness of freedom of the will (see, e.g., 42).

Notes

1. This translation is borrowed from Bunnin (2013). Note that *intellectual intuition* in this citation is the translation of Mou's Chinese term *zhi de zhi jue* (智的直覺). In the rest of this chapter, this term will be translated into intelligible intuition. See note 2.
2. Mou's concept of intelligible intuition is explained in detail in Mou (1974) and Mou (1996). In this chapter, I follow Lo (2010) in the translation of Mou's Chinese term *zhi de zhi jue* (智的直覺) into "intelligible intuition" instead of "intellectual intuition".
3. I shall discuss the meanings of *jue* in the next section.
4. All English translations of Confucian texts are mine.
5. In this chapter, all references to Liu's works are cited from Liu (1996), which is a six-volume collection in Chinese. The two numbers in brackets are the volume and the page(s), respectively. All English translations are mine.

References

Bunnin, Nicholas (2013). God's Knowledge and Ours: Kant and Mou Zongsan on Intellectual Intuition. In: *Journal of Chinese Philosophy* 40(Supplement), 47–58.

Chan, Wingtsit (1963). *A Source Book in Chinese Philosophy*. Princeton, NJ: Princeton University Press.

Liu, Zongzhou (1996). 劉宗周全集 (*The Collected Works of Liu Zongzhou*). Taipei: Institute of Chinese Literature and Philosophy, Academia Sinica.

Lo, Suet-kwan (2010). 理智的直觀與智的直覺 (Intellektuelle Anschauung and Intelligible Intuition). In: *New Asia Journal* 28, 239–260.

Mou, Zongsan (1974). 智的直覺與中國哲學 (*Intelligible Intuition and Chinese Philosophy*). Taipei: Taiwan Commercial Publisher.

——— (1996). 現象與物自身 (*Phenomena and Noumena*). Taipei: Student Book Company.

19 Kant's Revolutionary Doctrine of *Anschauung*[1] and the Philosophical Significance of Mencius' "Original Mind"

Suet-kwan Lo

1. Kant's Doctrine of *Anschauung* and Its Innovative Insights

Throughout the *Critique of Pure Reason*, Kant provides the form of a revolutionary new philosophy completely distinct from the Western philosophical tradition. In Kant's own words, it is: "complete reform, or rather a new birth of it, according to a previously unknown plan" (*PFM* 4:257).[2] In traditional Western philosophy, as Kant indicates: "Hitherto it has been assumed that all our cognition must conform to *Gegenständen*".[3] But Kant no longer supposes that cognition conforms to *Gegenständen*, but rather that *Gegenstände* must conform to our cognition. He said (Bxvi), "if we suppose that *Gegenstände* must conform to our cognition. This would agree better with what is desired, namely, that it should be possible to have cognition of *Gegenstände a priori*, determining something in regard to them prior to their being given."

First and foremost in terms of Kant's doctrine of *Anschauung* (usually translated as "intuition") and the innovative insight that moves from "*Anschauung* must conform to the constitution of the *Gegenstände*" into "the *Gegenstand* (as an object of the senses) must be subject to the character of our ability of *Anschauung*" (Bxvii).[4] That is to say, Kant's doctrine of *Anschauung* proposes such a new model as its foundation. And in accordance with this revolutionary doctrine, Kant specifies (Bxxv): "That space and time are only forms of sensible *Anschauung*, and so only conditions of the existence of things as appearances." And (Bxxvi): "We can therefore have no cognition of any *Gegenstand* as thing in itself, but only in so far as it is an object of sensible *Anschauung*, that is, an appearance." Critique teaches us that the object is to be taken *in a twofold sense* (Bxxvii), namely as appearance and as thing in itself. Furthermore, referring to his argument in the Analytic of Concepts, Kant conveys the following innovative insight (Bxvii).

> the *Gegenstände*, or what is the same thing, the *experience* in which alone, as given *Gegenstände*, they can be cognized, conform to those

concepts . . . and understanding has rules which I must presuppose as being in me prior to *Gegenstände* being given to me, and therefore as being *a priori*. They find expression in *a priori* concepts to which all *Gegenstände* of experience necessarily conform, and with which they must agree.

Nonetheless, such concepts are based on the spontaneity of thought (A68/B93), in contrast to *Gegenstände* which are thought solely through reason, and indeed as necessary, but which can never be given in experience (Bxviii). Accordingly, Kant put forward "all *Gegenstände* are divided into phenomena and noumena" (A235/B294).

According to the distinction between appearance and thing in itself, and the division of all *Gegenstände* into phenomena and noumena, Kant justifiably divides philosophy into two parts: *theoretical* and *practical* philosophy, namely, the theoretical as *philosophy of nature* and the practical as *moral philosophy* (*CPJ* 5:171). Kant argues that the concept of nature certainly makes its *Gegenstände* representable in *Anschauung*, but not as things in themselves, rather as mere appearances, while the concept of freedom in its object makes a thing representable in itself not in *Anschauung* (175). Kant thus overturned traditional Western practical philosophy. In the Western tradition, practical philosophy is viewed as theoretical knowledge, while on the contrary, Kant requires a separate part of philosophy for practical philosophy alone, alongside the theoretical part (173).

For Kant, practical philosophy rests upon a supersensible (*übersinnlichen*) principle (*CPJ* 5:173), and this principle rests on supersensible things (*Übersinnlichen*), "which the concept of freedom alone makes knowable [*kennbar*] through formal laws" (173); "the practical legislation of reason in accordance with the concept of freedom" (171) is morally practical (*moralisch–praktisch*). Accordingly, Kant indicates that the domain of the concept of freedom, as supersensible (176), and the realm of concepts of nature, as the sensible (175), are two different realms. Meanwhile, Kant claims (175):

> Understanding and reason thus have two different legislations on one and the same territory of experience, without either being detrimental to the other.
> The possibility of at least conceiving without contradiction the coexistence of the two legislations and the faculties pertaining to them in one and the same subject was proved by the *Critique of Pure Reason* . . .

Pursuant to Kant's new doctrine of *Anschauung* and critique of pure understanding, we are justified in accepting the following conclusion (A51/B75): "Our nature is so constituted that our *Anschauung* can never be other than sensible; that is, it contains only the mode in which we are affected by *Gegenstände* . . . . The understanding can intuit nothing, the senses can think nothing. Only through their union can cognition arise." As mentioned before, the validity of Kant's concept of things can be understood from a twofold standpoint: not only "as *Gegenstände* of the senses and of the understanding", in connection with experience, but also "as *Gegenstände* which are thought merely" (Bxix). This is what Kant elsewhere (A251) refers to as: "The cause of our not being satisfied with the substrate of sensibility, and of our therefore adding to the phenomena noumena which only the pure understanding can think." In consequence, we are able to understand Kant's claims about the critique that marks the limits of our sensible cognition, about why supersensible things are possible, and how these two claims are linked. He argues that, as sensible *Anschauung* does not extend to all things without distinction, there remains room for other and different objects, and that therefore such supersensible objects cannot be absolutely denied (A288/B344). Namely, we can have "a space which we can fill neither through possible experience nor through pure understanding" (A288/B345), as this space is the field of supersensible things [*Felde des Übersinnlichen*][5] (Bxxi).

For the following reasons, I find the validity of Kant's arguments hold true: If *Anschauung* must conform to the constitution of *Gegenstände*, I do not see how we could know anything of the latter a priori; and if concepts must conform to the *Gegenstand*, I do not see how I can know anything a priori in regard to the *Gegenstände* (Bxvii). Through Kant's "changed mode of thinking", we are able to explain how there can be cognition a priori. Therefore, Kant claims that nature is regarded as "the sum of the *Gegenstände* of experience" (Bxix) and that, with our ability to cognize a priori (*unseres Vermögens a priori zu erkennen*), we can never transcend the limits of possible experience; moreover, our a priori cognition of reason (*Vernunfterkenntnis a priori*) has to do only with appearances and must leave the thing in itself as indeed real *per se*, but as not known by us (Bxx). Thereof Kant claims that "the territory of pure understanding is an island enclosed by nature itself, within unalterable limits; it is the land of truth (enchanting name) surrounded by a wide and stormy ocean" (A235/B294–295).

The field of supersensible things resembles a wide and stormy ocean. Prior to Kant, this ocean had become "the native home of illusion"; it incessantly "deluded the philosopher with empty hopes and thus entangled him in adventures that he could never abandon and was unable to carry to completion" (A235–236/B295). According to the history of Western philosophy, we know, on one hand, that rationalism assumed a previous intellectual *Anschauung* as the primary source of the pure concepts of the understanding and of first principles; it assumed "the *harmonia praesiabilita intellectualis*" (C 10:131). It encourages philosophers to construct a supersensible "system of intellectual cognition

[*System intellektueller Erkenntnis*]", which undertakes "to determine its objects [*Gegenstände*] without any assistance from the senses" (A280/B336). On the other hand, empiricism and skepticism are dogmatic in their attitude towards ideas and audaciously deny whatever is beyond the sphere of intuitive cognitions (A471/B499). Certainly, Kant indicates that empiricism itself commits the mistake of immodesty, which thereby causes irreparable detriment to the practical interests of reason (A471/B499). In Kant, the practical interests of reason are "foundation stones of morality and religion" (A466/B494). As Kant indicates, pure empiricism deprives both morality and religion of their force and influence; so in empiricism, moral ideas and principles lose all validity and fall along with the transcendental ideas which served as their theoretical support (A468/B496).

Fortunately, Kant does not merely critically refute rationalism, empiricism, and skepticism, but he also proposes a new mode of thought, for he points out: we seek the cognition of supersensible things, not from objects, but from the morally practical subject—namely, free will; the domain of supersensible things belongs to the domain of the concept of freedom (*CPJ* 5:176). They are grounded entirely on the concept of freedom, to the complete exclusion of the determining grounds of the will from nature (173); the concept of freedom alone makes supersensible things cognizable by means of its formal laws (173), i.e., moral laws. Hence, Kant says (195): "Reason prescribes laws a priori for freedom and its peculiar causality as the supersensible thing in the subject, so that we may have a purely practical cognition."

2. The Concept of a Freedom That Cannot Be Given in *Anschauung*

In *Critique of Pure Reason* (e.g., B421), Kant indicates that we must divert our self-cognition from fruitless and extravagant speculation to fruitful practical employment. We must therefore seek cognition of the domain of supersensible things not just from the *Critique of Pure Reason*, but also proceed to the *Critique of Practical Reason*; we must not only explain supersensible things as just "noumena" and "ideas", but also proceed to prove the objective reality of some supersensible things. In particular, Kant proved the objective reality of three supersensible things: freedom, immortality, and God. In the *Critique of Judgment*, Kant states (*CPJ* 5:474): "Of the three ideas of pure reason, God, freedom, and immortality, that of freedom is the one and only concept of the supersensible-thing which (owing to the causality implied in it) proves its objective reality in nature by its possible effect there."[6] The consciousness of freedom of the will is not empirical consciousness, nor is it the consciousness of self (apperception),[7] but "consciousness of existing in and being determined by an intelligible order of things" (*CPrR* 5:42).

The realm of the natural concept (as the sensible) and the realm of the concept of freedom (as supersensible) are two distinct realms. Therefore, there are two different problems. The former (*CPrR* 5:45),

> as belonging to the Critique of pure (speculative) reason, requires the explanation of how *Anschauungen*, without which no object at all can be given and without which, therefore, none can be recognized synthetically, are possible a priori; and its solution turns out to be that *Anschauungen* are without exception sensible, and therefore, do not render possible any speculative cognition which goes further than possible experience reaches . . .

This realm refers to *Gegenstände* of possible experience (46). Kant indicates (42): "Not principles but instead pure sensible *Anschauung* (space and time) was there the first datum that made a priori cognition possible and, indeed, only for *Gegenstände* of the senses." The latter "belongs to the *Critique of Practical Reason*", requires explanation of only "how reason can determine maxims of the will", but requires no explanation of "how objects of the faculty of desire are possible" (45). And its solution turns out to be (44) that "the will is to be the cause of the objects [*Objecten*], so that its causality has its determining ground solely in the pure faculty of reason, which can therefore also be called a pure practical reason." Moreover, "pure reason might also be practical and might be a law of a possible order of nature not empirically cognizable" (45); this practical realm requires an explanation "of the determining ground of volition in maxims of volition, whether it is empirical or whether it is a concept of pure reason (of its lawfulness in general), and how it can be the latter."

I agree with Kant that the *Critique of Practical Reason* may and must begin with pure practical laws and their reality. Instead of *Anschauungen*, it takes as its basis those laws and the concept of their existence in the intelligible world—i.e., the concept of freedom (*CPrR* 5:46). How are the objects of the faculty of desire possible? Kant indicates: "For that, as a problem of theoretical cognition of nature, is left to the *Critique* of speculative reason" (45).

Allen W. Wood (2011, 24–25) claims that since "Kant takes cognition, properly speaking, to consist in an intuited content grasped through concepts" (see A19/B33; A51/B75–76), it is problematic that Kant claims that freedom is the only idea of reason whose possibility is cognized *a priori*, though without having insight into it (*CPrR* 5:4). However, if one requires a theoretical proof that we are free, this would require that causality from freedom cannot work independently of determination by alien causes—that is, causality from freedom would not be free. This is obviously paradoxical. If one requires the validity of the moral law independent of the presupposition of freedom—namely, if a person requires that the moral law is nothing more than a natural law, he or she "thus deprives us of the moral law itself, which admits no empirical principle of determination" (94). In the words of Kant, this is "to exhibit empiricism in its naked superficiality" (94).

In his Preface to the *Critique of Practical Reason*, Kant has indicated (*CPrR* 5:3): "Inasmuch as the reality of the concept of freedom is proved by an apodictic law of practical reason, it is the *keystone* of the whole system of pure reason, even the speculative." He confidently asserts "the fact that freedom actually exists, for this idea is revealed by the moral law" (4). He explicitly states that "practical reason itself, without any concert with the speculative, assures reality to a supersensible object of the category of causality, viz., *freedom*, although (as becomes a practical concept) only for practical use; and this establishes on the evidence of a fact that which in the former case could only be conceived" (6).

In the Preface, Kant expresses the conclusion: "the fact that freedom actually exists" (*CPrR* 5:4), and that freedom is "established on the evidence of a fact", is based on the Analytic (*CPrR* 5:19–41). Kant states (42):

> This Analytic shows that pure reason can be practical, that is, can of itself determine the will independently of anything empirical; and this it proves by a fact in which pure reason in us proves itself actually practical, namely, the autonomy shown in the fundamental principle of morality, by which reason determines the will to action.

But it has seemed to a number of Kant's interpreters that it is important whether the concept of freedom refers to something that can be given in *Anschauung*; answering negatively, they require supersensible things to be exhibited in *Anschauung*. We must recognize that these requirements are paradoxical. Such an interpreter, in Kant's words (*GMM* 4:452), is "inclined to expect behind the objects [*Gegenständen*] of sense always something invisible and for itself active, but is corrupted by the fact that [human understanding] wants to make this invisible [thing] once again into something sensible, i.e., into an object [*Gegenstande*] of *Anschauung*, and thereby does not become by any degree the wiser."

3. The Philosophical Significance of Mencius' "Original Mind"

All in all, I can state the thesis I will defend as follows (*CPJ* 5:474): "freedom is the one and only concept of the supersensible-thing which (owing to the causality implied in it) proves its objective reality in nature by its possible effect there." I agree with Kant that the moral law is itself laid down as a principle of the deduction of freedom through a causality of pure reason (*CPrR* 5:48).

Of course we know that many scholars attack Kant's account of the moral law and freedom.[8] They deny that there is any common criterion and law, which, if "it is to be valid morally, i.e., as the ground of an obligation, has to carry absolute necessity with it" (*GMM* 4:389). In other words, they do not admit that the moral law is true. They deny also (440) "the will through which it [the will] is a law to itself (independently of all properties of the objects of volition [*Gegenstände des Wollens*])." Furthermore, they do not admit that "the will is nothing but practical reason" (432), or that pure practical reason includes a universally legislative will. That is, they consider that both the moral law and freedom of will are chimerical ideas without truth.

In this chapter, I do not wish to belabor the dispute with those scholars who deny morality. I shall merely try to support Kant's moral philosophy by revealing the philosophical significance of Mencius' concept of "original mind".[9] Limiting my attention to the main points related to issues concerning *Anschauung*, I would like to make a summary description as follows. First, I must point out that Confucius (孔子, 551–479 B.C.) started the tradition known as Confucian philosophy, and Mencius (孟子, 385–304 B.C.) inherited Confucius' thought. Confucius' "*ren*" (仁)[10] constitutes the keystone of the whole tradition of Confucian philosophy, just like freedom of will is the keystone of Kant's philosophy.

Confucius' *ren* is the human being's faculty, which everybody has, of prescribing laws *a priori* and acting according to a universal and supreme principle. It is the universal law that we call *tianli* (literally, universal principle, 天理)—namely, the supreme principle of morality (i.e., what Kant calls "the moral law"). *The Analects* (論語 6:30) states: "The Master said, '*ren zhe* [仁者][11] desires to set himself up, seeks also others to set themselves up; desiring himself to achieve, he also makes others achieve'." We can say that "desires to set himself up" and "desiring himself to achieve" relate to the mental faculty of desire generally, and can be regarded as a higher faculty—in Kant's words, "as a faculty containing autonomy" (*CPJ* 5:198). Thus, we can state that *ren* is the human being's higher faculty of desire. Meanwhile, Mencius' above-quoted statement is an expression of the highest moral principle. As such, we can state that *ren* is a faculty which gives universal law. In Kant's words, *ren* includes a will "through which it is a law to itself (independently of all properties of the objects of volition)" (*GMM* 4:440). That is, *ren* includes the autonomy of the will, or as it is also called, the freedom of will.

Mencius inherits Confucian philosophy, for he clearly proposes (*The Mencius*, 孟子 11:11): "*ren* is man's mind." Here "man's mind" means "original mind"; Mencius also names it "*ben xin*" (本心). We can see, according to Confucius and Mencius, *ren* (i.e., *ben xin*) as the faculty of the mind (*Seelenvermögen*) originally containing the faculty of desire (*Begehrungsvermögen*), which are considered as higher faculties—i.e., reason legislating universally is related to the determination of the

faculty of desire. Confucius says (*Analects* 7:30): "Is *ren* a thing remote?
If I desired *ren*, *ren* would be right at hand." Here "I desired", (just as
"desires to set himself up" and "desiring himself to achieve") expresses
the higher faculty of desire, which distinguishes human moral desire from
natural desire. Mencius states (*The Mencius* 11:10):

> I desire fish, and I also desire bears paws. If I cannot have the two
> together, I will let the fish go, and take the bear's paws. So, I desire
> life, and I also desire *yi* [義]. If I cannot keep the two together, I will
> let life go, and choose *yi*.

In Mencius, "desire life" refers to human natural desire: Mencius names
it "*xiao ti*" (小體);[12] "desire *yi*" refers to the human moral desire which is
rooted in the original mind, which Mencius names "*da ti*" (大體)—that
is, "the function of the mind is reflecting [心之官則思]" (11:15).[13] *Si*
(思) means nothing more than the *tianli*. In Kant's words, "*si*" means "a
rational being has the faculty to act in accordance with the representation
of laws, i.e., in accordance with principles, or a will" (*GMM* 4:412), for
"the will is nothing other than practical reason." Accordingly, we can
suggest that Mencius' "the mind" (i.e., the function of *si*) corresponds to
free will—i.e., to pure practical reason; it is our own subject as an intelligible being. Mencius states (*The Mencius* 11:15): "Those who follow
their *da ti* are great men (*da ren*, 大人); those who follow their *xiao ti* are
little men (*xiao ren*, 小人)." Using Kant's words, little men merely reverse
the moral order of their incentives in incorporating them into their maxims,[14] so the problem is not simply that they have natural desire. Mencius
states (11:15): "Let a man first stand fast in his '*da*' (大), and the inferior
part will not be able to take it from him. It is simply this which makes
the great man."[15]

Continuing with the above explanations, we may identify "*ben xin*"
(original mind, 本心) with *ren*, as the higher faculty of desire—i.e., reason legislating universally in the faculty of desire. Thus we may propose
the original mind is the categorical principle—that is, "*xin ji li*" (心即
理)—just as Kant indicates that the freedom of will and the unconditional
practical law reciprocally imply each other (*CPrR* 5:29). Mencius says
(*The Mencius* 11:7):

> Men's mouths agree in having the same tastes; their ears agree in
> enjoying the same sounds; their eyes agree in recognizing the same
> beauty. Shall their minds alone be without that which they similarly
> approve? What is it then of which they similarly approve? It is, I say,
> *li* [the universal principle, 理], and *yi* [righteousness, 義].

Later (13:21) he adds: "*Ren* [仁], *yi* [義], *li* [禮], *zhi* [智] are rooted in the
original mind."

According to Mencius' words, the moral law originates from everyone's original mind. The Song and Ming Confucians (1017–1529), who inherited what Mencius achieved, clearly propose *"xin ji li"* (the original mind is the categorical principle, 心即理).[16] For example, Lu Xiangshan (陸象山, 1139–1193) said:

> The original mind is one and *li* [universal principle, 理] is one . . . The original mind and *li* can never be separated into two.
>
> (Lu 1963, 1:3b–4a)

> There is only one mind. My mind, my friends' mind, the mind of the sages thousands of years ago, and the mind of sages thousands of years to come are all the same.
>
> (35:10a–b)

> All men have this mind, and all minds are endowed with this *li*. The original mind is *li*.
>
> (11:5b–6a)

> The Four [i.e., *Ren, yi, li,* and *zhi*] are all originally present in the self. Nothing need be added.
>
> (35:22a)

Similarly, Wang Yangming (see note 14, above) said (Wang 1963, Article 3): "The original mind is *li*. Is there any affair in the world outside of the mind? Is there any *li* outside of the mind?"

Accordingly, we can see that Mencius' doctrine of the original mind contains two main points: (1) the faculty of desire is reason (i.e., free will), which is practical, without the mediation of any sort of pleasure; and (2) reason universally legislates—that is, *"xin ji li"*. Liu Jishan (劉蕺山, 1578–1645) states (Liu 1836, 10:611): "It is will (*yi,* 意) that makes the mind into the mind [意則心之所以為心也]." Later (12:695), he adds: "In terms of the master of the mind, the mind is called the will [意心一也，自其主宰而言謂之意]." And at 9:538 he writes: "Will is a compass giving the direction." As Mou Zongsan (牟宗三, 1909–1995) says: "Here, *yi* does not have the sense of [conscious] intention [*yinian,* 意念]. Rather, it corresponds to free will [自由意志]."[17]

According to the above quotations, we can point out that the original mind legislates to set up the universal principle that we comply with. The universal principle includes both universality and absolute necessity. In the tradition of Confucius' philosophy, "The original mind is the universal principle" (*xin ji li*), which includes the meaning of autonomy of the will. Just as Kant said, "The autonomy of will is the supreme principle of morals [*Sittlichkeit*, 德性]."[18] Kant continues (*GMM* 440):

> Autonomy of will is that property of it by which it is a law to itself (independently of any property of the objects of volition). The principle of autonomy, then, is: Always so to choose that the same volition shall comprehend the maxims of our choice as a universal law.[19]

Kant discovers that "morality (*Moralität*, 道德) exists in all actions in relation to legislation . . . But this legislation must always be found in the rational being himself, and can originate from his will" (434).

Many scholars think Confucius' thought revolves around the ideas of intuitionism, sentimentalism, and situation ethics. Chung-ying Cheng (2010, 85) says: "*ren* is a naturally born quality that can be directly and intuitively grasped. It is within the reach of our natural consciousness as a human being, because we can love others as we will." No doubt, *ren* must involve showing love for others, but *ren* does not therefore involve sentimentalism. We must emphasize that *ren* is not a *Gegenstand* of *Anschauung*. As we have repeatedly stressed, the first and essential meaning of *ren* is "*xin ji li* [心即理]"—namely, freedom and autonomy of the will.

Likewise, we cannot think the original mind as a *Gegenstand* of *Anschauung*. One's original mind is real; it reveals itself through the *tianli* (universal principle, 天理). Similarly, Kant indicates (*CPrR* 5:4): "freedom is real, for this idea reveals [*offenbart*] itself through the moral law." The original mind (i.e., free will) is not presented (*darstellen*) in any *Anschauung*, but we cannot thus infer that the original mind is not revealed. Scholars who grasp that "freedom is not presented in any *Anschauung*" must also acknowledge Kant's claim that "freedom cannot reveal [*offenbart*]".[20] If we recall Kant's distinction between the theoretical and practical faculties of cognition, we can regard the former quote as expressing the theoretical and the latter as expressing the practical cognition of reason. According to Kant, the objective reality of the concept of freedom is denied by theoretical (speculative) cognition (*CPrR* 5:6): we cannot be immediately conscious of freedom, because we have no *Anschauung* of freedom. Yet the objective reality of the concept of freedom is affirmed by practical reason: Kant claims that freedom actually exists, for this idea is revealed by the moral law (4). He affirms "freedom, although (as becomes a practical concept) only for practical use; and this establishes on the evidence of a fact that which in the former case could only be conceived" (*CPrR* 5:6). He later adds, after introducing his famous thought experiment of a man facing the gallows if he gratifies his lust (30): "He judges, therefore, that he can do something because he is aware that he ought to do it and cognizes freedom within him, which, without the moral law, would have remained unknown to him."

To put it simply, we cannot think of the original mind as our authentic nature, and *tian* as the *Gegenstand* of intelligible *Anschauung*. Although Mou Zongsan has provided a famous theory of *chih te chih chuek* (智的直覺), I would argue that it is wrong to identify *"chih te chih chuek"* with Kant's *"intellektuell Anschauung"*. I translate *"chih te chih chuek"* into English as *"intelligible intuition"*. As Kant argues (A256/B312), "only *cognitions* are either intellectual or sensuous. What can only be a *Gegenstand* of the one or the other kind of *Anschauung*—i.e., the objects—must be entitled intelligible or sensible."

Mou announced (1996, 44–45; cf. Cai 1996, 42–43): "Kant's philosophy is the starting point to understand Western philosophy. In the West, Kant is the unique bridge linking Eastern and Western philosophy, since it is the only way to integrate both at the core." I believe that, by following Kant's approach, the combination and integration of the Eastern and the Western could be actualized, thus bringing us one step closer to realizing the goal of creating a harmonious world. Of course, I have to admit that there are still a lot of problems to be solved; the road linking Eastern and Western philosophy is long.

Notes

1. *"Anschauung"* is generally translated into English as "intuition"; but "intuition" cannot adequately express the meaning of *"Anschauung"*. Therefore, I leave *"Anschauung"* untranslated throughout this chapter.
2. PFM 4:257. All quotations from Kant are my own translations.
3. Bxvi: "alle unsere Erkenntnis müsse sich nach den Gegenständen richten". In citing the *Critique of Pure Reason*, I have made extensive use of Norman Kemp Smith's translation, but I have made some changes, such as replacing "knowledge" with "cognition"; I translate *"Objekt"* into English "object". As *"Gegenstand"* cannot properly be translated as "object", I leave *"Gegenstand"* untranslated throughout this chapter. Any errors in translation remain entirely my own responsibility.
4. Kant's German here reads: "die Anschauung sich nach der Beschaffenheit der Gegenstände richten müßte"; "richtet sich aber der Gegenstand (als Objekt der Sinne) nach der Beschaffenheit unseres Anschauungsvermögens".
5. The field of supersensible things is called the world of the understanding (e.g., A255/B311), or the intelligible world (e.g., A257/B313).
6. In quoting from the *Critique of Judgment*, I have made extensive use of James Creed Meredith's translation, but I have made some changes, such as replacing "supersensible" with "supersensible-thing". I also used the Cambridge Edition translation of Paul Guyer and Eric Matthews.
7. In the *Critique of Pure Reason*, Kant says (B428): "The proposition, 'I think' or 'I exist thinking', is an empirical proposition. Such a proposition, however, is conditioned by empirical *Anschauung*, and is therefore also conditioned by the object [that is, the self] which is thought [in its aspect] as appearance. It would consequently seem that on our theory the soul, even in thought, is completely transformed into appearance, and that in this way our consciousness itself, as being a mere illusion, must refer in fact to nothing" (B428). He later continues (B428–429): "Thought, taken by itself, is merely

the logical function, and therefore the pure spontaneity of the combination of the manifold of a merely possible *Anschauung*, and does not exhibit the subject of consciousness as appearance; . . . in the consciousness of myself in mere thought I am the being itself, although nothing in myself is thereby given for thought."

8. As Allison (1990, 180) indicates, there is "a line of objection that deserves to be termed 'classical' because of its long and distinguished history. This line can be traced back to some of Kant's most important contemporanes and immediate successors, most notably Schiller and Hegel, and it reappears in the work of influential present-day writers such as Bernard Williams." For a detailed discussion, refer to my book, Lo 2009, Part III.

9. For a detailed discussion, refer to Lo 2012 and 2014.

10. As there is no natural equivalence for translate *ren* (仁) into English "benevolence" generally, but "benevolence" cannot adequately express the meaning of *ren*. Many words of the Confucian philosophy are not translated appropriately and rises misunderstanding. Therefore I will first transliterate these Chinese words into phonetic symbols in my essay, then give an explanation.

11. *Ren zhe* (仁者): the truly good person.

12. Mencius says: "There is no part of himself which a man does not love, and as he loves all, so he must nourish all. There is not an inch of skin which he does not love, and so there is not an inch of skin which he will not nourish. . . . Some parts of the body are noble, and some ignoble; some great, and some small. The great must not be injured for the small, nor the noble for the ignoble. He who nourishes the little belonging to him is a little man, and he who nourishes the great is a great man. . . . A man who only eats and drinks is counted mean by others; because he nourishes what is little to the neglect of what is great. If a man, fond of his eating and drinking, were not to neglect what is of more importance, how should his mouth and belly be considered as no more than an inch of skin?"

13. Wang Yangming (王陽明, 1472–1529) properly explained this sentence. He clarifies (Wang, Article 167) that "'*si*' means '*rui*' [思曰睿]" and that "*si* is nothing more than the *tianli* [思莫非天理]."

14. Kant says (*GMM* 4:36): "It follows that the human being (even the best) is evil only because he reverses the moral order of his incentives in incorporating them into his maxims. He indeed incorporates the moral law into those maxims, together with the law of self-love; since, however, he realizes that the two cannot stand on an equal footing, but one must be subordinated to the other as its supreme condition, he makes the incentives of self-love and their inclinations the condition of compliance with the moral law, whereas it is this latter that, as the supreme condition of the satisfaction of the former, should have been incorporated into the universal maxim of the *Willkür* as the sole incentive."

15. Mencius speaks of human natural desire when he says (11:15): "The senses of hearing and seeing do not *si* (思), and are obscured by external things."

16. Many phrases of Neo-Confucian philosophy are impossible to translate appropriately. Inappropriate translations tend to mislead the reader; therefore, I will occasionally transliterate these phrases into phonetic symbols throughout this chapter. I hope this approach can be accepted by the non-sinologue readers who have a specialist's knowledge of Neo- and New Confucianism.

17. See Mou 2007 and Mou 2014, 173.

18. "Die Autonomie des Willens als oberstes Prinzip der Sittlichkeit" (*GMM* 4:440).

19. "Autonomie des Willens ist die Beschaffenheit des Willens, dadurch derselbe ihm selbst (unabhängig von aller Beschaffenheit der Gegenstände des Wollens) ein Gesetz ist. Das Princip der Autonomie ist also: nicht anders zu wählen als so, daß die Maximen seiner Wahl in demselben Wollen zugleich als allgemeines Gesetz mit begriffen seien" (*GMM* 4:440).
20. The two words, "*darstellen*" (represent, 展現) and "*offenbart*" (reveal, 呈現) are translated into Chinese as "呈現" ("reveal") without distinction; this makes an implausible reading.

References

Allison, Henry (1990). *Kant's Theory of Freedom*. Cambridge: Cambridge University Press.

Cai, Jenhou (1996). 《牟宗三先生學思年譜》 (Mr. Mou Zongsan's Academic Thoughts and Chronicles). Taipei: 學生書局 (Xueshengshuju).

Cheng, Chung-ying (2010). Incorporating Kantian Good Will: On Confucian Ren (仁) as Perfect Duty. In: S. R. Palmquist (ed.), *Cultivating Personhood: Kant and Asian Philosophy*. Berlin: Walter de Gruyter, 74–96.

Confucius, *The Analects*.

Liu, Jishan (1836). 劉子全書 (*Complete Works of Liu Zi*). Taiwan: 華文書局 (Huawenshuju).

Lo, Suet-kwan (2009). 《康德的自由學說》 (*Kant's Theory of Freedom*). Taiwan: Lernbook.

——— (2012). Revival of Confucianism and a Return to Kant—Enlightenment through Reason and the Reestablishment of Philosophy. Unpublished essay presented for the research seminar of the Department of Philosophy, University of Tübingen, on 18 June 2012.

——— (2014). 《孔子哲學傳統—理性文明和基礎哲學》 (*Confucius' Philosophical Tradition: Vernunft Civilization and Basic Philosophy*). Taiwan: Lernbook.

Lu, Xing-shan (1963). Selected passages trans. Wing-tsit Chan, *Complete Works of Lu Xing-shan* 《象山全集》. In: Wing-tsit Chan (ed.), *A Source Book in Chinese Philosophy*. Princeton, NJ: Princeton University Press, 574–587.

Kant, Immanuel (1783). Trans. J. Fieser, *Prolegomena to Any Future Metaphysics*. Online at: www.sacred-texts.com/phi/kant/proleg.txt, 1997. Accessed July 14, 2018.

Mencius, *The Mencius*.

Mou, Zongsan (2007). 《牟宗三先生晚期文集》 (*Anthology of Late Writings of Mou Zongsan*), in 《牟宗三先生全集》 (*Mou's Collected Works*). Taipei: Lianjing.

——— (2014). Trans. J. Clower, *Late Works of Mou Zongsan, Selected Essays on Chinese Philosophy*. Leiden: Brill.

Wang, Yangming (1963). Selected passages trans. Wing-tsit Chan, *Instructions for Practical Living* 《傳習錄》. In: Wing-tsit Chan (ed.), *A Source Book in Chinese Philosophy*. Princeton, NJ: Princeton University Press, 667–691.

Wood, Allen W. (2011). Preface and Introduction (3–16). In: O. Höffe (ed.), *Kant: Kritik der Praktischen Vernunft*. Berlin: Akademie Verlag, 21–36.

20 The Paradox of Representation in Nishitani's Critique of Kant

Gregory S. Moss

1. The Progress of Subjectivity in Kant's Copernican Revolution

Kant's *Critique of Pure Reason* demonstrates that it is impossible to have knowledge of the thing in itself by means of either concepts or intuitions. The great student of Kitarō Nishida and Martin Heidegger, Japanese philosopher, Keiji Nishitani (1900–1990), does not seem to dispute Kant's claim that the thing in itself cannot be known by means of reason or indeed by any act of consciousness whatever. But for Nishitani the *Critique* does not demonstrate that it is impossible to experience or obtain awareness of the thing in itself through purely *non-subjective, non-representational*, and *non-conceptual* means. In what follows, I reconstruct Nishitani's formulation of *the paradox of representation* and show how his method of resolving the paradox provides an argument against Kant, that one can know the thing in itself by non-conceptual means.[1] For Nishitani it appears that the impossibility of knowing the thing in itself by means of reason shows a new path forward. Rather than attempt to know the thing in itself by means of reason or subjectivity in general, we can still gain access to the thing in itself by transcending reason and subjectivity altogether. To state this even more generally: insofar as philosophy itself performs its rational work from the standpoint of subjectivity (whether implicitly or explicitly), we can apprehend the thing in itself by transcending the standpoint of philosophy. In Nishitani's terms, the only way to know the thing in itself is by "breaking through self-consciousness" (Nishitani 1983, 16–17).

According to Nishitani, traditional dogmatic metaphysics attempts to know what things are insofar as they are *independent of subjectivity*. The traditional metaphysical attempt to know things insofar as they are independent of subjectivity contains a paradox. Nishitani calls this paradox "the paradox of representation" (Nishitani 1983, 109). Since the claims of traditional metaphysics also aim to establish the independence of the thing from the subject's *representations* of the object, in traditional dogmatic metaphysics, the independent determinations of the substance of things is also thought to be *independent of representation* in general.

Nonetheless, Nishitani points out that the claim that "x lies outside subjectivity" is still an act of subjectivity in which the thing is *represented* as that which is independent of representation (Nishitani 1983, 108). Since the thing is represented as that which is independent of representation, it is *covertly* and unknowingly treated as an *object of representation* for subjectivity. By thinking of the thing as something that is independent of representation and subjectivity, an implicit though unrecognized reference to representation and subjectivity is made. Accordingly, the paradox of representation is evident: that which is *posited* as independent of subjectivity cannot be independent of subjectivity. Instead, the dogmatist covertly takes a *stand on subjectivity* as the *center* of one's philosophizing. For Nishitani, subject and object are correlative terms: just as the subject is *of* an object, the object is *for* a subject. Since the implicit appeal to representation remains uncovered in traditional metaphysics, the paradox of representation also remains uncovered (134–135): traditional metaphysics has not "penetrated into the depths of the paradox of representation."

Whatever objections we might make to Nishitani's representation of dogmatism in the Kantian sense, it does reveal one philosophical motivation for the way pre-Kantian metaphysics is represented in the traditions of Kantian philosophy and German idealism. In Hegel's *Encyclopedia*, for example, pre-Kantian dogmatic metaphysics is represented as an attempt of the subject to know the object by *conforming* its representations to the independent object (Hegel 1975, 25).[2] In this model, the relation of knowing to its object is conceived in terms of the opposition of consciousness, of subject and object, and *truth* is conceived as the *correspondence* of the subject to the independent object. Of course, *prima facia* such a representation of pre-Kantian metaphysics appears both *anachronistic* and uncharitable, since pre-Kantian metaphysicians, such as the ancient Greeks, medieval philosophers, and others, would not characterize their own thinking in terms of subject and object. Nonetheless, from Nishitani's perspective, this way of representing pre-Kantian metaphysics is justified, since the appeal to the subject and object of knowing is *implicitly and covertly present*. For this reason, the Kantian philosophy, which explicitly conceives of knowing in terms of the opposition of consciousness, knows its own predecessors better than they knew themselves. Indeed, Kant might well be correct that other philosophers know our thought better than we know it ourselves (A313–314/B370).

Of course, the turn toward subjectivity as the locus of knowing and being precedes the Kantian philosophy and is characteristic of modernity in general, as is made sufficiently evident in Descartes' *cogito*. Still, Nishitani writes that "Kant followed this orientation all the way to the end" (Nishitani 1983, 132). Indeed, it is only in Kant wherein "the standpoint of subjectivity is radically and thoroughly sounded to its depths." For Nishitani, Kant's *Critique of Pure Reason* makes important advances in two main areas, which are most clearly evident in Kant's fundamental principle of the transcendental synthetic unity of apperception, namely that *"the I think must accompany all of my representations"* (B131, my emphasis). First, the activity and constitution of self-consciousness determines the constitution of the object of consciousness, and cannot be conceived independently of the existence of the object of consciousness. Since Nishitani takes subject and object to be *correlative* terms, Kant represents a philosophical advance upon Descartes and his other predecessors. For Kant, self-consciousness is simultaneously consciousness of an object, each of which is inseparable from the other. Second, in the *Critique of Pure Reason* the awareness of the competence of the subject "reaches its highest point" (Nishitani 1983, 133). The subject is competent in the realm of phenomena: it is able to know the universal and necessary relations of phenomena, but is unable to know the noumena. As is evident from Nishitani's critique of dogmatic metaphysics, since all conceptual determinations of an object are *subjective representations*, Kant is absolutely justified that subjectivity (whether this be through any one or all of the faculties of sensibility, understanding, or reason) can only know what is *for us* or what is phenomenal, and subjectivity is forever barred from knowing things in themselves.

For Nishitani, "the only change [from pre-Critical to Critical epistemology] is that the relationship between the object and its representation which operated as a covert basis in the former [metaphysics] was made overt in the latter [Kant] and given approval" (Nishitani 1983, 134). Since for both conceptions of philosophy, namely pre-Critical and Critical, knowledge is constituted by a relation of subjectivity to objectivity, Nishitani claims that the "objective-representational point of view" is basic to both conceptions, pre-Critical and Critical philosophy. As Nishitani writes (111),

> once the circumstances lying behind the formation of the concept of substance are brought to light, it is natural to propose, as Kant did, the basic position that all objects are representations and therefore "appearances" and to interpret substance as one of the *a priori* concepts of pure reason, something that "thought thinks into" [*hineindenkt*] objects.

Traditionally, substance has been conceived as the underlying subject of attributes and accidents of an independent thing, a subject that cannot be a predicate. Nishitani's point seems to be that Kant, rather than cease to employ the concept of substance, re-appropriates it as a category of the understanding, which synthetizes the intuitions given in sensibility. In this way, Kant does not abandon the view of objects as substances, but applies it in a novel way that is consistent with the subject as a representing activity. With Kant the philosophical tradition in the West becomes *self-aware* by uncovering the categories that have been at work without being recognized. In Nishitani's words "Kant marks a milestone" (Nishitani 1983, 111). By overtly conceiving philosophy as taking place on the field of consciousness, the traditional understanding of the relation of subject to object is fundamentally altered: since the object is always already determined by subjectivity on the field of consciousness, the object can no longer stand as a ready-made thing, independent of consciousness. Rather, the self-awareness that is generated by bringing to light philosophy's implicit appeal to subjectivity as the ground of the object thereby *inverts* the relation of object to subject: it is the object which must conform to the constitution of subjectivity and its self-consciousness. Nishitani makes clear that, although Kant's philosophy makes explicit the relationship of representation that is covert in traditional metaphysics, he does not solve the paradox of representation (111).[3]

2. Transcending Subjectivity: Toward the Thing in Itself

From the standpoint of reason, how must the thing in itself necessarily appear? Insofar as the thing in itself transcends reason, the only way that the thing in itself could appear from the standpoint of reason is in the form of *paradox* and *contradiction* (Nishitani 1983, 118, 120). From the standpoint of reason, the thing in itself appears as *non*-rational. Indeed, this is consistent with one of Kant's lessons from the Antinomies section of the *Critique of Pure Reason*: any attempt by reason to transcend what is *for us* and know what is *in itself* leads to paradox. As what transcends reason and sensation, reason and sensation are the "negatives of things themselves" (130).

Representation, the mode by which subjectivity relates to things, always keeps the thing at a *distance* from itself; the thing, insofar as it is *for* the subject, becomes an *object*, and the subject thereby fails to access the thing *as it is*. Formulated in positive terms, it is only from within the midst of the thing in itself that the thing in itself can be revealed: "things reveal themselves when we leap from the circumference to the center— into their selfness" (Nishitani 1983, 130). By overcoming every mode of representation, things become, in Nishitani's terms, present in their "home ground", where they *dwell* as themselves.

Since for Nishitani knowledge of things in themselves requires the complete abandonment of the field of consciousness, and thereby *cognition*, of which categories and intuitions are constituents, the "knowing" of things in themselves can be described as a "non-cognitive knowing of the non-objective thing in itself" (Nishitani 1983, 139). The knowing is non-cognitive because it transcends the cognizing subject. Naturally, this sense of "knowing" deviates from Kant's technical sense, as the knowing is "non-cognitive". The thing in itself is "non-objective" because it *transcends* the field of consciousness in which the thing is given as an *object* of consciousness. In other words, the knowing of things in themselves is a *docta ignorantia*, a doctrine of ignorance (139). Since the knowledge of the thing in itself transcends conceptual determination and all relations of representations, it is not a *mediated* knowing as is constitutive of *representation*. Knowing things from within their midst or in their "home ground" could be described as an *immediate experience* of the thing in itself (129). One might imagine that the immediate, non-conceptual experience of the thing in itself would, in Kant's terms, be properly described as an *intuition* of the thing in itself. Nonetheless, Nishitani is hesitant to employ the term "intuition", for it implies that there is a separate subject that intuits an object, and relates to it immediately. Nishitani is clear that the knowing of the thing in itself "breaks through consciousness" and for this reason cannot be constituted by a relation such as intuition that takes place on the field of consciousness (154).[4]

Despite all appearances to the contrary, Nishitani's philosophy does not constitute a return to dogmatic metaphysics. Dogmatic metaphysics models itself and its representations after things as its standard, and according to Nishitani, *covertly* relates to the thing from the standpoint of subjectivity. Dogmatic metaphysics erringly conceives of reason as the means by which things in themselves are revealed. In Nishitani's words, "we straighten ourselves out by turning to what does not respond to our turning, orienting ourselves to what negates our every orientation" (Nishitani 1983, 140). For Nishitani, the light of reason is not the true light; the true light is the "light of all things" (140). Rather than return to dogmatic metaphysics, Nishitani *transcends metaphysics* altogether. Accordingly, Nishitani's "knowledge" of the thing in itself ought not be understood either in terms of the pre-Critical or Critical philosophy.

Of course, Nishitani's knowledge of the thing in itself is just as much a negation of philosophy as metaphysics. Nishitani follows Kant's now famous dictum that the *Critique of Pure Reason* should make room for *faith* (Bxxx). Faith is usually understood as an orientation of the subject in which the subject trusts *that* something is true in a way that transcends demonstration, or is in some sense indemonstrable. According to Nishitani, knowledge of things in themselves is constituted as a kind of faith, for this knowledge necessarily *violates* the norms of reason. Yet there is more. Nishitani goes further: the conversion from philosophy to faith does not just demand a new mode of orientation for some subjectivity, but instead the *throwing off of subjectivity* altogether.[5] For Nishitani, the kind of faith necessary for knowing things in themselves is one that transcends both reason and subjectivity. As Nishitani puts it (Nishitani 1983, 26): "In religion, however faith comes about only on a horizon where this field has been overstepped and the framework of the 'ego' has been broken through"; likewise, "true personality comes forth when a person . . . forgets his or her self" (130).

What is at the heart of Nishitani's objections is that the Kantian categories *lack self-reference*. If cognition is always of a possible object of experience, and the categories *as categories* are not possible objects of experience (for they make experience possible), then there cannot be any cognition of the categories themselves. The knowing that constitutes transcendental subjectivity forbids *self-knowledge*, yet this is exactly what is demanded of the critique of pure reason. From these reflections, it should come as no surprise at all that Nishitani thinks the resources for knowing the being of transcendental subjectivity are unavailable from the perspective of transcendental philosophy itself. Given this restriction, knowing transcendental subjectivity requires a standpoint *outside* of transcendental subjectivity from which transcendental subjectivity itself can be known.[6] This may remind us of Fichte's methodological claim that to know what grounds experience one must *transcend experience* altogether.[7] Since knowing subjectivity as it is requires transcending that subjectivity, knowing subjectivity requires transcending what is merely "for us" to what is *in itself*. Indeed, Nishitani makes it clear that "we can get in touch with ourselves only through a mode of being that puts us in touch with things from the midst of those things themselves" (Nishitani 1983, 10). Because subjectivity insofar as it *is* cannot be an *object* of subjective knowing, the subject as it *is* must be "non-objective". Such a non-objective subject would be a subject that transcends the field of consciousness altogether, a *self–in–itself*. Likewise, because the knowing or being of subjectivity *itself* cannot be established on the field of consciousness or self-consciousness, the *knowing* of such a self-in-itself must be "non-objective". In Nishitani's terms, knowing the being of subjectivity must be a "non-objective knowing of a non-objective self–in–itself" (154). This passage makes it clear that for Nishitani it is not only the thing in itself that can be known only by transcending reason, but subjectivity itself is also not knowable in any other way.[8]

From Nishitani's perspective, Kant cannot help but overstep the limits he has imposed on reason itself. Subjectivity as it *is* can only appear as a paradox from the perspective of reason. Of course, Nishitani is not the first philosopher to grapple with this issue in Kant. Many philosophers in the Western tradition have grappled with this paradox and attempted to solve it in different ways. Fichte appeals to intellectual intuition to ground experience (Fichte 1982, 29–85). Hegel (1969) develops a logic of self-reference, whereby reason can ground itself. And Husserl (1969, 122) re-thinks the relation of subject to object by attempting to develop a categorial intuition in order to make it possible for categories themselves to be objects of experience. In these various approaches, subjectivity and reason are re-conceived in order to maintain a philosophical way out of the problem. What distinguishes Nishitani's approach is (i) his attempt to transcend philosophy and the field of subjectivity altogether by (ii) showing how the lack of self-reference inherent in categories and things leads to (iii) *absolute nothingness* as the ground of subjectivity.[9]

On the one hand, Nishitani's Kantian legacy can be traced back to the way in which the Kantian philosophy may be employed to motivate key elements of Nishitani's philosophical approach. On the other hand, Nishitani's negation of subjectivity transforms Kant's concept of phenomena and noumena as well as the way they are accessed, such that the "thing in itself", as well as the way the philosopher is aware of it, no longer has the same significance in Nishitani as it had in Kant (Nishitani 1983, 107). In order to see the contours of this transformation, we should follow Nishitani's critique of the standpoint of subjectivity. When we "turn the light to what is directly underfoot" (4), as the Zen phrase so eloquently expresses it, we discover that *absolutely nothing* lies at the ground of subjectivity. The inability of reason to specify the being of subjectivity is a reflection of the "primal fact" that nothing at all lies at the ground of the subject. In this way, from Nishitani's perspective, Kant cannot be held accountable for failing to know subjectivity *in itself*, but he can justifiably raise the objection that Kant failed to see the contradiction in the very attempt to perform the critique of pure reason. In this sense, Wittgenstein's recognition that setting limits to reason is senseless (Wittgenstein, 108) represents an advance upon Kant's thinking. As one Hegel commentator puts it (Mure 1974, 1), although Kant asked the question concerning the possibility of natural science, metaphysics, and mathematics, he failed to ask *whether and how the Critical philosophy itself was possible.*

Notes

1. Although Kant insists that one cannot know the thing–in–itself, Nishitani argues that the thing–in–itself is knowable. Certainly it is not Kant's position that the thing in itself is knowable. Indeed, in order to make his argument plausible, Nishitani develops a distinct sense of the term "knowledge", which deviates from the technical sense of Kant's term. The novel sense of knowing employed by Nishitani will be further elucidated in the course of this chapter. For an excellent paper in defense of Kant and his claim regarding the unknowability of the thing in itself, see Palmquist 1985.
2. See Hegel's discussion of the First Attitude to Objectivity, Section III paragraph 26.
3. Rather, Kant's success lies in making the presence of subjectivity explicit. Despite this, for Nishitani the distinction between phenomena and noumena reiterates the problem again, though in a different form: the noumenon transcends subjectivity and its structure of representation. Yet, the subject represents the noumenon as that which transcends representation. As is well known, this paradox of representation that arises at the intersection of the for us and the in itself later becomes a driving force in the epistemology and metaphysics of German idealism to expunge philosophy of the thing in itself.

4. In "Kant's Noumena and Sunyata", Laura E. Weed (2002, 75) writes: "So, my conclusion on the Buddhists and Kant on the self will be that their views are similar and compatible, but Kant did not articulate the consequences of his thinking on these topics in the level of detail that the Kyoto school did." Since Nishitani's thought demands breaking through consciousness, and Kant's account of objectivity requires consciousness as the transcendental principle thereof, I am much less inclined to claim that Kant and Nishitani's thought have compatible positions. Rather, Kant's critique opens up the possibility of a further critique that undermines consciousness as the ground of objectivity.

5. To enter into the spirit of Nishitani's critique of Kant, we are well reminded of Wittgenstein's preface to the *Tractatus* (Wittgenstein 2007, 27). In order to set the normative limits of reason, one must also know, in some sense, what limits reason. What limits reason cannot be internal to reason itself; rather it must transcend reason. Accordingly, in order to set regulative standards for the use of reason, one must violate those very standards in the process. Thus, in order to set normative limits to the use of pure reason, one necessarily transcends those very limits. Or we might enter into this reflection in the spirit of Hegel's Introduction to the *Science of Logic* (Hegel 1969, 45): for a science of reason to begin appears paradoxical. In order to ground the legitimacy of the authority of reason, one's assumptions cannot be garnered from reason itself, for this begs the question. Nishitani recognizes that to fulfill the critique of pure reason, one must question the very legitimacy of the authority of reason to perform the inquiry into the limits of rational inquiry in the first place. The critique of pure reason cannot be fulfilled by taking reason for granted; instead it is only by transcending reason and philosophy that the critique of pure reason can be fulfilled.

6. In order for transcendental subjectivity to be subject to transcendental analysis by the transcendental philosopher, transcendental subjectivity must be. To enter into the spirit of Nishitani's critique of Kant from another angle, we might entertain a question posed by the late Schelling: what are the ontological conditions for the possibility of subjectivity? (See Gabriel 2013, ix.) Given that the transcendental subject must be, it is not evident that transcendental subjectivity possesses the resources for elucidating its own being. If we take "being" in the sense of sein, we know from Kant's famous critique of the ontological argument that "being" is not a predicate (A596/B624). When we say of some concept that it is (or has being), we mean that it is given in intuition. The concept of one hundred dollars has being because it is given in intuition. But transcendental subjectivity as such is not given as a whole in intuition. If it were, it would be an object contained within another transcendental consciousness, which would engender an infinite regress. Still less can we say of transcendental subjectivity that it "exists" or "possibly exists" or "necessarily exists", for these are modalities which are contained in the understanding. Since the categories of the understanding apply to intuition, and not to themselves, we cannot say of the understanding or transcendental subjectivity as a whole that it "exists", "is possible", or "is necessary". To put the problem yet another way, we might also ask whether transcendental subjectivity is itself a phenomenon or noumenon. If transcendental subjectivity were a mere phenomenon, any analysis into the structure of subjectivity would be an appearance of what it is rather than what it is simpliciter. What is more, it would be contained within itself, which would initiate an infinite regress, and an infinite series of transcendental subjectivities would be presupposed in which it could appear. But if transcendental subjectivity were a noumenon, its structure and contents ought to remain utterly inscrutable to the transcendental

philosopher, which would consequently reduce the contents of the *Critique of Pure Reason* to a mere nullity. The further we penetrate into the question regarding the very being of transcendental subjectivity, the more skeptical we may be that Kant's transcendental philosophy has the resources to address the issue.

7. Fichte (8) writes: "Now philosophy must discover the ground of all experience; thus its object necessarily lies outside all experience."
8. As Hegel might put it (see 1969, 26–27), if anything deserves the status of at least a thing, it would be the understanding.
9. In this short chapter, I have only had space to develop the first point at any length. For an in-depth exploration of these points, especially the second and third, see my forthcoming paper, "An Ontology of Non-Discriminatory Love: The Resurrection of the Triune Self in Ueda Shizuteru's Appropriation and Critique of Meister Eckhart", which is to appear in the forthcoming Springer companion to Ueda Shizuteru.

References

Fichte, Johann Gottlieb (1982). Trans. P. Heath and J. Lachs, *Science of Knowledge*. Cambridge: Cambridge University Press.

Gabriel, Markus (2013). *Transcendental Ontology: Essays in German Idealism*. New York: Bloomsbury.

Hegel, G. W. F. (1969). Trans. A. V. Miller, *Science of Logic*. Amherst: Humanity Books.

——— (1975). Trans. W. Wallace, *Hegel's Logic*. New York: Oxford University Press.

Heidegger, Martin (2008). Trans. T. Carman, *Being and Time*. New York: Harper Perennial Modern Classics.

Husserl, Edmund (1969). Trans. D. Cairns, *Formal and Transcendental Logic*. The Hague: Martinus Hijhoff.

Mure, G. R. G. (1974). Hegel: How, and How Far, is Philosophy Possible? In: F. G. Weiss (ed.), *Beyond Epistemology*. The Hague: Martinus Nijhoff, 1–29.

Nishitani, Keiji (1983). Trans. J. von Bragt, *Religion and Nothingness*. Berkeley: University of California Press.

Palmquist, Stephen R. (1985). The Radical Unknowability of Kant's "Thing in Itself". In: *Cogito* 3(2), 101–115.

Weed, Laura E. (2002). Kant's Noumena and Sunyata. In: *Asian Philosophy* 12(2), 77–95.

Wittgenstein, Ludwig (2007). Trans. C. K. Ogden, *Tractatus Logico-Philosophicus*. New York: Cosimo Classics.

Contributors

Lucy Allais is jointly appointed as Professor of Philosophy at the University of the Witwatersrand and as Henry Allison Chair of the History of Philosophy at the University of California, San Diego. She has published largely on Kant's theoretical philosophy, especially on transcendental idealism and non-conceptualism about intuition, including her 2015 OUP book, *Manifest Reality: Kant's Idealism and his Realism*. She has recently published on Kant's racism as well as on Kant on giving to beggars, and is currently working on his account of the flawed nature of human agents (evil) and the way this involves moralized self-deception, in particular in relation to Kant's account of injustice, as well as on Kant's account of the metaphysics of free will, and Kantian accounts of forgiveness.

Xi Chen is a PhD candidate at Martin Luther University, Halle-Wittenberg (MLU). She received an MA in Philosophy from Peking University in June 2009 and a BA in 2005.

Jack Chun obtained his PhD at the University of Toronto as Canadian Commonwealth Scholar. Currently he is Interim Director of the General Education Centre in the Hong Kong Polytechnic University. His publications are mainly in applied ethics and comparative philosophy. He has written a philosophy textbook, *Being Philosophical* (McGraw-Hill, 2011), and chapters in *General Education as Social Ethics* in Chinese (Oxford University Press, 2012). He is co-editing an anthology on leadership and integrity with Heiner Roetz. Interested in pedagogies of philosophy, he has launched a MOOC on Life and Death and developed a mobile app on ethics in comics.

Robert R. Clewis is professor of philosophy at Gwynedd Mercy University, Pennsylvania. He is the translator of Kant's (1784/85) "Mrongovius" anthropology lecture (Cambridge University Press, 2012), the editor of *Reading Kant's Lectures* (Walter de Gruyter, 2015), and author of *The Kantian Sublime and the Revelation of Freedom* (Cambridge University Press, 2009) as well as "The Place of the Sublime in Kant's Project" (*Studi kantiani*, 2015) and "The Feeling of Enthusiasm" (*Kant and the Faculty of Feeling*, 2018).

Jieyao Hu has been a PhD student at the Department of Philosophy of Sun Yat-Sen University since 2013. Her dissertation focuses on Kant's theory of intuition and perceptual experience. With the financial support of China Scholarship Council she studied for two years (2014–2016) at Humboldt University of Berlin.

Tze-wan Kwan, Dr. phil., Bochum University, is Professor Emeritus and former chair of the Department of Philosophy, at Chinese University of Hong Kong. He was concurrently founding director of the Research Centre for Humanities Computing and of the Archive for Phenomenology and Contemporary Philosophy, CUHK. His books include: *Die hermeneutische Phänomenologie und das tautologische Denken Heideggers* (1982); *From a Philosophical Point of View* (1994); *Articulation-cum-Silence: In Search of a Philosophy of Orientation* (OUP, 2008; and Peking UP, 2009). He has authored (in Chinese, English, or German) some 80 articles or book chapters on Kant, Husserl, Heidegger, Jakobson, Benveniste, Wilhelm von Humboldt, Unamuno and various philosophical topics.

Dan Larkin completed his PhD at the University of Memphis in the spring of 2017. He has recently taken up a tenure track position at Georgia Southern University. His research focuses primarily on the history of philosophy, including both ancient and modern. In addition to his dissertation on Platonic methodology and divine inspiration, his work on Kant's aesthetics is forthcoming in *Proceedings of the 12th International Kant Congress* (de Gruyter, 2018).

Suet-kwan Lo is Professor of Philosophy at New Asia Advanced Chinese Study Institute in Hong Kong. Her publications (Taiwan: Lernbook) include: 《康德的自由學說》 (*Kant's Theory of Freedom*), 2009; 《物自身與智思物—康德的形而上學》 (*Thing in Itself and Noumena—Kant's Metaphysics*), 2010; 《孔子哲學傳統—理性文明和基礎哲學》 (*Confucius' Philosophical Tradition: Vernunft Civilization and Basic Philosophy*), 2014; and 《康德的批判哲學—理性啟蒙與哲學重建》 (*Kant's Critical Philosophy: Enlightenment from Reason and Reestablishment of Philosophy*), 2014.

Brandon Love received his PhD (August 2018), with a dissertation entitled "Kant's Baconian Method as a Transformation of Aristotelian Transcendental Philosophy—A Propaeduetic", from Hong Kong Baptist University, where he is currently a part-time Lecturer in the Department of Religion and Philosophy. His areas of research interest are Kant, philosophy of religion, the history of philosophy, metaphysics, Aristotelianism, and moral and political philosophy. He has published several articles and book chapters on Kant and Tillich.

Chun-yip Lowe, after obtaining his Dr. phil. in Germany, works as a part-time lecturer at the College of International Education, Hong

Kong Baptist University. His research interests include Kant's moral and political philosophy, Rawls, Lao Sze-kwang, and modernity/modernization.

Guy Lown is a retired officer of the Hong Kong Police Force, who now works with the World Wildlife Fund. He has a degree in Biochemistry and an MBA. His interest in philosophy arose around concern for the environment. He has attended over two dozen philosophy conferences around the world, having presented a paper jointly with Brandon Love on the philosophy of Gilles Deleuze at Shue Yan University (2014). He is interested mainly in Aristotelian and Continental philosophy. He has been a regular presenter and moderator at the Hong Kong Philosophy Cafe since its inception in 1999.

Werner Moskopp is a Lecturer in Philosophy at the University of Koblenz-Landau, in Koblenz. He does research on various topics in moral philosophy, applied ethics, methodology in cultural studies, aphorism, epistemology in Kant and German Idealism, etc.

Gregory S. Moss is currently an Assistant Professor of Philosophy at Chinese University of Hong Kong. He specializes in post-Kantian German philosophy and has a growing interest in its intersection with the Kyoto School. He has published in a variety of philosophical journals, such as *Northern European Journal of Philosophy* (Routledge, 2018). Before completing his PhD on Hegel under Richard Winfield, he was a Fulbright Fellow with Markus Gabriel in Bonn. He is co-editor with Robert H. Scott of *The Significance of Indeterminacy* (Routledge, 2018) and author of *Hegel's Foundation Free Metaphysics* (Routledge, forthcoming).

Xing Nan earned his Dr. phil from Ludwig-Maximilians-Universität, München, with a dissertation entitled "Kant on Intuition and Experience". He is now Assistant Professor of Philosophy at Peking University. His teaching and research interests include virtually all aspects of Kant's philosophy, as well as many Kantian themes in contemporary philosophy.

Sebastian Orlander is a PhD student at Keele University (UK), working on a dissertation on Kant's notion of the world and its systematic function in both Kant's theoretical and practical philosophy. He studied at Miami University of Ohio (BA), the University of Memphis and the University of Luxembourg (two separate MAs). Apart from working on Kant, from the *Critiques* to topics in history and political philosophy, he is also interested in the history of early modern philosophy (Spinoza and Hume), as well as early 20th century philosophy (particularly Husserl and Carnap).

Gregg Osborne is Associate Professor and chair of the Philosophy Department at Washington and Jefferson College, in Pennsylvania.

He received his PhD from the University of Chicago and previously taught at the American University of Beirut. He is especially interested in Kant's analogies of experience and has published articles in such journals as *Kant-Studien, Hume Studies, Journal of Philosophical Research,* and *Areté.*

Stephen R. Palmquist is Professor of Religion and Philosophy at Hong Kong Baptist University, where he has taught since earning his doctorate from Oxford University (1987). His 190+ publications (translated into 12 languages) include 100 refereed articles and book chapters. Among his 12 books are *The Tree of Philosophy* (1992/2000), *Kant's System of Perspectives* (1993), *Kant's Critical Religion* (2000), *Cultivating Personhood: Kant and Asian Philosophy* (2010), *Comprehensive Commentary on Kant's Religion* (2016), and *Baring All in Reason's Light: An Exposition and Defense of Kant's Critical Mysticism* (forthcoming). In 1999 he founded the Hong Kong Philosophy Café, now with over 800 members.

Krishna Mani Pathak, alumnus of Heidelberg University with a doctoral dissertation on Kant's Ethics, is Assistant Professor in the Department of Philosophy at Hindu College, Delhi University. He has recently been Visiting Professor at the MGI, Mauritius. His publications in various national and international journals cover a range of topics from theoretical to applied philosophy. He has taught at Heidelberg University and served on various administrative committees at Delhi University. He has also been associated with reputed international organizations such as SAGE Publications and SSHRC (Canada). He is a founding member and Joint Secretary of India's Ludwig Wittgenstein Philosophical Society.

Hoke Robinson received his BA from George Washington University (1969), his MA from University of Texas, Austin (1971), and his PhD from Stony Brook University (1978). He taught briefly at Rice University and Southern Methodist University before taking a tenured position at the University of Memphis, where he has been Emeritus Professor since 2015. A Humboldt Fellow (1983–1984 and 1990–1991), he was a long-time member of the Kant-Gesellschaft and founding president of the North American Kant Society. He organized the 8th International Kant Congress (Memphis, 1995) and edited the *Proceedings.* His publications focus on Kant's theoretical philosophy.

Bart Vandenabeele is Professor of Aesthetics and Philosophy of Art at Ghent University. His areas of research include aesthetics, the philosophy of Schopenhauer, the philosophy of Kant, and post-Kantian philosophy. His books include: *The Sublime in Schopenhauer's Philosophy* (Palgrave Macmillan, 2015) and *A Companion to Schopenhauer* (ed., Wiley–Blackwell, 2012). He has been Visiting Scholar and Visiting Professor at several universities in the USA, Europe, and Africa, including the University of Oxford, Missouri Western University, and The University of Stellenbosch.

Simon Sai-ming Wong has recently completed his doctoral studies in the Department of Religion and Philosophy Hong Kong Baptist University. While his doctoral research is about Rawls' and Kant's political philosophy, he also specializes in Confucian philosophy, Kant's Critical philosophy, and the dialogue between the two. His research interest in this respect is notably inherited from his MA supervisor at the New Asia Institute of Advanced Chinese Studies, Prof. Lo Suet-kwan, who shares the same aspiration as her own mentor, Mr. Mou Zongsan.

John H. Zammito is John Antony Weir Professor of History at Rice University. He works in history of philosophy and science, concentrating on the German Enlightenment, especially Kant and Herder, and the emergence of life sciences in eighteenth-century Germany. He also works on theoretical issues in science studies and in historical theory. His books include: *The Genesis of Kant's Critique of Judgment* (Chicago, 1992); *Kant, Herder and the Birth of Anthropology* (Chicago, 2002); *A Nice Derangement of Epistemes: Post-Positivism in the Study of Science from Quine to Latour* (Chicago, 2004); and *The Gestation of German Biology: Philosophy and Physiology from Stahl to Schelling* (Chicago, 2018).

Ellen Y. Zhang holds a PhD in Philosophy of Religion from Rice University. She is Associate Professor in the Department of Religion and Philosophy at Hong Kong Baptist University and a research fellow at HKBU's Centre for Applied Ethics. Her research projects are related to Chinese philosophy, ethics, and comparative studies. Recent publications include "When the Ground of Being Encounters Emptiness: Tillich and Buddhism" in *Paul Tillich and Asian Religion* (Walter de Gruyter, 2017) and "*Zheng* as *Zheng*? A Daoist Challenge to Punitive Expeditions" in *Chinese Just War Ethics: Origin, Development, and Dissent* (Routledge, 2015).

Zhengmi Zhouhuang is Associate Professor of Philosophy and a member of the Center for Studies of Values & Culture at Beijing Normal University. Her main research areas are: classical German philosophy, Kant's practical philosophy, and aesthetics. Her publications include: *Der Sensus Communis bei Kant. Zwischen Erkenntnis, Moralität und Schönheit. Kantstudien-Ergänzungshefte* (de Gruyter, 2016) and "The Development of Kant's Theory of Moral Feeling" in *Con-Textos Kantianos* (2017).

Index

In this Index, "*see*" indicates that pages where the preceding term (i.e., the main entry) occurs are listed elsewhere, as stated; "*see also*" indicates that *additional* pages where the main entry's term occurs are listed at some point under the stated index entry/entries; "*cf.*" points to entries for concepts that are closely related to the main entry, *other than* those containing the main entry's term. Page numbers in *italics* indicate that the word is used in a Figure on that page rather than in the main text.

Ertl, Wolfgang 19, 22
Euclid xv, 23–27, 29n4, 29n5, 30;
　see also geometry; space
Evans, Gareth 65n4, 66
exemplary necessity 173

faith 5, 13, 18–19, 22, 148, 156n7,
　279; *cf.* belief; God
Falkenstein, Lorne 30, 35, 37, 41n5
feeling: aesthetic 148–149, 161,
　194; *a priori* 187; intellectual 163,
　165n4, 165n5, 165n6; moral xx,
　144, 148–149, 170–174, 175n5,
　176n6, 179, 186–188, *189*, 242;
　oceanic xix, 139, 155, 157n17,
　159; sphere of 141, 147; spiritual
　147, 150, 163; *see also* beauty/-
　iful; displeasure; freedom; *cf.*
　Geistesgefühl; *Lebensgefühl*; life;
　pain; pleasure; purposive/-ness;
　respect; spirit (*Geist*); sublime
Fei, Robert Yufeng xxviii
Ferrarin, Alfredo 112, 118n10, 120
Fichte, Johann Gottlieb 157n20, 244,
　247n9, 280, 283n7
Firestone, Chris L. 131, 135
Fitz, Hope K. 212n10, 213
Foessel, Michaël 191
force(s) 142–143, 153, 163; original
　185; vital 162–163, 165n5, 183;
　see also incentive(s)
Forman, Robert 130, 135
Förster, Eckart 97, 116, 120
Frank, Manfred 198, 199
freedom xvii, 14, 19, 21n14, 69,
　76–82, 84n7, 84n9, 85, 85n13,
　112, 119n20, 124, 134n5,
　141–143, 145, 149, 151, 153–154,
　158, 160, 163–164, 165, 176n11,
　177, 179, *189*, 190, 191n6, 201,
　211, 239–241, 243–244, 247n6,
　248, 265, 267–269, 271, 274;
　actuality of 77–78, 83; causality of
　77–81, 240, 246, 266; cognition
　of xvii, 69, 76–77, 79, 81, 160,
　271; concept of xiii, 13–14, 18,
　78, 84n9, 139, 153–154, 160,
　263, 265–267, 271; consciousness
　of 77, 79, 119n20, 260, 265,
　271; deduction of 267; effect of
　15; empirical 145, 147; feeling
　of 161; idea of 119n20, 175,
　240, 265–266; internal 149, 190;

intuition (*Anschauung*) of 160–161,
　271; laws of 139; moral 141,
　156n4, 174–175, 230; negative
　163–164, 188, *189*; noumenal
　143; positive 163–164, 188;
　practical xxiii, 163–164, 267, 271;
　presupposition of 266; problem of
　243; rational 157n15; reality of 78,
　240–241, 271; supreme principle of
　82; transcendental 143, 149–150,
　163–164, 240; *cf.* feeling; moral
　law; nature; reason
Freud, Sigmund xix, 139, 155, 156n2,
　158, 159, 165
Friedman, Michael xv, 23–25, 29n2,
　29n3, 29n4, 30

Gabriel, Markus 282n6, 283, 286
Gardner, Sebastian 107, 120
Garfield, Jay L. 134n3, 134n8, 135
Gegenstand xii–xv, xx, xxiii, xxxn6,
　3–19, 19n1, 20n1, 20n2, 20n6,
　20n7, 20n8, 21n10, 21n11, 21n12,
　21n13, 21n14, 38, 114, 198n2,
　241, 262–268, 271–272, 272n3,
　272n4, 274n19; *cf.* object(s);
　objective reality; objective validity;
　Objekt
Geistesgefühl 146–148, 150,
　156n13, 163, 165n6; *cf.* feeling;
　Lebensgefühl; life; spirit (*Geist*)
genius 149, 151–152, 154, 156,
　157n22, 161
geometry xiv–xv, 24–26, 30, 31–33,
　35–36, 38, 41n1, 55, 71, 111;
　Euclidian xv, 23–24, 26–29, 33;
　Non-Euclidian xv, 23; *cf.* Euclid;
　mathematics
Gibbons, Sarah 172, 177
Ginsborg, Hannah 105, 105n3
God xvii, xxi, 23, 38, 69, 77–79,
　85, 130, 134, 135, 141, 167, 201,
　207, 213n11, 260; attributes of
　208; belief in xvii, 69, 85n14, 131;
　cognition of 82, 85n14; concept of
　144, 212n11; as *Ens perfectissimum*
　145; as *Ens realissimum* 145;
　existence of 21n14, 85n14, 207;
　experience of 131; idea of 19,
　76, 265; as original being 144;
　possibility of 78; reality of 207,
　265; *cf.* belief; faith; reason
Godlove, Terry 29n6, 30, 30n10

171–173, 180–188, *189*, 191n2;
feeling of 150; formal 180;
inner 150; objective 190; subjective
180–181, *189*; *cf.* beauty/-iful;
pleasure

qualia 194
quantity 113, 133, 181, 184; category
of 40, 133; moment of 180–181,
183; saturation of 135n9; schema
of 107; *cf.* magnitude

Raju, P.T. 212n3, 214
Rao, K. Ramakrishna 136
rational belief (*Vernunftglaube*) *see*
belief
rational idea(s) 119n20, 151–152,
161, 163, 168, 171, 182, 186; *cf.*
reason
realism/-ist 5, 18, 21, 22, 65, 85,
101, 105, 121, 213, 284; empirical
xv, xx, 4, 10, 192, 195, 198n2; *cf.*
idealism/-ist(ic)
reason: idea(s) of 19, 21n14, 76,
84n5, 119n20, 143, 145, 151–152,
154, 161, 163, 168, 171, 173, 182,
184, 186–190, 240, 265–268, 271;
cf. freedom; God; immortality;
rational idea(s)
recognition: of powers of reason
160, 162, 170; synthesis of
91–92, 95–96; *cf.* apprehension;
reproduction
reflection xxiii, 40, 142–143, 145,
147–149, 151, 163, 180–181,
184–186, 190, 195, 201, 234,
242, 281, 282n5; aesthetic 141,
188, 191n4; concepts of 55; pure
179–180; transcendental 22,
53–54, 141
Refutation of Idealism *see* idealism
Reid, Thomas 162
Relativity: General Theory of 26–27,
30; Special Theory of 26; *cf.*
Einstein
ren (仁) 252, 259, 268–269, 273n10,
273n11, 274
representation: empirical 105;
faculty of 188, 207; figurative 111;
immediate 61, 72–73, 122; innate
45; intuitive 35, 38; mediating
109; mental x, xxi, 123, 200–203,
210, 212n5, 212n6, 212n7, 213,

214; metaphysical 41n5; non-
conceptual 86–87; paradox of xxiv,
275–276, 278, 281n3; perceptive
126; power of 185; sensory xvii,
48–50, 190, 212n5; singular 29,
38, 206; spatial 34, 45; unconscious
210; universal 29; *see also* space
reproduction: synthesis of 91–92, 96,
110; *cf.* apprehension; recognition
respect: experience of 147–148;
feeling of 142, 147–149, 171, 174,
176n6, 187; inward 153; moral
170–171, 174; *cf.* moral law
Robinson, Hoke xv, 23–30, 287
Rodemeyer, Lanei 119n15, 121
Rogozinski, Jacob 177n14, 178
Rolland, Romain 139, 155, 156n2,
158, 159
Romanticism 155, 157n20

Sardesai, Arundhati 213n15, 214
Schafer, Karl 70–71, 75, 78, 82, 84n6,
85
Schelling, Friedrich Wilhelm Joseph
193, 198n1, 199, 247n9, 282n6
schema/-ta 48, 107, 109–110,
114–116, 118n5, 118n7, 118n13,
131, 190; immediacy of 108; pure
110; *see also cf.* category/-ies;
quantity; schematism; space; time
schematism xviii, 107–110, 113–117,
117n1, 118n8, 119n17, 119n18,
121, 151; secondary 112; *see also*
category/-ies; *cf.* schema/-ta; space;
time
Schenkl, Karl 235n8, 237
Schlegel, Friedrich 196
Schmitz, Christoph 223, 227
Schopenhauer, Arthur 159, 175n1,
178, 196
Schrader, G. 141, 158
Schulting, Dennis 35, 37, 41n2, 42,
65, 65n5, 66, 97, 109, 118n3,
118n9, 118n11, 121
Scott, Robert 226, 230, 237
Sellars, Wilfrid 100, 106, 124–125,
136
sensibilism xv, 36; *cf.* conceptual/-
ism/-ist(s); intellectualism; non-
conceptual/-ism/-ist(s)
sensibility xvii–xviii, 4, 16, 22,
35–36, 39–40, 42, 44, 47–48,
50, 54, 61, 63–64, 92, 98–99,